Inventing
Elsa Maxwell

Also by Sam Staggs

Born to Be Hurt
When Blanche Met Brando
Close-up on Sunset Boulevard
All About "All About Eve"

Inventing
Elsa Maxwell

How an Irrepressible Nobody Conquered High Society,
Hollywood, the Press, and the World

Sam Staggs

St. Martin's Press ᴍ New York

INVENTING ELSA MAXWELL. Copyright © 2012 by Sam Staggs. All rights reserved. Printed in the United States of America. For information, address St. Martin's Press, 175 Fifth Avenue, New York, N.Y. 10010.

www.stmartins.com

Library of Congress Cataloging-in-Publication Data

Staggs, Sam.
    Inventing Elsa Maxwell : how an irrepressible nobody conquered high society, Hollywood, the press, and the world / Sam Staggs.—1st ed.
        p. cm.
    Includes bibliographical references and index.
    ISBN 978-0-312-69944-4 (hardcover)
    ISBN 978-1-250-01775-8 (e-book)
    1. Maxwell, Elsa.   2. Socialites—United States—Biography.   3. Actors—United States—Biography.   4. Television personalities—United States—Biography.
I. Title.
    CT275.M464718S73 2012
    974.7'23044092—dc23
    [B]

                                                                    2012026406

First Edition: October 2012

10 9 8 7 6 5 4 3 2 1

For Ron Bowers
and
Joann Kaplet Duff

Contents

My life has been incredible. I don't believe a word of it.
—Madame Du Barry

Speak of me as I am, nothing extenuate,
Nor set down aught in malice.
—*Othello*

Society is always diseased, and the best is the most so.
—Henry David Thoreau

I The Sun Never Sets on Elsa Maxwell

Elsa Maxwell, introduced by Jack Paar on his late-night talk show in 1958: "Elsa, your stockings are wrinkled."

Her response: "I'm not wearing any. Those are varicose veins."

———·———

I first met Elsa Maxwell in the summer of 1922. I found her dynamic, gay, bursting with energy, courageous, insanely generous and, to me, always kind.

—Noël Coward, in his introduction to Elsa Maxwell's
last book, *The Celebrity Circus*, 1963

———·———

"Elsa was one of my aversions," Walter Winchell wrote in his memoir. "Now along comes Mr. Paar and makes a brand-new life and career for Elsa, who'd publicly announced that she had 'never had a man in her life.'

"The Lez said about it, the better."

———·———

While filming *The Black Rose* on location in England in 1950, Tyrone Power sent a picture postcard to Clifton Webb back in Hollywood. Power, in costume, is holding a prop from a banquet scene: a boar's head on a silver platter with an apple in its mouth. On the back he scrawled: "I'll be home on the 15th. As you can see, I ran into Elsa Maxwell over here and she's in fine fettle. Ty."

—·—

Elsa Maxwell? Just another pretty face.
—Hermione Gingold

—·—

I went to a big party she gave in Paris. I don't know why she bothered to ask me. I think it was because she needed extra men at these affairs from time to time, and I had a clean shirt.
—Claus von Bülow to author, 2009

—·—

The ugliest woman I have ever seen.
—Giovanni Battista Meneghini, divorced husband of Maria
Callas. (He hated Elsa for her lesbian designs on his wife.)

—·—

A fat old son of a bitch!
—Maria Callas

—·—

As I remember every single person who was ever kind to me, I remember that often maligned woman very well.
—Maria Riva (daughter of Marlene Dietrich)

—·—

"I May Not Be Good Looking but I'm Awfully Good to Ma"
—one of many songs composed by Elsa,
this one published in 1909

—·—

Old battering-ram Elsa always gives the best parties.
—the Duke of Windsor

———·———

The old oaken bucket in the Well of Loneliness.
—the Duchess of Windsor's vicious epithet
during their noisy feud in the mid-1950s

———·———

Elsa Maxwell was part of the old generation, a generation for whom sexuality was not intrinsic to public identity, whose community—even if predominantly with homosexuals—was defined more by class and privilege than anything else.
—William J. Mann, *Behind the Screen: How Gays
and Lesbians Shaped Hollywood, 1910–1969*

———·———

Elsa to the formidable Alma de Bretteville Spreckels, wife of sugar baron Adolph Spreckels and, like Elsa, a San Franciscan: "How old are you, Alma?"

A. de B. S.: "Old enough to remember when there was no such person as Elsa Maxwell." (She meant it figuratively, since they were born the same year. The remark implies, also, that Elsa's social status as a girl in San Francisco was not of the highest rank.)

———·———

She preferred rich women with large houses in which she could stage her parties. What most people regard as amusing interludes were to Elsa a profession.
—R.V.C. Bodley, a military attaché at the British embassy in Paris after
World War I, when Elsa was making an international name for herself.

———·———

Shaped like a cottage loaf with currant eyes.
—Stanley Jackson, *Inside Monte Carlo*

———·——

Monte Carlo. Elsa Maxwell, the cumbersome butterfly, staged her night parties with unbelievable mixtures of the great and near great.
—film director Jean Negulesco, recalling his youth
on the Côte d'Azur in the Roaring Twenties

———·——

Asked why Elsa hadn't been invited to a celebrity bash at his famed Hollywood restaurant, con man and faux Russian royalty "Prince" Mike Romanoff replied, "No phonies."

———·——

Personal and Confidential Memo to J. Edgar Hoover from E. E. Conroy, an underling at the FBI, dated July 26, 1945:

"Miss Elsa Maxwell has been a Special Service Contact of this office since September of 1942 but contact has been had with her infrequently. The Bureau is aware, of course, that presently she is writing a column for the *New York Post* and for some time now she has enjoyed the reputation of a successful hostess at gatherings which she arranges for socially prominent people. However, it has come to the attention of this office in the recent past that generally they consider her now to be a person of somewhat unsavory background and reputation. In addition, the Bureau itself has evidence of the fact that she is indiscreet and not entirely trustworthy, as is indicated in G-2 reports forwarded as enclosures to this office with a letter from the Bureau dated January 8, 1943.

"For the reasons outlined above it is deemed advisable therefore to discontinue the services of Miss Maxwell as a Special Service Contact and this will be done unless the Bureau advises to the contrary."

———·——

Elsa's indictment of racism, from her column in the *New York Post*, November 16, 1943:

"Let's look this matter of prejudice straight in the eye. I'm sick and tired of all the pussyfooting that's been going on about Jim Crow. Either we are believers in the principles of democracy—as we piously declare, three times a day—or we are a collection of the greatest frauds the world has seen.

"For generations the conventional and learned citizens of this republic have stood stolidly silent while the American Negro has been vilified, libeled, and denied almost all access to the privileged places of sweetness and light. . . . Democracy has been wayward in the cause of democracy."

———·———

Although as lively and perky as a sparrow, Miss Maxwell never strikes me as being a particularly happy woman herself. She has unsmiling eyes. She is restless. One of her idiosyncrasies is to eat chocolate continually between the courses of meals—which is to me only less disconcerting than that abominable habit of smoking between the courses.

—"The Talk of London," a pseudonymous column by
"The Dragoman" in the *Daily Express*, October 22, 1932

———·———

Headline in the *New York Herald-Tribune*, 1957: ELSA MAXWELL ORDERED TO PAY $840 TO FAROUK FOR INSULT, which, decoded, was reporting that a court in Paris had ordered Elsa to pay that amount to the deposed King of Egypt for defamation of character. While still on the throne, he had invited her to one of his parties. Elsa replied with a telegram to his equerry which read, "I do not associate with clowns, monkeys, or corrupt gangsters." An intemperate reaction, surely, from the author of *Elsa Maxwell's Etiquette Book*, published around the time of the king's party. In it, Elsa wrote that "whenever you are asked to be a guest you are paid a compliment. Your host or hostess, in effect, looks upon you as someone who will contribute to the success of their party. A prompt reply will express your appreciation of the invitation."

———·———

Elsa Maxwell took a bad fall on the Guinness yacht in Monte Carlo. The yacht is expected to recover.

—Earl Wilson's column, 1961

———.———

Telegram sent from the White House, May 31, 1963, to Elsa at the Park Sheraton Hotel in New York: "Thank you very much for your birthday message. It was kind of you to remember me on this occasion, and I am most appreciative of your thoughtfulness. John F. Kennedy."

The following day, Western Union notified the White House that the telegram was undelivered because Miss Maxwell was on the high seas aboard the SS *France*. It was her final trip abroad. (The telegram was missent to the Park Sheraton Hotel, rather than the Delmonico, where Elsa lived at the time. Had the address been correct, she would have received the telegram before departure. The great irony is that both Elsa and President Kennedy celebrated their last birthdays in that month of May 1963. She died on Friday, November 1, exactly three weeks before the assassination.)

———.———

In 1969, the director of Ferncliff Cemetery and Mausoleum, in Hartsdale, New York, assured Mickey Deans, widower of Judy Garland, that "your wife will be the star of Ferncliff. Jerome Kern rests here, and Moss Hart, Basil Rathbone, and Elsa Maxwell, but your wife will be our only star."

—Anne Edwards, *Judy Garland,* page 305

———.———

As this book goes to press, there are 133 memorial "flowers"—i.e., kitschy floral icons and visual bric-a-brac—posted on findagrave.com at Elsa's page (or should I call it her ePlot?). Many bear weepy sentiments such as "Happy Heavenly Birthday, Dearest Angel" (posted May 24, 2011) forty-eight years after Elsa's death) and "Rest in peace, Great Lady." But Judy Garland remains, as predicted, the star of Ferncliff, at least electronically; she has 6,150 tributes.

2   The Duchess of Keokuk

$\mathcal{K}$eokuk is a place name that elicits chuckles, like Peoria or Ketchikan. And like Dubuque—another titillating name owing to *The New Yorker**—Keokuk is in Iowa, a state that has better served as shtick for comedians than, say, the state of Maine. Add to Keokuk, Iowa, the fact that its most famous scion is Elsa Maxwell, and you've got the making of a stand-up routine—or so you might have had sixty years ago, when Elsa Maxwell was as famous a name as Martha Stewart or Joan Rivers today.

Elsa is often remembered as a "party girl," a superficial mischaracterization. True, Elsa was best known as party giver for the rich, the royal, the famous, and for herself—she threw some three thousand during her long life, and if you count the ones she attended or otherwise enlivened, the number rises to ten thousand by Elsa's own tabulation. The statistic seems incredible, but there is no one to contradict it. Long before the end of her life, Elsa had become a one-woman Coney Island of entertainments in palaces, hotels, yachts, casinos, stately homes, even once in the Egyptian desert. Some called her the doyenne of cafe society, but she preferred that "cafe" be omitted.

---

*In a 1925 prospectus for the magazine, founding editor Harold Ross famously stated that "*The New Yorker* will be the magazine which is not edited for the old lady in Dubuque."

Parties, however, make up a mere third or fourth of the Maxwell story, for she was songwriter, newspaper columnist and magazine feature writer, press agent, host of a radio show, film and stage actress, lecturer, talk show guest, author of books on entertaining, on etiquette, on celebrities, and on herself. She was also a gadabout, and a virtual Smithsonian of name dropping. Unlike many such, however, she knew all those whose names she dropped. Empires rose and fell while Elsa busied herself with the twentieth century. She was Mount Rushmore with jowls.

THE TABLE CAUGHT FIRE, BUT THE MAGAZINE DIDN'T

Two of Elsa's more interesting journalistic ventures are *Elsa Maxwell's Etiquette Book*, which often reads like a novel, and *Elsa Maxwell's Cafe Society*, a magazine that lasted for only one issue.

In the etiquette book, she concludes her chapter on "Manners in Public Places" with this anecdote: "I well remember how, when I was dining with Noël Coward, our table caught fire." (It was caused by a chafing dish, and Noël, like a suave character from a Coward play, poured his glass of water on the flames and treated it as a joke, "assuring our waiter that everything was quite all right.") Elsa, who loved conversation but warned against "tactless blunders," cited these dreadful statements that, she vowed, had been made in her presence:

"Your husband's eyesight is much worse, isn't it? He couldn't recognize me at all tonight."

"You must be very lonely since your son's death."

A young actress in Hollywood, trying to impress a certain director, asked: "Why are you seen with that girl? She walks as if her mother had been frightened by a chimpanzee." He replied: "She is my sister." Elsa added that "then the laughter died, and I suspect the girl wished she could have, too."

In 1953, the Dell Publishing Company secured Elsa's name for a celebrity magazine that resembled a mélange of fanzines, *Police Gazette*, scandal sheets like *Confidential* and *Whisper*, with a foreshadowing of *Vanity Fair*. The dozen or so articles, ostensibly written by Elsa but helped along by staff writers, include "The Mystery of the Marrying Gabors" (Zsa Zsa on the cover), Elsa's nemesis King Farouk, Charlie Chaplin, stripteasers, debutantes, playboys, the royal family, and Tommy Manville (married thirteen times to eleven different women).

Keokuk, surely, lacked panache as the birthplace of a rara avis like Elsa Maxwell. Throughout her life, therefore, instead of the prosaic truth, Elsa gilded the circumstances of her debut in the world. In her ghostwritten autobiography, *R.S.V.P.*, published in 1954, she claimed to have been born in a box at the Keokuk Opera House during a performance of Ambroise Thomas's *Mignon*, "just as a road-company prima donna was struggling through her big aria. It was never established whether the whole thing was due to my father's love of music or my mother's inability to count by the calendar."

The undramatic truth, as confessed by Elsa to an Iowa writer a few years before her death, is that she was born in the home of her maternal grandparents on North Fourth Street. Fabricated beginnings were not unusual in those days, especially for anyone with social or show-biz aspirations. What's more surprising than Elsa's cock-and-bull story is that it was rarely questioned, and often reported in such reputedly reliable media as *The New York Times* and *Time* magazine. Was no journalist aware that Victorian ladies did not go out in an advanced state of pregnancy?

Later, finding herself in the public eye, Elsa shaved two years off her age. During her lifetime, and up to the present, her date of birth has been given as 1883. In fact, she was born May 24, 1881, and baptized eleven months later, on April 16, 1882, at St. John's Episcopal Church on North Fourth Street in Keokuk, just down the street from her birthplace. She was christened Elsie Wyman Maxwell. At some point in late childhood or adolescence, she amended her given name when, taken by her father to a performance of *Lohengrin*, precocious Elsie decided that Wagner's Elsa bore a more elegant cognomen than her own.

A few months after the christening, Elsa's parents, David and Laura Maxwell, left Keokuk to return to San Francisco, where they had lived since shortly after their marriage, in 1878. According to Elsa, they had made the long journey back to Iowa so that their first, and only, child could be born in the home of her mother's parents.

At this point we plunge seventy years into the future. It is 1951, and Bartholomew House, Inc., Publishers, of New York, have just brought out *Elsa Maxwell's Etiquette Book*. A lively read, it is full of common sense and good-heartedness. In her foreword, Elsa posits that "good manners spring from just one thing—kind impulses."

After "Introductions," "Manners in Public Places," "Engagements," "Weddings," and the like, comes the chapter titled "Parties, Parties, Parties." Whether by coincidence or design, it's in the very center of the book, and it opens with an odd anecdote, one that fascinated me as a child when I first laid hands on an aunt's copy and which accounts, in part, for my long curiosity about Elsa Maxwell the phenomenon.

"When, as a schoolgirl in San Francisco," she writes, "I lay weeping on my bed, I vowed: 'Someday I'll give the most extraordinary parties in the world. And I'll invite whom I want. People won't be asked just because they are rich!'

"Across the street from us lived Senator James G. Fair and his family. His daughter, Virginia, named for the Virginia Mines which contributed to the Senator's wealth, was about to marry William K. Vanderbilt, Jr. Great preparations were in progress. Florists were moving in palms and ferns and flowering shrubs. And caterers' men were erecting a huge tent on the lawn.

"I came home from school that afternoon, I remember, and throwing my strapped books on the hall table, found my mother standing at the parlor window.

"'It's going to be the most wonderful party!' I sought to share my excitement.

"My mother smiled and said nothing.

"'What's the matter?' I demanded.

"'Nothing, nothing, Elsa,' she replied.

"Trying to cheer her up, I said, 'I'm so glad you and Father will be going to that party. What a great time you will have . . .'

"'Your father and I are not going, Daughter,' my mother said. 'We were not invited.'

"It was then I stamped out of the room and up the stairs and, slamming my bedroom door behind me, burst into tears."

What a story, provoking sympathy and indignation. And, like so many tales in Elsa's books, not to be taken literally at all. Throughout her life, Elsa claimed to be a poor girl who conquered the ramparts of celebrity through her own talent and grit. In her last book, *The Celebrity Circus*, she summarized her climb as that of "a short, fat, homely piano player from Keokuk, Iowa, with no money or background, who decided to become a legend and did just that." A few years earlier, in *R.S.V.P.*, Elsa sounded like a latter-day Marie Antoinette playing milkmaid behind a barn at Versailles as she claimed her favorite part of celebrity was "getting into confidential conversations with taxi drivers, chambermaids, and store clerks, the people of my class, the ordinary, common people who struggle with uncommon valor to pay their bills and educate their children and observe the rules of decent behavior."

Viewed from one angle, Elsa's working-class fantasy is jiggery-pokery. From another, it's a transparent half truth—who wouldn't hail an ordinary Joe after a day with the Windsors? Then, too, throughout her bejeweled, cosmopolitan existence, Elsa kept one toe planted, if not exactly in the cornfields back home, at least in California. She was as American as crêpes suzette.

And not good at fiction. Had Elsa tried her hand at novels, she might have turned up at the bottom of a *New Yorker* page as one of "Our Forgetful Authors." For instance, those school days. In another one of her books, she wrote that her father, disliking formal education, taught her at home. Elsa said that she, like Virginia Woolf, Edith Wharton, and so many others, had educated herself in her father's library.

Until her mother intervened, after many parental arguments, and entered Elsa in public school, which lasted only a month. Then David Maxwell pulled his daughter out and took her with him on a business trip to Japan. Four years later, according to Elsa, her mother made one more attempt. She enrolled Elsa in "Miss Denham's private school, but that lasted only six months." In all, Elsa said, she received less than two years of formal education. Which I cannot disprove, but there was no "Miss Denham's School" in San Francisco. Instead, Elsa attended the all-girls Denman Grammar School on Bush Street, housed in an Italian Renaissance-style building whose four spacious floors and mansard roof give it the stately look of a Nob Hill mansion. The original school survives only in photographs; it was destroyed in the earthquake.

Elsa's friend Anita Loos, born in 1888, also attended this school. Whether the little girls knew each other there is unclear. Loos described the school as "so cosmopolitan that many schoolmates were Chinese, French, Spanish, and Japanese."

Elsa's lowering of herself on the social ladder is appropriately theatrical, along the lines of a play by Clyde Fitch or one of those rich-girl-slumming-as-poor-girl stories like *Stage Door*, where Katharine Hepburn plays a society girl in pursuit of Broadway success sans family money and connections. And Elsa was theatrical, almost without trying. It would take a team like Kaufman and Hart, with an assist by Edna Ferber, to dramatize her unlikely narrative, not to mention the resplendent cast. Call it "Every Name in the Book."

"The people of her class" were, from the start, several rungs up the social ladder from taxi drivers and store clerks. To understand where Elsa came from, and also her reasons for devaluing her rank, we return to Keokuk and the wedding of Elsa's parents.

On November 7, 1878, the local newspaper carried a two-column feature titled "Brilliant Wedding," which led with: "The marriage of Mr. J. David Maxwell and Miss Laura Wyman, which has occupied a prominent place in the public mind and been the theme of conversation in society circles for some time past, took place at St. John's Episcopal Church yesterday afternoon at 3 o'clock." The second sentence conveys fairly conventional details of the event: "Over fifteen hundred invitations to the wedding were sent to friends here and elsewhere, and as many of this number as the church would comfortably accommodate were present to witness the nuptials."

But wait: fifteen hundred is an astounding number for a town of some sixteen thousand. And the original St. John's, consecrated in 1852, was a small wooden structure intended to seat no more than a couple of hundred parishoners.* Consider that 750 attended the wedding of John F. Kennedy and Jacqueline Bouvier in 1953, with 1,200 invited to their champagne reception, and it's staggering to think that a frontier town outdid Newport. Even if "1,500" is a misprint for "500," or even "150," the implication is that, contrary to Elsa's later account, she sprang from a monied background.

The panting newspaper story continues with details of altar flowers, Professor Reps the organist and the "Bridal Procession" from *Lohengrin*, and the bride's "elaborate costume, of an exquisite shade of pale gold silk, trimmed in ruby velvet, made in the new Princess style, with a deep train, cut square, the front of the skirt being trimmed with shell trimming of silk," and so on, with hardly a flounce or a sleeve left undescribed. The piece concludes with the information that "after the ceremony the bridal party repaired to the residence of Dr. Wyman [the bride's father], where they were entertained with a sumptuous lunch. . . . The bride and groom took the evening train for St. Louis, where they will remain a day, and then leave for New York."

If Elsa were recounting the event, it might unfold more like a ragtag parlor wedding from an old Hollywood movie, with Susan Hayward or Ann Sheridan as the bride, a bouquet plucked from the front yard by the parson's wife, and a handful of poor-but-honest relatives to wish them well as they head out west in a buggy.

When I referred to Keokuk as a frontier town, I didn't mean to equate it with a place like Deadwood, where gunfights erupted on the hour and a whorehouse flourished on every street. Keokuk, although new—a village in 1829, it was incorporated as a town in 1847—was civilized and settled, if less rooted than Boston, say, or Savannah. (The town is named for Chief Keokuk, of the Sauk and Fox tribes. Elsa, in a lecture in 1942, flippantly described the chief as "an old Indian who did something, I don't know what.")

---

*The present stone structure, which I visited recently, was begun in 1884, and apparently unseen by Elsa. Howard Hughes, although born in Texas, was baptised in this church in 1905.

Located in the extreme southeast of the state, at the confluence of the Des Moines and Mississippi Rivers, Keokuk was part of the Louisiana Purchase in 1803. Its location, favorable to commerce and culture, ensured the town's prosperity. During the Civil War, Keokuk boomed as a point of embarkation for troops heading to fight in southern battles. Several hospitals were established to treat injured soldiers returning from those battles, as well as a national cemetery for those who did not survive. Elsa's maternal grandfather, Dr. Rufus H. Wyman (1817–1881), was commissioned surgeon of the 21st Regiment Missouri Volunteer Infantry in 1861.

Details of her parents' wedding obviously contradict Elsa's poor-mouth fabrications. Since she succeeded so well, however, in concealing the truth, and thus convincing the world of her down-and-out origins, I offer further proof of her family's wealth and social standing, followed by possible reasons why Elsa toned herself down rather than up. (Even close friends like Noël Coward knew nothing of her early years. In his 1937 autobiography, *Present Indicative*, he devoted several pages to their friendship, beginning in medias res because, he said, "to write the true story of Elsa's life would be worth doing, but unfortunately quite impossible, for the simple reason that the details of it, the real mysteries and struggles and adventures, are untraceable. The only authority for data would be Elsa herself, but to appeal to her would be worse than useless.")

Elsa's father, James David Maxwell (1850–1904), known as David, was given an entry in *The History of Lee County, Iowa*, published in 1879. The volume is misleadingly titled, for it is not solely a narrative history of the county but also a biographical directory of leading citizens past and present. Twenty-nine at the time, and married one year, Maxwell was titular head of his own company—"general fire, life, accident, and marine insurance." We are told that he had spent several years in St. Louis, Texas, New Orleans, and San Francisco, having come to Keokuk in 1877. "He married Miss Laura Wyman; she is associated with her husband in the insurance business."

For those who, like me, possess meager knowledge of insurance-business profitability, I offer the parallel of former Supreme Court Justice John Paul Stevens. Jeffrey Toobin, in a *New Yorker* profile, wrote that "the Stevenses were prominent citizens of Chicago. The Justice's grandfather James Stevens had gone into the insurance business, and, with the profits, he and his sons Ernest and Raymond bought land on South Michigan Avenue and built what was then the biggest hotel in the world." (Stevens *grand-père* would have been a contemporary of Elsa's father.)

Scattered across both branches of Elsa's family tree, the Maxwells and the Wymans, are doctors, lawyers, bankers, judges, and politicians. The geographical spread is mainly midwestern, with offshoots in Mississippi, Arizona, and Northern and Southern California. Elsa's uncle, Cortes Maxwell, graduated with honors from Yale and joined the Eastern Establishment. Described in a newspaper article as "the son of a very rich man," he later bought his own newspaper in Iowa. When David Maxwell's sister, Elizabeth, was married in Illinois in 1881, the local paper's lavish details equaled those of the Keokuk paper when Elsa's parents were wed. Of interest, also, in reconstructing Elsa's provenance is the fact that the Maxwells and the Wymans formed virtually a single large clan, with close-knit, ongoing business and social relations among several generations. (That "very rich man," Elsa's paternal grandfather, was Andrew Maxwell, who lived from 1820 to 1876. He was born in Ireland and made his fortune in Missouri, in the meatpacking business. Elsa always referred to her father, and to herself, as being of Scottish ancestry. That could mean that her forebears emigrated from Scotland to Ireland, and thus arrived in America as Scotch-Irish. Or perhaps she chose Scottish to set herself apart from the many Irish immigrants of the late nineteenth century.)

Another filament in Elsa's fabric is slightly puzzling: Dr. Wyman's house, Elsa's birthplace, although spacious at 2,700 square feet, is not a showplace compared with many of the other Victorian residences in Keokuk. Built around 1860, the two-story house set high above the street is plain-faced except for a bow window on the southeast corner of its facade, and large set-back porches on both the first and second levels. Today, its Italianate shape might remind you of an ungentrified country house in Tuscany. According to the 1880 census, Dr. Wyman and his wife, Susan, lived there with three of their four adult children, one of whom was Laura Maxwell. Her husband, David, was also a resident, along with two live-in servants. One can speculate that the house is relatively unadorned because a small-town physician's home was expected to be sober; otherwise, he might be thought to overcharge the sick. On the other hand, an architect assures me that the house, though more modest than many in the town, has been stripped of Victorian decorative elements offensive to the modern sensibilities of the 1950s. If the original house was less than a showplace, it could be that the Wymans (and the Maxwells), though affiliated with the Democratic Party and leaning toward genteel progressivism, had no flamboyant ambitions, aesthetic or otherwise. Their milieu was the conservative Midwest, and they adhered to its customs.

3 An Oasis of Civilization
in the California Desert

$\mathcal{U}$ntil the advent of Elsa, who was just passing through.

Her parents had settled in San Francisco shortly after their marriage in 1878. Returning to Keokuk in 1880 for the birth of their child, they stayed on there until shortly after Elsa's christening in the spring of 1882. After that, David and Laura Maxwell remained in California for the rest of their lives, with occasional visits back to Iowa. These were reciprocated by members of the Maxwell family, who seem to have loved Laura as a sister, and by the Wymans, for whom David Maxwell was more like a brother than a brother-in-law. On one occasion, in 1891, the *San Francisco Bulletin*'s "Events in Society" column reported that "Joseph D. Redding entertained at dinner during the week, at the Bohemian Club, Dr. and Mrs. W.J. Younger, Mr. and Mrs. J.D. Maxwell, and Mrs. Marie Wyman Williams." The latter was Laura's sister.

THE BOHEMIAN CLUB

Founded in 1872, the Bohemian Club was originally instituted for "gentlemen connected professionally with literature, art, music, the drama, and those having appreciation of the same." A later member, the celebrated photographer Arnold Genthe, declared that "the best a man could have in those days in San Francisco, if he were to enter into its life, was membership in the Bohemian Club." David Maxwell, as correspondent and reviewer for the New York *Dramatic Mirror*, was eminently qualified on cultural grounds. A businessman-dilettante, with money and social standing, he possessed the right mix of raffish charm and secure background to delight other off-beat gentlemen without threatening members of the San Francisco elite (e.g., Charles Crocker, of the $2,300,000 mansion on Nob Hill; Senator William Sharon; various males of the Spreckels clan). Among the honorary members in 1899 were S. L. Clemens (aka Mark Twain) of Connecticut; Bret Harte; Sir Henry Irving and Sir Arthur Sullivan, both of London; and Joaquin Miller, an outré poet and proto-hippie with long flowing hair who was persona non grata in the higher purlieus of the city.

One writer described the club's Red Room as a place of "famous feasts," where epic banquets were held for such notables as Sarah Bernhardt and another legendary actress, Helena Mojeska. Oscar Wilde dropped in, and later said, "I never saw so many well-dressed, well-fed, business-looking Bohemians in my life." Another visitor was showman DeWolf Hopper, remembered for two dubious feats: his endless recitations of the baseball poem "Casey at the Bat" and his fifth wife, Hedda.

Today, the Bohemian Club has evolved into something depressingly different. Alex Shoumatoff, writing in *Vanity Fair* in 2009, described its members as "2,500 of America's richest, most conservative men, including Henry Kissinger, George H.W. Bush, and a passel of Bechtels, Basses, and Rockefellers. . . . Many of the guys, in other words, who have been running the country into the ground and ripping us off for decades." When I phoned the club recently to ascertain the exact years of David Maxwell's membership, I was dismissed with a "not at liberty to divulge"—rather redundant secrecy, considering that various nineteenth-century memberships appear online.

If Elsa were alive, she surely wouldn't be invited to visit her father's club. In the unlikely event of an invitation, however, she might reply with a rebuking telegram like the one she sent to King Farouk, back on page 5.

Beginning with the Gold Rush, San Francisco was a powerful magnet. In the case of Laura and David Maxwell, the city's pull is unclear, though they seem to have required a more varied playing field than Iowa provided. Perhaps the insurance business was more lucrative on the West Coast. One wonders, also, whether, by Iowa standards, David and Laura were slightly too carefree, and not chained to the Protestant work ethic. Proper, certainly, but perhaps more at home among the fleshpots of San Francisco than their kinsmen might have been.

They had Elsa's horoscope cast when she was seven, a method of divination better suited to San Francisco than to Keokuk. Elsa recalled years later that the astrologer told her parents, "This little girl will become world famous." She added, "I can't say that I take astrology very seriously, but when I hark back to that first prediction, it *does* make me think." Elsa rarely portrayed her two parents together, but in one scene they resemble characters in the novels of a midwestern regionalist such as Booth Tarkington. In her 1957 book *How to Do It, or The Lively Art of Entertaining*, she warns that destructive gossip can taint the atmosphere of a party. "My father had a wonderful way of handling malicious gossips," she wrote, "and I have often followed his example, always with the looked-for result." Elsa recalled that at home, David Maxwell would tolerate gossip only up to a point. "When one of my mother's friends came to call he would sit quietly by, listening to the two of them as they huddled over their coffee cups droning out the long litany of They Says—'They say that she . . . ' 'They say he *saw* her . . . ' and on and on, until he could stand it no longer.

"'You're speaking of So-and-So?' he would ask suddenly, with the air of someone brought abruptly out of his own deep thoughts. 'Funny you should mention her. I ran into her only last night and we were talking about you. She certainly thinks highly of you—went on at great length about what a fine woman you are.' When the visitor left, and Laura asked whether David really had seen Mrs. So-and-So, he would answer, 'I never heard of the woman in my life before today.' "

We may assume that these scenes played out on the days of Laura Maxwell's "at home," listed in San Francisco's *Our Society Blue Book* for 1901 as the third Thursday of each month.

The historian Edward Wagenknecht reminds us that in the 1890s, and into the next century, "most of the country west of the Alleghenies still lay as God had made it. Only Chicago and San Francisco had much place in the minds of dwellers on the eastern seaboard." The entire Pacific Coast had a population of about one million, and almost half of that number—some 400,000—resided in the vicinity of San Francisco.

Simon Winchester, leading up to the 1906 earthquake in his book *A Crack in the Edge of the World*, notes that in the post–Gold Rush decades "fine restaurants and music halls and bars and high-class brothels sprang up . . . the streets of the plutocracy were fast being paved with cobbles . . . and the luxury of piped water brought in from small reservoirs was being offered to all residents fortunate enough to live in the gleaming center of the new city." By 1876, and the American centenary, San Francisco had "something like 600 saloons, 40 bookshops, a dozen photography studios . . . omnibuses and hackney coaches" to transport passengers around town.

Evelyn Wells, who interviewed many nineteenth-century denizens for her 1939 book *Champagne Days of San Francisco*, spotlights rapid developments in the fin de siècle city. "The past few years had introduced new miracles—the telephone, the electric light, the automobile . . . there had been startling changes, and not the least of these was in the point of view of the 'end-of-the-century girl.' " San Francisco's nascent feminism, as set forth by Wells, stops just short of corset burning. "Among certain circles of young women there was a growing conviction that while the world was made entirely for the males, something might be done about it. There was an increasing antagonism to marriage. There was more talk of votes for women. The 'end-of-the-century girl' was refusing to wear shoes several sizes too small. Her whalebone stays were laced less tightly. Her skirts were shorter, and a few daring girls bobbed their hair." These young women also "defended the nude in art, were stirred by Ibsen's Nora, by the poetic passions of Ella Wheeler Wilcox, and the impudent observations of an obstreperous young Irishman, George Bernard Shaw."

One of these young women was Anita Loos, Elsa's contemporary and friend. Loos, in her witty memoir *A Girl Like I*, wrote that "there were five other little girls scurrying around the environs of San Francisco, getting ready to invade the planet. They were Gertrude Stein, Alice B. Toklas, Elsa Maxwell, [the novelist] Gertrude Atherton, and Frances Marion, who became rich and famous writing movie scripts." (Loos left out Isadora Duncan, also a friend of Elsa's.)

Simon Winchester used the oxymoron "bohemian normality" to characterize San Francisco in the years preceding the earthquake, and I borrow it here as a label for Elsa: applicable not only to her San Francisco days, but in varying degrees to her entire life. Indeed, based on scant evidence, it is appropriate for Elsa's parents, as well, especially her father. At the Bohemian Club, and elsewhere around the city, David Maxwell took part in entertainments involving pranks and practical jokes, often with costumes and elaborate scenarios. Elsa's later high jinks in London, Paris, and elsewhere were probably influenced by her father's boisterous socializing.

Elsa called David Maxwell "the rarest of all nonconformists—a Scotsman who had absolutely no interest in money. He casually went through the motions of selling insurance to earn a living, but his major attention was wrapped up in a job that barely paid his expenses. He was the Pacific Coast correspondent for the New York *Dramatic Mirror*, a newspaper devoted to the theatre, music, and the performing arts." Recalling that he was paid ten dollars for his weekly column of news and comment, Elsa is certain that he would gladly have paid the paper for the privilege of "breathing the same air with the artists he admired." David Maxwell's obituary in the *San Francisco Chronicle* in 1904 contradicts Elsa's assertion; according to the paper, "He prospered in business until his health began to fail three years ago." According to that obituary, he was also active in the Democratic Party.

Elsa described her mother as "practical, economical, a meticulous housekeeper and a bit of a fanatic on keeping up appearances. She was a stiff disciplinarian." Despite their contrasting temperaments, David and Laura complemented each other perfectly according to Elsa, even though, she said, "my mother's sense of propriety must have been outraged constantly by the odd assortment of people my father cultivated." He once brought home a sailor, whose purpose in the Maxwell household is left unspecified. He presented a pet monkey to young Elsa. Scandalized, Laura berated the monkey for his endless mischief and Elsa for her tomboyish propensity for simian tricks. Max, as the monkey was dubbed, proved to be Elsa's "first and most appreciative audience" when she began rehearsing her destined role as life of the party.

Little Elsa, no doubt, was a handful by any parental gauge, and at some point in her young adulthood a rift occurred between her and Laura which was never completely patched up. The reason for it is likely to remain obscure. One factor in the mother-daughter estrangement may be simply the clash of two strong, controlling personalities. Whatever her strengths and shortcomings, however, Laura qualifies as one of those "end-of-the-century girls," perhaps even a proto-feminist. She helped her husband run his insurance business in Keokuk and in San Francisco. After his death in 1904, she herself ran the company for many years. She also voted in California state elections as early as 1912, years before the Nineteenth Amendment to the Constitution gave all women the right to vote. Laura remained on the voter-registration rolls until 1930, five years before her death. There is evidence, although slight, that David and Laura lived apart for a time: different addresses in phone books and city directories, and the 1900 voter-registration roll lists David's address as the Palace Hotel.

The biographer's crystal ball reveals only so much; at times a cloud cover descends on the past. Having no version of Elsa's San Francisco childhood but her own, I offer a précis of her adventures during the first two eventful decades of her life, as Elsa recalled them many years later. After that, the newspapers of San Francisco and Oakland began to notice her, and in no time at all she had launched her invasion of the planet. Elsa's imagination notwithstanding, there are reasons to accept the bulk of her autobiographical reporting. For instance, a number of friends and cohorts were alive in 1954, when Elsa published *R.S.V.P.*, who presumably would have challenged major fictions. Then, too, given San Francisco's high self-regard, someone—e.g., columnist Herb Caen—would have set the record straight had Elsa filled her book with whoppers. Moreover, the well documented later decades of her life are even more crowded with incident than her crying-in-the-wilderness period, meaning that if things didn't happen to her, she made them happen. And I'm convinced she did so from the start.

Here, in newsreel style, Elsa's Act One.

At sixteen months, Elsa wins a beautiful-baby contest in competition with four thousand other infants (more likely "400" or even "40") . . . David Maxwell hires as Baby's nurse Hi Foo, a Chinese thug who is later hanged for murder . . . Caught by her father turning the clock ahead an hour when she is five, Elsa explains that she always looks forward to tomorrow . . . When the great soprano Adelina Patti comes to lunch, Elsa announces that she can sing, too, and that her favorite song is "Comin' Thro' the Rye," whereupon the preemptive diva sings it first. When she is finished, Patti asks the little girl, "Did you like the way I sang your song?" Elsa's cheeky rejoinder: "No, I can sing it better." And starts to warble. Next day, a messenger delivers a package that contains a gold bracelet and a note: "To my best and only singing teacher.—Adelina Patti."

ADELINA PATTI CAME TO OUR HOUSE TODAY

In her last book, *The Celebrity Circus*, Elsa wrote: "It will be my fate, I suppose, to go down in social history as Elsa the Party-Giver. But only my close friends know that the balls, the banquets, the bridge tables, and even the celebrities, all pale in the face of my one serious passion: music. If I have one consuming regret, it is that I never found the time nor the discipline really to develop my own musical talent, a talent that might have proved outstanding if I'd ever given it half the proper chance." For Elsa, the piano was the supreme instrument, followed by the operatic voice. Like many youngsters who can play by ear, Elsa did just that—all her life, and never got around to serious sight reading, though she later composed a number of songs. By her own admission, she could play any piece of music perfectly after one hearing—songs, symphonies, and arias—transposing keys at will and adding embellishments to delight herself and her audiences. No one ever complained of a sour note, and she played for Noël Coward, Cole Porter, Artur Rubinstein, and Maria Callas—many photos show Elsa at the piano and Maria, with her hair down, singing pop hits and show tunes like a Greek Doris Day.

Elsa's first celebrity, she always claimed, was Adelina Patti, who came to San Francisco many times. In 1884, Patti sang in *La Traviata* and *Rigoletto* and caused a riot unsurpassed even by Elvis or the Beatles. Throngs surrounded her hotel. Tickets for opening night cost seven dollars, but scalpers upped the price to fifty. Lines formed at dawn and soon stretched from the Grand Opera House on Mission Street to the corner, around it, and along Third Street all the way to Market. Contentious ticket buyers pushed, shoved, swore, and an angry fan even challenged another to a Wild West duel with revolvers.

The adulation was surely justified; Verdi called Adelina Patti the greatest singer he had ever heard. Born in Spain to Italian parents who later moved to New York, Patti (1843–1919) grew up in the Bronx. After making her debut at sixteen in *Lucia di Lammermoor* at the Academy of Music in New York, she performed throughout the world. In 1862, she sang "Home, Sweet Home" for President and Mrs. Lincoln at the White House. The Lincolns, who had recently lost their son Willie to typhoid, were moved to tears and requested an encore. In the coming years, this sentimental air became one of Patti's signature songs.

Her luncheon with the Maxwells took place in 1887. Elsa wrote, "I can recall the letdown when I saw her step from her carriage. I'd expected someone who looked like a star. The frail, rather diminutive diva who climbed our front steps didn't look at all important." (In photographs and paintings, Patti's dark, purposeful eyes dominate her lean face, and on her lips a sneer seems at the ready.)

A couple of nights later, as Patti sang the last notes of *Lucia* in the final performance of her San Francisco run, a deranged seventy-year-old socialist threw a bomb on the stage "with the idea of annihilating the whole of San Francisco society in one grand explosion," according to historian Julia Altrocchi in *The Spectacular San Franciscans*. "The bomb fizzled out with only a minor bang and sputter. Patti, in the wings, thinking that this was some additional enthusiastic Western salute to her genius, emerged gaily, tripped to the front of the stage, shook a merrily admonitory finger at the audience, her mischievous eyes twinkling, signaled the orchestra conductor, and sang 'Home, Sweet Home.' Many considered this an act of supreme composure and courage, and

San Francisco fell in love with her all over again."

In a different medium—the Broadway musical—Adelina Patti's great-grand-niece and namesake, pop diva Patti LuPone, draws similar adulation today.

Elsa, homeschooled, never sees a *McGuffey's Reader* or a spelling book, though by age eleven—already in training as a honky-tonk intellectual—she knows her Plato and Aristotle, her Keats and Browning . . . For her thirteenth birthday, at her parents' cottage on Belvedere Island, Elsa hijacks a fourteen-foot boat, loads it with trusting kiddies, sets sail across the bay, almost capsizes in the backwash of a passing freighter, and next day braves a visit from the chief of police . . . "If you're going to act like a tomboy," harangues Mother Maxwell, "you'll look like one." She picks up scissors, cuts off Elsa's hair, and makes her wear pants. "I didn't mind the penalty at all," said Elsa of her transvestite youth. "I didn't have to comb my hair and the pants gave me more freedom of motion." (At many a masquerade over the next half century, Elsa comes in drag: as Benjamin Franklin, Herbert Hoover, Einstein, Sancho Panza, a baseball player. As Elsa's friend Dorothy Parker might have said, but didn't: "How could they tell?")

Perhaps the rift between Elsa and Laura began on that Mommie Dearest day. A mother who could purposely disfigure her child, even temporarily, must have been rigid and somewhat cruel.

At sixteen, Elsa fell in love. In *R.S.V.P.*, she devotes several pages to this teenage crush, and a strange affair it is in the telling. That's because it's Elsa's coming-out story cross-dressing as a romance of the time, almost a parody of a sweet tale by some lady novelist with three names. But Elsa's forte wasn't fiction, and so the shape of her story is all wrong, disharmonious.

Letting us know in the first line that this heterosexual "complication" was her first and last, Elsa recounts climbing Nob Hill with fresh fruits and vegetables for her mother when, passing in front of the Von Schroeder mansion, she couldn't resist peering through an open window. She lost her balance; tomatoes, potatoes, and apples rolled down the famous hill.

"May I help you, Fräulein?" said Baron Charming, who, Elsa soon learned, was Alexander von Schroeder, a recent graduate of the University of Bonn. He was the younger brother of Baron Johann Heinrich von Schroeder, who had married San Francisco's very wealthy Mary Ellen Donahue, and her money. Alex, as Elsa was soon calling him, was "a handsome young man with a deep scar on his right cheek" who clicked his heels before gathering up Elsa's wayward produce. If we deconstruct this meet-cute device crossed with Erich von Stroheim, it suggests that Elsa's fictions were about as convincing as those of the lady novelists.

He walked her to her humble abode. (Elsa often forgot to reconcile her "poverty" with the Maxwell dwelling on Nob Hill.) She, losing the "maidenly reserve" that she never had to begin with, urged him to come back the next day. "He was handsome and rich—and I had read enough romantic novels to realize that a girl could not afford to be too coy under the circumstances." Spoken like Myra Breckinridge in search of an author.

He came, and came, and came again—to read poetry aloud and sing in his rich baritone, to Elsa's impeccable accompaniment. At night they went to the theatre, where, on one such outing, they ran into Johann Heinrich himself. Like any good Prussian, he was rude and brusque.

It was a dark and stormy night, although the sky was clear. After the show, Alex blurted out a somewhat queeny opinion: "I think, Liebchen, you should wear an evening dress occasionally." Elsa, though wounded, saw his point, for although she had, by now, escaped her boyish garb, she wore the same outfit all the time: "an inexpensive black velvet suit that didn't fit too well to begin with, and constant wear had not improved its style."

Surmounting her distress, Elsa played the poverty card. "I have no money to buy a new dress," she fairly wailed. Alex, like a Teutonic Daddy Warbucks, offered to take her shopping the very next day. "I will buy you a beautiful décolleté gown."

Insulted for the second time that evening, Elsa flounced, sobbing, into her house. David Maxwell, by this time accustomed to drama offstage as well as on, gave Elsa a twenty-dollar bill (an amount that poor fathers rarely carried in their pockets in 1897). Next day Elsa bought a black chiffon evening frock with pink velvet belt, reduced from $35 to $18.75. Still relatively svelte from climbing Nob Hill, young Elsa gazed in the mirror and beheld a buxom nymph. That night, Alex throbbed with passion. The dress was stunning! "Oh yes, and you are, too, of course, mein Liebchen," he remembered to say. He grabbed her in his arms and kissed her as cable cars rolled and lurched. Surely her mouth was sweet, as he— "You brute!" she screamed, shoving him away. "You've ruined everything!"

It's curious that Elsa was so astonished; after all, she had read those novels, although not *Odd Girl Out* or *Woman in the Shadows*, for Ann Bannon was not yet born. But now she knew. Elsa knew that the kiss of a man must nevermore soil her lips. She raced to her bedroom, ripped off the chiffon dress, wiped her mouth, and quickly changed into the old velvet suit. Alex, stunned, remained seated in the parlor. Eventually Elsa descended and sat on a sofa far across the room.

He apologized. He told her he was in love with her, although back in Prussia his parents had arranged an aristocratic bride for him, but his desire was to marry this woman before him, this *schöne kleine* Duchess von Keokuk. "I don't want to hear about it!" Elsa cried out. "I'm not in love with you. Besides, I never intend to get married. That spoils everything." Elsa's antimarriage tirade had nothing in common with Isadora Duncan's, who perhaps at that very moment was burning her parents' marriage license in another part of San Francisco, and proclaiming that "any intelligent woman who reads the marriage contract, and then goes into it, deserves all the consequences." Isadora wanted free love and lots of it; Elsa wanted nothing a man could give.

Until she changed her mind. One night at dinner in the Poodle Dog they argued and Alex called her a prude. Had his accusation been true, however, she never would have accompanied him to the Poodle Dog, which functioned not only as a restaurant but also as a *maison de rendez-vous* with bedrooms conveniently located on the upper stories.

"You're right," said Elsa, in an odd switcheroo. "I will marry you." He removed the family signet ring from his finger and whispered, "*Ich liebe dich.*" By coincidence, Elsa knew this one German phrase; it was there in a song by Grieg that Alex had taught her. (Victor Herbert couldn't have done this scene any better. Picture Jeanette MacDonald and Nelson Eddy in "Naughty Elsa.")

Unlike most of the straightforward stories in Elsa's writings, this burlesque episode was most likely an elaborate hoax intended to tip off savvy 1950s readers that she had once brushed awkwardly against the other sex. A neat ending to her fable would have been that her heart was broken and never again could she trust masculine love.

Instead, however, she prolonged the climax, turning it, at long last, into a sad anticlimax. For a month they were engaged. "Alex began to teach me German. After a stiff session of declining irregular verbs, we read Goethe and Schiller aloud for relaxation." With that, Elsa, who lacked a sense of camp, penned a line worthy of Patrick Dennis. (And Elsa should have known that you *conjugate* verbs.)

As we near the end, Alex goes to New York for a month. He returns to Nob Hill, and— "The moment I saw him I knew that our relationship had ended." Elsa asked whether there was another woman, and his reply might have come from the lips of someone doing Arnold Schwarzenegger on *Saturday Night Live*. "Ven you say another voman, you imply there are two vimmen in my life. That is wrong. There is only one voman, but she is not you. You are a fine person, but there is something in you that will always stop you from becoming a voman."

Elsa's pro forma devastation took the form of tears, though she knew he was right. "Alex bowed formally, clicked his heels and left." She concludes her narrative with the unsurprising statement, "I was not meant to marry Alex or any other man."

And that's how Elsa outed herself.

There is a coda, however. Years later, just before World War I, Elsa visited Alex and his *gnädige Frau* in their palatial home in the Tiergartenstrasse in Berlin. By this time, Alex was on the kaiser's staff, and he took Elsa to Potsdam to meet Wilhelm II, the first royalty she ever encountered. "I think I embarrassed Alex by the inept curtsy I gave the kaiser," she said.

In another, more credible version, Elsa was playing piano at the Wintergarten, a variety theatre in Berlin that wasn't looked on as a proper setting for "a fine American girl." Alex begged her to quit, Elsa said, "for the sake of my immortal soul." In this telling, there is of course no introduction to

Alex's wife, no visit to their home, and certainly no introduction to the kaiser. Alex returned to his "palace," and Elsa kept "pounding the keys."

A few years later, in 1916, Elsa read in a New York newspaper that Baron Alexander von Schroeder had been killed in action on the Western Front. Unlike most lesbian fables of the time, in Elsa's it's the man who dies.

I said at the outset of this romantic tale of Elsa's that it's a strange affair in the telling. It became even stranger when I located an alternate version. In September of 1917, the *Oakland Tribune* published an item under the following headline, which has the tabloid decibels of present-day "news": BRIDE WOULD TAKE GIRL FRIEND ON TOUR.

The ostensible news is that Elsa Maxwell has returned to the Bay Area on a visit after an absence of a decade. The heart of the story, however, recounts an unusual episode, dating back to 1898, of teenage Elsa and her "bosom companion," Ethel Cook. "The two girls were of very different types, but adored each other in the way of romantic girls in their teens. When Sterling Postley came along and induced the beautiful Ethel to marry him, Elsa Maxwell grieved as only sixteen can grieve when deserted by a chum. Not so the fair young bride, and everyone wondered at the equanimity with which she faced separation from her inseparable companion. After the wedding ceremony, the reason was forthcoming. The bride had no intention of separating from her friend. She had quietly made every arrangement, including the purchase of a railroad ticket, for Miss Maxwell to accompany them on their honeymoon jaunt. It was a nice little surprise for everyone, including the bridegroom, but no one seemed to think much of the scheme except the bride, and she grew tearful and refused to go at all unless accompanied by her friend. Finally she was convinced that the only proper honeymoon is the honeymoon *à deux*, so with many tears and fond farewells, she left Miss Maxwell behind."

This second story of thwarted teenage love is both charming and poignant. Elsa's story of balking young love with German barons and crying scenes lacks verisimilitude. I suspect she invented it as a safe parallel to the truth, a way of recalling her affection for Ethel. The second account, even in old-timey newspaper prose, and told with innocence, nevertheless leads to consternation: Were these girls really so naive, or can we read Ethel and Elsa, in hindsight, as trying to free themselves from traditional female roles and the restraints of marriage? Did their devotion trigger scenes of parental rebuke, and did this romantic interlude provoke Elsa's discord with her mother? Who gave the story to the newspaper, and what reactions did it elicit among readers two decades after the fact—especially Ethel and Elsa?

Ethel Cook's marital history deepens the mystery, even as it suggests partial answers to our questions. On November 13, 1898, the *San Francisco Call* announced the engagement of Miss Ethel Cook, daughter of Mrs. Horace Nelson Cook, to Sterling Postley, son of Commodore Clarence Postley of New York City. "The wedding will take place on Wednesday, the 30th of November, at the pretty villa of the bride's mother at Belvedere." This marriage, of course, is the one for which Elsa was wanted as a third party.

The marriage lasted a dozen years, until Ethel divorced Sterling Postley in Paris in 1911. Shortly thereafter, she secretly married Ross Ambler Curran, who was previously married to Elise Postley, sister of Sterling Postley, and thus Ethel's former sister-in-law. *The New York Times* reported the marriage of Ethel to Ross Ambler Curran in an article that began, "A complicated matrimonial tangle which involves two prominent families in New York and San Francisco society circles and those in Paris came to a climax in Pasadena Sunday with the secret marriage of . . ."

The item continues with the information that the new Mrs. Curran— i.e., Ethel Cook—"when reigning belle of San Francisco several years ago, was made famous by Grand Duke Boris of Russia, who drank a toast with champagne out of one of her slippers at a banquet and declared that she was the most beautiful American woman he had ever seen."

Two months later, in May 1911, the *Times* reported the marriage of Guernsey Curran, brother of Ross Ambler Curran, to Elise Postley, his brother's ex-wife, who now became Ethel's sister-in-law for the second time, as well as the former wife of Ethel's present husband! Among the headlines generated by this marital kaleidoscope: LOVE GONE AMUCK AMONG MILLIONS and THE ROMANCES OF THE IDLE RICH CURRANS. (Ethel later divorced Curran, in 1933.)

Our interest in this swapping is, of course, Elsa, and her connection with the dizzying quadrille. First, her friendship with Ethel, who came from great wealth and social position, belies Elsa's self-portrait as a poor Cinderella at home in the ashes. In truth, she ran with the fast set of San Francisco, young people with enough money to live it up and, in some cases, to burn. Then, too, her ongoing connection with Ethel (whom she visited in 1917 on her trip back home to San Francisco, and with whom she maintained contact until Ethel's death), suggests a lively, and continuing, interest in her own sex, Elsa's denials notwithstanding. And whatever Victorian mores the Maxwells brought with them from Keokuk were given short shrift by Elsa, whose bohemianism suited her for the social experiments rife in San Francisco.

Elsa's name began appearing in Bay Area newspapers when she was a teenager, always in the context of social propriety. One of the first mentions is from August 4, 1895, when the *San Francisco Chronicle* reported, in a full-page article, on "Belvedere's Night in Venice," the theme of a summer fête. All of Belvedere Island was decked out in carnival garb, with thousands of lanterns, "draperies that floated to the water's edge and upon its surface," pennants and flags, yacht races in the cove, and an immense Ferris wheel. "One small boat, J.D. Maxwell's *Casa Linda*, was a Turkish gem. It was canopied with satin, so heavy with gold embroideries that the fairy boat almost sank to the water's edge. Jeweled lamps glittered and were reflected a hundred times. The twinkling lanterns showed that the ten occupants of the boat, headed by Miss Elsie Maxwell, all wore fezes." Later in the article, almost as an afterthought, it was mentioned that among those in attendance were Governor James Budd; and "Mayor Sutro was the guest of J.D. Maxwell at Casa Linda."

(Casa Linda was the name of the Maxwell house as well as the name of their boat. They lived for a time on Linda Vista Avenue, as well as on another street. Belvedere Island, narrowly separated from the mainland, lies due north of San Francisco and northeast of Sausalito. Today one crosses a bridge to the island, though it was once connected to mainland Marin County by two roads built on sand bars that could only be seen at low tide. The hilly island was where well-to-do city residents built country homes in the late-nineteenth and early-twentieth centuries.)

In 1900, the *Chronicle* reported on a society wedding at Trinity Church (dating from 1849, it is the oldest Episcopal church on the Pacific Coast). One of the four bridesmaids was "Miss Elsie Maxwell." Later that year, the *Oakland Tribune*'s society column noted that "Miss Hazel Curtiss of Oakland and Miss Elsie Maxwell of Belvedere were guests at a luncheon given yesterday by Mr. and Mrs. Hunt of San Francisco." In 1904, the same paper announced that "a merry party of Oaklanders will leave June 1 to spend two weeks at Lake Tahoe, and the outing promises to be one of the most delightful of the summer season." Among the thirty young people of both sexes, with chaperones: Miss Elsie Maxwell. (In the various Bay Area newspapers, she is sometimes "Elsie" and at other times "Elsa," suggesting that her hometown identity was still in flux.)

The same year, Miss Elsie Maxwell was a guest of Mrs. A. M. Rosborough and her son, Joseph Rosborough, at "a picturesque garden musical recital given in the grounds of their East Oakland home." In 1906, the *Chronicle*'s society columnist, "Lady Teazle," reported that "Miss Elsie Maxwell was hostess last Saturday at a delightful informal evening at her pretty home in Linda Vista. Miss Maxwell's talent and versatility, combined with her magnetic cordiality, make her a perfect hostess, and one whose enthusiasm inspires all whom she gathers about her." Such items appeared regularly until Elsa left town in 1907.

Given so much irrefutable proof that Elsa was anything but poor, we may well ask why, throughout her life, she labored at pretending to be. It's likely that even Elsa herself had no full explanation. The indefinable urge behind such charades often lies buried in the heart. To blur one's past is a distancing device; it coats tender emotions, and also deters those who would come too close. Perhaps the answer to such psychological enigmas could come only from a Proust or a Henry James.

Gazing into the lives of the dead, however, we do find glimmers in the dark. For a showboat personality like Elsa, a dull résumé indeed would be one that stated, "Born into a family of midwestern burghers that wasn't wealthy enough to reach the heights of the Spreckels, the Vanderbilts, or the Rockefellers, though well-placed on the second or third tier." Seen in this light, how greater the drama for her, a pauper girl, to have grappled the towers of high society (or that lower circle, cafe society) through her own grit and craft.

Or, suppose that Elsa knew, in her lingering resentment, that it would needle her mother, and others in the family who took Laura's side in the rift, to declare herself lacking support, whether material or otherwise? Then, too, there might have been a sliver of masochism in Elsa's equation: I'm unattractive, a sexual misfit, and therefore no matter what success I have I'll punish myself with the sorrows of an unlovely youth—a script that Elsa may well have come to believe. Or perhaps the family did, indeed, lose a lot of money in the various financial crashes and recessions of the Gilded Age, like so many Americans a century later owing to robber barons of the Bush years. With financial loss would have come social demotion.

That would explain a slight but revealing variation in Elsa's story, which, as far as I can ascertain, is a change she made but once. In an interview in 1941, she said, "When I was a kid in San Francisco, my mother told me that we weren't invited to the big parties on Nob Hill because we weren't rich enough. I resolved then and there that some day I would give parties—big parties, expensive parties—to which no rich people would be invited. That is, of course, unless they also happened to be nice people or talented people as well."

The big parties, plural. I believe that Elsa focused on Senator Fair's party, and his snub to her parents, because she found him especially distasteful; we will soon see why. It was convenient to combine all those invitations that never came into one enormous affront. Elsa also found it efficient to demonize the shady, wealthy, but unpopular Senator Fair, when in reality others of San Francisco's super rich slighted the Maxwells. Seen in this light, Elsa is like many overachievers. They dress the wounds of childhood with immoderate success.

4 Where Were You at 5:13 A.M. on Wednesday, April 18, 1906?

By 1900, Elsa had grown past her rakehell adolescence. Although never mistaken for a Gibson Girl, she was, if one made liberal allowances, "just another pretty face," although that description of Elsa at nineteen lacked the wicked irony of Hermione Gingold's barb. Owing to her father's status as a critic for the New York *Dramatic Mirror*, to her intelligence and her omnivorous reading, and to her enthusiam for the arts, especially music, she was welcomed into various literary societies and regularly cast in amateur theatricals.

Although Elsa claimed to have appeared in productions of Ibsen, Strindberg, and Hauptmann that introduced these dramatists to the Pacific Coast, the truth is that traveling professional companies presented those revolutionary plays before they filtered down to the local talent. Edmond Gagey, in *The San Francisco Stage*, reels off a roster suggesting that one could go every night to the theatre in the first years of the new century: while the plays of George Bernard Shaw "might reach San Francisco late, eventually they came—*Mrs. Warren's Profession, Man and Superman, The Devil's Disciple, Caesar and Cleopatra*, and *Pygmalion*. Oscar Wilde's *Salome* reached the city in 1907. J.M. Barrie was ably interpreted by Maude Adams in *The Little Minister, Peter Pan*, and *Quality Street*." Other British and continental playwrights whose works were performed in the city include W. Somerset Maugham, John Galsworthy, Edmond Rostand, and Henrik Ibsen. (Such actresses as Mrs. Fiske and Alla Nazimova, not Elsa and her merry play-makers, introduced *Hedda Gabler* and *A Doll's House* to San Francisco.)

In addition to the theatres, there were three opera houses and a number of orchestras, libraries, and museums. Simon Winchester, in an eleventh-hour panorama of the golden city, names "the great and glittering hotels, with the St. Francis just opened and the Fairmont just about to; restaurants to rival those of New York and Paris, and sex on an equally grand scale; ten-story, steel-framed skyscrapers and grand municipal buildings with churchly domes and acres of gold foil; a domed, sixteen-story building at the corner of Market and Third Streets, the tallest building in the American West, owned by Claus Spreckels, the sucrose magnate whose fondness for younger women is said by some to have given us the term 'sugar daddy'; a brand-new City Hall that had taken twenty-six years to build."

But also, Winchester adds, barely out of sight of this "gaudy grandilo-quence, gaity and hyperbole, San Francisco in 1906 was in fact a big, dirty, brawling, vulgar, smoggy, sooty, and corrupt town," befogged by coal smoke, with streets fouled by "the leavings of thousands of horses that pulled freight and passengers around the city . . . and though in the city center and up on Nob Hill and out at Land's End there were fine buildings, built to impress and to last, farther afield the structures were gimcrack and ugly—shacks and lean-tos and hastily cobbled together cuboids of brick and lath, smoky and insanitary and ill planned and likely to burn or fall down at the slightest excuse." Anyone depressed by such squalor could drop in at the Opium Den, 614 Jackson (listed in the San Francisco Blue Book) and smoke away his cares.

Elsa always said that as her father lay dying in 1904, he summoned her to his bedside and imparted four rules that guided her through life. Whether or not the deathbed scene played out literally is less important than Elsa's philo-sophical inheritance, which does seem the cornerstone of her unusual life.

"It won't be easy for you after I'm gone," he said quietly. "You are plain and plump and as time goes by you will get plainer and plumper. You can turn your looks into an asset because no woman will be jealous of you and no man will be suspicious of you." Then, Polonious-like, he imparted his rules for living, telling Elsa that he believed they would work for her because she was so much like him. "First, never be afraid of what *They* say. *They* exist only in your fears. What you *do* is the only thing that counts. What *They say* means nothing. Second, the more you own, the more you are possessed. Keep free of material things and enjoy life as it comes. Third, take serious things lightly and light things seriously. Fourth, always laugh at yourself first— before others do." (This fourth one David Maxwell surely remembered from Latin class, because Seneca said it first: *"Nemo risum praebuit qui ex se ce- pit,"* meaning "No one becomes a laughingstock who laughs at himself.")

Another adage that Elsa sometimes attributed to David Maxwell was this: "Mix talented people without money with the rich without talent and you will do well." This last one is suspect, however, since he couldn't have foreseen Elsa's career. Far more likely that Elsa herself coined the epigram, since it applies to her more than to anyone else.

After the death of David Maxwell, his friends remembered Elsa with invitations to the gala events she loved, not forgetting the pleasures of the table. (Nowhere does Elsa imply that her mother was involved in these out- ings.) If one must grieve, Elsa decided, San Francisco was the perfect setting for it. "The city had the vitality of a boom town and an urbane tradition that made it the cultural center of the United States second only to New York," she recalled. "Fees were so lucrative that musical giants of the stature of Paderewski, Caruso, and Kubelik made the long, uncomfortable trip across the continent to perform in San Francisco, and Broadway hits with the original casts played to sellout performances."

And so, a couple of hours before dawn on April 18, 1906, Elsa Maxwell lay in bed, wide awake, reliving the thrills of the night before and scripting, in her overstimulated mind, the witty stories with which she would regale Enrico Caruso at lunch in a few hours. She had dined, the previous evening after the opera, with the legendary tenor at Zinkand's, one of San Francis- co's esteemed restaurants. Caruso had just sung Don José in *Carmen*, to great acclaim. Also at supper was Antonio Scotti, another cast member. They had come to town for the spring season of the touring Metropolitan Opera Com- pany. Half a century later, Elsa recalled the performance: "Olive Fremstad sang the 'Habañera' so brilliantly that the applause actually drowned out the orchestra and stopped the opera. Scotti was a superb toreador, but the mounting excitement reached a tremendous crescendo to Caruso's 'Flower Song' in the second act. The audience cheered and screamed for ten minutes, an ovation that almost exhausted Caruso with all the bows he was forced to take."

In her bed, with *Carmen*'s hot-blooded tunes pounding in her brain, Elsa clutched her memories of the previous night. "Caruso was a notorious lady's man and could have enjoyed delectable hunting among the alluring females ready to swoon at his feet. He took an immediate shine to me, though, when I went to the piano and, without music, played his famous arias. But Caruso didn't like the name Elsa or anything that smacked of Wagner's operas." So he nicknamed her *"mio pappone"*—Elsa omits the translation, but the tenor had dubbed her his piglet. "Several hours—and much champagne—later, Caruso took me home and asked me to have lunch with him the next day at the St. Francis Hotel."

Later, it was remembered that during the previous day animals had seemed restless: dogs bayed like coyotes, cats leaped to mantels and swung from draperies, nervous horses threatened to run away. Conversely, an unnatural silence had fallen over the rural areas along the San Andreas Fault. Some even recalled that a peculiar silvery light had hovered over the city and the bay, seeming to keep the birds agitated and chirping long past their usual retirement. In Elsa Maxwell's bedroom, it was opera dreams that kept the young woman awake, at least until a distant rumble like the thunder of an approaching spring storm interrupted her happy thoughts. A second later, the house trembled "as though a giant hand were shaking the foundations," she said later.

Jack London, reporting on the great disaster for *Collier's* magazine, wrote that a minute after the earthquake struck, "flames were leaping upward. In a dozen different quarters south of Market Street, in the working-class ghetto, and in the factories, fires started. There was no stopping the flames. There was no organization, no communication. All the cunning adjustments of the twentieth-century city had been smashed."

Within an hour, according to London, "the smoke of San Francisco's burning was a lurid tower visible a hundred miles away. And for three days and nights this lurid tower swayed in the sky, reddening the sun, darkening the day, and filling the land with smoke."

Elsa at first had no clear idea of what was happening. She knew only that calamity had struck. Terrified, she jumped from bed and ran down the hall to her mother's bedroom. Elsa's account of those moments, recorded much later, erred in one particular detail: ". . . to my mother's room," Elsa said, "which she was sharing with a woman friend who was staying with us." The "friend" was actually Elsa's aunt Mary (aka Mollie) Johnson, her father's sister, who had joined the household after David Maxwell's death two years before.

Elsa woke her mother and her aunt. Dazed with sleep and terror, the three of them "managed to reach the front door before it was jammed by the walls, which were heaving crazily. We were halfway down a flight of marble steps leading to the street when it buckled and pitched us headlong to the cracking pavement. We lay there too stunned to speak while the house collapsed behind us. We were engulfed by a roar so deafening that it seemed to well up from every point of the compass. I tried to help my mother to her feet to escape the debris raining down on us from crashing houses, but both of us were immediately knocked down by a violent jolt."

Elsa's journalistic skills are evident in this passage from *R.S.V.P.* As if to confirm it, several weeks later a newspaper in Illinois ran an item under the headline MOTHER OF ROCK ISLAND LADY LOST ALL IN SAN FRANCISCO CATASTROPHE:

"Mrs. Mattie M. Williams [Elsa's first cousin] has received word from her mother, Mrs. M. Johnson [Elsa's aunt Mary] of San Francisco that the home in which Mrs. Johnson and her sister-in-law, Mrs. Laura Maxwell, resided was practically destroyed by the earthquake, and both of the ladies were cared for at the Mare Island Hospital and both are now practically well, though Mrs. Johnson is still suffering from lameness. Although their home was not burned, they lost practically everything of value in it, the articles being carried away by thieves and looters after the disaster."

Francis Moffat, in *Dancing on the Brink of the World*, cites many instances of those who, like Elsa and Laura and Mary, rushed out of toppling houses. "San Francisco society, dressed in their robes, stood in front of their houses amid the rubble of fallen chimneys and broken ornament. From Nob

Hill, the residents could see a stream of refugees moving slowly west and north. They moved away from the fire, pushing carts and wheelbarrows and dragging trunks filled with their belongings; a few were even pushing bulky upright pianos. All the guests, including Enrico Caruso and the Metropolitan Opera Company, fled the Palace Hotel." Arnold Genthe saw, near the ruins of his home and studio, "an old lady carrying a large bird cage with four kittens inside, while the original occupant, the parrot, perched on her hand."

Writing about the disaster nearly half a century later, Elsa chose not to linger over the devastation. "My recollection of the earthquake is unique in only one detail," she said. "I must have been the only one of the victims whose first reaction was not concerned with safety or salvaging personal possessions. True to form, I thought only of keeping my luncheon appointment with Caruso."

But Caruso regrets he's unable to lunch today.

At quarter past five, the thirty-three-year-old opera star jerked awake and felt his room at the Palace Hotel swaying like a ship at sea. There are at least half a dozen versions of what he did next—he dressed in a tuxedo; he went into the street in a nightshirt; he repaired to the St. Francis Hotel for a tranquil breakfast (the building was undamaged and the food free); he rushed to the opera house, hoping to retrieve the company's costumes, only to learn that the building had burned down along with the eight carloads of wardrobes and stage settings—with only one fact clear: as soon as possible he and his colleagues took the ferry to Oakland, and from there a train to New York. He vowed never to return to San Francisco, and he never did.

Elsa, of course, had no way to learn his whereabouts, so she elbowed her way against the flow of humanity fleeing the doomed city. The only others moving against the tide were the occasional stray horse, a wildly honking automobile steered by an apparent maniac, a preacher with a lapel card that read "A Servant of God. Let Me Help."

And John Barrymore, twenty-four, the future matinee idol of stage and screen, who had been appearing in an uncelebrated play in San Francisco. He was due to sail for Australia at noon. In anticipation of monotonous weeks at sea, Barrymore had reveled all night. When Elsa spotted him he was still in white tie and tails, though his ensemble was now soiled and askew. As he and Elsa stood exchanging stories—both had attended *Carmen* the night before, and their surreal conversation zigzagged from arias and applause to the carnage at their feet—Jack London happened by, and then George Sterling, the poet. This motley bunch, hearing Elsa's madcap scheme, agreed that she was insane to imagine lunch at the St. Francis. They had heard that the hotel was in ruins and Caruso dead in the rubble.

Apparently unscathed, Elsa seems curiously insouciant about the welfare of her mother and her aunt as she obsessed over that missed lunch date with Caruso. Since she left neither diaries nor revealing letters from this period, we have little to go on. From sources such as the newspaper item quoted above, I learned that both women were treated at the hospital at Mare Island, which is actually a peninsula alongside the town of Vallejo, some twenty miles northeast of San Francisco. At the time of the earthquake, Mare Island was the site of an important naval shipyard, and as such would have had facilities for a number of the injured and homeless. (In 1958, the newspaper columnist Jack Anderson, writing about naval issues of the time, mentioned that "famed party-giver Elsa Maxwell threw one of her first parties on Mare Island, where she stayed as a refugee from the San Francisco earthquake in 1906." The account of that apocryphal party is poetically accurate, if not literally so.)

But did Elsa take the disaster as lightly as it seems? If so, one might suspect that she held a funeral for her emotions and buried them deep. I attribute her airiness to bravado: she's giving a performance on the page as she did in many areas of her life. It's true that Elsa didn't look back; she lived in the present and the future. Although not one to show her vulnerability in public, she was by no means insensitive. It's just that sometimes you must laugh in order not to cry. In private, Elsa talked at length to a younger friend, Susan Smith, who became a columnist for the *San Francisco Examiner*. In April 1956, on the fiftieth anniversary of the earthquake, Smith wrote: "Elsa Maxwell tells stories for hours of the sights and horrors which she witnessed during that day of April, 1906. Often she has held me spellbound as she painted a picture in words of our burning city.

"Houses crumbling under the quake; people kneeling in the streets, praying, fearing it must be the end of the world; a young woman in evening clothes stopping a group of refugees and screaming as she begged them to take her into their buggy and to go to Bush and Leavenworth, where she had left her two children alone; men, women, children walking, walking, overtaken by the fire as it encroached on what had been a point of safety; the variety of precious things saved, only to be abandoned as too heavy; the anguish for the pets, the birds, the animals; businessmen trying to save their records, and in one case tying ropes to the handles of a copper boiler which they filled with their books and dragged away to safety." This account suggests that Elsa, in quiet moments, was forever haunted by the catastrophe.

Caruso, or no Caruso? I now summon a surprise witness whose testimony calls into question Elsa's account of how she spent the eve of the earthquake. In a scrapbook at the California Historical Society, I came across a clipping from the *Oakland Tribune*, dated January 20, 1952. A columnist for the paper quotes a letter he has recently received from Joseph Rosborough, whom we met when he and his mother hosted Elsa at a garden party in 1904. Recalling Elsa half a century later, he wrote: "Few people know that this musical genius and world entertainer started her career here in the Bay Area. My family spent a summer in Belvedere where I first met and became acquainted with her.

"I was to attend the Grand Opera on Mission Street as her guest the night of April 16, 1906, with Caruso in the cast. Needless to say, the performance never came off. The earthquake and fire drove many families across the Bay to Oakland and among them came Miss Maxwell, who immediately established a salon which became the rendezvous of artists, writers, and musicians." (Does he mean April 18? The performances of April 16 and April 17 took place *before* the earthquake struck, early on the eighteenth.)

Rosborough, like Elsa, would have been close to seventy in 1952, and only a Hercule Poirot could discern whether he remembered those April nights clearly, or whether his report is no more substantial than a wisp of San Francisco fog. He *seems* to mean that he and Elsa had tickets for *Carmen* on Wednesday night, but that the earthquake that morning obviated the performance. What his letter does prove, however, is the ambiguity that shrouds every biography, from Jesus to JFK.

5 Now Voyager, Sail Thou Forth

 an Kurzman, in his book *Disaster!*, wrote that "San Francisco has lived two lives—one before the earthquake and fire and one after." The same might be said of Elsa. "My easy, sheltered life went up in the smoke of ruined San Francisco," she said, forgetting that she was "poor." She continued candidly, "I had never earned a penny and it was high time I did. My father's entire estate was a $10,000 life-insurance policy," but medical and funeral expenses had reduced the amount to four thousand dollars, which, according to Elsa, resided in the joint bank account of her and her mother. "It was obvious that I could not go on being a burden to my mother. The very best I could do was to support myself." (Ten thousand dollars in those days had the purchasing power of roughly a quarter of a million dollars in present-day money, meaning that Elsa's father left his wife and daughter far from destitute.)

By all accounts, San Francisco's recovery was a swift success. Kurzman asserts that the obliterated city had to be "rebuilt physically, economically, and socially—a feat miraculously accomplished in a few years." One year after the earthquake, on April 18, 1907, the *Coast Seaman's Journal* editorialized that "the immediate effects of the disaster have been beneficial in the main. San Francisco is today the busiest city in the world, and where that condition exists there is little time, and generally little occasion, for lamentation. On the whole, we think that the people of San Francisco are justified in looking with satisfaction, if not pride, upon the events of the past year."

Much of puritan America looked askance at the city's rapid healing. Julia Altrocchi, in *The Spectacular San Franciscans*, cites "sermonizers in the East" who "thundered sulphurously that the 'Sodom of the West' had been punished and laid low 'by Almighty God,' but San Francisco had no such sense of guilt." The *New York Evening Post* chastized San Francisco's "*gaieté de coeur*" so soon after the disaster. (Fundamentalists never shut up. A century later they were still foaming over God's "punishment" of New York on September 11 and New Orleans by Hurricane Katrina.)

Elsa, too, wasted no time in reestablishing her social calendar. Less than four months after the earthquake, on August 7, 1906, the *Oakland Tribune* reported that "Miss Elsie Maxwell was hostess Saturday evening at a delightful affair given at her Linda Vista house. [Meaning the Maxwell cottage on Linda Vista Avenue, Belvedere Island.] The evening was enjoyed by a score or more guests and the hostess and others contributed musical numbers to an interesting and varied program."

It is unclear whether Elsa, her mother, and her aunt had taken up residence at the cottage or whether they used it only for weekends and vacations. On August 10, 1906, the same newspaper reported that "Miss Elsie Maxwell and Miss Beatrice Fredericks have been spending a few days in Marin County." That item suggests that Elsa's permanent residence was still in San Francisco. On August 16, the paper again reported that "Miss Elsie Maxwell has been visiting in Belvedere. The Maxwell country home has been purchased by Mr. and Mrs. L. Adams." Later in August, she entertained with a musical evening on Linda Vista Avenue; in September she was once more in Belvedere; "her former residence in the pretty suburb makes her well known there among a host of friends." These society jottings continue throughout 1906 and into 1907, which is the time, according to Elsa's chronology, that she left San Francisco. The sale of the Maxwell house on Belvedere Island suggests postearthquake financial need.

"I didn't have a single accomplishment that vaguely resembled a commercial asset," she said. "I could play the piano well enough to entertain at parties, but not well enough to make a career of it. The truth was inescapable. I was nothing but a dilettante with no usefulness in my home town."

The four thousand dollars in Elsa's and Laura's joint account would have amounted to the equivalent of nearly a hundred thousand dollars today. They were well above the poverty line, though obviously in reduced circumstances. Elsa's claim, however, that in 1906 "it would be gone within the year" is absurd, unless her mother was as flighty a spendthrift as Elsa. Then and throughout her life, Elsa's solution to low funds was always to spend more money. Whatever prior quarrels had taken place between her and Laura, Elsa's next move was perhaps the coup de grâce to mother-daughter harmony.

Elsa withdrew two thousand dollars from the account, presumably her share. Or perhaps not: in later years she was accused more than once of financial irregularities verging on grand larceny. For instance, the novelist Dawn Powell, in a diary entry for 1950, wrote of a recent visit to Gerald and Sara Murphy: "They spoke of Elsa Maxwell and how she raised money for Russian Ambulance in World War I, absconded with the money, then returned to social success after three years." In 1960, Dick Nolan, a columnist for the *San Francisco Examiner*, included this accusatory item: "I don't know how much will be left for the San Mateo Crippled Children's Auxiliary from the proceeds of that Elsa Maxwell party in the Palace. Now Elsa has billed the Auxiliary for $1,100 to pay for her gown." The accusations, however, are suspect on various counts. Dawn Powell suffered from alcoholism, the Murphys were not involved in charity work except through hearsay, Elsa was not away from "social success" for three years and therefore made no "return," and top designers like Edward Molyneux gave Elsa more dresses than she could wear as free advertising for their *maisons de couture*.

In any case, two thousand dollars ended up in Elsa's incapable hands. Had she invested this birthright in a hot dog stand, or a ladies' detective agency, she might have stood on a firmer foundation than sinking it into a questionable Shakespearean stock company that was touring the wilds of California. Elsa, however, chose dramatic art as her financial instrument, the catalyst for her unwise investment being an English thespian, Constance Crawley. If Elsa had consulted a wise businessman, a reliable showman, or even her mother, she would have learned that competition was formidable: in the first decade of the twentieth century, some 2,500 stock companies worked the United States from top to bottom.

CONSTANCE CRAWLEY

Born in London in 1879, Crawley enjoyed moderate success on the stage in Britain, America, and Australia in the early years of the twentieth century. Her repertoire ranged from Shakespeare to Oscar Wilde; indeed, in 1910 she appeared in a Broadway production of Wilde's last play, *Mr. and Mrs. Daventry*, a drama dealing with the injustice of the divorce laws in England. Earlier, she had made her debut in London under the management of Sir Herbert Beerbohm Tree, the actor-manager who, in 1904, founded the Royal Academy of Dramatic Art. Whatever her own talents as an actress-manager, she surely had spunk, for she formed her own company and traveled thousands of miles with it while still in her early twenties. Those of her reviews captured online are mostly favorable, although the *Oakland Tribune* on September 29, 1906, struck a hesitant note: "Perhaps most of us liked Constance Crawley less in *Hedda Gabler* than in anything we have seen her attempt." Interviewed by that paper the following year, Crawley revealed that the mining town of Tonopah, Nevada, had built a theatre especially for her. "It took just a month to build," she said, "and it's beautifully fitted up, with all modern conveniences, and lighted by electricity." Throughout the interview, she sounds provincially pretentious as she unfolds grandiose plans for playing Shakespeare in "my beloved Italy." And then, "I'm going to Brussels, too, and maybe Norway." When the interviewer inquired about plans to stage the Norwegian play *Beyond Human Power* in Oakland, Crawley replied that she would take the leading part. "Let me see," continued the journalist, "who wrote that play?" But Crawley couldn't remember. "Really," she said, "I'm not sure; but I think it was Bjornson. Let me see—I have the manuscript here." (She was right; Bjørnstjerne Bjørnson had won the Nobel Prize three years earlier.)

In 1913, Crawley went to Hollywood, where she appeared in fourteen films before her death in 1919. Among these are such picturesque titles as *Thais* (which Crawley codirected with Arthur Maude), *Jephtah's Daughter*, and *The Virgin of the Rocks*. In addition, she is credited as writer on eleven other pictures. George Sterling, the local poet we met crawling out of the earthquake, wrote a poem "To Miss Constance Crawley," which contains the florid sentiment "Sing as I might, I could not sing / A fairer dream than thou."

As for Arthur Maude, whom Elsa accused of chicanery, he acted in some forty pictures in Britain and Hollywood, and directed thirty-one. Elmer Harris, also associated with Elsa's brief career as impresario, later wrote a number of Broadway plays, the most famous one being *Johnny Belinda*, the basis for the 1948 motion picture.

Many a gentleman has lost money on "hopeful" actresses. Instances are rare, however, of a twenty-five-year-old woman with the wherewithal and bad judgment to do the same. Nevertheless, in Elsa's view "fate intervened" in the guise of Miss Crawley. As so often in Elsa's life, details are murky. How the two came to form a partnership no one knows, though it's likely that Elsa, well known in San Francisco for her theatrical endeavors, helped to welcome visiting stage luminaries to the city. And Crawley's sculptural profile, her big hats with plumes, and her susurrous gowns would have quickened Elsa's heartbeat.

Constance Crawley "had a fairly good following in London," Elsa recalled, but, having made the arduous journey to California, "Constance was seized by a strange delusion," namely, that the California desert was athirst for precisely what she and her strolling players had to offer: Shakespeare. Elsa implies that the troupe was at best third-rate, offering as evidence the fact that Arthur Maude, manager of the Crawley company, offered Elsa herself the choice of Juliet, Lady Macbeth, or Ophelia!

The way Elsa got rooked resembles more closely a Molière farce than anything Shakespearean. "At a reception given for Constance," Elsa said, "someone with a perverted sense of humor played her a cruel trick. Constance was told that I was a wealthy, stagestruck heiress who would be only too ecstatic to bail her out of the jam"—the actors were stuck without a cent. Suddenly the room was filled with theatrical endearments: "Dahling Girl, I have heard of your wonderful creative work even in far away London."

Though Elsa's London reputation lay at least a decade in the future, she was enormously flattered by such folderol.

Soon they were bosom buddies, with Elsa at tea in Constance Crawley's "shabby hotel," where, Elsa recalled ruefully, "the troupe couldn't have greeted me more effusively had I been the British consul with free transportation back to England." For hours they petted Elsa, who plumed herself over the attention and the sudden opportunities. All of Shakespeare lay at her feet, with modern drama and popular comedies thrown in. Arthur Maude, with Dickensian unctuousness, stepped forward to announce, "We shall be delighted to have you join our company, dear lady. But let me ask you a question. How much do you wish to invest in our enterprise?"

Wine having been poured into the teacups, Elsa felt the world spinning as she had not since the earthquake. "Twenty thousand dollars," she caroled, and Constance Crawley's pet monkey, Doodles, shrieked his approval.

A crooked smile crossed the lips of Arthur Maude. "You must realize, Miss Maxwell, this is an unparalleled chance for a girl of your tender age and relative inexperience," and so on, seducing Elsa even further. Scarcely pausing, she upped her promised investment to thirty thousand, becoming instantly the co-owner, co-manager, and star of—what, exactly? This down-at-the-heels company did exist, unlike Elsa's twenty and then thirty thousands, but its pulse was irregular, and, without a massive transfusion, rigor mortis would soon set in. For a short while, however, the honeymoon was on, and Pleasure reigned alongside Art.

On September 17, 1906, the *Oakland Tribune* reported that "Miss Elsie Maxwell was hostess Saturday evening at an enjoyable reception given at her Linda Vista home with Mrs. Constance Crawley and Arthur Maude as honored guests." On December 8, that same paper (which tracked Elsa with doglike devotion) reported that the Independent Stage Society, of which Elmer Harris, having replaced Arthur Maude, was director and stage manager and Miss Elsa (no longer Elsie) Maxwell secretary-treasurer, would present Oscar Wilde's *The Importance of Being Earnest* at Ye Liberty Playhouse on December 12, with Elsa as Lady Bracknell, proceeds to benefit Providence Hospital. The article also reported that, preceding the play, Constance Crawley "will make an address explaining the plan and purpose of the organization and will introduce the players."

The newspaper explained that "the society has been organized for the purpose of presenting literary and high-class dramas, and all the talented folk around the bay will participate in the various productions planned for the future." The next play in the series was to be *The Misanthrope*. All of this suggests that the group was legitimate and respectable, though Elsa's account presents it as unyieldingly shady, with a mixed bag of amateur and professional actors. (Reviewing *The Importance of Being Earnest*, the *San Francisco Call* opined that "the acting ranged from bad to rather fair. Elsa Wyman Maxwell, who played Lady Bracknell, seemed to have a sure grip on the requirements of her role and the ability to meet them." Overall, however, the production sounds ghastly: "If the characters had been of Missouri birth and breeding, the absence of what goes to make British upperdom so atmospherically distinct could not have been more pronounced.")

In Elsa's tangled version of her theatrical fiasco, she invested the two thousand dollars and then skipped town with the stock company. Her assertion raises the question: What did the company think of two thousand rather than the promised thirty thousand dollars? Elsa claims to have mailed a valedictory letter to her mother without so much as a good-bye kiss: "My Dearest, I am running away. I am not in love and I am not going to have a baby. I simply can't stand this life. I want to make my own way and I'll never amount to anything if I stay in San Francisco. I won't come back until I'm somebody."

The fact that the Independent Stage Society lingered for close to two years in the Bay Area belies Elsa's melodramatic leave-taking. It's likely that Laura Maxwell, no doubt displeased at Elsa's unwise investment, knew all that went on and even attended the plays. Since Laura had by then recovered from injuries received in the earthquake, she would certainly have known about Elsa's soirees at the family cottage on Belvedere Island, even if she wasn't there. One could speculate endlessly, and, in truth, apart from the scant information in *R.S.V.P.* and the newspapers, speculation offers the only insight into this pivotal time in Elsa's life.

According to her, she left town with Constance Crawley and the other actors. They ended up in Texas flat broke; the railroad depot in San Antonio caught fire and burned their scenery and billboard posters; Elsa was demoted from playing Juliet to Juliet's nurse; angry words were exchanged and tears gushed from various eyes; Elsa wired her mother for money and received two hundred dollars; a projected "triumphant world tour" lasted ten months without crossing an international border; and Elsa scraped together enough dough to get her to New York with three dollars in her purse.

Another version, from the *San Francisco Chronicle*, does little to clarify Elsa's departure from the Bay Area. Under the headline PROFESSIONAL STAGE IS A DISAPPOINTMENT, the item leads with: "Telegrams to her friends in San Francisco, Berkeley, and Oakland from Miss Elsa Maxwell in Kansas City brought the news yesterday that she had met with disappointment in her first venture on the professional stage." Suggesting that Elsa left town under a cloud, the piece states that "Miss Maxwell said little to her friends here of her plans, and to some of them her telegrams received yesterday contained the first knowledge they had that she had gone on the professional stage. Miss Maxwell desires to return to Berkeley and her friends have come to her assistance." But the real shock comes in the last paragraph: "Miss Maxwell is a young woman of great beauty. . . . Her friends say that she has received many offers of a stage career but refused them all until importuned by Constance Crawley to join her company."

This version implies that Elsa did not appeal to her mother for funds, but rather to everyone but Laura Maxwell. Whatever the breach between them, it seems irreparable by this point. In press accounts of Elsa's later visits to the Bay Area, there is never mention of Mrs. Maxwell. Indeed, one item pointedly identifies Elsa as "the daughter of the late James David Maxwell," without noting the mother who lived nearby.

Notwithstanding the financial assistance of friends, Elsa soldiered on with the ragtag drama troupe. (Perhaps she had no intention of returning home, and sent those misleading telegrams only to procure funds.) September 1908 finds the company's three principals in Edwardsville, Illinois, where the *Edwardsville Intelligencer* devoted an entire front-page column to the news, CONSTANCE CRAWLEY PLAYERS TO PRESENT DRAMA. The presentation was H. V. Esmond's *One Summer Day*, to be given on the lawn of a private home as a benefit for the Humane Society. Appearing in the play with Crawley were Arthur Maude, "an actor of renown," and "Miss Elsa Maxwell, secretary to Miss Crawley."

6 Send Me a Tenor

$\mathcal{O}$n *R.S.V.P.*, Elsa recalls that she first arrived in New York in 1907. (The city's first motorized taxicab arrived the same year.) Her stated time of arrival raises several questions, however. Did she come with Constance Crawley and others in the stock company? It's unlikely that the New York theatre would have summoned them, since it had a full complement of professional players and then, as always, hordes of amateurs in search of stardom. (Crawley made her one short-lived Broadway appearance in February 1910.) It's conceivable that Crawley and her ill-assorted troupe thought to storm the New York ramparts and, being disappointed, took their show on the road to Edwardsville, Illinois, and elsewhere in the provinces.

Accepting Elsa's chronology, we encounter once more her insistence that she was broke, along with her claim that she "didn't know a soul in the big, overwhelming city," an assertion she soon contradicts. She said she had three dollars and no idea where to look for work. As always, Elsa is eager to convince the reader not only of her poverty, but also of her own resourcefulness. She walked a mile in the rain to a boardinghouse in Hell's Kitchen recommended by a conductor on the train. Lacking the requisite twelve dollars a month demanded by the landlady, payable in advance, she remembered Mrs. Fiske—the great actress Minnie Maddern Fiske, a star who had often played in San Francisco and who had visited the Maxwell home. Mrs. Fiske's niece, Merle Maddern, had also appeared in San Francisco productions under the auspices of Elsa's and Constance Crawley's Independent Stage Company. Then, too, Mrs. Fiske's husband, Harrison Fiske, published the New York *Dramatic Mirror*, for which Elsa's father had been stringer and critic. (In *All About Eve*, George Sanders tells Anne Baxter that she's "too short for that gesture" and that "it went out with Mrs. Fiske.")

Throwing herself on the great lady's mercy, Elsa cried out, "I am the late J. D. Maxwell's daughter, he was your friend," beseeching Mrs. Fiske to help his orphaned girl find work. Learning of Elsa's agility at the piano, the Fiskes sent her to a nickelodeon in the West Thirties, where she was hired to play from noon to midnight seven days a week.

At this point one may sigh, "Permit me my doubts," and indeed the events unroll like the scenario of a melodrama playing right there in Elsa's nickelodeon—or something on the order of Thomas Edison's version of Mark Twain's *The Prince and the Pauper*, Edwin S. Porter's *The Dream of a Rarebit Fiend* and *The Kleptomaniac*, a one-reel version of *Ben-Hur*, or D. W. Griffith's first film, *The Adventures of Dollie*, all of them on offer in the city at that time. (Despite Elsa's Orphan Annie scenario, it's likely that Mrs. Fiske received her with tea and cordiality as an old acquaintance, if not exactly as a colleague.)

Starry-eyed newcomers to New York are not known for slavish devotion to fact; the process of reinventing oneself obtrudes. *This* Elsa, the Elsa nearing the end of act one, was ready for a change. She didn't have the next Elsa clearly focused, but in every direction she heard music. It came from the Metropolitan Opera, Broadway, Carnegie Hall, Tin Pan Alley, a thousand concerts and symphonies, and musical evenings in the mansions of Fifth Avenue. And she heard her own songs, all of those she knew she could write, and play, and sell, to charm the world with her melodies. More than anything else, Elsa wanted a life filled with music.

Whatever Elsa's prevarications, it's true that New York was not a tender place, especially for an unchaperoned single woman who, by age twenty-six, had grown portly and increasingly plain. Her discomforts were physical as well as sociological for, as the historian Edward Wagenknecht reminds us, "women held themselves together with stiff, whalebone- and steel-fortified corsets, which the most fashionable laced as tightly as possible, and often they wore boned collars too. The hourglass figure was much admired."

(To be sure, Elsa had the makings of an hourglass, though her proportions were not stacked in the usual order.) In a sense, women, like children, were to be seen and not heard, and similarly disciplined, even in New York, where a woman could be arrested for smoking in public. Nevertheless, many women migrated to the city to escape worse oppressions at home.

And to experience the greatest concentration of vitality in America. Just a handful of attractions in 1907: at Fifth Avenue and Fifty-ninth Street, the Plaza Hotel opened on October 1; Clyde Fitch, widely considered the country's greatest playwright, had three new plays and two revivals on Broadway that year, including *Captain Jinks of the Horse Marines* with Ethel Barrymore as star; Florenz Ziegfeld opened his first *Follies*; Gustav Mahler conducted at the Metropolitan Opera.

And by 1907, Tin Pan Alley had turned popular music composing into an assembly-line industry. Originally a specific place in New York—West Twenty-eighth Street between Fifth and Sixth Avenues—it soon became a metonym for all of music publishing. Most of the country's best composers had some connection with Tin Pan Alley, and some of its worst. Edward Wagenknecht points out that those who ran it understood two things extremely well: "how to write songs about what people were interested in, and how to make them aware of the songs' existence." Put another way, Tin Pan Alley marketed the lowest common denominator as relentlessly as television would do in later decades. The extraordinary thing is that so much genius found its way to the top: countless songs by George M. Cohan, the Gershwins, Cole Porter, Jerome Kern, and many others.

When Elsa first looked toward Twenty-eighth Street, however, the songs that filled the air were not of the Porter-Gershwin-Kern calibre. Sophistication must wait a decade or so. "Even when the lyrics were imbecilic," says Wagenknecht, "the tunes might be unforgettable." Who hasn't heard such grandmother's delights as "Wait 'til the Sun Shines, Nellie" (1905), "Shine On, Harvest Moon" (1908), and "Let Me Call You Sweetheart" (1910)? They'll run forever in family pictures from the studio era, and on TV under the mad-cow baton of Lawrence Welk.

In 1909, Elsa took a sheaf of songs to Leo Feist, a leading publisher of popular music. In one of the cubbyholes at his publishing house, each one with its own piano, she played and sang her tunes. "They're lousy," he said.

Then, after a cunning pause, he added as though doing her a favor, "That one you call 'The Sum of Life' is not as lousy as the others." He offered her ten dollars for it, and Elsa imagined all of New York at her feet. Such swindles were not uncommon. Elsa's claim, however, that she didn't sell another song for six years is patently untrue.

Harrison Fiske, who had become her benefactor, scoffed when she told him the news. "Don't you know better than to sell a song outright for a paltry ten dollars without getting the usual royalty rights?" But Elsa didn't care. "I never regretted the deal," she said. "Feist sold 200,000 copies of 'The Sum of Life,' and the thrill of seeing 'Words and Music by Elsa Maxwell' on the cover of the sheet music was all the reward I wanted."

News of Elsa's success reached San Francisco, and newspaper accounts named local singers who had added her work to their programs. The hometown papers also reported that she was composing a "grand opera, selections of which have startled New York musicians on account of the marvelous orchestral harmony of which she shows a mastery." That work was never finished.

Elsa claimed that her visits to Mrs. Fiske at the theatre sustained her during this lean period. There's a faint echo of Eve Harrington in her account, minus any designs on the leading lady's spouse or any wish to become her understudy. Elsa haunted Mrs. Fiske's dressing room and, with her garrulous gladhanding, soon got to know a number of theatre people. It was backstage after one of Mrs. Fiske's performances that Elsa "met an exquisite girl who was to change the entire course of my life with a casual word."

She was Marie Doro, and Elsa doesn't exaggerate in calling her "one of the biggest and unquestionably the most beautiful of all the stars on Broadway." Born Marie Katherine Steward in Pennsylvania in 1882, she made her Broadway debut in 1902 and appeared in seventeen plays and musicals over the next twenty years, as well as in eighteen films between 1915 and 1924. Onstage, she starred in works by Sir James M. Barrie, Clyde Fitch, and Gilbert and Sullivan.

Marie Doro's hair was long and midnight black, her large, dark, widely spaced eyes set in a startlingly white face, and her expression was one of bemusement, as if she were trying to figure out how to escape from the beauty that framed her. She felt imprisoned by it. According to Mercedes de Acosta, a friend and possible lover, "If you never knew Marie intimately you could never have known all her tricks for hiding her beauty. I was immediately aware of her, even when she dressed herself up like a pixie to conceal it." In her profound, intelligent beauty, she resembled Keira Knightley, though without Knightley's angularity.

Marie was actress, singer, and composer, and it was music that brought her and Elsa together. "I understand you play the piano very well," Marie said, and asked Elsa whether she would come to her house the following night to help entertain a few guests.

It was a small after-theatre party for a few old friends—of Marie's, and, as it turned out, of Elsa's, as well. William Gillette was there, the actor and playwright who had cast Marie in several of his plays; John Drew, the matinee idol; his nephew, John Barrymore, and another alumnus of the San Francisco earthquake, Enrico Caruso, who remembered Elsa, and enlisted her as both pianist and accomplice for his unpleasant practical joke: he cooked an Italian dish with face powder substituted for flour, a risky prank in a roomful of actors and singers with sensitive vocal cords. Caruso sang, and so did Elsa and Marie, and John Barrymore told "Rabelaisian stories" of his adventures on stage and in the bedroom—Elsa's phrase, meaning "stories that would make them faint in Keokuk."

As Elsa and Marie became more intimate, Elsa discovered that Marie was surely the only actress who could "read an ode in the original Greek while removing her makeup." She learned, too, that Marie was something of an authority on Shakespeare's sonnets and on Elizabethan poetry in general. Another interest was religion, and after leaving the theatre in the early 1920s, Marie studied for a time at Union Theological Seminary, in New York, a liberal Protestant institution. Afterward, she grew increasingly reclusive, and died in obscurity in 1956.

Elsa said, "We got along so well that Marie added me to her entourage as a companion, to play the piano at parties and to balance her supper tables, which always were top-heavy with men." The first part of this pregnant sentence could mean that they became lovers for a time; or it could mean merely that Elsa was terrific company, as many others described her in later years. For a sensitive soul like Marie, Elsa's brash head-on with the world would have provided a buffer. Elsa's eventual claim that Marie took her up because "the contrast in our appearances set off Marie's beauty" doesn't ring true; after all, Marie was renowned for downplaying that very beauty, which she regarded as a handicap. (Could she be the only woman who ever envied Elsa's looks?) Elsa's averral sounds like facile closure to an affair—or a friendship—grown cold.

Elsa does not specify how Marie changed her life. It's true that Marie wangled a part for her in *The Richest Girl*, one of Marie's lesser starring vehicles—the play ran on Broadway for twenty-four performances in March 1909. Then they went on tour, and Elsa luxuriated in the star comfort they shared: a private rail car, with maid service and a French chef to prepare each meal.

Unfortunately for Elsa, Marie's domineering mother joined them on the tour and took an instant dislike to Elsa. As soon as the tour ended, Elsa washed up once more on the shores of New York. There she lived in grubby boardinghouses, writing songs all day, emerging to look for jobs she couldn't get, eating in greasy cafeterias. Then, at night, she became half a Cinderella: no dazzling gown, no tiara nor coach and four, though she did attend the ball—many a ball, like one given by some of Caruso's friends, who invited her to play the piano (for pay, no doubt, for Elsa had sure ways of making known her needs). "I marched straight to the piano and, as usual, began to play for my supper. An extraordinary-looking woman came over to listen and, after humming along with me for a few minutes, asked whether I could play something from *Pagliacci*."

Elsa asked which aria she would like, her fingers poised for Nedda's happy song to the birds, known as the "Ballatella." Instead, the woman replied with supreme confidence, *"Vesti la giubba"*—the opera's signature tenor aria.

"Who's going to sing it?" Elsa demanded.

"I am," said the strange woman.

"In what key do you want me to play it?" Elsa, with her unusual ear, could transpose from one key to another with no effort.

"Exactly as it's written. For a tenor."

With enormous misgiving, Elsa played the opening bars . . ."*Recitar! Mentre preso dal delirio* . . ." And from the throat of Dorothy Toye came a perfect rendition of Canio's show-stopping aria. "I almost fell off the stool,"

said Elsa. "Not only was her voice amazing but it had the quality and tim-
bre of a pure tenor."

They all laughed at Elsa because she hadn't heard of the Trick Voice, the
veteran vaudevillian Dorothy Toye. (Toye was the Yma Sumac of her day.
Sumac was said to have a vocal range of five octaves. Elsa described Dorothy as having "a strong, true voice in any register above baritone.")

If Toye made recordings, they are extremely obsure today. Nor is much
biographical information to be found. Her one Broadway appearance was
in *Marie Dressler's "All Star Gambol"* in 1913 (which lasted for five performances). A Canadian review from the same period refers to her "international fame," adding that "she has traveled throughout Europe, as well as
America, and is now back for a period of rest with her home friends [in
Canada]." That Canadian program included songs by Puccini, Dvorak,
Tchaikovsky, Grieg, Mascagni, and Leoncavallo. The reviewer mentions her
"fine dramatic expression and technical brilliancy" in soprano arias from
Manon Lescaut and *La Bohème*. "Her songs for tenor voice included the
familiar 'La Donna è Mobile' and the 'Siciliana' from *Cavalleria Rusticana*,
both being sung with the manly ring and resonance of a well trained male
tenor, and it was difficult to believe that both tenor and soprano voices came
from the slender throat of the attractive girl who stood before the large and
fashionable audience."

Surely it was Dorothy Toye, more than Marie Doro, who changed the
entire course of Elsa's life. Before Elsa stood up from the piano that night,
she was hired as Dorothy's accompanist. Elsa soon guessed that the curtain
had gone up on the next act of her life, the long act two that would play for
the next fifty years.

7   I've Written a Letter to Mother

During the following months, Elsa was happier, she said, than at any time since her father's death: "For the first time in my life I was accepted on my own merits without the aid of another person's influence." She portrays Dorothy Toye as an easygoing and considerate boss, unpretentious and comfortable in her own skin. And she paid well. With Elsa at the piano, she toured the East Coast vaudeville circuit until a cablegram arrived offering Dorothy an engagement in England. According to Elsa, Dorothy didn't have money enough to take her along on the same boat, and of course Elsa was flat broke, as always. Elsa accompanied Dorothy to the ship, waved as it floated off down the Hudson, and trudged back to her desk to write more songs that the world could wait to sing.

Elsa is not self-aggrandizing when she points out her lifelong good luck, her knack for putting herself in the right place at exactly the right moment, and her faith in small, happy miracles. In the words of a satirical song published the same year that Elsa met Dorothy Toye, "Heaven Will Protect the Working Girl." And it did, with a phone call from Marie Doro, who had been out of town for several months. Marie was sailing for Europe that very day—without her draconian mother—and would Elsa like to follow on the next boat? Marie would pay her passage.

At this point in Elsa's narrative, you could swear that her inspiration was *I Love Lucy*. Like that show, it's a funny farce, one you enjoy far more if you don't peek behind the curtain or demand that it conform to truth. With Marie's travel money, Elsa settled "some bills which could not be dodged"—meaning she might otherwise face arrest at the dock—and used the amount remaining to book passage on a cattle boat. (That term, which Elsa deftly used to underline once more her poverty, is somewhat deceptive. Such boats, which indeed carried livestock and other cargo, were actually comfortable, with dining rooms, salons, and the like.) A dozen other passengers had chosen this conveyance, including a Captain and Mrs. Sands, he a Master of Fox Hounds, who insisted that Elsa join them in Warwickshire for their first hunt of the season.

On arrival in England, Elsa received a message that Marie was on tour somewhere on the Continent. It was Friday, and the office of Marie's manager would not open again until Monday. Elsa had no notion of Dorothy Toye's location, and she had three pounds in her purse. So, with great misgiving, she accompanied her shipboard friends to the dreaded fox hunt. Having planned to ditch them in Southhampton and rush off to London to join Marie, Elsa had claimed boastful expertise as a horsewoman: "All Californians are born to the saddle." In truth, she had never mounted a horse. After a mighty struggle getting on, and clinging to the dreaded mare, she finally tumbled off, bedraggled and disheveled. Believing herself safe at last, she hitched a ride with a groom on a two-wheeled cart, which promptly hit a deep rut and threw its cargo, Elsa, to the ground. Finally she escaped these rural hazards, having recalled more than once Oscar Wilde's characterization of a fox hunt as "the unspeakable in full pursuit of the uneatable."

Back in London, and no Marie, no Dorothy, she found a dingy hotel in Russell Square, Bloomsbury, near the British Museum, and spent her days there in the Reading Room. It's entirely possible that Virginia Woolf, who would later write, "There is, in the British Museum, an enormous mind," was reading there, or writing a book review for the *Times*, within sight of Elsa.

Walking down Oxford Street one day, Elsa saw a placard announcing "Dorothy Toye/Double Voice Phenomenon/Empire Music Hall Now." Reunited with her patroness, Elsa forsook the elevated thoughts of Bloomsbury and resumed playing the piano, two shows a day, for ten pounds a week. After a tour of the British Isles, she accompanied Dorothy on engagements in France and Germany, which occupied them for over a year and a half, or so Elsa said.

Her chronology, however, is distorted, and after much attention devoted to the matter, I have concluded that the reasons for her wavering time line are 1) her habit of inflating successes even as she denigrated her social standing and her family's wealth; 2) a genuine lack of concern for precision in matching events with their proper dates; and 3) the factor of age, for Elsa was past seventy when she hurriedly threw together the bare bones of her life story and entrusted it to a slipshod ghostwriter.

During this period, Elsa was writing to her mother back in San Francisco, and Mrs. Maxwell, with contacts at the *Oakland Tribune*, was a proud informant of Elsa's triumphs. On August 1, 1909, the paper reported that "Miss Elsa Wyman Maxwell, a former society girl of the Linda Vista set, has made a great success in the East, and is fast becoming famous as a song writer. . . . She is now receiving a royalty on twelve songs and is writing, in collaboration with Marie Doro, an opera." (Elsa's assertion that she didn't sell another song for six years after Leo Feist bought "The Sum of Life" is wrong. The British Library has at least nine of her songs with 1908 and 1909 copyright dates, several of them published by Feist.)

By 1910, her letters home had become grandiose with exaggeration. The Oakland paper reported on February 20 of that year that Elsa had been "presented at court and has been given presents by King Edward of England and the King and Queen of Austria. In letters received by her mother the news of Miss Maxwell's success has come to friends in Berkeley." The piece continues with the news of her association with Dorothy Toye in London: "Recently the two young women gave a benefit for crippled children, and in token of appreciation King Edward presented them with two beautiful loving cups."

These apocryphal court appearances, if they took place at all, would likely have seen Elsa and Dorothy in a vast crowd of honorees, and not, as the newspaper implies, tête-à-tête with royalty. Two foreign vaudevillians, both lacking the beauty to attract the king's eye, would not have raised Edward VII from his sickbed. Often ill, he was nearing the end of his life, and died in the spring of 1910. The tottering Hapsburg Empire of Austria-Hungary, headed by an elderly emperor, was already in such turmoil that the outbreak of World War I seemed an anticlimax. And nowhere in her writings does Elsa mention a brush with the British royal family earlier than the 1920s, when she first met Queen Mary, and also the queen's son, the Prince of Wales, later Edward VIII, and later still the Duke of Windsor, her longtime friend in spite of Elsa's spats with his American wife, the Duchess.

Elsa puts the date of her departure for the Union of South Africa, its official name at the time, as 1909. If not that year, it would have taken place no later than 1910. Dorothy Toye had received an invitation to perform in that remote British colony, but was reluctant to go until Elsa, always the adventuress, persuaded her. Eventually, Dorothy accepted a month of engagements in Cape Town and Johannesburg.

With what expectations Elsa set sail for the bottom of the African continent, we don't know. The magnificent scenery took a backseat to society, as Elsa concentrated her energies on social lions rather than wildlife. She captured Sir Henry Scobell, a luminary of the Boer War and later commander of the British garrison in Cape Town. Sir Henry introduced her to his former enemy, the Boer General Louis Botha, who was charmed by Elsa's piano tunes. When she learned of his great fondness for Viennese waltzes, she played so many of them that the general—a handsome man of Hemingwayesque mien and sparkling brown eyes—invited her to dine with him and his wife. When word got around in the provincial city that both Sir Henry and General Botha had taken a shine to the animated American, she was flooded with invitations. Such unaccustomed attention went to her head like a Cape cabernet, and her tongue was loosened. "I concocted a glittering background," she admitted. She told them her father was a pioneer in the California Gold Rush. "My fling in vaudeville was laughed off as a typical eccentricity of a headstrong, enormously wealthy heiress. I began to tell barefaced lies in front of Dorothy," who let Elsa cut up and have her fun, then berated her in private.

When Dorothy's month was over, and she was packing to sail back to England, Elsa informed her that she herself would not be on the boat. She added that playing the piano was not what she intended to do for the rest of her life, though it was unexplicit, even to Elsa, which activity she might find to replace it. Social climbing was the immediate candidate, for she was invited to be the house guest of Sir Lionel and Lady Phillips at Arcadia Farm, their estate near Johannesburg. Florence, Lady Phillips, had taken a great liking for Elsa, who soon addressed her as "Florrie."

"Frankly speaking, I was too eager to stay in South Africa to worry about the various whys of Florrie's invitation," Elsa said cryptically, without revealing those "whys." Sir Lionel was a mining magnate and politician, a protégé of Cecil Rhodes. Lady Phillips was an art collector who helped establish the Johannesburg Art Gallery and later presented it with works from her own collection, including paintings by Pissarro, Monet, Sisley, and Walter Sickert. A boldly handsome woman whose face suggested both the plainness and the robust character of a wheat field, Lady Phillips posed for several painters, including Giovanni Boldini, and her own portraits hang in several museums.

Elsa said she was "responsible for everything worthwhile in Johannesburg. She financed theatres, art galleries, hospitals, and newspapers. She kept an open house for artists and writers. She knew everything about everybody." In 1913 Lady Phillips wrote a book, *A Friendly Germany: Why Not?*, which urged Britain and Germany to unite against the anticolonialist movements among Africans and Asians, which to her represented "the Black and Yellow Perils."

Sir Lionel, according to Elsa, was "a nervous little person with a soft voice and a diabolical sense of sarcasm who wasn't fooled by me for a minute. I think he took to me because he was rather amused by the bill of goods I had sold the gullible upper crust of Johannesburg." In his own Boldini portrait, Sir Lionel does indeed look nervous, with the pinched face of a sad prune. Such a specimen might well be amused by Elsa, whose energy never flagged and who, throughout her life, provided entertainment for the bored rich. Elsa remained at the Phillipses' estate for more than a year. While there she helped Lady Phillips edit *The State*, the first illustrated magazine to be published in Johannesburg. Elsa also occasionally conducted the Wheeler Light Opera Company, and founded a Browning Society. To help swell its membership, she gave weekly readings from the poet's works.

Another of Elsa's projects may strain the credulity of most readers. I believe it because even Elsa wouldn't invent something so absurd: "I took a course at the local university in farm irrigation and canal construction; I took up wine-making and persuaded local winegrowers to put sneakers on natives who previously had been treading on the grapes with their bare feet. . . . I don't know whether my innovation improved the end product, but it certainly was more sanitary." Though not an oenophile, Elsa must have pictured herself as an agricultural missionary of sorts in covering a body part heretofore left exposed.

Elsa's year in South Africa sounds idyllic. When not involved in local culture and agriculture, she spent her days "in Florrie's gorgeous drawing room, composing what I thought was great music." So happy were these days in South Africa that Elsa considered permanent residence there . . . until her gypsy nature overruled that whim. "You're making a mistake," warned Lady Phillips.

"Leaving a patroness as kind and generous as Florrie was a severe wrench," Elsa wrote, and the following sentence turns a curious spotlight back on this one. That next sentence may well be the most significant one Elsa ever wrote: "On the boat I met a tall, stunning girl who was—and still is—the best and most helpful friend I have ever known." The reason this sentence lights up the previous one is because the "tall, stunning girl" was to be Elsa's companion for the next fifty years. With two such point-blank sentences fired so close together, one ponders whether the "severe wrench" on parting from Lady Phillips was owing to a romantic liaison that had run out.

8 Dickie

S ome marriages, both legal and de facto, are aesthetically perfect when observed by an outsider, whatever the internal reality of the match. Such alliances as Leonard and Virginia Woolf; Gertrude Stein and Alice B. Toklas; even, rather chillingly, the Duke and Duchess of Windsor—whatever the genius of an individual partner, or the baseness, the two together create a greatness in the room. Their stories provide the pleasure of a well-constructed novel.

Elsa Maxwell and Dorothy Fellowes-Gordon, or "Dickie," as she was usually called, never agreed on much, not even on where they met. "On the boat," said Elsa.

"We met in Durban," countered Dickie, as though adding lyrics to Lerner and Loewe's "I Remember It Well."

"I was in South Africa for about two weeks, in Cape Town and Durban," continued Dickie. "I told her, 'You've been here long enough. It's time you came back to Europe and did something with your music.' " After the long voyage back to England, they didn't meet for several months, until "she appeared again," said Dickie mysteriously. "We became great friends, and we took this little furnished house, three guineas a week, very extravagant we thought. It's still there, in Drayton Gardens. I passed it one day, it has a nice garden, a nice little house."

Drayton Gardens, in South Kensington, runs between the Old Brompton

Road and Fulham Road, a mile or so from the Thames and a bit farther than that from Harrods. Dickie, who lived one hundred years and eight days, was speaking almost literally from her deathbed. In May of 1991, the biographer and historian Hugo Vickers took a tape recorder to the care home where Dickie was a resident and spent several lively hours with her; three months later she died. Much of my information about her comes from Hugo's generosity in lending me those tapes.

Americans are sometimes perplexed by the nuances of British social rank. Placing Dickie in the proper context, therefore, is more difficult than locating Elsa's niche in Keokuk and San Francisco. Dickie's family belonged to the landed gentry, helpfully defined in Terrick V. H. Fitzhugh's *The Dictionary of Genealogy* as the class between the aristocracy and the middle class. Fitzhugh, referring mainly to the nineteenth century, when Dickie was born, explains that the gentry "had much in common with the aristocracy, but on a smaller scale. They were armigerous, had private incomes and were educated at public schools and universities. The heads of county families inherited manor houses, and younger sons became officers in the navy and army, or barristers, clergy, and bankers. The pedigrees of many gentry families have been published from time to time in *Burke's Landed Gentry*." And there, indeed, we find Dickie (along with her distant cousin, the actor and Oscar-winning writer—for *Gosford Park*—Julian Fellowes).

Fitzhugh's definition suggests a homogeneity that does not exist, however, for among the landed gentry are rich and insolvent, British and foreign, pedigreed and otherwise, and indeed, landed and landless. Some families trace their lineage to the twelfth century, others only to the nineteenth. The novelist Anthony Powell, in an essay on the subject in 1969 included in *Burke's* 18th edition, volume 2, estimated the total number of living members of the landed gentry at around eighty thousand in a total United Kingdom population of some fifty million. Perhaps the neatest definition of the landed gentry, if not the most accurate, is "the untitled aristocracy."

Dickie belonged to the Fellowes-Gordon family of Knockespock, Aberdeenshire, in northeast Scotland. Her father, Arthur William Fellowes-Gordon (1864–1922), married her mother, Beatrice Green, in 1887. They divorced in 1904, and in 1906 her mother said to fifteen-year-old Dickie, "Do you mind if I marry Alec?" She was referring to her fiancé, Colonel

Alexander Keith Wyllie. Dickie, an only child, answered, "No, as long as you don't have any children by him." His family had made a fortune in the coal industry, which Dickie's mother quite reasonably expected to insure comfort for her daughter. For a few years this scenario played out as planned.

On May 26, 1911, the *Times* of London reported: "At the court held by their Majesties the King and Queen* on Wednesday the following presentations were made." Among those named was "Miss Dorothy Fellowes-Gordon, by her mother, Mrs. Alexander Keith Wyllie." Not long afterward, however, Dickie's mother died, and to distract Dickie from her grief her stepfather invited her, and two cousins, to accompany him to South Africa, where he had fought in the Boer War. On the eventful voyage back to England, with Elsa in tow, Dickie and her stepfather had a vicious quarrel. "We didn't speak to each other again," she said, and indeed she left his house in London and went to live with other relatives until, some months later, she and Elsa moved to Drayton Gardens.

Dickie, accustomed to a comfortable bank account, now found herself impecunious because her stepfather laid hands on money that her mother had left in trust for her. "I didn't get it until he died," she said, "a long time later." Dickie's wait was almost two decades, for Colonel Keith Wyllie lived until 1928. "Impecunious," however, is a relative term, and in Dickie's case it meant one or two servants rather than half a dozen. Dickie's "poverty," like Elsa's, did not preclude costly entertaining at home, dinners in fine restaurants, fashionable frocks, travel on the Continent, and transatlantic steamship tickets.

Before proceeding, I must digress on the subject of marriage. Earlier, when I referred to Dickie as Elsa's companion, I implied a same-sex marriage long before that concept existed in a modern sense. It's true, they were companions, but only recently has that word become synonymous with "spouse" or "lover." The truth is, we do not know for certain whether Elsa and Dickie were "companions" in that euphemistic sense. Dickie had many affairs with

---

*King George V and Queen Mary

men, including eight years with the seventeenth Duke of Alba (1878–1953). She discussed these affairs freely with Hugo Vickers, and yet she did not clarify her relationship with Elsa. Dickie, in her matter-of-fact style, perhaps assumed that everyone knew. Or else she was being cagey, like Gertrude and Alice: as "out" as they now seem to have been, theirs was a *friendship* to all but a select group.

Although many friends assumed that Dickie and Elsa were lesbian lovers, ambiguity remains. Philip Hoare, who befriended Dickie in her later years, included this statement when he wrote her long obituary in the *Independent*: "The notion of their being lovers is largely speculative, based on contemporary rumour and circumstantial evidence (such as the double-bed discovered by a cousin, turned over and laid out with two pairs of pyjamas)."

Given the risks and repressions of the fifty years that Elsa and Dickie spent together, their lack of candor is understandable. One could say they had a "Boston marriage," described as the relationship of two women who decide to live together, with or without sexual intimacy. My own opinion is that they had an open marriage, and I will write from that point of view. Marriage, however, of this kind or that, is perhaps the least interesting facet of either woman's life.

It is ironic that Dickie, in South Africa, prodded Elsa to return to Europe and pursue her music, since Dickie herself had the raw materials of a great operatic star. But, as a late starter, she lacked the requisite drive. "I had a very beautiful voice," she told Hugo Vickers. "I can say that without conceit. I mean, God gives you that. Toscanini very kindly said he'd be interested, and recommended a teacher in Milan. I went to Milan and stayed on and off for about two years." While there, Dickie attended the famous premiere of *Turandot* on April 25, 1926, at La Scala, with Toscanini conducting. Puccini had died a year and a half earlier, leaving the opera unfinished. When Toscanini reached the point in the final act where Puccini had left off, the conductor stopped the music, put down his baton, turned to the audience, and said, "Here the Maestro laid down his pen."

By the time Dickie went to study in Milan, she was approaching forty.

Her full social calendar, with and without Elsa, collided with the iron discipline and the sacrifices of a diva. Life called, and Dickie answered. The American soprano Grace Moore, a close friend of Elsa and Dickie, described Dickie as "humorous, bitchy, and charming . . . she has never done much with her own beautiful voice though she has made a career out of telling everyone else exactly how to run their life."

On the subject of music, and Elsa's piano playing in particular, Dickie told Hugo Vickers that the Maxwells wouldn't let Elsa take piano lessons. "They very stupidly thought they shouldn't interfere with this talent and that Elsa shouldn't be tied down by technique of any kind, which was ridiculous. She could have been a concert pianist." Since Dickie knew Elsa better than anyone else ever did, we can read this revelation as a key reason for Elsa's resentment of her mother, and also as Elsa's spur to succeed in multiple endeavors. Elsa herself said, "I was exhibited, exploited, told how too, too marvelous I was—and never once taken seriously. I never had a music lesson in my life."

Physically, Dickie was Elsa's type: tall, a near-beauty with dark hair and intense black brooding eyes that blazed when kindled by emotion. And, of course, musical. She and Elsa had noisy rows, and friends like Noël Coward dubbed her "the Black Bitch" owing to her difficult and demanding ways. (Years later, Elsa's devastating crush on Maria Callas conjured the early years with Dickie.)

In 1912, when Elsa and Dickie set up housekeeping in Drayton Gardens, London was in ferment. Fear and suspicion hung like fog over the city, for German militarism grew more ominous each day. The kaiser's soldiers were massed on the Belgian border, and rumors proliferated that Germany was ready any day to march across Belgium and into France. British nerves were taut. Letters to and from Germany were routinely opened by the Secret Service Bureau, founded in 1909. The military establishment in Britain saw no alternative to war.

Through it all, however, London kept on singing. Peter Ackroyd, in *London: The Biography*, reports twelve music halls in central London at the time, with forty-seven just outside the center. Other sources claim several hundred music halls throughout the vast city. For Elsa, this hungry musical market offered the chance to peddle her wares. Dickie's connections proved useful to Elsa, who shook each new hand as if gripping a higher rung. In no time, she had become a familiar name in the lower echelons of show business.

In 1913, Elsa wrote a song for the American vaudeville star Grace La Rue, who was appearing in London. That song was "A Tango Dream," which La Rue recorded in 1914 and which you can hear on YouTube. It's Elsa's best song by far. One might mistake it for early Coward, or for a number that Gertrude Lawrence or Bea Lillie performed in *Charlot's Revue*, a series of highly successful musical productions staged in London and New York from 1912 to the 1930s by the French impresario André Charlot. "A Tango Dream" combines chic wistfulness in the lyrics with a world-weary tune, at least in Grace La Rue's version. When Elsa herself recorded it in 1958, she sounded like a truck driver backed by an orchestra of sugary strings. (Isadora Duncan loved the song, and when Elsa visited her in 1917 at her beachfront cottage on Long Island, Isadora had her sit down at the piano and play it.)

The song was a hit, Elsa earned two hundred pounds in royalties, and her foot was in the door. She wrote "additional music" for several revues, such as *The Whirl of the Town* in 1914 and *Stage Struck* the following year; the latter was described in the *Observer* as "a musical comedietta" presented at the Victoria Palace. In 1915, the *Daily Mirror* ran a picture of Elsa with a caption informing that her "new revue will be produced shortly. She has written songs for Miss Ethel Levey and well-known artists." (Levey, the ex-wife of George M. Cohan, appeared on the London stage in 1912 in the revue *Hullo Ragtime*. Impressed by Elsa's songs, she hired her as accompanist and promoted her socially among London's theatrical elite.)

Soon Elsa was appearing in the London gossip columns. When the American actress Doris Keane opened in *Romance* at the Duke of York's Theatre, the *Daily Mirror* noted celebrities in the audience, including "Lady Alexander in a black and white gown, sables and many diamonds . . . Miss Elsa Maxwell, the composer, with a party of friends."

The British Library owns sheet music for some two dozen of Elsa's songs, ranging from rowdy music hall crowd-pleasers like "Ragtime Valentine" to sentimental ballads ("Don't Hesitate in Love," "From a Bagdad Window") and more serious attempts, namely "Deux Morceaux Pour Violon & Piano," which a friend of mine compared to music played on the *Titanic*.

Elsa wrote of this period, "I had money in the bank and champagne in the icebox. Dickie and I hit it off perfectly. I was busily, and gainfully, occupied in the mornings writing special material songs for vaudeville stars. I was busier in the afternoons and evenings making a widening circle of friends." One of these was the actress Maxine Elliott, along with "the fascinating artists and intellectuals she attracted to her home." It was there, at Elliott's mansion, 20 Abbey Road in Maida Vale, that Elsa first met Lady Randolph Churchill, and her son, Winston, one of Maxine's many admirers. For decades to come, Sir Winston Churchill would receive Elsa's unsolicited advice on how to run the world.

It was at Maxine Elliott's, also, that Elsa first encountered Lady Cunard (née Maud Alice Burke, in San Francisco). They loathed each other instantly. "I understand, Miss Maxwell," cooed Her Ladyship, "that you have met a great many nice people in London. Isn't it odd?"

"Not so odd," Elsa retorted, "as to have met you *last*."

MAXINE ELLIOTT

She was the Elizabeth Taylor of her age, an international beauty worshipped for her looks but whose acting was often denigrated. And with a profligate appetite that, late in life, made her more gawky than grand. Nevertheless, such were her power and wealth that she opened her own Broadway house in 1908, the Maxine Elliott Theatre, with the help of J. P. Morgan, a close friend and rumored lover whose financial advice helped make her stunningly rich.

Born in Maine in 1868, Jessie Dermot—who took the name Maxine Elliott in New York at age sixteen while an acting student—served a long apprenticeship in minor roles. In 1895, her career zoomed, and for the next two decades she was a top star in New York, London, and distant provinces of the British Empire. King Edward VII was another rumored lover; his grandson, the Duke of Windsor, a frequent house guest, along with the Duchess. When Elsa made her acquaintance, Maxine owned a large estate, Hartsbourne Manor, in addition to her house in London. She became a luminary of British society. There was, it seemed, a princess or an earl on every landing of the stairs.

Following her success in *Joseph and His Brethren* in London in 1913, Maxine suspected that this hit marked the apogee of her career. She acted only occasionally during the next seven years, and gave her final performance in 1920. Perhaps her greatest role, exceeding any of her stage work, came in World War I, when, as a Red Cross volunteer, she became one of the first women permitted at the battle front, except for professional nurses. She had her automobile refitted as an ambulance; she scrubbed floors, cooked, bathed wounded soldiers, soothed the dying and encouraged the living. After the armistice, she received the Belgian Order of the Crown, along with decorations from Britain and France.

Refusing to resume her career, she said, "I wish to grow middle-aged gracefully." Long after middle age, she told an interviewer, "All I care about are my friends, and peace." She might have added bridge and rich foods to that list, for according to her niece and biographer, Diana Forbes-Robertson, she tired of Hartsbourne and remodeled the Abbey Road mansion to be closer to the bridge-playing world. "She let it absorb her completely," her niece wrote. "She became a member of a bridge club and stayed there often until five in the morning."

Eventually Maxine regained a measure of self-control. Missing the friends of earlier years, and their witty repartee, she hurried off to Paris in the mid-1920s, and joined the partying set: Elsa, Noël, the Cole Porters, Isadora Duncan, Maugham, Scott and Zelda. A few years later she retreated to the Riviera, and ordered construction on the lavish Villa de l'Horizon, near Cannes. The cost: $350,000. The site was dynamited from sheer stone, and a swimming pool scooped out of remaining rock. A chute was installed so that swimmers could slide from the pool into the sea below.

By this time, Maxine had eaten to the point of weighing two hundred pounds. The architects of her villa measured the famous derrière to make sure it would fit into the chute. In her late sixties, she suffered a mild stroke. Her doctor ordered a bland diet, the notion of which made Maxine chortle. One day at lunch, Elsa watched Maxine devour a full-course meal. In a classic instance of the pot and the kettle, Elsa admonished, "If you go on eating that way, you're going to kill yourself."

"There's only one better way to die," replied Maxine, reaching for a hefty slice of *gâteau au chocolat*, "and I'm too old for *that*." "Oh darling, surely the doctor said no cake," another guest remonstrated. Maxine's reply: "But he didn't say no *chocolate* cake." Leo Lerman, in his waspish memoir, described Maxine near the end: "Her beauty, as it became immersed in fat, grew more concentrated, her exquisite face diminished to coin size and set in a vast flabby medallion." Her illustrious guests flocked to the villa until 1939, and then she closed the doors. In 1940, she died.

Life felt good to Elsa. Then, on June 28, 1914, Archduke Franz Ferdinand was assassinated at Sarajevo, and the Great War began. The American embassy urged citizens to return immediately to the United States, and Elsa considered doing so. Until, in 1915, two close friends of hers and Dickie's were killed in action, the poet Julian Grenfell, and, two months later, his brother Gerald. On the morning that the latter's death was announced in the *Times*, Elsa encountered the young men's father, Lord Desborough, who, in spite of his grief, raised his hat to Elsa and murmured, "Lovely morning." Such courage persuaded Elsa to stay on in London. In *R.S.V.P.*, she claimed that she returned home that very day and wrote England's first war song, "The British Volunteer." (The title is actually "My Volunteer," though two lines in the lyric are "You feel you want to cheer / The British Volunteer.")

Introduced by the singing actress Violet Lorraine at the London Hippodrome, "My Volunteer" became a patriotic hit, though Elsa didn't earn a penny from it. The song was her contribution to the war effort. She wrote a couple of other such patriotic songs, including "Carry On," aimed at the

Royal Navy ("Carry on, that our ships / May ever rule the sea / Who lives if England dies?").

As the situation in London became more desperate, the government urged residents not actively engaged in the war effort to leave the city. Elsa and Dickie found accommodations in an inn at Marlow-on-Thames, some thirty miles away. Small-town life was boring, however, and the two women found little of interest to fill their disrupted lives. Then, on May 7, 1915, a German U-boat torpedoed the British passenger ship RMS *Lusitania* off the coast of Ireland, killing 1,198 of the 1,959 aboard. Among the dead was the theatrical producer Charles Frohman, a connection of Elsa's through Marie Doro, whose career he micromanaged, and through Maxine Elliott and other show business friends.

Frohman's death, and the worsening situation in Europe, changed Elsa's mind about staying on in England. Like many other Americans at the time, she wanted the United States to enter the war in support of its allies. So far, however, President Woodrow Wilson had avoided doing so. Elsa, whether naïvely or not, imagined that, back in the U.S., she "could help alert America to the menace of Prussian militarism."

Dickie's version of their departure for New York lacks the Union Jacks and bugle calls of Elsa's. She said, "One morning, we were reading the newspaper, I looked at the sailings, and I said to Elsa, 'How would you feel about sailing to New York?'" (Dickie had recently inherited some money upon the death of an uncle.) They booked passage on the SS *Rotterdam*, with lifeboats out in case of enemy attack. "We took a maid with us," Dickie recalled, and when they reached New York they took a double room, with maid's room, at the Ritz-Carlton for seven dollars a day. They stayed in America for four years, returning to England in 1919.

9 A Night at the Suffragist Opera

$\mathcal{D}$oes the name "Vanderbilt" make you drowsy? If, like me, you consider it a chloroform clan, here's an iconoclast among the bromides. To be sure, she was only a Vanderbilt by marriage, and that a limited run, for Alva Erskine Smith married William K. Vanderbilt in 1875 and divorced him twenty years later.

Born in Mobile, Alabama, in 1853, Alva could have taught Scarlett O'Hara a thing or two. She divorced Vanderbilt in 1895, a move so rare and scandalous among the elite that a divorcée was expected to retreat into veiled purdah. Alva, however, took a different view. With her ten-million-dollar settlement, in addition to several estates in New York and Newport, she buzzed past the Four Hundred with chutzpah flying. To show them she felt no contrition, she marched into St. Thomas Episcopal Church, a patrician stronghold on Fifth Avenue, with her daughter, Consuelo, on one arm and son-in-law, the young Duke of Marlborough, on the other. Hoisting the hymnbook, she sang out like a newly minted saint.

A year after her divorce, she committed the unthinkable act of remarriage—and to a man who was half Jewish. The groom was Oliver Hazard Perry Belmont, five years her junior, the son of a Rothschild banker. Cleveland Amory, in *The Last Resorts*, wrote that Mrs. O.H.P. Belmont (as she came to be known in her dowager years) "embarked upon Good Works and at the same time endeavored to keep up with her rivals" in high society.

It was rumored that Mr. Belmont's death, in 1908, was brought on by the strain of his wife and the rigors of life in the upper crust. Alva, however, thrived. With elaborate self-pity, she commented, "I know of no profession, art, or trade that women are working in today as taxing on mental resource as being a leader of Society."

Needing a change from soup kitchens, slum clinics, and campaigns for birth control, she shouldered the cause of women's suffrage. The year her husband died, she convened a suffragist conclave in her eleven-million-dollar cottage in Newport. To a discouraged delegate, she offered this advice: "Brace up, my dear. Just pray to God. *She* will help you."

Was it God, or Mrs. Belmont, who first heard that Elsa Maxwell had docked in New York? No doubt the latter, who, unlike the Diety, was seeking a collaborator. When Elsa came to call, Mrs. Belmont beheld a junior version of herself, for these two willful, outspoken, slightly naughty women, though bodily corseted, had flung off the corsets of convention. Their alliance came about like this: in 1895, Mrs. Belmont's daughter, Consuelo, had married the Duke of Marlborough, who was a cousin of Winston Churchill. The Marlboroughs, Churchill, Elsa, and Dickie often met up at Maxine Elliott's soirees. Elsa, therefore, arrived in New York with a letter of introduction from the duchess.

Mrs. Belmont and Elsa had much in common besides an interest in society, for the Vote was mother's milk to Elsa—almost literally, for, as we have seen, Laura Wyman Maxwell was on the California register long before the vote was universal. Mrs. Belmont had devoted the years of her widowhood to the suffrage movement. To name but a few of her activities: she donated large sums to it; founded the Political Equality League in 1909 to encourage New York State politicians who supported women's suffrage; led parades; and was instrumental in founding the National Woman's Party.

And she had written a feminist opera, which she titled *Melinda and Her Sisters*. More precisely, she had written the libretto, or at least the bare bones of it. What she needed to lead her opus to completion was a songwriter-lyricist. "I became one of Mrs. Belmont's protegées soon after arriving in New York in 1915," Elsa said. And they set to work.

To call *Melinda* an opera, or even an operetta, is to inflate the merits of the work. Allowing for different tastes a century ago, and wildly dissimilar levels of sophistication, *Melinda and Her Sisters* will remind you all the same of spoofs like *The Pleasant Peasant*, Lucy and Ethel's fund-raiser for their women's club. Mr. and Mrs. Pepper, nouveaux riches "out West," are awaiting the arrival of seven of their eight daughters, who have been away to absorb culture and refinement. These seven, having acquired proficiency in the arts, perform their various specialties: singing, dancing, tragic acting, and the like. Then Melinda, the black sheep, enters unexpectedly, "with children of the poor holding on to her skirt and men and women in every walk of life following her in the procession: laborers, factory girls, salesladies, etc." All hoist banners proclaiming their demands for equality. Melinda and her little army march to center stage, where she begs her mother to welcome her. A family friend exclaims, "Good heavens, I actually believe the creature's a suffragette! No wonder they never spoke of her except behind closed doors."

Marie Doro, having just finished a run on Broadway, played Melinda. There was a row over whether she would wear classical sandals—her preference—or the sensible shoes preferred by women on the march. Others in the cast: Marie Dressler as Melinda's mother, Josephine Hull (who won an Oscar in 1951 as Best Supporting Actress in *Harvey*), soprano Frances Alda of the Metropolitan Opera, the architect Addison Mizner (famous for his buildings in Palm Beach, and the subject of the Sondheim musical *Road Show*), Maud Kahn and Kitty Bache, the daughters of prominent Wall Street bankers, along with New York debutantes and suffragists. Dickie played one of Melinda's sisters.

After six weeks of rehearsals, *Melinda* played for one performance, a benefit on February 18, 1916, at the Waldorf-Astoria (the "old" Waldorf, which stood on the site of the Empire State Building) with ticket prices up to one hundred twenty-five dollars. It raised over eight thousand dollars for the National Woman's Party. The New York papers, always intoxicated by society, swooned in their reporting of the evening's success. The work was never revived, although later that year *The New York Times* reported that "a smart entertainment for the benefit of the Permanent Blind War Relief, an invitation affair, is to be given in the Ritz-Carlton ballroom on the evening of May 17." Top price for a box was a hundred dollars, and the evening was under the direction of Elsa and the California artist Robert Tittle McKee. The *Times* account added that "by special request the fox-trot from

Melinda and Her Sisters will be given" and "Miss Maxwell will sing some of her new songs at the piano."

If not for Elsa's presence, this event would have no surpassing significance here, and could be ticked off as a typical charity frolic among the New York beau monde. Elegant dinners preceded, and intimate suppers followed the benefit, which included not only music and dancing but short sketches and tableaux vivants featuring famous stage and screen actors. Since it was a benefit for afflicted soldiers in Europe, young society girls dressed in Belgian and French peasant costumes handed out programs and flowers throughout the evening, and at the end everyone rose to sing "La Marseillaise."

What sets the evening apart is this: for the first time Elsa Maxwell occupied the unique place she would retain for the next half century in literally thousands of such swank events. The *Times* account on the following day gleams with names that soon would gild Elsa's own conversations, her newspaper columns, radio broadcasts, and eventually her books. Mrs. Belmont, of course, was mentioned as a patroness of the benefit, along with Mrs. John Astor, Mrs. Cornelius Vanderbilt, Mrs. Harry Payne Whitney, and Mrs. Herman Oelrichs. The mayor of New York, John Purroy Mitchel, was there, and the governor's wife, along with the celebrated Edwardian hostess Lady Colebrook, Mrs. M. H. de Young of San Francisco, Mrs. Hamilton Carhart of Detroit, Will Rogers, and Lady de Bathe (aka Lillie Langtry). The actresses Ina Claire, Madge Kennedy, Elsie Ferguson, Emmy Wehlen, and Cathleen Nesbitt. Star of the opera, Mary Garden, and opera star manqué Dorothy Fellowes-Gordon. From the London stage, Sir Herbert Beerbohm Tree; Mrs. Otto Kahn representing Wall Street; and the cover of the evening's program designed by Charles Dana Gibson, the graphic artist famous for his early-twentieth-century creation, the Gibson Girl. Had a painter captured the evening and its splendors, the tableau might have been called "The Apotheosis of Elsa Maxwell's Dream."

Elsa's position was unique because she occupied a top spot in the hierarchy of the evening, while remaining psychologically—and socially—distant. And so she always would. Highly placed as songwriter, entertainer, friend of Mrs. Belmont and of many others in attendance, and connected already, or soon to be, with the sundry interests represented: high society, and the demi-monde; the American stage, the British stage, Hollywood, the opera; the art world, the world of music; politics; high finance. And central, also, like the eye of a camera, as observer of romance—all kinds, sanctioned and otherwise, though herself a partial participant at best. She and Dickie lived together, but Dickie had an eye for the gents. Elsa herself, that night and forever, endured the discomfort of belonging to an erotic caucus whose name she dared not speak in public.

That night, and throughout her countless public nights to come, there were two Elsa Maxwells. One Elsa venerated these swirling entertainments, where her kind of conviviality and élan guaranteed membership. The other Elsa, shrewd and unillusioned, looked past the charade and recognized herself on the outside peering in because of what she lacked: the credentials of an American princess, despite her social position in San Francisco; feminine charm; the lovely lineaments and gliding grace of a great lady.

Such lofty musings detained her but a moment, for already she envisioned her own evenings—a bit like this one, perhaps, though superior. Elsa's heart beat faster to imagine whom she would invite, the music, the games, the ballrooms, the panache, the money raised and the money spent. Over the sound of the orchestra playing Melinda's fox-trot, over "La Marseillaise," above the strident voice of Mrs. Belmont, the future called out to Elsa Maxwell. The title of her later book echoes that vocation: "I Married the World." *

Elsa and Mrs. Belmont remained friends, though Elsa once stormed out of the mansion in outrage when Alva threw a plate at her long-suffering butler, who, after years of service, had surely grown accustomed to such violence. "If he is that bad," Elsa demanded, "why don't you fire him?"

"Oh, I couldn't do that," said Mrs. Belmont. "He was so devoted to my late husband. I've soothed his ruffled feelings by giving him an extra week's pay."

Elsa herself often benefited from such unpredictable charity, including a lavish trip to Egypt in 1930, where she staged a party in the shadow of the

*This is the British title of *R.S.V.P.*, Elsa's autobiography.

pyramids. Three years later, Mrs. Belmont died. She had requested that services be held at the Cathedral Church of St. John the Divine, in New York, with a female minister officiating. Such a funeral proved unfeasible on several counts, however. First, there were no female clergy in the Episcopal Church at that time. Then, too, Mrs. Belmont had quarreled with the arch-conservative Bishop William Manning. Upon becoming bishop of New York in 1921, he removed her as chairwoman of a church charity because she was a divorcée. "I suppose it's perfectly proper, though, for you to accept my tainted money," she snapped, just before she took it all elsewhere.

And so Mrs. Belmont ended up once more at St. Thomas's, on Fifth Avenue, the "Vanderbilt church." Her final provocation must have shivered the collective Episcopal spine, for the body was borne by female pallbearers, and a female guard of honor followed with feminist banners held aloft. (One marvels that the bishop didn't declare the service eccesiastically illegal.) Music, chosen in advance by Mrs. Belmont, was appropriate to the occasion: "Still, Still with Thee" by Harriet Beecher Stowe; "The March of Women" by Dame Ethel Smythe; and then, sung by a girls' choir, a hymn that Mrs. Belmont herself had written:

No waiting at the gates of Paradise
No tribunal of men to judge!
The watchers of the tower proclaim
A daughter of the King.

10 Fifty Million Frenchmen

Owing to Mrs. Belmont's overbearing prestige, Dickie's finances, and her own ambitious energy, Elsa soon established herself as a New Yorker to be noticed and talked about—a supporting player in the pageant of social Manhattan. By 1917, although not yet positioned to engineer the lively parties that would become her trademark, Elsa had climbed from spear carrier (piano player and minor composer) to speaking roles in the larger arena, as publicist and organizer of publicity-getting events. This new success owed much to her war activism, for, by her own admission, "I was so fervently pro-British that, like all rabid propagandists I had no patience with objectivity or another viewpoint. . . . I was hoping to rally support for the Allies."

Her grand opportunity to do so came in May of 1917, with the arrival in New York of a European delegation whose mission was to seek humanitarian aid and, if possible, to nudge the United States into an active role in the Great War. Leaders of the delegation were General Joseph Joffre, the sixty-five-year-old Hero of the Marne, so called because of a decisive victory over Germany in 1914; former French prime minister René Viviani; and British foreign secretary Arthur Balfour.

Joffre, forced into retirement after the calamitous Battle of the Somme in 1916, and thus a defeated hero in France, nevertheless commanded rock star idolatry in an America aflame with war fever and antipathy toward the kaiser's Germany. Welcoming crowds in New York and elsewhere reached unprecedented numbers. (Although the United States had declared war on Germany on April 6, 1917, some weeks before Joffre's arrival, this country had not yet begun to fight.)

Despite his setbacks at home, Joffre had been elevated to the lofty position of Maréchal de France, a title of military distinction, not rank, reaching back to the twelfth century. In France, a *maréchal*, or marshal, merits the genuflection of a founding father in America. From afar, Elsa spied Joffre as the nexus of her burning interests: patriotism, Francophilia, the rallying of high society to a magnificent cause, and a golden window flung open for her to quaff great gusts of recognition.

A grand muddle surrounding the French mission might have been avoided if Elsa had been running New York, either from City Hall or from distant Albany. The mayor and the governor loathed each other, and each one's political apparatus vied for glory as the visiting satraps approached. So belligerent were the two camps that Joffre and Company almost ended on the casualty list of a New York turf war, with Washington firing salvos of its own.

First, as reported in *The New York Times*, Joffre was to speak at City Hall; then not. A gala at the Metropolitan Opera was expected to raise eighty thousand dollars for French war relief—then "doubt was raised," as the *Times* demurely put it, whether Joffre would attend. (Continuing its dainty policies, the paper avoided direct mention of political strife on its doorstep.) Caruso would sing; no, he was to sail for South America. The French tenor Lucien Muratore would step in, but suddenly he was hospitalized. Then Joffre was quoted as saying that he could not attend a benefit at which citizens were charged admission for the sole purpose of seeing him (which was not the case, in any event; the gala was to be a night of stars, with a peek-in by Marshal Joffre near the final curtain. And the purpose, of course, was to raise funds for his desperate country.) On and on went the cockeyed controversy, the *Times* accounts sounding daily more absurd. Anyone who knew the complete story took it with them to the grave; and so, a jump cut to Elsa's twenty-three-year-old accomplice who, in a decade or so, would start producing famous films in Hollywood, among them *Queen Christina* and *Cleopatra*: Walter Wanger.

Elisabeth Marbury, one of the first female theatrical tycoons—literary agent, producer, businesswoman, and longtime lover of actress Elsie de Wolfe, whom we will meet presently after she has left the stage to become an interior decorator—hired Wanger in 1915, and the following year put him in charge of Cole Porter's debut production on Broadway, *See America First*. The musical closed after fifteen performances; one critic advised, "*See America First*, last." (Porter said that Wanger managed his show "with professional éclat." The young Clifton Webb, a future friend of Elsa's, was in the cast.)

A fledgling producer and stylish man about town, Wanger had a lot in common with Elsa. Like her, he was a San Franciscan on the rise in New York. Also like Elsa, he excelled at making useful friends. Shortly after the United States declared war on Germany, Mayor John Purroy Mitchel appointed Wanger to the city's Committee on National Defense, whose function was to promote the war effort through propaganda (recruiting posters, a reenactment of Paul Revere's ride, and the like). Elsa, meanwhile, was named by New York Governor Whitman to the Program Committee of the opera gala, along with Mrs. Harry Payne Whitney (née Gertrude Vanderbilt), Jacques Coppeau of the Théatre Français de New York, and two others.

As plans for the Joffre spectacle began to go awry, and confusion ran rampant, Elsa and Walter Wanger joined forces in spite of his supposed allegiance to the mayor and hers to the governor. Elsa claimed later that she came up with the opera gala. "I sought the advice of Mrs. Harry Payne Whitney," she said, who considered it "a wonderful idea." There were problems, however. Because France was losing the war, Mrs. Whitney was informed by the U.S. State Department that it was best to keep "the old man"—Joffre—out of sight.

Elsa persuaded Mrs. Whitney to fall in, however, and soon Elsa stormed the Met, begging the fiery general manager, Giulio Gatti-Casazza, to lend her the opera house for the occasion. (The husband of Frances Alda, who had performed in *Melinda and Her Sisters* the year before, Gatti-Casazza was thus amenable to Elsa's pleas, despite his initial reservations.) Meanwhile, Wanger's phone calls to Washington were rebuffed as he attempted to reach Marshal Joffre.

Elsa sent Wanger to Albany, where he obtained a stack of official stationery from the governor, a rubber stamp of the governor's signature, and permission to send out letters to fifty prominent New Yorkers summoning them to a meeting "of utmost importance and urgency" at the Met. At that meeting, Elsa promised not only an appearance by Joffre, but also by Caruso and his colleague Geraldine Farrar, as well as the pianists Paderewski, Artur Rubinstein, and a panoply of other international musicians. Elsa's promises were based on bravado. Rubinstein, for instance, was in England, and Gatti-Casazza's offer was grudging, at best. Nevertheless, she obtained pledges for seats amounting to ninety-two thousand dollars.

Soon, however, Elsa herself was caught up in the maelstrom of political self-interest swirling from New York to Albany to Washington. As her scheme began to unravel, she rushed off to D.C. and bluffed her way into Joffre's hotel suite. He liked the brazen *Américaine*, even forgave her French (*"comme une vache espagnole,"* we can imagine him muttering to his aide-de-camp as Elsa massacred his language), and agreed to appear at the Met in spite of the grotesque political football being kicked all over the East.

Next, Elsa lured Maude Adams (the Meryl Streep of her day) out of retirement; Paderewski interrupted a tour and hurried to New York for the privilege of playing for the great Frenchman; and a cluster of Met employees was added to the program. At last, despite twists of fate and close calls with failure, the night arrived. And Joffre was nowhere to be found.

The doors opened at nine o'clock. Toward nine thirty, when Joffre was due, the orchestra began to play the rousing "Sambre et Meuse," his favorite march. When the march ended, all heads turned to J. P. Morgan's box, where the general was expected to stand up. It was empty. The conductor, Pierre Monteux, rapped on the podium and the orchestra played the piece again.

"The Diamond Horseshoe never was more somber—or more impressive," Elsa recalled. (This was, of course, the old Met, at Broadway and Thirty-ninth Street.) "All the women wore black evening gowns unrelieved by jewelry as a mark of sympathy for the terrible losses France was suffering during the war." Men were asked to omit evening clothes in favor of the less formal frock coat. (Miffed, the mayor did not attend. Absent, also, were many others who ordinarily would have occupied front-row seats at such an event—these either casualties of political carnage, or overlooked.)

Elsa, meanwhile, scurried from post to post backstage, then peered anxiously out the Fortieth Street entrance in search of the missing prize. She signaled the conductor to play "Sambre et Meuse" once more. That completed, Paderewski played three selections by Chopin. Audience restlessness morphed to backstage panic as Elsa rushed about, imagining high-toned Met patrons tearing her to pieces, Fury-like. Mrs. Whitney fled to some dark recess. Gatti-Casazza raved in Italian.

Paderewski began his fourth piece, this one Chopin's "Military Polonaise," and in the very middle of it, "Marshal Joffre, by the side of Governor Whitman, stepped into a box fronting the stage. The great audience swept to its feet, forgetting that Paderewski was playing a masterpiece. The Marshal, with a wide sweep of his right hand, saluted as his allies and admirers cheered and sang the Marseillaise." Thus, the *Times*' front-page account, on the streets a few hours later.

Joffre made a speech, ending with "Long live the United States! Long live the city of New York!" The Metropolitan Opera chorus sang "God Save the King" and "Hymn Garibaldi," followed by Louise Homer, of the Met, who sang "The Star-Spangled Banner." At the end of the American national anthem, Joffre and the governor left the box and made their way out of the opera house.

There followed, onstage, a series of tableaux vivants representing the nations allied against Germany. Ethel Barrymore posed as "America." At the end of the evening, Léon Rothier, of the Met, sang "La Marseillaise," while Maude Adams stood in the guise of Joan of Arc. The following day, a check was presented to Marshal Joffre for eighty-six thousand dollars in aid of the war orphans of France.

"The Joffre success," claimed Elsa, "established me as a triple-plated wonder-worker, and in the months that followed I was asked to join every committee in sight staging benefits for the Allies."

II   A Perfect Blendship

Elsa admired talent anywhere she found it, whether onstage at the Met or in a smoky cabaret. Around the time of *l'affaire Joffre*, she befriended one of America's greatest future composers, Cole Porter. Her version of their first encounter strikes me as doctored up, but not even Porter contradicted her story.

According to Elsa, she and Dickie were invited to a soiree at the home of Mrs. Bridget Guinness, whom Elsa described as "the type of society woman I admired and, frankly, was trying to cultivate. She was cultured, progressive, and made her beautiful home on Washington Square a salon in the European tradition." Indeed, Mrs. Guinness was an international hostess, very rich, and known for entertaining show business luminaries along with society. Elsa and Dickie were acquainted with Mrs. Guinness because of their involvement with the New York Allied Bazaar, a sort of miniature indoor World's Fair set up to raise money for "the blind, starving, and homeless" in the affected nations of Europe. Although they saw Mrs. Guinness night after night in her booth at the bazaar, which was near theirs, she treated them coldly to the point of disdain. Other volunteers—among them many New York stage stars and socialites—were invited to the Guinness home for dinners and musicales, but not Elsa, and not Dickie.

"Why does she ignore us?" Elsa asked Dickie.

"Why, indeed?"

"I grieved and fretted," Elsa confessed. "The desire to be invited by Bridget became a major obsession in my life."

Finally Elsa asked Alexandra, Lady Colebrook: "Why does Bridget dislike me?"

"I'd rather not discuss it" was the answer.

A long conversation took place, with rumors and veiled insinuations repeated by Lady Colebrook. "You know, Plumpy, I like you, I always have, but then not everyone is as broad-minded as I am. You see, Bridget thinks . . . Well, she thinks . . ."

"That I'm . . . ?"

Elsa, who later claimed to be furious at such insinuations, assured Lady Colebrook that such slanderous rumors were totally false, and soon Elsa and Dickie made it onto the Guinness guest list.

Elsa claimed that she and Dickie were so excited by the invitation to Mrs. Guinness's party that they arrived fifteen minutes early and strolled around the Square until time to enter. (The excitability was all on Elsa's part; more than a society hostess was required to arouse the splenetic Dickie.) The pair were arguing, rather fiercely, the merits of the Met's Lucien Muratore, who was to be guest of honor, versus Caruso, whose rival he was said to be, with Elsa unyielding on the virtuosity of her old acquaintance from San Francisco. Changing the subject to circumvent Dickie's stubbornness—"matched only by her temper," said her companion—Elsa began praising a young Broadway composer who was also invited for the evening. Although his first show had been unsuccessful, Elsa had heard the music and considered it "unusually promising."

As they approached the Guinness mansion, Dickie said, "The fellow must be a false alarm. The show was a flop."

"Pardon me for eavesdropping, but are you paging me?" an unfamiliar voice chimed in. It belonged, of course, to Cole Porter.

It was not love at first sight. Elsa disliked Porter at first because she thought he was trying to be cute. "I've always been allergic to that approach in men and women, adults and children," Elsa said. Nor did she like his attire: his outfit struck her as too snappy. "I pegged him for a phony," she confessed, and practically told him so: "You must be flat broke or else you wouldn't dress so well." (Later, she admitted the rudeness of her remark.)

The friendship seemed stillborn. He irritated her further with the airy information that his wealthy grandfather's money had put those threads on his back. Cole was also "tight," and Elsa never cared for those who drank too much. "I walked away from the irritating little man," Elsa said forty years later, after they had laughed about it many times.

Mrs. Guinness required those who attended her parties to take part in the entertainment. Often the contribution involved music, though a recitation or a somersault would do in a pinch. All eyes turned to beautiful Dickie when she sang. Elsa went unnoticed until she sat down at the piano and played one of her London music hall songs, "They Call Me Ivy Because I Cling." Later she accompanied Muratore. At the end of their performance, Cole winked at Elsa. "Now it's my turn to sing for my supper," declared the cheeky upstart. He played a few bars from his late musical. Conversation buzzed on. No one knew the tunes, and so at first they thought, Why bother? Soon, however, the assembly quieted. Elsa recalled that everyone strained "to catch the droll nuances of his lyrics. He held a critical audience enraptured for fully a half hour while he ran through his repertoire. At the end of that half hour I was a wild fan." To Elsa, he became "Coley," a pet name used by no one else.

In 1935, "Coley" included Elsa as a character in *Jubilee*. The premise of this musical, with book by Moss Hart, is the diamond jubilee of the king of a mythical country who, along with the queen and two of their royal children, are eager to escape the palace and have some fun. Their ruse is a rumored revolution in the country, which enables them to quit the formalities of court and become plain "Mr. and Mrs. Smith"—the title of one of the show's thirty-plus songs. It can't compare, however, with the four that later became standards: "Why Shouldn't I?," "When Love Comes Your Way," "Begin the Beguine," and "Just One of Those Things."

Having loosed the royal fetters, the king indulges his chief hobby: rope tricks. The queen develops a crush on a muscular actor known for playing "Mowgli" on the screen in a loincloth (translation: Johnny Weissmuller as Tarzan), the princess falls for a young playwright with a resemblance to Noël Coward, and the crown prince finds a showgirl who reminded some theatregoers of Ginger Rogers. Eva Standing, who is "standing in" for Elsa Maxwell, is a nonstop party giver. May Boley, a minor character actress onstage and in films, played Eva. (By odd coincidence, she was Elsa's exact contemporary: 1881–1963.) The best known cast member at the time was Mary Boland as the queen. She is best remembered for scatty roles like the Countess de Lave in *The Women* (1939) and as Mrs. Bennett in *Pride and Prejudice* (1940). Fifteen-year-old Montgomery Clift had a small role as the youngest child of the king and queen.

Cole was said to be delighted by May Boley's Elsa-like portrayal of Eva Standing, a role to which she brought the right balance of satire and sympathy. (In the book, Moss Hart described the character as "a small, delicate mouse-like creature" who was "as helpless as the Bethlehem Steel Company and as delicate as Jack the Ripper.") Eva happens on the king expertly twirling his rope in a municipal park. Not guessing his true identity, she invites him to perform at her "Come as Your Favorite Book-of-the-Month Club" party for several hundred of her most intimate friends. One of them, she tells "Mr. Smith," is George Gershwin—who has already created a sensation by promising *not* to play the piano. (Gershwin was known for playing his own songs nonstop at parties, allowing no one else a chance to entertain.)

According to Steven Bach, in *Dazzler: The Life and Times of Moss Hart*, Eva Standing's party "gave Porter a chance to raid his trunk and use a song he had written in the 1920s for a birthday party for the real Elsa Maxwell. It lampooned her claim that every celebrity freeloading at her table was 'My Most Intimate Friend.' More important, the party served as the big finish toward which the show might build and provided an occasion for the royal runaways to reunite for a happy ending."

In spite of a strong cast, a better-constructed book than most Cole Porter musicals had, jokes and in-jokes to please every taste, a homoerotic subtext, set design by Jo Mielziner, and rave reviews, the show closed after 169 performances.

In 1938, when *Leave It to Me* opened on Broadway, a reviewer who otherwise praised the show took a small swipe: "Of course, Mr. Porter still appears to feel that no score of his is official without reference to Elsa Maxwell."

The reviewer had a point. If you collected the references to Elsa in every Porter song, you could publish a pamphlet. In *Leave It to Me*, she pops up in "Tomorrow," a novelty number filled with references to such topical events as Orson Welles's *War of the Worlds* broadcast, and the New Deal: tomorrow, as happy days return under FDR, "plumpish ladies who are heavier than whales" will lose all that weight and Elsa Maxwell "will no longer break the scales."

Owing to copyright restrictions, I can't include that Elsa pamphlet here. And besides, reading Cole Porter's lyrics isn't half the fun of hearing them sung. Therefore, a few titles and snippets will suffice. According to Robert Kimball, editor of *The Complete Lyrics of Cole Porter*, "I'm Dining with Elsa" ("and her ninety-nine most intimate friends") was a surprise birthday present from Cole to Elsa in Paris in the late 1920s. The lyric survives, though the music seems to have been lost. According to Elsa, "I had at least a dozen kings, or near kings, coming to dinner. It was my birthday, and after the soup I was too impatient to wait longer. I demanded, 'Where is my present?' Cole got up, ran to the piano in the corner of the Ritz dining room, and played the song." ("My Most Intimate Friend," in *Jubliee*, is apparently a reworking of this song.)

While Elsa was press-agenting for Venice in the twenties, Cole wrote "The Scampi" to amuse some of his friends. Along with Elsa, he named Lady Cunard and Princess Jane di San Faustino. In 1941, when *Let's Face It* opened in New York, the cast included Danny Kaye, Eve Arden, Vivian Vance, and Nanette Fabray. Elsa was there in the song "Farming," along with Fannie Hurst, Fanny Brice, Lady Mendl, Garbo, and half a dozen others. A year earlier, in *Panama Hattie*, Ethel Merman introduced "I'm Throwing a Ball Tonight," which starts out "My life was simply hellish" then, like a pop-gun going off, quickly rhymes "relish," "swellish," and "Elsa Maxwellish."

Elsa's up-tempo disposition complemented Cole Porter's moods. Porter's life, however, must be viewed as a two-act tragicomedy, or perhaps a comitragedy: Act I, before the catastrophe, and then Act II. His time in New York, Paris, and Venice in the twenties and early thirties—Cole's first forty-six years—took place in the sunny first act. The rest of his life, up to the end in 1964, stretched in shadow and anguish. At a house party on Long Island in 1937, the horse he was riding reared and fell back on Cole, crushing both legs. From then on, he was severely crippled and in anguish, even after dozens of operations. His great talent, however, came through unscathed. Some of his best work belongs to the latter period, including *Kiss Me, Kate*, which opened on Broadway in 1948 and ran for more than a thousand performances.

Elsa's devotion never wavered. According to Porter's best biographer, George Eells, Elsa and Clifton Webb visited him in the hospital two days after the accident. There, "they found him under heavy sedation. Even so, upon sight of Elsa, he whispered, 'It just goes to show, fifty million Frenchmen can't be wrong. They eat horses instead of ride them.' Elsa, touched by this show of spirit, reported the remark in a letter published in *Harper's* magazine."

Eells adds that later on, Cole played a game with Elsa, naming his left leg Josephine and his right Geraldine. "Each, according to its response to treatment, was given a personality. Josephine was a docile creature who gave as little trouble as possible." Geraldine, however, Cole described as "a hellion, a bitch, a psychopath." In January 1938, Elsa gave a surprise "coming out" party at the Waldorf for Josephine and Geraldine, ostensibly to celebrate the removal of Cole's casts even though, in reality, they would remain on for many months to come. Cole, still so sedated by morphine that he hardly knew where he was, said of the party, "I'm sorry I missed it." Among the five hundred guests were Cecil Beaton, Grace Moore, Alfred Lunt and Lynn Fontanne, Richard Rodgers, Gertrude Lawrence, Clifton Webb, and Dickie Gordon.

Cole and Elsa quarreled occasionally, but never stayed mad for long. Following the death of Cole's wife, Linda, in 1954, Cole suffered a long depression. He told George Eells, "How can one help being depressed when all those you're closest to are dying? I asked Elsa, and she said, 'Rise above it! Rise above it!' " Then, according to Eells, Cole shook his head, and said, "I'm afraid she cares about no one but Elsa."

No doubt he soon realized that he hadn't been fair to his old friend. She was there for his seventieth birthday party on June 9, 1962. By then, Elsa's own health was declining, but she acted as mistress of ceremonies onstage at the Orpheum Theatre in downtown Manhattan, where a revival of *Anything Goes* was playing. After a special midnight performance, a seven-tiered cake was rolled out. Several hundred friends, colleagues, and well-wishers sang "Happy Birthday" along with Elsa, then all raised their glasses in a toast. "This will be a real shot in the arm for Cole," Elsa proclaimed, even though he was not well enough to attend. In happier days he would have savored the irony: no one, including Elsa, noticed that they were a year late, for Cole had turned seventy in 1961.

Elsa's efforts to cultivate Mrs. Guinness succeeded better than even she hoped for. Some months after her first invitation, the *Oakland Tribune* reported on September 23, 1917, that Elsa, back in the Bay Area for the first time since her departure a decade earlier, was "being feted by the smart set" and "with Lady Lister-Kaye, Miss Maxwell has been the house guest of Mrs. Benjamin Guinness." The item ended with the information that Elsa would "return East next week with the Guinness family." Mrs. Guinness's son, eleven-year-old Loel, the future socialite and member of parliament, would have formed part of the entourage.

Another newspaper reported that "Miss Maxwell has brought to San Francisco the official films of the Russian revolution, which will be displayed here for charity, first at the Fairmont Hotel and probably later at one of the local theatres. They were shown once in New York and created a tremendous sensation." Elsa's friends in the haute bourgeoisie must have viewed these revolutionary films with curiosity and consternation. Since the revolution had taken place only a few months earlier, American capitalists had not yet hardened their positions. And yet many among the wealthy and socially prominent would have cheered the American refusal to recognize the new Soviet government. (Diplomatic recognition finally came in 1933.) Whether or not Elsa sympathized with the Bolsheviks, she herself lived a vaguely Communist life: scorning material possessions, she never owned a home and refused to accumulate capital. Nevertheless, if Nicholas and Alexandra had invited her to the Winter Palace, it's doubtful that Elsa's Pavlovian response would have been other than a resounding "Da!"

12 A Funny Thing Happened on the Way to Versailles

On November 11, 1918, the Armistice was signed that officially ended the Great War. Immediately, the Allied victors began planning a peace conference, which convened in Paris early in 1919. Apart from its political importance, and eventual notoriety, the Paris Peace Conference was an enormous media event and also a launch party for the Roaring Twenties. No international political gathering in recent decades is comparable; the nearest present-day equivalent might be the Academy Awards crossed with the Olympics, and a royal wedding thrown in.

For Elsa, getting Marshal Joffre to the Met amounted to a finger snap compared with getting herself to Paris. "Everyone I knew was trying to get boat accommodations to Europe," she said. "Paris might just as well have been on Mars." Her chance at the most lavish social spectacle of the new century seemed nil, but only for the nonce. As always in Elsa's charmed life, a backer appeared—if not Lady Luck herself, then at least Dowager Luck. In 1919, this figure was Eva Stotesbury, a Philadelphia socialite whose husband, the banker Edward Stotesbury, was said to own assets in excess of one hundred fifty million dollars. Eva's divorced daughter by a previous marriage, Louise Cromwell Brooks, a frisky beauty approaching thirty and in search of her next husband, needed a chaperone—respectable, but not zealously so. No one qualified in stodgy, Quakerish Philadelphia, but in New York, Mrs. Stotesbury had heard the buzz, everyone was talking about that indefatigable fund-raiser, the adorably chubby piano player who lived with an opera singer and was doted on by Mrs. Belmont. She was terribly amusing and surely no competition for Louise in the looks department. Their sailing put them in Paris just in time for April.

Elsa claimed, unconvincingly, never to have been taken on a free trip as a "companion" or a "chaperone," two words she detested. "A companion," she said, "suggests a handmaiden or a stooge who truckles to the whims and vanity of the person picking up the checks. A chaperone in my book is a dried-up, professional killjoy. Mrs. Stotesbury, and all the other women who cultivated my friendship, did it for one reason. I was a gay and amusing guest." Still, since unthrifty Elsa didn't pay her own bills, she was in effect the paid companion of many rich women and their daughters. No doubt they enjoyed her company, for her energy never flagged, she had upscale connections everywhere, titled and otherwise, and she took a laissez-faire attitude to the activities of her sponsors. No governessy scruples interfered with their frolic.

In Paris, Elsa and Louise Brooks (not to be confused with the silent film star) put up at Mrs. Stotesbury's house on the rue des Saints-Pères. Dickie, of course, joined them. Elsa's charge fancied men in uniforms; moreover, she had made up her mind to land one of high rank. Elsa said that she had never given big parties until she became Louise's hostess. Now, with an inviting town house and unlimited funds, Elsa applied the skills that so far had remained latent. Her parties helped Louise land Douglas MacArthur, who at age forty was already a brigadier general and would soon rise higher. Their marriage took place in 1922, although before those troths were plighted, Louise had an affair with General John J. Pershing, one of America's most highly regarded military officers. The *on-dit* had it that Louise was also seeing one of Pershing's aides on spare evenings. Elsa, highly skilled at writing between the lines, confirms the testosterone in their residence: "Louise Brooks's house was the unofficial headquarters of the American military delegation and the younger set of foreign army officers attached to the various embassies. . . . Louise's Saturday-night dances were enlivened by General Pershing's liquor and my piano playing." Imagine *La Traviata* without the fatal illness, and voilà! It's Louise as Violetta, and Elsa as her deep-voiced cohort, Flora.

Even with both hands on the piano, and one eye on Paris at play, Elsa turned the other eye to the politics of the peace conference. You get the feeling that she understood the maneuvers of the various nations, and that she, like everyone from President Woodrow Wilson to Louise's majordomo, believed that this had been the war to end all wars, and also that the League of Nations, an outgrowth of the conference, might indeed make the world safe for democracy. Everyone in Paris was wildly idealistic—or at least, those on the winning side were. A few years later, Elsa witnessed the broken treaties at home and abroad. She blamed the United States Senate for its blockage of the Treaty of Versailles and thus American participation in the League of Nations. Had Elsa been born fifty years later, and lived in the era of Margaret Thatcher and Hillary Clinton, she might have groomed herself for politics. In addition to a grasp of government tactics, she possessed the requisite amount of fakery, she thrived on control, and she specialized in spending other people's money.

By her own admission, Elsa in Paris in 1919, aged thirty-eight, didn't know what she wanted to be when she grew up. Although she helped Louise plan the parties and choose the guests, then entertained them at the piano, she had not given a party since her days in San Francisco, those tame musical evenings for local friends on Belvedere Island. "No one in Paris, New York, or London had less money or fewer qualifications for the nebulous distinction of international hostess," she recalled.

Very late one night Elsa awakened to a terrible row in the garden below her bedroom. Two drunken officers, one British, the other Italian, where tilting at each other with swords, or perhaps carving knives—darkness made the weapons hard to distinguish. Throwing on her wrapper, Elsa descended and heaved herself between the combatants. "Gentlemen! Gentlemen! Let's have a cup of coffee!"

A bit later, slightly sobered, the two men all but kissed to cement the friendship of their great nations, et cetera. They invited Elsa for cocktails next day at the Ritz. The following morning, hearing about the ruckus, Louise assumed the duel was fought for her, though in truth, Elsa confided to Dickie, they were both in love with the beautiful Miss Fellowes-Gordon. Years later, telling the tale, Elsa implied that their passion was not reciprocated.

OF MICE AND MUSIC

In her memoir *D.V.*, Diana Vreeland wrote: "Do you remember Mary Borden's *A Woman with White Eyes*? In that book is a marvelous description of fat white hands galloping over the keys. They were Elsa's." Borden (1886–1968) must have scrutinized Elsa, for in the novel, published in 1930, she based a lost-generation character named Marcella Macintosh squarely on her. "Marcella, round as a pumpkin, terrible to behold in her mannish coat and skirt, with her face like a suet pudding and her eyes like currants, would plump herself on the piano stool and then—well, madness would fill the room. It came from her fat fingers that pounded out the irresistible, insistent, syncopated rhythm of the tom-tom. Faster and faster, louder and louder, wizard fingers, wizard hands, monstrous, magical, they scrambled like fat white mice over the ivory keys, but they were made of iron, they had the strength of steel hammers."

Marcella, expressionistically described, occupies a dozen of the novel's three-hundred-plus pages: "Like the ten plagues of Egypt she swept over Europe, leaving a desert behind her. She destroyed Paris. She filled its streets with noise and made the pale gray stones of its beautiful proud eighteenth-century houses echo and shake with American jazz. The head waiter of the Ritz Palace cringed to her. The men at the Bourse did her bidding . . . Anything was better than being alone. Marcella was an absolute guarantee that you never would be . . . Marcella's gang were well trained in parlour tricks. They danced beautifully, made love gracefully, played expert bridge. They were indeed such expert performers that one forgot in one's delight at the performance who they were, what they were, how old they were, and how hopeless they were."

As Elsa and her comrades left the Ritz bar next afternoon, "an elderly, chic woman" stopped her at the door. "Aren't you Elsa Maxwell," demanded the stranger, "the woman who sings those risqué songs?"

"I'm Elsa Maxwell, but off-color songs are not my stock-in-trade!"

(True, but they *were* a sideline. Today those blue lyrics sound as innocent as Mother Goose.)

The impatient woman waved aside Elsa's demurral. "Never mind. I'm giving a tea at my home tomorrow for some of the diplomats of the Peace Conference and I'd like you to help with the entertainment." When the woman introduced herself, Elsa was astonished and then flattered, for the name was on the lips of *le tout Paris*.

"I'm Elsie de Wolfe," said that "elderly, chic woman," who was, in reality, a youthful fifty-four, a dynamo who could stand on her head until the day she died. The introduction was superfluous, akin to "I am Greta Garbo." Everyone knew the name, and what she was famous for. Born in New York in 1865, Elsie de Wolfe inherited roughly the same uneven social prominence there as Elsa in San Francisco. Her father, a physician, managed money badly, so that the family fortunes swung from fat to lean. Elsie's Scottish mother had connections in the British Isles, and after her schooling, Elsie was sent to Scotland for added polish. There she stayed with her mother's cousin, who was Queen Victoria's chaplain at Balmoral. She was presented to the queen in the 1880s, and by 1891 she had embarked on a career as an actress. She starred with luminaries of the day, such as John Drew and Maude Adams. Ethel Barrymore was her understudy; Clyde Fitch wrote a play for her.

Possessed of a small but persistent talent, de Wolfe was better known for her Paris wardrobe than for her power to move an audience. In 1904 she left the stage to take up her second career, for which she is best remembered today: she invented interior decoration. According to Diana Vreeland, in the introduction to Jane Smith's biography *Elsie de Wolfe*, "She simply cleared out the Victoriana and let in the twentieth century. She was the first person who pulled up the blinds, let in the sunshine, cleared out the smelly tasseled curtains within curtains—loaded with cigar smoke and dust—and replaced them with clean English chintz and French *toiles*." (Many of Elsie's new-fangled ideas came from Oscar Wilde, who had been her guest in New York in the 1890s.)

Her lover was Elisabeth Marbury, the theatrical tycoon. They lived together for over thirty years, and around the turn of the century they bought and renovated the Villa Trianon, in Versailles, which Louis XV had built in the eighteenth century as a retreat from the main palace. During World War I, both women worked heroically to aid the wounded. Elsie was awarded the Croix de Guerre, with two citations for bravery under fire, and later the Légion d'Honneur. It was noted by her friends that, unlike most volunteers, she had gone through the rigors of war accompanied by a French maid on the battlefields.

Elsie de Wolfe's third career—that of hostess and party giver—overlapped the second. Indeed, her vast earnings as *the* society decorator financed the lavish entertainments at the Villa Trianon, at her apartment in Paris, and in her New York apartment. Diana Vreeland again: "Her parties were a mixture of artists, beautiful people, high society, and young people who were on their way up." Janet Flanner, in a *New Yorker* profile in 1938, described de Wolfe's parties as "ostentatious in their elaboration, preparation, and ocular details," although never stuffy. "She enjoys two hundred guests to dinner, counts her friends in crowds. . . . She has created a sort of social gigantism of which she remains the expert manipulator." No better mentor existed for Elsa Maxwell, who, like Elsie de Wolfe, had the innate gift of creating parties and, again like her exemplar, found her vocation only in middle age.

The two women blended exceptionally well, in view of so many competitive possibilities. A quarrel or two notwithstanding, they remained fast friends until Elsie's death in 1950. Except for a love of parties and a talent for benign social climbing, however, the two were opposites. Elsie de Wolfe was the total aesthete. She breathed beauty and suffocated in vulgar or impersonal surroundings. Perfect furniture, curtains, walls, objets d'art, gardens—and Elsie herself disciplined in body and soul, trim, immaculately groomed, as though posing for an early *Harper's Bazaar*.

Elsa Maxwell, by contrast, looked like an unwelcome guest in her clothes. Her girth became her trademark, and recipes for rich food were as beloved by her as the poems of Keats and Shelley. Elsa loved a rip-roaring good time, and relished the impersonality of hotel rooms. Her own apartment on the twenty-sixth floor of the Waldorf Towers, when Edward R. Murrow visited her for *Person to Person* in 1953, might have been a generic display in Macy's furniture department. "I own nothing," Elsa told Murrow. "I don't own a single thing." Watching the interview, one takes her almost literally. She sits on an ordinary sofa, with pillows and a predictable lamp on an end table. In the bedroom, a plain bed with a lamp on a nightstand, lace curtains, a floor lamp, some books and magazines on tables and divans, nondescript pictures on the walls. On a table in the sitting room, a few framed photographs and roses in a vase. Certainly, the place was comfortable, but even if she had received Ed Murrow in one of those catchpenny hotels from her early days in New York, Elsa's credo would have varied little: "Never in my life have I been depressed, and never tired. And never worried, Ed. I've just sort of been happy. That's why I never drink. Never have to."

To parse what Elsa learned from Elsie de Wolfe would be impossible, since no party outlives its own brief hour. Attempts to recapture those swirling amusements lead to frustration, since party scenes wilt faster than bouquets. In general, however, one might say that a de Wolfe affair had visible structure and unity, a beginning, middle, and end. She operated within the lineaments of French formality, whereas Elsa's parties typically seemed more like impromptu carnival events, often with a one-damn-thing-after-another giddiness. Although thoroughly planned and organized, they were nevertheless so loosely structured that the middle part might well occur at the end, with a finale to greet the crowd. ("Be different," she advised. "Run the party backward.") In dramatic terms, a de Wolfe evening unwound like a classic drama by Racine, while at Elsa's you might expect a Falstaffian romp, a midsummer night's costume party, or a barn dance punctuated by mooing cows and cackling hens. (Although not referring to de Wolfe's elegant style, Elsa said, "It was the monotony of most people's parties that drove me to invent my own.")

Elsie de Wolfe's private life chimes with her philosophy of social gatherings. When the moment arrived to become Lady Mendl, she assumed the role with panache, as though donning the sword and *habit vert* of the French Academy. In 1926, she married Sir Charles Mendl, a press attaché at the British embassy in Paris. This *mariage blanc* served them both well. She cherished the title, he increased his bank account, and they remained friends as before, since they maintained separate residences in Paris, with the Villa Trianon as common turf.

On June 28, 1919, the Treaty of Versailles was signed, ending hostilities between Germany and the Allied powers. Other treaties were signed between other warring parties, but this primary one came to symbolize both the end of the Great War and the seedbed of the next one. At the Villa Trianon, said Elsie de Wolfe in her autobiography, *After All*, "On the day of the signing of the Peace we kept open house. Afterwards our guests went back to the Galerie des Glaces in the Château to affix their signatures to the Treaty."

Arthur Balfour, former British prime minister and now foreign secretary, came in for tea and gave details of the dramatic day.* Late in the afternoon, Elsie and her guests watched President Wilson and his entourage drive out through the gates of Versailles. That evening, at dinner, she entertained Balfour; Sir Ian Malcolm, commander-in-chief of the British army in the Dardanelles; Alexandra, Lady Colebrook; Consuelo, Duchess of Marlborough; the French aviator Jacques Balsan (who, two years later, would marry Consuelo following her divorce from the Duke of Marlborough); Sir Oswald Mosley (a Conservative MP at the time, and future leader of the Union of British Facsists, who, in 1936, would marry Diana Mitford in Berlin, at the home of Joseph Goebbels, with Adolf Hitler as one of the guests); and Elsa Maxwell.

Elsie de Wolfe described Elsa Maxwell as "the star of the party as she sat all evening at the piano, singing and playing, in her inimitable way, all of the latest songs. Arthur Balfour was among the most delighted of our guests, and told me, on leaving, that he had never passed a more amusing evening."

Elsa, expanding on her entertainment for the dinner guests, contradicted her pique at Elsie's reference, the previous day, to risqué ditties: "I played and sang some of Cole Porter's 'secret' songs. Balfour's eyebrows became an

---

*Balfour's name is well remembered, and highly controversial, in the Middle East, owing to the so-called Balfour Declaration of 1917. In a letter to Lord Rothschild, a leader of the Jewish community in Britain, Balfour wrote: "His Majesty's government view with favour the establishment in Palestine of a national home for the Jewish people. . . ." Those displaced by the state of Israel cite the letter's disregarded caveat that "nothing shall be done to prejudice the civil and religious rights of existing non-Jewish communities in Palestine."

extension of his hairline when he first heard the irreverent lyrics, but his reserve soon cracked and he laughed uproariously as I dipped deeper into Cole's private stock." By secret songs, Elsa presumably meant those written for various college musicals at Yale from 1909 to 1914, and for *See America First*. One such, "We're a Group of Nonentities," published in *The Complete Lyrics of Cole Porter*, rhymes "sword of Damocles" with "a box of Rameses"—i.e., condoms.

Although Cole didn't write "Anything Goes" until the thirties, it would have been a suitable anthem for those gathered in Paris in 1919, and for sophisticates and progressives in many cities. The twentieth century had finally arrived in astonishing form: the Jazz Age. Elsie de Wolfe's snapshot of that heady time: "A tremendous change took place in the pace of society. Old conventions were cast aside. Old barriers were torn down. Cabarets, cocktails, all-night parties, became the prerogatives of youth—of the girls as well as of the boys. The release from the hardships and self-sacrifice of four long years had its reaction in a license of speech and action unheard of since Elizabethan days. Life was broken up into a mad patchwork."

Looking back on the dawn of modernism, Elsie de Wolfe recalled that in 1919, "If one wanted to be in the thick of things one had to set one's mind to work creating new diversions." Perhaps she advised Elsa Maxwell to do just that. In any event, Elsa yearned to be in the thick of things, and Elsie de Wolfe's dinner party on June 28, 1919, marks her debut as creator of new diversions. Her titillating presence that evening assured that invitations from Elsa would be enthusiastically accepted. She lost no time in issuing them. Arthur Balfour, on his way out of the Villa Trianon, complimented Elsa and said, "I should like to see you again."

"Why not dine with me?" she rejoined.

"I should be charmed," smiled the foreign secretary, for whom it had been a day of political triumph and social boisterousness.

"How about a week from tonight at the Ritz?" said Elsa with more confidence than she actually possessed.

"I shall be there," he said, with a bow.

13 A Footnote as Big as the Ritz

Elsa's flamboyant invitation landed her in a jam. She was, of course, flat broke. As long as she dined and entertained at Louise Brooks's house, her needs were amply met. Dickie and various friends paid the bills in restaurants and cafes, the tacit agreement being that Elsa's showmanship and vivacity compensated for her shallow pockets. But dinner at the Ritz with a prime minister, even a former one—it was, as all the world knew, the most expensive restaurant in France.

Fortunately for herself, and for our narrative, Elsa had no shame. Lady Colebrook, whom she knew from New York and the Belmont fêtes, and who was also a guest at Elsie de Wolfe's dinner, had overheard Elsa's brash invitation. Always the operator, Elsa put it to Her Ladyship without a blush, telling her what a pickle she had gotten herself into.

"Don't worry, Plumpy," cooed Lady Colebrook. "I'll see to it that you don't let down my country's foreign secretary. I'll stand treat for the dinner." Even Elsa, who expected good fortune, reeled at the next offer, for her patroness, with the offhand remark that eight guests make a nice number for a dinner party, began jotting names: Mrs. Keppel (Elsa knew, like everyone else, that she had been the favorite mistress of Edward VII); Princesse Edmond de Polignac (née Winnaretta Singer, of the American sewing machine family); Lord d'Abenon (banker and diplomat); Sir Ronald Storrs (military governor of Jerusalem); Lady Ripon, a celebrated beauty; her friend, the Grand Duke Alexander of Russia; and the Marquis Boni de Castellane. (Number eight, of course, would be Arthur Balfour; Elsa herself, as hostess, didn't count among that number.)

"There," said Lady Colebrook, looking up from the page. "That will balance your table quite nicely."

When Elsa lamented that she had never laid eyes on any of the guests except the foreign secretary and Mrs. Keppel, Lady Colebrook waved it aside. "I'll see to it that they all come," she soothed.

"I have nothing to wear except my old black chiffon dress," wailed Elsa, whose resemblance to a very mature Orphan Annie wasn't lost on Her Ladyship. The unexpected solution to this dilemma was a new scarf that someone had recently given Lady Colebrook. "I'll paint some Chinese sampans on it and the effect will be so striking that it may even start a new fashion." The promise of such adornment left Elsa speechless, and drew many a stare when she wore it to the Ritz. Elsa was terrified of ordering the dinner with Olivier Dabescat, the very mention of whom caused frissons throughout the gourmet world, for he was the Louis XIV (and, some said, the Genghis Khan) of maîtres d'hôtel. According to Elsa, Olivier—who was known only by his given name—"was a towering iceberg of etiquette who had been known to freeze grand dukes with a glance."

Elsa claimed that in 1919 her knowledge of ordering dinners was limited to asking for "blue-plate specials in a cafeteria," which is a patent exaggeration. Whether she herself ordered or not, she had dined at Maxine Elliott's, at Mrs. Belmont's, and at many another fine table. No one would confuse her with Oliver Twist.

Nevertheless, she was not the Elsa Maxwell yet to come, though she suspected that Olivier and the Ritz, and her table d'hôte there, might bring her destiny into clearer focus. Elsa knew that one's destiny requires homework, and to this end she sped to the Paris office of the *New York Herald* where she dipped into dusty files to locate a famous prewar dinner given by none other than the formidable Boni de Castellane, who was soon to sit at her very own table. That stupendous menu retrieved, Elsa memorized the courses and the wines served with each one. Next stop, Olivier, who, Elsa said, ceased writing her order after the first two courses, fixed her with a stare, and proclaimed with dry eloquence, "This dinner, Mademoiselle, lacks only one thing to make it perfect—the presence of the Marquis de Castellane." Elsa remembered it in French, as well: *"Ce dîner ne manque que la présence du Marquis de Castellane pour être parfait."*

During the day—during many days in 1919—the aging leaders of the Allied nations toiled to impose nineteenth-century imperialistic notions onto a dangerous new age. President Woodrow Wilson (1856–1924), French Prime Minister Georges Clemenceau (1841–1929), British Prime Minister David Lloyd George (1863–1945), and Vittorio Emmanuele Orlando (1860–1952), head of the Italian delegation—these led the victorious, whose Parisian dreams, ending in ultimate chaos, would long outlive them. The blundering hours of the day passed slowly for these men, for hundreds of their aides, for diplomats, minor kings seeking lost kingdoms, onlookers from foreign lands, and camp followers of every stripe.

At night, however, with anxieties and travails cast aside, workaday Paris became Paree, alive once more after four years of mourning. Those who had not previously savored the City of Light, and those fated never to come back, along with Parisians and frequent revelers, vowed to celebrate the end of slaughter, even though blood still drenched their memory. Their motto might have been Survival of the Merriest.

"It is difficult to describe the exhilarating atmosphere of Paris during the peace negotiations," Elsa said. "Every day was like a sparkling holiday. The city echoed to the music of bands welcoming returning soldiers. Shops, theatres, and cafes were jammed." The roundelay of parties surely gave Elsa ideas: some she attended, she hosted others under the auspices of Louise Brooks, and absorbed details of a thousand others.

Like an aspiring writer convinced his own books will outsell the bestsellers, or a zealous politician bent on reshaping the state, Elsa blueprinted the parties that she herself would like to give. Early on, she formulated a practical Theory of Parties that she adhered to for the rest of her life. Though she elaborated on it many times in books and magazines, and later on TV, the kernel of her theory remained constant: "The best parties are given by people who can't afford them. They must use imagination and ingenuity as substitutes for money. The glimmer of an original idea can make an evening more successful than a lavish dinner and a well-stocked bar." Years later, looking back across her famous landscape of conviviality and high jinks, she affirmed that the conclusive proof of her theory was her own career. "My parties were memorable for the entertainment, not the food and liquor I provided. Guests who heard Rubinstein, Milstein, Melchior and Coward perform for me didn't know, or care, what they had to eat. Anyone who participated in one of my scavenger hunts or murder parties didn't need the artificial stimulus of liquor."

Other important dicta in Elsa's theory: Never invite those you don't like just because you're obligated. "When drawing up a guest list," Elsa said, "consider only two qualifications. One is that you know and like the person. The other, that he or she has something to contribute to the success of the party." One key to Elsa's artistry was the illusion of spontaneity: "Carefully studied effects must appear just to happen, and the joy of the hostess in her own party must be the first element encountered by a guest." The corollary to this seeming effortlessness by the happy hostess runs like a knife blade through Elsa's party advice: "Ruthlessness is the first attribute toward the achievement of a perfect party," and Elsa's instances of it show her unflinching control. She turned away a Vanderbilt matron who begged for an invitation because "this party is for my friends, and you are not one of them." When Elsa discovered bores at one of her large dinners, which sometimes happened, she put them all at the same table where, she swore, they amused one another with great boring panache. Woe to anyone who appeared bored by the party itself, for Elsa would call that tedious person aside and present him with a book, saying, "Darling, I can tell you aren't having a good time. You'll be so much happier at home reading this," and out he went. (She kept current bestsellers on hand for the purpose.) Among the do's of a good party, Elsa listed flowers, appropriate music—not too loud—games, good food, and entertainment, whether charades, cards, or a concert by the world's greatest musician. And always lively conversation.

ELSA AND DICKIE MEET THE LOST GENERATION

So much has been written about Americans in Paris during the Jazz Age—Hemingway, the Fitzgeralds, Gertrude Stein and Alice B. Toklas, Gerald and Sara Murphy—that it's easy to overlook the other side of their mythology: not everyone found them enchanting. Elsa, for one. Her summation: "The dreariest bunch were the half-baked mediocrities who took sniveling refuge behind Gertrude Stein's convenient catchall phrase, 'the lost generation,' to excuse their inadequacies. The lost generation's self-pity, a philosophy alien to me, further was exposed as a superficial doctrine by its chief drumbeater, F. Scott Fitzgerald. I met Fitzgerald on several occasions and he never was sober enough to carry on a coherent conversation with anyone."

Elsa said she couldn't recall meeting Hemingway—"although he mentioned me twice in books written during that period." I have located only one of Hemingway's references to Elsa. In his 1950 novel, *Across the River and into the Trees*, the narrator reminisces about his experiences in World War I: "At the Etoile I took Elsa Maxwell's butler prisoner. It was a very complicated operation." The reference is pointless, even silly.

F. Scott Fitzgerald annoyed Dickie mightily: "He used to get crying drunk, and I can't bear that. I had dinner with him and Zelda once, and he started crying, he said, 'Oh poor Zelda, poor dear, and poor Dickie.' I said, 'Leave me out of it, I'm quite all right. I'm not poor anything.'"

Still the neophyte in 1919, Elsa surfed the waves of hilarity with the younger set. Flaming youth, whether young or not, all trusted the dogma of insouciant, riotous Paris as infallible. While many of them barely concealed the desperation beneath their laughter, Elsa had no patience with the world-weary. She took an interest in everything and everyone, from the Moulin Rouge and *le jazz hot*, which heated up her own piano, to the alluring personalities who had descended on the city. Paderewski, for example, whom she hadn't seen since Joffre night at the Met. Newly elected as prime minister of Poland, he had not a spare moment to pay her a visit, or even to play his own piano, as he toiled on behalf of his downtrodden land. Queen Marie of Romania, occupying twenty rooms at the Ritz, was out of reach, though Elsa set her traps and a few years later, in Venice, staged an alfresco dinner for Her Majesty. Elsa's old friend from South Africa, General Botha, and her more recent one, Winston Churchill, had both descended on Paris.

Others in town were unknown to Elsa, though they, too, seemed in rehearsal for destiny: the erudite young diplomant Harold Nicolson, of Bloomsbury, whom Elsa would meet a few years later in San Francisco; Allen Dulles, who would found the CIA three decades later; Lawrence of Arabia, stirring the pot in Paris on behalf of many an Arab cause; Marcel Proust, who shuffled into the Ritz late at night in an overcoat as a scenery change from his cork-lined bedroom, who adored Olivier and presented this unique maître d'hôtel with one of the first copies of *A la recherche du temps perdu*; Eleanor and Franklin Roosevelt, married for fourteen years, he an assistant navy secretary and she displeased by his excessive attention to other ladies; Ho Chi Minh, the future hero of Vietnam, who in 1919 was a busboy at the Ritz. Sarah Bernhardt, seventy-five, the fabled actress whose destiny lay behind her, starred in charity galas every night, or so it seemed. Elsa's young cohort, Walter Wanger, had also arrived in town. Having served in the war, he now worked as an aide to James T. Shotwell, an advisor to President Wilson.

Indeed, more names than even Elsa could drop, though in due course she would host a high percentage of this teeming cast. So fantastic was that assemblage, so intertwined their encounters, that David A. Andelman, in his book *A Shattered Peace: Versailles 1919 and the Price We Pay Today*, speculates on one fanciful meet-up: "While there is, of course, no real record, it is not unreasonable to ponder whether Ho Chi Minh might have been clearing the tables after the dinner party Elsa Maxwell gave for Arthur Balfour, or when Marcel Proust demanded that Harold Nicolson describe every nuance of the Peace Conference deliberations."

Meanwhile, back at the Ritz, Elsa confessed to Olivier that she had indeed purloined this menu from Boni de Castellane, adding, with a soupçon of one-upmanship, that the marquis himself would indeed be one of her guests. Elsa apparently melodramatized her descriptions of Olivier's *froideur* in order to spotlight herself as the shrinking violet she never was. Her old San Francisco habit of grouping herself with the frontier urchins persisted, even in the arrogant and opulent purlieus of Paris. It was, as always, a pose, for there, more than anywhere, without a measure of assertiveness and self-assurance, one would be trampled. Elsa did not fall in with the herd; more often, she charged ahead as social bellwether. Perhaps Elsa placed herself among the humble owing to low self-esteem. Or did she do it for the sake of snappy prose?

Marie-Louise Ritz, widow of the hotel's founder, wrote in 1938 that Olivier "is the most modest of men" with "infinite tact and courtesy." How would Elsa's story read if she had merely ordered the dinner from Olivier, and he assented, "*Oui, Mademoiselle*"? The answer: she created his bullying stereotype so that she could win him over, as it were, thereby aggrandizing herself as conqueror hostess. In *R.S.V.P.* she announced that "years later, Olivier wrote his memoirs and paid me a supreme compliment by stating that only three people in all his experience knew how to order a dinner properly—the Prince of Wales, afterwards Edward VII; Prince Esterházy of Hungary; and Elsa Maxwell."

If Elsa had read Marie-Louise Ritz's biography of her husband, César, the hotel's eponymous founder, she might have omitted Olivier's glacial *snobisme*, for Madame Ritz had heard it all before: "Fashionable ladies who write their memoirs do not consider their task achieved unless they are able to drag in—if only by the heels—an anecdote mentioning 'Olivier of the Ritz.' Olivier anecdotes mount and mount in the stacks of this type of literature." Madame Ritz liked to tease Olivier about his reputation by asking, "Did this happen?" and "Did you really say . . . ?" According to her, "His left eyelid droops, he bows from the waist, stiffly. 'It is quite possible,' he replies." (Olivier's memoir exists, if at all, as a phantom. Neither the Bibliothèque Nationale, repository of all books published in France, nor other sources, have a listing for it. It is possible, of course, that the memoir was privately printed, circulated in manuscript, or printed in a magazine.)

Elsa claimed that "the big night passed in a daze for me. The food tasted like ashes and the wine was as flat as water in my parched mouth"—surely a revolutionary reaction with someone else footing the bill. Ahh, but her guests: "Balfour went into raptures. Mrs. Keppel remarked on my flawless menu. The Grand Duke Alexander raved that the white wine was the best since 1897"—the kind of boisterous self-promotion that makes us want to leave the room until Elsa regains her equilibrium.

Balfour probably did say, however, as quoted by Elsa, that after such an enjoyable meal he dreaded the return to his hotel. If anyone could transgress his famous aloofness, surely it was she. After all, Elsa previously had sung him naughty songs and made him laugh. Leaving the Ritz, she said, "How would you like to go to the new night club Paul Poiret has just opened?" The foreign secretary was game, so off they went.

Poiret, the fashion designer, had recently created an entertainment mecca called l'Oasis in the garden behind his couture establishment on the Avenue d'Antin. For a time, this became the rage, owing to the elaborate theme events in which guests took part. One might find oneself on a tropical isle, in a circus, or at a costume party where everyone was dressed in orange, black, and silver. Although an article and photographs in *Vogue* in November 1919 portrayed l'Oasis as respectably chaste, on the night Elsa took Balfour the attraction involved "undressed French chorus girls and ribald jokes." Departing after four hours, he said, "My dear Miss Maxwell, allow me to thank you for the most delightful and degrading evening I ever have spent."

Poiret's parties may have inspired some of Elsa's own. According to one source, "These huge fêtes were elaborate" and ran the gamut of entertainment, from "dancers and orchestras to immense buffets and hundreds of carafes filled with exotic drinks. One party even featured a python, a monkey merchant, and a garden of wild animals."

News of Elsa's coup in nabbing a table of international luminaries spread like a virus. She claimed that the Balfour dinner "launched me as a hostess." Exactly who, people asked, some grudgingly, is this jolly elf of a woman, and how does she gain top-notch entree without working at it for years? If Elsa's unprecedented success had taken place a decade earlier, Proust himself might have pastiched her for his novel. Already he had immortalized the bohemian hostess Madame Verdurin, who, though common and provincial, rhapsodizes over beautiful piano playing, laughs so hard at questionable humor that she dislocates her jaw, and eventually rises to the pinnacle of snob society as the Princesse de Guermantes.

Elsa came along too late for Proust, but not for R.V.C. (Ronnie) Bodley, a military attaché at the British embassy in Paris. His novelistic portrait of Elsa in 1919, and extending a few years later: "I do not know how she existed or why she is still alive [he was writing in 1931] as she never went to bed before three all the time I knew her, and I believe that to this day she lives in the same way. Her powers of organisation were immense, her 'entrain' [i.e., zest, wholeheartedness] indefatigable, and she just made people about her keep on the move until they dropped out from sheer exhaustion. She had an astonishing flair for those people who would be useful to her, and everyone had for her some particular value. It might be money, it might be position or good looks or piano playing or a sense of humour, but it had to be something and as long as one had this 'something' to give, one was Elsa's best friend." (Dickie revealed to Hugo Vickers that she had an affair with Ronnie Bodley at the time.)

BONI DE CASTELLANE

I was born in the year 1867 at Rochecotte, in Touraine, a part of France particularly associated with historic châteaux. . . . My ancestors exercised the prerogative of coining money—a fact worthy of notice, since most of their descendants appear to have been mainly endowed with a capacity for spending it." So begins the *Confessions of the Marquis de Castellane*, and money remains a motif throughout.

Madame Ritz, in her book, described Marie Ernest Paul Boniface de Castellane-Novejean—"Boni" to his friends—as a "leader of Paris fashions who understood the art of entertaining and the art of dining as almost no one else of his time." Dandyism didn't count against him during the Belle Epoque, for European society reserved an elevated seat for foppish gentlemen, especially those with titles. Boni, the perfumed aesthete, resembled a heterosexual Oscar Wilde, or a straight version of

Proust's friend Count Robert de Montesquiou, whom the novelist immortalized as the Baron de Charlus.

Boni de Castellane is best remembered today for his capture, in 1895, of Anna Gould, daughter of the American robber baron Jay Gould. One of the many "dollar princesses" of the era, she brought fifteen million dollars to the match, which she swapped for the title of marquise. To the euphemistic French, these alliances were "*les mariages transatlantiques.*"

"She'll never know how much I loved her," said the husband, "for her money." By then, he had spent seven or eight million on a new mansion, other women, and sumptuous parties (an elaborate fête in the Bois de Boulogne cost a quarter of a million dollars). Fed up with Boni's habits and his ungallant bon mots (he said of his plain-featured wife that "her swarthy face would not have caused comment if seen peering out of a wigwam"), Anna packed up her five children and the servants, doused the electricity in the Paris mansion, and filed for divorce in 1906.

Unable to snare another heiress, Boni spent his last twenty-five years as a minor antiques dealer, interior decorator, and fashion consultant. He attended a few of Elsa's parties, though they gave each other a wide berth. Elsie de Wolfe remained a close friend, and even after his descent into reduced circumstances, she kept a full-length portrait of the witty marquis in the entrance hall of her Villa Trianon.

14 I Love the Nightlife

When Louise Brooks left Paris for the United States in 1922 to marry Douglas MacArthur, Elsa and Dickie took an apartment in Montmartre for which they paid less than one hundred dollars a year, owing to rent controls imposed by the government at the start of the war and continuing after the armistice. "A single woman," said Elsa, "has three major items of expense—rent, food, and clothes." Lodged under the famous rooftops of Paris, Elsa dined out, and lunched out, at the invitation of sundry hosts and hostesses who found it stylish to be seen with this feisty Yankee dumpling, though none among them could explain how Mademoiselle Maxwell had so quickly situated herself as a monument. Hemingway's moveable feast became, for Elsa, boot camp for self-promotion.

She stood out among the best-dressed as their polar opposite: Elsa's "uniform" consisted of one dark suit and one dark dress, or so it seemed, varied occasionally with a Molyneux or a Jean Patou. Whatever the outfit, it enveloped a few more pounds each month, thus helping to seal her reputation as "*une originale*," an eccentric, although one to be cultivated for her connections. For instance, a line of titles that stretched like can-can dancers at the Moulin Rouge.

There was Lady Mendl, of course. And Princesse Edmond de Polignac, née Winnaretta Singer, of the sewing machine family. A famous lesbian patroness of the arts, she entered a "lavender marriage" with the homosexual

Prince de Polignac in 1893. Elsa's entree to "Princess Winnie," as she was fondly called, came about through Dickie, whose distant cousin, Reginald Ailwyn Fellowes, married Winnaretta's niece, Marguerite Séverine Philippine Decazes de Glücksberg—better known as the beautiful Daisy Fellowes, heiress, socialite, fashion icon, and editor of the French *Harper's Bazaar*. After Daisy's mother, Isabelle-Blanche Singer, committed suicide, the girl was raised by Winnaretta, the dead woman's sister. Elsa omits Dickie's important connections in Paris, leaving the impression that she, the impecunious pioneer gal, climbed the Eiffel Tower of Parisian society one princess at a time. But even Elsa's fierce ambition required a supplemental nod from a person of rank. Dickie herself, unimpressed by her own milieu, acquiesced in Elsa's patrician pursuits, though in private she sometimes snarled and called Elsa names.

Another link in Elsa's golden chain was Princess Jane di San Faustino, née Campbell and born in New Jersey, who married Prince Carlo Bourbon del Monte in 1897. Someone said of the princess that "she collects human beings as others collect postage stamps or moths." (The same could be said of Elsa.) Elsa described her as looking like "a figure out of a medieval painting," and with "the tongue of a fishwife when she turned it on arrogant poseurs." According to Elsa, Princess Jane "ruled social Rome with an iron hand—as she did the Lido Beach in Venice." Gianni Agnelli, head of Fiat for thirty years beginning in 1966, was Princess Jane's grandson. As a friend of Elsa's, he once donated a ten-thousand-dollar deluxe automobile from his company to a charity raffle held by Elsa to benefit blind babies of the New York Lighthouse.

These women, and many others like them, were never Elsa's intimates, nor did she claim more than their acquaintance. (Elsie de Wolfe, Lady Mendl, was an exception.) Rather, they served as distant mentors, templates for how a strong-willed, determined American woman might set up her own Social Republic in a sophisticated European capital. In Elsa's case, this must be done without benefit of good looks, titled husband, or family fortune, though with the aid of Dickie's social ballast. Unlike the princesses and their fixed realms, Elsa envisioned for herself a floating fiefdom, informal, carefree, filled with music, laughter, food, games, and bonhomie. And portable: wherever Elsa went, the party followed, and as the 1920s progressed, Elsa

Maxwell indeed became an international institution—Paris, Venice, Monaco, New York, and the world.

At times, however, from around 1920 until midpoint in the decade, it seemed that her apprenticeship would never end. Sir Oswald Mosley, whom Elsa first met at Elsie de Wolfe's on the day the Treaty of Versailles was signed, wrote in his autobiography, *My Life*, that Elsa "in those days gave discreet parties, at least in Paris, without publicity of any kind . . . her simple and boisterous turns at the piano in these small parties had not yet been transmuted to a world-wide music hall with all participants displayed to the headlines in the grotesque acrobatics of superfluous wealth." (When Elsa met Mosley in 1919, he was a Conservative MP. She, like many other former friends, never forgave his later pro-Nazi fascism, and described a party he gave in Paris in 1953 as attended by "termites of all nationalities.")

After a decade together, Elsa and Dickie began spending long periods apart. In the early twenties, Dickie began an eight-year affair with Don Jacobo Fitz-James Stuart y Falcó, seventeenth Duke of Alba, a Spanish nobleman, diplomat, politician, and art collector. (Seventy years later, as Hugo Vickers interviewed her, a staff member of the care home in London offered Dickie a glass of sherry, which didn't quite meet her expectations. Recalling "Jimmy" Alba, Dickie sighed. "He used to send me cases of that, always." Then, "He was good looking, but he was a bore, frankly. I never went to Madrid, not then. Years later, I did go to Madrid and I went to the house for tea." That would have taken place, presumably, after the death of his wife, in 1934.)

In public, Elsa accepted Dickie's roving with equanimity. To Elsa, who stayed in Paris, Dickie was merely "in England or batting around the continent with her own group of friends." According to Anita Loos, however, "for long stretches Elsa was bitter about two of Dickie's suitors (both aristocrats, one British, and the other a Spanish duke)." Nevertheless, Loos considered that Elsa's and Dickie's battles "only accented their devotion to each other."

While Dickie roamed, Elsa had much to occupy her. She had formed an alliance with Captain Edward Molyneux, whom she accurately described as "a British war hero who was a rising star in the fashion hierarchy." Born

in London in 1891, Molyneux entered the world of fashion at age seventeen. His promising career interrupted by World War I, Molyneux recom-
menced in 1919 by opening his own couture house in Paris. He resembled
David Niven without the mustache, and had he become an actor the BBC
would surely have typecast him as a prime minister or a high commissioner.
Within two years Molyneux had built up an enormous reputation, and a
business with some twelve hundred employees.

In 1921, he and Elsa, in partnership, opened a nightclub called l'Acacia,
on the rue des Acacias. Elsa dreamed up the idea, she said, because she was
spending so much time at parties as piano player-in-chief, why not do it on
a grander commercial scale. According to her, Paris in 1921 needed her kind
of cabaret. Those looking for diversion after dinner or the theatre had three
unsatisfactory choices, she said: big hotels with dance orchestras—stuffy;
naughty clubs of international repute, like the Moulin Rouge and the Folies
Bergère, which lost their appeal after one visit; and most of the remaining
boîtes, which amounted to tourist clip joints.

According to Elsa, Molyneux liked her business plan: a high-end nightclub with top attractions for its floor show. Already, in two years, his *maison
de couture* had done quite well, but he needed a gimmick to keep up with
stiff competition, namely the established French couturiers. Elsa convinced
him that he must gain publicity, as much of it as possible, which would
serve him in two vital connections. First, a chic nightclub would attract the
glittery clientele he wished for his salon; indeed, his customers would surely
storm the gates of l'Acacia in their Molyneux garb. Then, too, their new
club would divert some of the crowd from rival Paul Poiret's l'Oasis, where
Elsa took Arthur Balfour for his "delightful and degrading evening."

L'Acacia borrowed its garden motif from l'Oasis, whose setting was indeed out of doors. They spent half a million francs, Elsa claimed, to trans-
form the room into an outdoor fantasy: trellises, climbing flowers, bubbling
fountains, bucolic benches, butterflies in the trees, and waiters dressed in
rustic garb. For snob appeal, the audience was limited to fifty, even though
the club could hold up to three hundred. Elsa and Molyneux, seated near the
entrance like an oddly matched pair of divinities, passed judgment on those
allowed in. An authentic Russian general from the late czar's army stood

watch at the door; a negative nod from the proprietors cued him to suggest other venues to those deemed unworthy of these Elysian Fields, informing them with deep regret that vacant tables were all reserved.

A night at l'Acacia soon became de rigeur for A-list Parisians. The price of admission having reached its zenith, those vacant tables were no longer "reserved"—every one was thronged with the elect. The first floor show starred thirty-two-year-old Clifton Webb, not yet a movie star but well known as a dancer who had performed in seven musical comedies on Broadway. His dance partner was Jenny Dolly, one half of the legendary Hungarian act the Dolly Sisters. Elsa recalled that Jenny made her nightly grand entrance in an enormous cape of fresh gardenias, which must have added a sweetly funereal touch to the gaiety.

A portent of the club's destiny, for it died in less than a year. L'Acacia should have been a gold mine, Elsa lamented, but "the trouble was that Molyneux and I were too busy having a good time to check incoming revenue against outgoing expenses." She accused chefs and waiters of stealing liquour from l'Acacia and selling it to other bistros and restaurants. A London newspaper at the time reported the problem from a different perspective: the proprietors had run afoul of French licensing laws, and the police closed it down.

Before l'Acacia wilted, however, it was visited by the future Queen Mother of the United Kingdom, who, in April of 1921, was still the unmarried Lady Elizabeth Bowes-Lyon. Hugo Vickers, in his biography *Elizabeth the Queen Mother*, wrote that "friends of Elizabeth asked Dickie Fellowes-Gordon if she could arrange the visit. Dickie sent a message back saying that all Elizabeth had to do was to ask for Elsa's table." Vickers points out that a visit to a nightclub was "a rare treat for Elizabeth, easier to accomplish in Paris than in London," owing to the punctilio expected of high-born young women at the time, and of this one in particular, who had already received a proposal from the future King George VI.

Dreamers who open businesses do not readily accept defeat, convinced of the infallibility of their marvelous idea. Shortly after the demise of nightclub number one, Elsa and Molyneux, with financial backing from a third party, opened a new venture, Le Jardin de Ma Soeur, on the rue Caumartin just off the boulevard Haussmann. Anita Loos described it as "the most elegant place in which to greet the Paris dawn. It occupied an ancient town house with a lush, well-kept garden where we dined and danced out of doors, weather permitting; when the rain came down, activities moved inside."

That rather domestic name—My Sister's Garden—although accurate, lacked punch. It might better have suited a greengrocer's shop than a night-club featuring Josephine Baker, and yet there she was, newly arrived in Paris and not yet the sensation in scanty feathers and multiphallic banana skirts that she would soon become. Already she had star quality, and patrons of Le Jardin—who streamed in wearing furs, gowns, beaded chemises, and other elegant outfits designed by Molyneux—begged her to teach them the Charleston.

Elsa called Le Jardin de Ma Soeur "a great success," adding, "it made so much money that it took the employees two years to steal us blind." To be sure, this nightclub flourished from 1922 until 1924, though Elsa lasted for "just one season," according to Dickie, who considered the financial ar-rangement "ridiculous, because they paid Elsa just so much a week, when she should have had a share in the business. We had a great row about that. She said, 'Nonsense, it's very kind of them to pay me at all to enjoy myself every night.' But she could have made a lot of money with it."

Elsa's departure from Le Jardin did not leave her idle; she could play piano at parties every night, all over town, if she chose. She had also become known among savvy hostesses as someone who could throw a party with more zing and pizzazz than the ones they themselves had been putting on for years. The novelty of this tireless party giver, and the surprising freshness of her ideas, upped her demand in the chic arrondissements. As Elsa exited Le Jardin, Edward Molyneux, with whom she remained friends for the rest of her life, found another patron to appreciate her talents, this one as reckless as Elsa herself.

15   Jean, Joy, and Noël

His name: Jean Patou, and Elsa's job title in his firm was social secretary, though in reality she functioned as press agent, advisor, critic, friend, gambling buddy, and watchdog. He and Edward Molyneux were amiable rivals, for Patou designed dresses and, unlike Molyneux, he concocted new perfumes, as well. When word got around Paris that Elsa had changed partners, this joke buzzed through the fashion houses: Do you know why Eddie sent dear Elsa over to Jean? Because Patou can't bankrupt himself fast enough.

Meredith Etherington-Smith, in her biography *Patou*, describes him as "more than a couturier with some fascinating clients, but certainly the broad spectrum of women he dressed reflects his almost universal appeal during the twenties. There was Suzanne Lenglen, the champion tennis player, and Elsie de Wolfe, doyenne of expatriate society in Paris. There was Mona Harrison Williams, later the Countess Bismarck, who was always cited in the popular American press as one of the best-dressed women of her time." Other clients included the Dolly Sisters (the Hungarian twins Jenny and Rosy; the former had danced with Clifton Webb at l'Acacia), Gloria Swanson, Mary Pickford, Pola Negri, Lady Diana Cooper, and countless others from society high and low. He even dressed Elsa, and made her not just passably chic but stunning. In a 1930s glamour photograph by George Hoyningen-Huene, she wears a simple dark Patou suit, a narrow-brim hat that slenderizes her face, and flattering makeup—dark lipstick, full brows, eyeshadow. In the picture, Elsa could pass for forty, though she was well past fifty, and her contemplative expression recalls some distinguished personage like Dame Sybil Thorndike or Schiaparelli. In the picture, Elsa is so striking that one almost suspects a retoucher's brush.

Jean Patou (1880–1936) matched the decade of his greatest fame and achievement, the years from the armistice to the crash of 1929. Etherington-Smith places him in context: "Like Hispano-Suiza tourers, suntans, green hats, cubism, jazz, and the Riviera in summer, Patou was part of the bright patchwork of new ideas, new people and a new, more modern way of life that spelled the spirit of the twenties. His personality, with all its faults, evasions, and virtues, echoes the paradoxes of the Jazz Age. He was immensely disciplined and at the same time excessively volatile, a private man who wore a cleverly contrived public mask. A spendthrift and a brilliant businessman. A ladies' man who loved no one woman and yet who preferred to go shooting or fishing with his father and his brother-in-law. A modernist with a strong sense of tradition." She sums up his fashion credo: "The essence of a Patou design was that it was so beautifully cut and the workmanship so exquisite that you lived in it until it wore out. With the exception of his wedding dresses and some of the more elaborate solidly sequinned evening gowns, Patou's clothes were made for real life, made to wear and wear again, not for show."

Elsa's account of working with Patou jumps with excitement. In *R.S.V.P.*, she devoted six pages to him, more space than she allotted to most of her intimates, including Dickie and Noël Coward. Only Cole Porter and Barbara Hutton exceeded Patou, with ten or twelve pages apiece.

Elsa explains his contradictions and his recklessness as the result of his four years in the trenches of World War I. Many who lived through these horrors lost hope in a future. Chaos could come again, the only insurance being the pleasures of the fleeting present. "He possessed the fastest cars, boats, and women on the Continent," Elsa said. "He entertained on an incredibly lavish scale. His gambling was an incurable disease that mounted in intensity with his losses. It is safe to say that Patou wagered, and lost, more money in the casinos of France and Monte Carlo than any gambler in history."

In 1924, however, when Elsa's association with Patou started up, his enterprise struck her as a paradox. Although a top designer with important connections throughout France, he was not attracting the desired clientele, nor the one that Elsa thought he needed. Why, he asked, as though man-to-man with a trusted confidant. Elsa pulled no punches. "Your appearance is driving customers away," she replied, a response that demanded sangfroid. Perhaps that's the reason Patou posed the question; he knew that Elsa would not flatter.

"You can't expect society women to come to you for chic clothes when you look like a cheap racetrack tout," she went on, for, according to her, he dressed like many Frenchmen of the period. His notion of a snappy outfit was "to wear an ensemble of the same color from hat to socks—and Patou's favorite color was a bilious green," she lamented.

"Get yourself a black Homburg, conservatively cut dark suits, white shirts with starched collars and cuffs and throw away those awful, garish ties," she ordered. "Put on a front that is in keeping with the elegance you're selling." In later photographs, he is indeed wearing a Homburg. His suit may be light or dark, but he looks as handsome and as well tailored as the young Gary Cooper, whom he resembles.

His image thus tweaked, Patou rose ever higher in the volatile, cutthroat world of Paris fashion design. His immortality, however, as they might say in the rag trade, comes not from the cut of fine fabrics but from perfume, and one scent in particular. Elsa's role in the story is second only to Patou's.

"Patou was happiest when he was planning a luxury for women, at once his business and his pleasure," Elsa recalled. "That was the purpose of our trip to Grasse, the town on the Riviera which produces the essences for France's best perfumes. Couturiers were developing perfumes as a profitable sideline, particularly in America, and Patou, a belated entry in the field, knew he had to come up with a unique article to crash the market."

He and Elsa spent three days sniffing samples at the establishment of a top perfume blender in Grasse, and yet nothing pleased them. According to Elsa, they were in search of an "elusive, special something," a literal je ne sais quoi. The perfumier, excitable and impatient as such acute specialists often are, grew exasperated as these impossible Parisians rejected first one of his specialities, then another. Finally, beside himself with frustration, he thrust a

"Let's give a party!"—The motto of fabulous Elsa Maxwell. (*Courtesy of Michael Willhoite*)

The Keokuk Opera House in Iowa, where Elsa claimed she was born during a performance of *Mignon*. *(Keokuk Public Library)*

Elsa's actual birthplace: the home of her maternal grandparents in Keokuk, much altered since Elsa's arrival in 1881. *(Photo by Sam Staggs)*

CHAIRMAN J. D. MAXWELL

Elsa's father, James David Maxwell, in a turn-of-the-century caricature from a San Francisco newspaper. He had just been elected chairman of a local Democratic Party ward. *(San Francisco Public Library)*

His visiting card. In *Elsa Maxwell's Etiquette Book,* she wrote: "In the dim Victorian days—and I undoubtedly am one of the few women alive who will admit remembering how formal and uncomfortable those days could be—visiting cards were a *must.*" *(Collection of the author)*

Mr. J. D. Maxwell

San Francisco, Cal.

Elsa's mother wrote in her daughter's name as an afterthought. Later, Elsa repaid the slight. *(Collection of the author)*

Mr. James David Maxwell

Miss Elsa Maxwell

Casa Linda,
Belvedere.

Elsa's mother, Laura Wyman Maxwell. In later years, she and Elsa were estranged. *(Collection of the author)*

Elsa at sixteen months, winner of a beautiful baby contest. "I am well aware that this revelation is a severe strain on anyone's credulity," she joked years later. *(Courtesy of Bob Kingdom)*

A pensive San Francisco tomboy in the making: Elsa at three. *(Courtesy of Bob Kingdom)*

In her twenties, Elsa joined an acting troupe that specialized in Shakespeare. She is third from right in front row. *(Collection of the author)*

Elsa at thirty, ready to storm the gates of New York. The gates remained standing until a few years later. *(Collection of the author)*

Elsa dined with Caruso the night before the San Francisco earthquake in 1906. His self-portrait dates from two years later. *(Collection of the author)*

Dorothy Fellowes-Gordon, ca. 1925. "Dickie" to her friends, she was Elsa's companion for half a century. *(Collection of the author)*

Maxine Elliott, the Elizabeth Taylor of her day, helped Elsa get a toehold in England. *(Courtesy of Fredrick Tucker)*

Elsa, at thirty-five, with the formidable Mrs. O.H.P. Belmont, whose patronage launched Elsa in New York society. *(Collection of the author)*

Rehearsing *Melinda and Her Sisters,* the feminist opera composed by Elsa and Mrs. Belmont. Elsa at far right; the cast includes Mrs. Belmont, Marie Dressler, Frances Alda, and Marie Doro. *(Library of Congress)*

One of Elsa's many songs, "Laughing Eyes," written for the actress Marie Doro to sing in a Broadway play. *(British Library)*

Alexandra, Lady Colebrook, who financed Elsa's first dinner party at the Ritz Hotel in Paris. *(Collection of the author)*

Elsa's "serious" works often sounded like music played on the Titanic. *(British Library)*

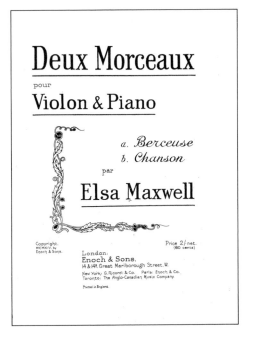

Elsa in Venice, ca. 1927. *(Collection of the author)*

The couturier Edward Molyneux. He and Elsa ran two night clubs in Paris in the twenties. *(Collection of the author)*

As Elsa's fame as party giver and gadabout increased, along with her girth, caricaturists found her irresistible. Here, drawn by Sem (Georges Goursat, 1863–1934). *(Collection of the author)*

Elsa in Somerset Maugham's *Our Betters* in summer stock, 1941. *(Photofest)*

Linda Darnell and Elsa in *Elsa Maxwell's Hotel for Women. (Photofest)*

Elsa played herself in the picture as a Park Avenue Ma Kettle. *(Collection of Robert Sanchez)*

In *Public Deb No. 1*, Elsa cross-dressed as Benjamin Franklin. *(Photofest)*

"Let me in!" Brenda Joyce and Elsa in *Public Deb No. 1*. *(Photofest)*

Elsa in the Warner Bros. short *Riding into Society*. *(Photofest)*

Elsa makes her first radio broadcast from the United Nations Conference in San Francisco, 1945. *(Charter Heslep Collection, American Heritage Center, University of Wyoming)*

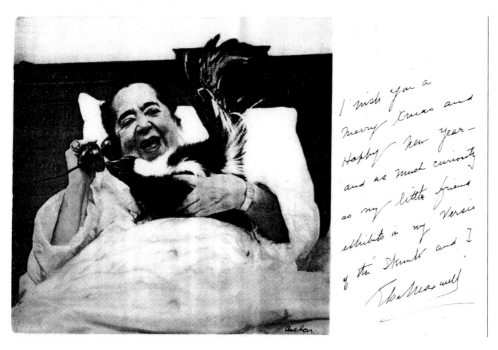

Anything for a laugh. On her Christmas card, she wrote, "I wish you a Merry Xmas and Happy New Year—and as much curiosity as my little friend exhibits in 'The Skunk and I.'" *(Courtesy of Bob Kingdom)*

From *Elsa Maxwell's Etiquette Book*: "Table manners, like all other etiquette rules, are meant to make living easier." Elsa found it easier to dunk her doughnut. *(Collection of the author)*

vial at them, more in sarcasm than in hope. "If you don't like this," he muttered, "I'll get a job herding goats."

Patou smelled it. Suddenly his face, his entire body, seemed as beatific as a Renaissance saint. He passed the vial to Elsa. They agreed: divine. This ultimate smell was made up from the combined aromas of the most precious rose and jasmine essences. (Ten thousand jasmine flowers, to be exact, and twenty-eight dozen Bulgarian roses per ounce.)

"Of course it's wonderful," snorted the perfumier. "It's made from the finest essences available. But you can't use it commercially. The price will be prohibitive."

Spoken like an oracle, for the two words "price" and "prohibitive" sent a simultaneous jolt through those two extravagant creatures, Elsa and Patou. "That's our angle," Elsa cried out. "We'll promote it as the most expensive perfume in the world. And I've got the perfect name for it. *Joy*." With a sudden vision of himself counting a million francs, the blender translated Elsa's proposed name into French: *Joie*, he pronounced, with a hint of superiority, as though correcting the foreigner's faulty pronunciation.

"No," Elsa replied in a firm voice, looking him in the eye. "*Joy*. It conveys a meaning that's understood all over the world. Wherever perfume is sold, Joy will be the standard of excellence, just as the Rolls-Royce is in cars." Dickie was there, too, and her version matches Elsa's.

This exclusive new product was not suited to an advertising campaign in the media. Instead, Elsa sent samples of the new perfume to two hundred and fifty prominent American women (all of them known to Elsa, or at one remove from her acquaintance). When it was introduced commercially in 1926, it sold at forty dollars an ounce, the highest price ever charged for a scent sold across the counter. (This year, the going rate is $450 for a one-ounce bottle.)

One might believe that Elsa had become a permanent resident of Paris during the early 1920s. That is not the case. "In those days," she said, "Dickie and I practically commuted between Paris and London." Elsa might have added Venice as the third point on their international triangle, for the two women spent as much time there as in the other two cities. They also made side trips to any point of interest. On one such, in 1922, they first met Noël Coward. That encounter took place in Oxford at a weekend party at the home of Lady Sybil Colefax, who quarried not only big names but also those with promise. She took up Virginia Woolf early on, who in turn devoted a good deal of energy to evading the Colefax clutches. ("I am always reading her scrawls or answering them," Virginia confided to her diary.)

Noël, at age twenty-three, had achieved a minor reputation as actor and playwright, though he was two years away from the sensation he would create when *The Vortex* opened in London. At Lady Colefax's estate, on the night in question, "the elms shuddered a little when a large car drew up at the door and disgorged, amid raucous laughter, the bouncing, Michelin figure of Elsa Maxwell," Noël wrote in *Present Indicative*. "She at once proceeded to whistle through the house like a cyclone, strumming the piano, laughing, talking, and striking the rose-white youth present into a coma of dumb bewilderment. I loved her at once. I loved her round friendly face, with its little shrewd eyes darting about like animated currants in a Bath bun. I loved her high spirits and her loud infectious laugh."

Elsa: "I was installed at my customary place at the piano and I could not help but notice a young man with an unusual, almost Mongolian, countenance watching me intently. After playing popular songs for a while, I drifted into my old meal ticket, 'The Tango Dream.' " (The young Noël did indeed have slightly Asian eyes.)

"That's a beautiful song, Miss Maxwell," he said. "I wish I could compose a number like that." (Coward's first published song, for which he wrote lyrics to Doris Joel's music, was "The Baseball Rag," in 1919.) His compliment, as recounted by Elsa, sounds genuine when you recall that "The Tango Dream," from 1913, suggests Elsa's influence on the sentimental future Coward of "Let's Say Goodbye" and "I'll See You Again."

As their conversation continued, Noël told her of his ambitions and his disappointments. Elsa offered pro forma encouragement, for at that point she had seen no example of his talent. Before leaving Oxford, she invited him to a party she was hosting in London the following week. Noël accepted, hoping to benefit from her example of how to make one's mark on the larger world.

"Elsa's party was great fun with social and Bohemian graces tactfully mixed," he wrote. There Noël met Dickie, who, like Elsa, would remain his lifelong friend. "Later on in the evening," he said, "when I was sitting talking to her in a corner, Elsa came over and joined us, and after they had both exchanged significant raised-eyebrow looks, Elsa said that they had a little proposition to make to me and that on no account was I to be offended. Then she explained that she and Dickie were going for two weeks to Venice, and wanted me to go with them as their guest. She added, as a palliative to my wounded honour, that they would feel far more comfortable with a man to look after them and that I would really be doing them a great favour if I would consent."

Noël, of course, saw through their ruse: "I knew perfectly well that they didn't in the least need anyone to look after them, but were only trying to gloss over for me the unmentionable horror of having my expenses paid by two defenseless women." Later he described his role as "a gigolo unimpaired by amatory obligations."

During his "glamorous fortnight" with Elsa and Dickie, Noël absorbed the atmosphere of Venice and "the strange decayed magic of old palaces rising out of green canals." In the lesbian and bisexual circles where he was introduced by his patronesses, he made several new friends, including Muriel Draper, society hostess to the fashionable world, who counted among her friends in Paris Gertrude Stein and Alice B. Toklas, Natalie Barney, and Romaine Brooks. Another addition to Noël's address book was Blanche Barrymore, aka Michael Strange, bisexual wife of John Barrymore (from 1920 to 1925), and mother of the ill-fated actress Diana Barrymore. Later, Noël recalled her "farouche Byronic locks flowing in the breeze and long billowing cloaks."

MICHAEL STRANGE

Elsa knew John Barrymore from his early stage appearances in San Francisco, even before she surveyed the earthquake rubble in his company. Perhaps through that connection she knew his second wife, Blanche; but they would have met in any event, since Blanche (née

Oelrichs) involved herself in the suffragist movement at the time of *Melinda and Her Sisters*. Under the pen name Michael Strange, Blanche wrote plays and poems; in 1940, she published her autobiography, *Who Tells Me True*.

That book of opaque prose includes this vignette: "In those days we all went about quite a lot with that odd miscellany of successful artists of the musical comedy and farce variety, rich travellers in a bright mood, and titled people somewhat chastened by events, who clustered around the buoyant overemphasis of Elsa Maxwell. I found Elsa very diverting; she took a childish, uproarious pleasure in cracking the whip over this ring in which she had persuaded so many prominent people to posture. And she had her disarming contrasts too, for on a night table by her bed could always be found the latest that was worthwhile in fiction, drama and poetry; as I recall it, her literary avidity only reined in before philosophy and mysticism; but I am unfailingly grateful to Elsa Maxwell for showing me a side that is not the one usually selected for report—the side of a serious friend, worried by my pangs and casting about with sensibility and intelligence to restore my attention to real duties instead of doomed hysterias."

At the end of his two-week introduction to Venice, Noël returned to London for rehearsals of his new play, *The Young Idea*. In 1923, Noël appeared with Gertrude Lawrence in the musical revue *London Calling*. The two had been friends since their days as child actors a decade earlier. Elsa and Dickie, back in town, had settled into their London pied-à-terre, a two-room apartment in a converted stable—or so Elsa described it in the American edition of her autobiography, leading the reader almost to imagine a manger and docile livestock. In reality, they occupied a stylish mews house half a mile from Buckingham Palace. How this tenancy came about involves a story that takes Elsa not exactly into the palace, but rather brings sometime occupants of the palace directly to Elsa's door.

16 Noblesse Oblige

Elsa described it as "the first party I ever gave for royalty," and claimed that her total cost ran to seven dollars for a dozen guests. Decades later, Elsa made a cardinal point in her theory of parties: "The best ones are given by people who can't afford them." That axiom recurs throughout Elsa's writings, and in interviews she gave. It's a slippery fish, however, since Elsa, from the start of her party-giving career, had the backing of Dickie's resources, followed by a caravan of wealthy donors who financed the splash and verve of Elsa's entertainments.

She hated the notion that she was hired to give parties; to her, that was an accusation. Elsa insisted instead that "fun" was her only means of exchange. When cornered, she coyly admitted that certain rich ladies contributed "Christmas presents" in cash as gratitude for her yearlong merrymaking. Such equivocation was unnecessary, however. There was nothing shameful in the truth, for Elsa gave good measure to all who engaged her services. Once she had a toehold in society, and the reputation of being indispensable for chic parties, the rich gave her carte blanche to organize and stage their entertainments. At her say-so, palaces, stately homes, town houses, vast apartments, hotel ballrooms, and the best restaurants were commandeered. These, by Elsa's fiat, were then transformed through the addition of elaborate decorations, orchestras, food and drink for a thousand guests, or, in miniature versions, the perfect dinner party for half a dozen. Or a treasure hunt, a boating excursion, a costume ball, champagne picnics in the world's most beautiful parks, a charity ball to raise a million dollars for any good cause. And yet: "I never give parties professionally," she snapped more than once at an interviewer.

In London, Elsa and Dickie's "converted stable" was indeed that. What Elsa omitted was the fact that it belonged to the wealthy Mrs. Guinness, at whose home in New York she had first met Cole Porter, and that many such buildings in London had been turned into dwellings with the advent of the automobile in the early twentieth century. Elsa and Dickie, when in town, occupied the mews house behind the grand Guinness home in Carlton House Terrace. Mrs. Guinness thoughtfully supplied a piano.

Meanwhile, in the big house, Mrs. Guinness was organizing a charity concert with Elsa's help. Or vice versa, since Elsa had long since become managing director of such events. The concert, when it happened, swarmed with royalty: Queen Mary, consort of King George V and grandmother of Queen Elizabeth II; Queen Victoria of Spain; Princess Marie Louise and her sister, Princess Helena Victoria, granddaughters of Queen Victoria. Also in attendance, according to the Court Circular—the daily record of royal engagements—but omitted from Elsa's memoirs, were the Duchess of Rutland; the Duchess of Devonshire; Adele, Countess Cadogan; Viscountess Burnham; Lady Louis Mountbatten; and a dozen or so others.

With help from various acquaintances in London, Elsa told how she "roped in a young tenor whom I'd met in America and believed had a great future, Lauritz Melchior. I asked him to sing a song of mine for which I would play the accompaniment." The florid Melchior, acclaimed as one of the great Wagnerians of his day, must have been nonplussed when asked to sing a Maxwell ditty rather than "In fernem Land" or "Winterstüme."

Protocol dictated that Elsa curtsy to Queen Mary and the Queen of Spain when passing in front of them en route to the concert platform, where Elsa introduced Lauritz Melchior, and again as she returned to her seat in the audience. The first curtsies went off nobly, but as she passed a second time before the queens, her foot slipped on the polished parquet. In a flash all of Elsa Maxwell—some two hundred pounds—landed like a sack of potatoes not at Queen Mary's feet, but on them. "If it was hideously embarrassing for me," Elsa said later, "it must have been extremely painful for her."

And yet, "without the slightest change of expression Her Majesty leaned down and helped me to my feet as though it were the most natural thing in the world. My face as red as a peony, I wanted to crawl into the woodwork and die of shame, but Queen Mary saved my mortification by breaking the ghastly silence and covering my retreat by complimenting Melchior on his singing." (Although it's a great story, it lost credibility when Elsa used it again and again to spotlight herself in various royal encounters. If she had fallen that often, she would have needed a nursing home more than a mews house.)

Embarrassment, for Elsa, was always a quick-change emotion. At the end of the concert she chatted up Princess Helena Victoria: "But, ma'am, why don't you come to a party in our little house?" Realizing that the princess must be properly escorted, Elsa nominated Lord Alington, who happened to be standing nearby. ("Naps" to his friends, the bisexual Alington was the object of Tallulah Bankhead's passion 'round about this time. Later, after his marriage, Bankhead walked into a restaurant where Lord Alington was dining with his wife. He pretended not to see Tallulah—who sashayed over to the Alington table and said, "What's the matter, dahling, don't you recognize me with my clothes on?")

Princess Helena Victoria's grandmother might not have approved of such company, but the old queen's notions of propriety were greatly watered down in postwar London. The princess accepted, and so did Lord Alington. (Her sister evaded the invitation, as did Queen Mary and the retinue of duchesses, viscountesses, and titled ladies. Since the princess was considered colorless, she was perhaps delighted with any invitation, however quirky.)

Another tenet in Elsa's theory of parties: they must never be dull or stuffy, nor must they drag; liveliness is all. In this instance, however, she faced a dilemma: how to entertain Queen Victoria's granddaughter minus the boring formality to which such a royal person was surely accustomed? Elsa's new friend Noël Coward came to mind. He was easily persuaded. Through him, Elsa and Dickie procured Ivor Novello, Beatrice Lillie, and Gertrude Lawrence. All of these played the piano and sang. "We all joined together in an imitation of French and Italian opera in which nearly everybody joined," Elsa recalled, naming her other guests as Lady Diana Cooper, Viola Tree, Lois Sturt (Lord Alington's sister), and Oliver Messel, who had just begun his career as painter and stage designer. Elsa claimed that her guests sat on the floor, and between entertainments munched hardboiled eggs and sausages and had the time of their lives.

In 1991, when Hugo Vickers asked Dickie about the party and about Princess Helena Victoria, she said, "I remember the old girl being there. I think she was there more than one night."

"And did you enjoy the parties that Elsa arranged?" he continued.

"Oh, very much," Dickie said. "She made people feel welcome and feel their best. She had that gift."

Already, Noël had dubbed Elsa "the Rose by Any Other Name-Dropper." He knew, of course, that unlike many such, she really knew all those whose names she sprinkled across her conversations and, later on, into her books, magazine articles, and newspaper columns. And they all wanted their names dropped.

PRINCESS HELENA VICTORIA

From the diary of Sir Henry ("Chips") Channon, a transplanted Chicagoan who became a socialite in Britain and eventually a Conservative Member of Parliament: "Princess Helena Victoria—of what?—died a few days ago and has been buried at Windsor. When I last saw her, a few weeks ago, it was difficult to remember that she had once been a bouncing, fat, jolly Princess . . . known to her intimates as 'the Snipe.' She was an old maid who may, however, have once known love. Certainly her first cousin, the Grand Duke of Hesse, wanted to marry her. . . . She is survived by her even duller sister, Princess Marie Louise."

Princess Helena Victoria (1870–1948) was the third child and elder daughter of Prince Christian of Schleswig-Holstein and his wife, Princess Helena, the third daughter of Queen Victoria. Kenneth Rose, in *Kings, Queens, and Courtiers*, an informal Who's Who of the Royal House of Windsor, explains that "in King George V's purge of German styles and titles in 1917, the two sisters retained the title of Princess but lost the territorial designation of 'Schleswig-Holstein.' They were also obliged to abandon the style of 'Royal Highness' and adopt that of 'Highness.' "

She was a great lover of music, which of course would have fostered a friendship with Elsa. During World War I, the princess arranged for the shipment of musical instruments and musicians to the Western Front for the entertainment of soldiers fighting there. She also visited British troops on duty in France.

In their later years, Princess Helena Victoria and her sister lived together at Schomberg House, London. When a German bomb damaged their home in 1940, they moved to Fitzmaurice Place, Berkeley Square. Confined to a wheelchair by the end of World War II, Princess Helena Victoria made her last major appearance at the wedding of her first cousin twice removed, Princess Elizabeth, to Lieutenant Philip Mountbatten, in Westminster Abbey in 1947.

17 Everything's Coming Up Elsa

Paris, June 1924: Edouard Herriot is the newly elected prime minister of France when Elsa invites a hundred or so guests to a costume ball. Everyone is to appear as a great statesman. Elsa garbs herself as Herriot, and indeed the resemblance is remarkable once she is *en costume*. Although she is nine years younger than the prime minister, she duplicates his jowls with little effort. The bushy mustache, of course, is false, and so are the Grouchoesque eyebrows. Kohl around her eyes adds age and gravitas, as do spectacles and a tuxedo. The French, who take politics very seriously, spot the controversial politician and—"As I drove to the ball," Elsa said, "a crowd followed. I was all but mobbed by hissing and cheering Parisians."

The uproar attracted two policemen, who zoomed up on motorcycles, demanding to know the reason for such disorder. One of them, approaching Elsa's car, stopped in amazement, doffed his hat, then looked again. "I'm Elsa Maxwell," she whispered. "I'm on my way to a ball. What shall I do?"

Gruff and annoyed at such tomfoolery, and also grudgingly impressed, the officer replied, "Then *be* Herriot, Madame!" And on his motorcycle he escorted Elsa's car, as she bowed first to those who booed (the right wing), and then to those cheering Frenchmen of the left-wing coalition that had elected Monsieur Herriot.

A few years earlier, during the Peace Conference, Elsa had attended a costume ball with Joachim, the sixth Prince Murat. He dressed as Clemenceau and she as Lloyd George, the respective leaders of the French and British delegations. "Passers-by caught a glimpse of us as we rode down the Champs-Elysées and thought we were the diplomats in the flesh," Elsa recalled. "In three minutes traffic was blocked by the dense, cheering crowd that surrounded the car." In later years, Elsa made a memorable Ben Franklin, a liverish Herbert Hoover, and disguised herself as still another French statesman, Aristide Briand.

If studio-era Hollywood had filmed *The Elsa Maxwell Story,* the years from around 1924 to 1930 would be quickly conveyed by calendar pages blowing across the screen, and intercut with a montage of nightclubs, fox-trots and the Charleston, champagne gushing from uncorked bottles, motor cars whizzing along a Mediterranean corniche, scenes of joyous abandon, outlandish costume parties, card games, roulette wheels spinning, liquor and laughter, and far off in a corner of the frame an almost subliminal shot of one or two women in tuxedos smoking cigars, followed by a shapely blonde in a backless gown who slowly turns to reveal . . . an oddly unreal decolletage below a beard and mustache. A shot of the Eiffel Tower; cut to Big Ben; and a gondola disappears under the Rialto bridge.

Elsa is the camera.

She recorded the nonstop gaiety of her life not on film but in words, and though she assures us repeatedly that she herself enjoyed the parties, dinners, outings, poker games, and nightclubs more than anyone, she seems nevertheless at one remove, like the master chef with a slightly jaded palate. And yet the great party, Elsa's *Mona Lisa* of glittering carefree pleasure, stayed seductively in the future, always one night ahead of Elsa. It would happen next week in Paris, or perhaps her masterpiece would open the season in Venice, or Rome, at the Waldorf, in the country, the king would attend, or the empress, a grand levee with titles enough to furnish a patter song by Gilbert and Sullivan or, later, by Sondheim: archduke, peer, grandee, marquis/landgrave, viscount, baronessa, Bart./maharani, margrave, chevalier, shah/nawab and—everybody ought to have an earl!

NOUVEAU IS BETTER THAN NO RICHE AT ALL

Jerry Sachs, a New York photographer who took pictures at Elsa's parties during her final years, observed General Maxwell's command of her troops. Sachs recalled her speed and efficiency in organizing an affair, the prebattle orders to hotels and orchestras, florists and caterers. And all done with aplomb. "The only time she was gruff," according to him, "was if one of them did something wrong." Recalling her brush-off to those she considered boring or nouveau riche, he said: "Some nouveau lady would call her up. Elsa would say, 'Oh, I don't think I can squeeze you in, my dear, this party is overbooked.' After hanging up, she would roll her eyes and say, 'Don't they ever stop? Pushy, pushy.'"

Occasionally, however, she invited the nouveaux because, she told Sachs, "They have all the money today. I let them in because it's money in my pocket." Asked why Elsa was so beloved, he said, "She always made her guests important, whether they were or not. Even the nouveaux. She knew that they have feelings too."

Elsa knew, by instinct, that every successful party requires a shape. Its architecture may be vast, intimate, nostalgic, avant-garde, formal, relaxed, symmetrical, impromptu, comic. Its rhythm can be presto, largo, or any tempo between. But like a symphony, an army, or a film, it needs a control freak in charge. By the mid-1920s, Elsa had assumed control. And why not? She possessed the instincts of an epic director, a female DeMille. Like him, Elsa was regarded, throughout her life, as too-too, not only by the respectably dull but even by the don't-give-a-damn. The majority of her gold-plated friends saw her as a dyke in the manger, and yet she overwhelmed the social worlds so completely that she could not be ignored.

For Elsa combined the traits of everyone in *Cinderella*: the homely stepsisters; their manipulative mother; and the neglected little afterthought with her feet in the cinders who trumps them all by stealing the party and its royal host. Most of all, however, Elsa was Charles Perrault narrating the tale and bending it to suit her ends. Again like DeMille, she marshaled her cast of thousands and never savored the camp, even as she drooled titles by the mouthful and flattered them in geysers of prose.

What would you do if one day you received this in the mail: XELM ALE-LASW SIVIETN OUY TO A RUTEARES THNU. LESSAEBM AT VEGA-BER QSEUAR ON RETAL NTHA 8 M.P.

If you knew Elsa Maxwell and her unpredictable tricks—and of course you would if you belonged to the London smart set in 1927—then you might well figure out the missive as ELSA MAXWELL INVITES YOU TO A TREASURE HUNT. ASSEMBLE AT BELGRAVE SQUARE NO LATER THAN 8 P.M.

In this instance, the smart set were quicker than Elsa credited. She expected a dozen or so to show up, but on the appointed evening, "staid old Belgrave Square became a bedlam of honking and shrieking," said Elsa. "As perpetrator of the disorder I was about to be haled off to jail when a handsome, golden-haired young man with blue eyes and a bowler hat drove up. He asked what was going on, waved the bobbies aside and joined the hunt. That was my first meeting with the Prince of Wales, now the Duke of Windsor. I was so impressed that I never have remembered who won the money." (A string of clues led the revelers around London and eventually to Maidenhead, Berkshire, some twenty-five miles distant. There a prize of one hundred pounds was hidden.)

Never one to spare royalty her charms, Elsa held on to the future king and, surprisingly, he held on to her. One may well ponder how this unlikely alliance flourished during the coming decades, and indeed the subject is worthy of a small separate volume. For now, however, a pause for social history.

"On or about December 1910 human character changed," wrote Virginia Woolf. Her famous whimsy echoes through any number of tomes on British society in the early twentieth century. For instance, David Cannadine, in *The Decline and Fall of the British Aristocracy*, notes that "by 1914 . . . it was widely believed that traditional high society had effectively ceased to exist. A new generation of Americans took over as leaders of society, and were much drawn to the Prince of Wales. But they counted for nothing politically, and unlike the patrician hostesses of yesteryear, they regarded social life as an end in itself."

Reading Cannadine's Spenglerian pages, one is amazed that the monarchy still exists, or country houses, titles, tiaras, Rolls-Royces, any upper-crust symbol or institution whatsoever, for in his version the barbarians hold dominion over all. "The old élite could no longer keep 'without the gates' the new international plutocracy that was clamoring for admission to high society in the 'world metropolis' [i.e., London]. By losing control of the admissions process, the aristocracy also lost control of the way society conducted itself. For the plutocrats lived far more loudly, lavishly, and luxuriously than the patricians, and it was they who increasingly set the social tone."

Cannadine is referring to the likes of J. P. Morgan and various Astors and Vanderbilts—plutocrats whose limitless wealth and nouveau riche vulgarity were seen as diluting the purity of the British aristocracy. Elsa, of course, was a "poor girl," and while we know the heightening of that part of her script, it is true that no fortune resided in her coffers. Nevertheless, the same wave that swept those American plutocrats through the sacred gates also swept Elsa.

In a chapter on "The Dilution of Select Society," Cannadine exhibits further evidence for the lamentable decline of Albion's blue blood: "the sudden increase in the number of brides from overseas, especially from the United States of America. Between 1870 and 1914, fully ten per cent of aristocratic marriages followed this novel pattern. Despite sensational press rumours to the contrary, the majority of these American brides were not especially rich, and many did not even come from New York." Now, if we see Elsa in some sense as a bride, then here is another explanation for her Napoleonic seizure of power and rank in the slippery British hierarchy: she "married" into it.

It is important to emphasize that while Elsa was "in" society in half a dozen countries—England, France, Monaco, Italy, the United States, even remote South Africa—she was not "of" it in the way that Dickie was. In Europe, Elsa remained forever a foreigner. She fits Louis Auchincloss's delineation of Henry James, who settled in England and was thus "acceptable to any class with which he chose to associate himself, and able to avoid the brambles of the rigid British hierarchical system." In Elsa's case, she had the advantage of eccentricity—seldom frowned upon in England—as well as those slightly risqué links with theatre and the music hall. An exotic colonial jester, she struck many a lord and lady as some amusing mix of Falstaff, Henrietta Stackpole, and Betsy Trotwood. Finally, though Queen Victoria supposedly refused to believe that such a phenomenon as lesbianism could exist, her descendants took a more sanguine view of sexual ambiguity. Naturally, neither Elsa nor Dickie ever frightened the horses.

Elsa's place in society cannot be divorced from her nonstop party giving, both made possible by the abatement of traditionalism among the British upper classes. "It was not just the aristocratic houses that vanished in the inter-war years," Cannadine points out. "It was also the aristocratic principle of formal entertaining. It was the era of the Bright Young Things, gossip columns, night clubs, cocktails, shorter skirts, and dancing."

As the mortified old guard retreated from the Jazz Age into sherry, whist, and evensong, "they were superseded by a new generation of transatlantic social leaders, like Elsa Maxwell, Laura Corrigan, Nancy Astor, Emerald Cunard, and Henry Channon." To David Cannadine, "it seemed at times as if London society was being run by an American syndicate."

Elsa told several versions of her first meeting with the Prince of Wales, the future King Edward VIII. More important than when and where they met, however, is the fact that they did so, and the possibility of a friendship between them. Forgetting Belgrave Square, she wrote in *R.S.V.P.* that she first met him in 1922 "at a party in Mrs. Cucco Belleville's house in Manchester Square." They seem to have exchanged no more than a hello and a handshake. "The next time I saw him and had an opportunity to talk to him was in 1927. On a short visit to London, I borrowed Lady Milbanks's house at 20 Talbot Square to give a cabaret party." No royalty was invited because the royal family was in mourning for Queen Mary's brother, the Marquis of Cambridge.

Grief, however, was not protracted. And since royalty needs no invitation, to Elsa's great surprise the Prince of Wales, along with two of his brothers and a sister-in-law—Prince George and the Duke and Duchess of York—crashed the party. (Elsa and the Duchess, formerly Lady Elizabeth Bowes-Lyon, were acquainted from Elsa's nightclub in Paris, l'Acacia.) Elsa remembered that "the band was blaring a hot number and the Duchess [the future Queen Mother Elizabeth], who had recently returned from a good-will tour of the South Seas with her husband, remarked that the dancing in London was more primitive than anything she had seen on the trip. To illustrate the point, she rose and did a charming, impromptu native dance, waving her arms and swaying her shoulders gracefully."

The Prince of Wales, meanwhile, had been drinking steadily, and when supper was served he requested that Elsa join him at the bar. Elsa recollected that he seemed bored. Then: "For want of something to say, I commented on the styles he had introduced in men's fashions—the Windsor tie, the backless waistcoat for evening wear, the boater hat.

"'It's depressing to think that's all I'm to be known for,' he muttered. 'Such trivial things.'

"He stared morosely at his glass, then blurted: 'I don't want to be king. I wouldn't be a good one.'

"It was an astonishing statement to make to a total stranger, but I learned later that it was characteristic of him. He was anxious to shirk the responsibilities of his heritage long before he assumed them." Elsewhere Elsa wrote that, after these initial encounters, she "never really knew the duke until 1946—and I wish I had never gotten to know him better." She delivered this little broadside in the mid-1950s, during her fierce quarrel with the Duchess of Windsor, a falling-out that will enter our story later.

Elsa's dropping of names, seen out of context, sometimes strains credulity. On my first reading of *R.S.V.P*, I doubted that the Prince of Wales would have said anything so indiscreet to an American arriviste. One goal of a biography, however, is to provide a landscape in which to view the subject, and also to discern her supporting cast. The biographer's gathered facts, and his interpretation of them, help to redraw prevailing boundaries. In this case, I now find it unexceptional that the future king should have expressed his displeasure over kingship. That royal disgruntlement popped up repeatedly.

For royalty changed, too, along with human character, though Virginia Woolf explored neither the date nor the consequences of the former. Ross

McKibbin, in *Classes and Cultures: England 1918–1951*, follows the steady decline of royalty in intellect, education, even common sense, from the time of Queen Victoria and Prince Albert. These two "could claim a good knowledge of the mental world of the European upper middle classes; they spoke several languages, read widely, and were actively, if somewhat distantly, aware of the main developments in the arts and sciences. This was less true of [their son] King Edward VII. . . . It was much less true of his son, George V (1910–1936) and his grandsons, Edward VIII (1936), and George VI (1936–1952)."

McKibbin disparages the meager efforts of the tutors and preceptors of these latter four kings, all of whom "failed in even the most elementary task of a royal education—the teaching of foreign languages. The most striking feature of the royal princes' education was its aimlessness." Sounding surprisingly unlearned, the lowbrow future Edward VIII on three separate occasions began a conversation with a lady of the bedchamber to his mother, Queen Mary, with these words: "Lady Desborough, I know you're a bookish sort of person. At the moment, I'm reading such an interesting novel. I think it would appeal to you. It's called *Dracula*."

Elsa—well read, psychologically shrewd, tactful, and gifted in the art of making anyone feel at ease—would have sized up the Prince of Wales, found him a specimen of interest, and told herself, perhaps, that while he wasn't the sharpest knife in the cupboard, she could use him in her address book. Their long friendship became warmer a decade after his abdication, by which time he and his wife were the Duke and Duchess of Windsor. In Elsa's writings, the friendship lacks depth. It seems rather loveless, even before the feud and certainly after they all made up. Nevertheless, she grappled this man to her bosom, first as prince, then as ex-king, along with his wife; she could not do otherwise. The Duke and Duchess of Windsor—those titles rolled off Elsa's tongue like molten gold.

Bold Elsa had learned, early on, a secret about kings and queens, whether present, future, or former: "It is *courtiers* who make royalty frightened and frightening: taken neat, they are perfectly all right. This does not mean that they are as others; but you can get on to plain terms with the species, like an ornithologist making friends with some rare wild duck." (The quote is from James Pope-Hennessy.)

But of what advantage to the Prince of Wales was the friendship of Elsa

Maxwell? McKibbin again: "The career of Edward VIII demonstrates the difficulties of someone who came to rely almost exclusively upon the mass media. It sometimes appeared as if he had no existence independent of them. He was the man of 'glamour' *par excellence* and inhabited a 'glamorous' world where other 'glamorous' upper-class figures like Lord and Lady Mountbatten, film stars, and, increasingly, sportsmen and women and popular entertainers, had much in common." In other words, he loved all that Elsa stood for. It became a symbiotic relationship, like the useful friendships, hyped in the media, of Diana, Princess of Wales, with such celebrities as Gianni Versace and Elton John, or Barbara Walters fawning on TV over a Christmas card from the late princess.

Guests assembled for the scavenger hunt? *Très bien*, here's what you must find and bring back to win the prize, a gallon jar of Joy, the new perfume by Jean Patou.

Elsa, in Paris in 1927, reads the list to her caffeinated guests, who thrill to the submerged eroticism of several objects in the quest. "The first player who brings back the most items in one hour, or the most unusual specimen on the list, wins the prize. First, a slipper taken from Mistinguett on the stage of the Casino de Paris. Second, a black swan from the lake in the Bois de Boulogne. Next, a *pot de chambre*; three hairs plucked from a redheaded woman; a pompom off the cap of a French sailor; an animal other than a dog or a cat; and a handkerchief from the house of the Baron Maurice de Rothschild."

They fanned out, a bit too riotously, in every direction. "A series of disturbances promptly broke out all over Paris," said Elsa. Half an hour later, two of her younger male guests unshod the chanteuse Mistinguett as she sang, in a throaty gargle, one of her signature songs, "Mon homme":

Je suis à bout,
Mais malgré tout,
Que voulez-vous—

A sudden scuffle, one man picked her up and the other plucked off not one shoe but both, and out the door they fled as pandemonium erupted in the Casino de Paris. The manager called the cops, reporting two hoodlums who had barged onstage and left the star with naked feet.

Elsa described the dignified Lady Mendl, who "tore through the rue de Rivoli, past the Ministère de la Marine, and snatched the hat from a sailor on duty, nearly causing an international incident." Indeed, she did cause one. Her husband, Sir Charles Mendl, served as a staff member of the British embassy in Paris. Next morning, the ambassador was informed that Lady Mendl had violated France's sovereignty by invading the ministry and stealing the cap of the sailor on guard duty. A chilly note of protest was delivered to the embassy. The incident was taken up in the House of Commons, where several members denounced the pernicious influence of one Elsa Maxwell upon the wife of His Majesty's civil servant in Paris.

Meanwhile, the black swans in the Bois lived up to their sinister reputation. One of them pecked his molester, who dropped the angry fowl and sought medical help. During this mayhem, Elsa's only redheaded guest, Solange, Duchesse d'Ayen, locked herself in the bathroom with a bottle of wine. Did she hear the commotion when a donkey, an animal borrowed from a street peddler, came clomping up the stairs to Elsa's flat? Unaccustomed to such confinement, the donkey kicked the plastered walls until the screaming landlady ordered it out—along with the baby crocodile, several crabs, and a bucket of fish that another guest had rounded up. None of the contretemps dimmed Elsa's fun, however, especially when "the Grand Duchess Maria of Russia came back with the trophy that won first prize: a chamber pot with two big, blue inquisitive eyes painted on the inside."

18 The Guilty Party

The period between World Wars I and II has been called the golden age of the detective story. The novels of Agatha Christie, the "queen of crime," were enormously popular, and everyone wanted to emulate her. Those who lacked the patience for novel writing found other ways to create and solve a crime.

For two weeks in 1930, cryptic messages appeared in the personals column of the *Times* of London; a typical one read, "Meet me at eight or else." Each one of these notices was signed "M." Toward the end of this two-week period, dinner-party invitations were sent by Lady Ribblesdale to twenty-five of her illustrious friends. The dinner would take place at her home near St. James's Park. Among the invited guests were the Duke of Marlborough (former son-in-law of Elsa's friend, Mrs. Belmont, although by now he and Consuelo were divorced) and Zita Jungman, a twenty-four-year-old model and much-publicized Bright Young Thing. (Cecil Beaton, who photographed her, described Zita as "a snake-like beauty, with a mysterious smile and a cold glint in her upward slanting eyes.")

On the appointed evening, the guests assembled for dinner at Lady Ribblesdale's baronial table. One place, however, was vacant: Zita's. With studied casualness, Lady Ribblesdale remarked, "Oh, just a girl who is staying with me. She must have gone out to dinner without telling me." Pause. "Yet she would hardly have done that." A worried look crossed her porcelain-figurine face as she instructed the butler to serve dinner without the missing guest.

Elsa, seated beside the duke, asked him for a cigarette between courses. Just as he handed his silver case to her, Lady Ribblesdale created a small disturbance by dropping a fork onto the floor and emitting a muffled scream. Every guest turned to observe her, and while all eyes were on the hostess, surreptitious Elsa slipped two Turkish cigarettes into the duke's case—cigarettes of an unusual brand which, she had ascertained, none of the other guests smoked.

Dinner resumed, but Lady Ribblesdale seemed anxious to the point of distraction. Finally, she instructed the butler to go to Zita's room, knock on the door, and inquire whether anything was the matter. Soon the butler returned and reported that the door was locked. Repeated knocking, he said, had brought no response.

Everyone was alarmed, no one more so than Elsa, who led the charge upstairs to investigate. Again, knocking yielded only silence from inside the bedchamber. "Break down the door!" Lady Ribblesdale shrieked. The butler ran below stairs and quickly returned with another servant, who helped him remove the door from its hinges.

A scene of horror: Zita Jungman lay stretched across the rumpled bed, a great red stain across her bosom and a revolver on the floor beside the bed. Lady Ribblesdale, on the verge of a swoon, clutched the arm of the gentleman nearest her.

Instantly, the butler commanded everyone to leave the room in order to preserve all clues. Elsa picked up a telephone and pretended to dial, informing the shocked assembly that she was calling Scotland Yard. In a few minutes, two detectives arrived. They searched the murder room and snorted loudly when they came upon a Turkish cigarette in an ashtray at the side of the bed.

"Please resume your places at the table," said the detectives to Lady Ribblesdale's guests. "And now, we must ask those present to submit one of their cigarettes for inspection." Several exhibits were scrutinized before it was the duke's turn. Then one detective opened the duke's silver case and nodded solemnly at his colleague. "This confirms our suspicions," he said, holding up a Turkish cigarette identical to the one in the ashtray upstairs. "Can you explain this, Your Grace?" demanded the detective.

The Duke of Marlborough was thunderstuck.

"Come now," resumed the detective. "We know all about it. You had a liaison with the deceased. We've been watching you ever since these threatening messages first appeared in the *Times*." Whereupon he removed from his pocket a batch of clippings. (Elsa noticed that, in the confusion of the moment, no one commented on the remarkable coincidence of the detective's having the clippings so readily at hand.)

"Your Grace," said the detective quietly, "why did you murder Zita Jungman?"

"That," said Elsa, "was the cue for the butler to plunge the room into total darkness. He knocked over a chair, stamped on the floor and slammed the door to produce the sound effects of a fleeing man. Lady Ribblesdale and I screamed. The detectives yelled, 'Stop that man!' Dishes crashed to the floor. The guests thrashed about in a wild turmoil for thirty seconds, and then suddenly the lights went on. Zita was sitting at the table nibbling on an olive."

The detectives, of course, were hired actors. Only four people were in on the plot: Lady Ribblesdale, Elsa, the butler, and Zita. The Duke of Marlborough, fifty-eight at the time, spluttered explanations, hardly realizing for several minutes that it had been a joke, and that it was now ended. He "maintained his reputation as a sportsman by smiling feebly at the hoax," Elsa reported blithely. The "austere" duke, as Elsa characterized him, was selected as suspect because "he was to be the top-ranking guest at the party and pointing the finger at him would create the greatest excitement." Although such a trick strikes us as cruel, perhaps even grounds for litigation, among that class, in those years, any antidote to boredom was acceptable.

The party made the news all over London next day. The *Daily Express* headlined, MAYFAIR PARTY "MURDER." *Girl "Stabbed" to Death.* CLUE OF DUKE'S CIGARETTE. Despite Elsa's claim of having "the devil to pay" when the newspapers got wind of the affair, the party was reported in good humor, and the day after the headlines, the *Daily Express* ran this small item inside the paper:

"All those whose curiosity about the 'murder' party at Lady Ribblesdale's house had been satisfied by the description of it which appeared in the *Daily Express* were talking yesterday about Miss Elsa Maxwell.

"Miss Maxwell, who organised this party as successfully as she has so many others in Paris, Venice, and Monte Carlo, has, indeed, a personality which compels attention.

"She is short, dark, and stout, and talks a great deal, rather wittily, with a slight American accent. An intense vitality seems to radiate from her and make her the central object of interest wherever she goes.

"'I wish she would arrange another murder party' was a sentence often uttered yesterday. One of the enjoyable entertainments organised by Miss Maxwell was a treasure hunt some four years ago on the Lido. The treasure—a 500-lire note pounded to pulp—was eventually discovered at the bottom of a glass of milk which Mr. Duff Cooper was drinking at the Excelsior bar!"

Reading the entries on Elsa in *The Duff Cooper Diaries*, it's easy to picture the scowl on his face when the cacophony of Elsa's harpies interrupts his quiet drink of—milk?—in a subdued bar in Venice. In 1922 he wrote, "She is a strange woman and she hates anybody giving a party except herself." Three years later: "I dined this evening with Elsa Maxwell—a ghastly party."

Duff Cooper started out as a Conservative member of parliament in the twenties. Later he became First Lord of the Admiralty, and in 1944 he was named British ambassador to France. Later still he was created Viscount Norwich. His wife, the Lady Diana Cooper, tolerated Elsa somewhat less allergically than her husband. Their son, John Julius Norwich (2nd Viscount Norwich), told me that his mother enjoyed Elsa "in small doses." In 1958, upon publication of Lady Diana's memoir, *The Rainbow Comes and Goes*, she did a book launch at W. H. Smith in Paris. Elsa turned up, sat down beside her old friend, and a moment later Elsa was energetically signing copies—at least, one hopes—*under* Lady Diana's signature and not above it.

"What did your mother think about that?" I asked John Julius Norwich.

"She just thought it was hilarious," he said. "Which it was."

By 1930, Elsa's reputation as party giver extraordinaire preceded her wherever she went in London, Paris, Venice, Monte Carlo, and New York. Her arrival at a hotel was a sign that an important party must be imminent. In Paris, especially, her name had great cachet, and sophisticated Europeans preferred her company to that of Americans such as the Fitzgeralds and the Hemingways, who often behaved like adolescent tourists.

Bricktop (1894–1984), the African-American performer and self-described saloon keeper whose club, Chez Bricktop, operated in Paris from 1924 to 1961, wrote in her memoir that Elsa and Fannie Ward, the American silent film actress and perennial flapper, "were in a neck-and-neck race to see who could outdo the other as the most popular hostess in Paris." Fannie, of course, didn't win, and her name is virtually forgotten.

Bricktop's fame in Jazz Age Paris owed more to her expertise at dancing the Charleston than to her singing, and it came about like this. Cole Porter visited her club, saw her Charleston, and found it sensational. Since the dance had not yet been introduced to Europe, he became its impresario, with Bricktop as artiste. "You have talking feet and legs," he complimented her.

A few nights after his initial visit, he returned, bringing Elsa and several others with him. Bricktop danced the Charleston, Elsa loved it, and Cole decided to give a Charleston party in his mansion at 13 rue Monsieur. He invited Bricktop to teach the new dance to his guests. Upon arrival for her first lesson, Bricktop discovered that the three-hundred-pound Aga Khan was to be a pupil (he later reconsidered). Elsa was there, too, along with some fifty others. "I was about to become the dance teacher to the most elegant members of the international set," Bricktop said. Describing the Charleston as "a fast dance" that "appealed to people who led fast lives," she regarded those dancing lessons as her entree to celebrity. "I began to meet the top hosts and hostesses of Paris," Bricktop said. "The best party-givers I knew were Cole; Elsa Maxwell; Dolly O'Brien [a socialite and onetime girlfriend of Clark Gable]; Arturo Lopez-Willshaw, the Chilean multimillionaire; the Rothschilds; Lady Mendl; Daisy Fellowes; and Consuelo Vanderbilt, who had married the Duke of Marlborough."

Bricktop's memories of Paris in the twenties, and especially of the city's party circuit, are valuable for the panorama they unfold. It becomes clear, in this context, that Elsa had stiff competition, and also that her reputation endures as top-of-the-line hostess because of her flair for variety and originality. Recalling a party given by Elsa at the Ritz, Bricktop said, "I brought along the Three Eddys, a team of dancers who did a comedy act. Like many entertainers of the time, Negro and white, they blackened their faces with burnt cork, wore white gloves and big eyeglasses. It was a great party, and the Three Eddys thought they'd gone over well."

Elsa, however, did not agree. Afterward she said, "Brick, don't use the Three Eddys again." Bricktop asked whether they had misbehaved, and Elsa told her they had not. But, having observed male guests kissing the hands of female guests, the Three Eddys decided that must be de rigueur. The result: a dozen women retrieved their hands to find them smeared with burnt cork. "And Brick," Elsa said, "if you don't know how hard that is to clean off, I do. I used to wear cork in vaudeville." Reading this anecdote, two aspects of Elsa's character stand out. One, her minute attention to detail, and also the absence of racism. The fact of black men kissing white female hands had nothing to do with Elsa's chagrin. A few years later, in writings that we will come to, she took a bold stand against the institutionalized bigotry in America.

Bricktop entertained for Elsa at many other parties. They stayed in touch for years, and Bricktop's shrewd observations on Elsa's nature surpass most such commentary. "I never got too close to Elsa," she conceded. "With her, the best thing to do was to be cordial. You could stay that way for a long time. I suppose that's why we remained casual friends and I never found myself on the wrong side of her sharp, cutting words. I could have gotten into a feud with her if I'd called her on her claim that she was responsible for my success. I could have reminded her that she took me up simply because Cole was interested."

Cordiality over intimacy—Bricktop grasped a vital component of Elsa's psychology. Deep emotional relationships held scant appeal, apart from those with her father, with Dickie, and with a few longtime intimates such as Noël and Cole. Indeed, even with her enormous energy, how could she have invested more than superficial interest in so many hundreds of friends? Elsa's charisma enveloped those around her: she listened, she complimented, she confided (though not about herself), she made them laugh, she warmed her friends like a fireplace in winter. And if they dropped dead on her threshold, Elsa had scant time for grief. Their party was over, but a hundred others were starting up.

Bricktop perceived, also, Elsa's penchant for self-aggrandizement—a superfluous need, since Elsa wielded the power that she wished to. By overstating her importance—for instance, insisting that she had launched Bricktop—she diminished herself to caricature. Eventually, every name she dropped, every puffed-up accomplishment, took on the comical excess of Elsa's signature on the title page of Lady Diana's book.

19 We Open in Venice

$\mathcal{B}$ack home in California, newspaper chroniclers kept readers abreast of Elsa's fabulous life in Europe. In 1927, the *Oakland Tribune* reported that "smart gowns were the order of the day at Miss Elsie Maxwell's dinner party, held last week at the Paris Ritz. Notable were three of Louise Boulanger's flowered chiffon dresses, an ivory satin model by Jean Patou, and Chanel's pailletted dress, this time in white instead of the original black."

Parties, however, even one or more a night, did not satisfy Elsa's oceanic drive. Endless energy—and the quest for money, which always slipped through her hands—compelled Elsa to expand her one-woman empire. (Today she would be a multinational: EM, Ltd.) "To turn a fast and reasonably honest franc, I became one of Europe's pioneer press agents," she said airily, as though such an enterprise were an afterthought. And for her it probably was. That very statement is a masterpiece of press agentry, for its kernel of truth resides under candy floss. Rarely, if ever, is Elsa mentioned in histories of public relations—an absence that does not detract from her effectiveness at it. The best press agents land their jobs on the fly. Insofar as I can reconstruct Elsa's PR career, more than half the credit she gives herself is accurate.

Venice hungered for press agentry, although local government had not realized its crying need until Elsa hit town and pointed it out. She and Dickie, like others of the cognoscenti, knew the pleasures of this city whose streets are paved in water. They were regulars from the early twenties. Cole and Linda Porter made Venice one of their homes-away-from, and a colorful phalanx of luminaries had long favored this unique otherworld. Nevertheless, in the decade following the Great War, two problems faced the mayor of Venice: how to lure prosperous Americans, and how to lure anyone at all during the sweltering months of July and August. The Lido, especially, languished for want of visitors. It was anything but the smart place to go.

By 1925, Elsa was known in Venice for the parties, masquerades, and treasure hunts she staged there. That year, upon Elsa's arrival in town, the mayor invited her to his office, and the two discussed ways to promote Venetian tourism among the well-heeled. According to Elsa, the mayor found it perplexing that women from all over the world came to Venice "to savor the romantic atmosphere of Byron, Shelley, and Browning. Our gondolas, museums, and famous landmarks are very popular with the ladies, but men seem to prefer other places. Why?"

Elsa told him that Venice should offer sporting events to the men. Among her suggestions: start a regatta; award trophies for aviation and water sports; make a golf course "on that strip of land about ten kilometers up the coast near Alberoni." You're hired, said the mayor, or words to that effect. A number of her suggestions were taken; for instance, the Venice Golf Club at Alberoni dates back to 1928. Elsa's most direct involvement with the promotion of Venice, however, seems to have been her formal dinners, beach parties, treasure hunts, and parties on Cole Porter's *galleggiante*—a floating nightclub and dance boat. (This craft, which seated one hundred fifty, made only one journey because the guests found it almost impossible to maintain their balance on the choppy waters. Then, too, Cole forgot to install bathrooms. After her maiden voyage, therefore, the *galleggiante* remained stationary in the dock for future fêtes.)

According to Elsa, her efforts brought such dazzling results that Mussolini gave her a medal in the mid-twenties "for giving Italian *turismo* a shot in the arm"—a decoration that she returned three years later when she discovered the true nature of fascism. It is perhaps easier to accept Elsa's version of her grand Venetian accomplishments as good PR rather than a factual account of what really happened. And yet—no one has disproved her. True, biographers of Cole Porter and of other habitués of Venice have put forth their own candidates as patrons of the city's Jazz Age popularity, and no doubt it was ultimately a joint effort. Still, Elsa more than anyone else seems the linchpin.

I wasn't convinced of her cohesive influence until I looked up the July 1934 issue of *Fortune* magazine. That issue, devoted to the Italy of Mussolini's "Corporative State"—i.e., fascism—included a feature on Venice titled "The Perfect Tourist City." Despite the slippery slope of Elsa's self-promotion in tandem with her promotion of Venice, and notwithstanding the conservative bias of Henry Luce's magazines (he published *Time* and *Life,* as well as *Fortune*), my account follows the reporting in that unsigned article.

The writer points out that the Lido, "that slim, sandy island some fifteen minutes by motor launch from the main cluster of Venetian islands," was an empty waste until the 1890s, when CIGA (Compania Italiana dei Grandi Alberghi), the company that built luxury hotels all over Italy, constructed several such on the Lido. The "biggest and swankiest," according to *Fortune*, was the Excelsior Palace. Thus, in the 1890s and the early years of the twentieth century, the Lido came to resemble the Riviera. But, continued the article, the Lido of those days was a very different place, "for in the early twenties something happened that changed it from a pleasantly smart Adriatic beach to *the* Place—magnet for the celebrities of two continents, rotogravure favorite, perhaps the best known beach in all the world. Just what that something was remains an argument. Some say it was nothing more complicated than the world boom, some say Fascism. And some insist it was just plain Elsa Maxwell who, alone and single-handed, put the Lido on the map."

But, like the hero of a fairy tale, Elsa had first to subdue and reconcile two ferocious dragons—in this case, a countess and a princess. The Contessa Annina Morosini, a haughty Medusa of the canals, ruled her elite set of blue bloods with a fascist fist that even Mussolini might fear. Before her, Venice trembled. She despised the Lido and the foreign, postwar trash that congregated there. She hated loud horseplay and scandalous informality, for she was descended from a line of doges. Her long-ago lover was Kaiser Wilhelm II, of the House of Hohenzollern.

In a rival palazzo dwelled the Principessa Jane di San Faustino—dwelled, that is, when she wasn't roaring as the social lionness of Rome. A mean gorgon who originated in New Jersey, Princess Jane wore mourning for twenty years after the death of her husband, the prince, and "looked as ethereal as a figure out of a medieval painting," according to Elsa. She beat her servants and spoke with the tongue of a fishwife. Although roughly the same age as the Countess Morosini—both were in their sixties—Jane had a youthful outlook. She loved the Jazz Age, adored the Bright Young Things, the flaming youth and flappers who washed up onto the Lido sands. "The Lido crowd which she led with inexhaustible verve was neither small nor very haughty nor particularly genteel," tattled the *Fortune* writer. "They were a noisy troupe consisting mainly of foreigners, including a large number of young men who might have been safely described as effeminate. This twittering, champagne-drinking group had nothing against old Venice. They merely ignored it."

Elsa's first task was to harmonize the two hostile courts. Her vision, like that of a latter-day Isaiah, was to make the wolf lie down with the lamb, the leopard curl up with the baby goat. And Elsa herself was cast as shepherd in the peaceable, watery kingdom. With enterpreneurial acumen, she realized that all of Venice—hotels, restaurants, antique shops, sellers of bibelots—would benefit from a truce between the two factions. Her plan was to make Lido goings-on so irresistibly seductive that the old guard would steal across the channel, risking the wrath of La Morosini to attend a twilight picnic for Queen Marie of Romania. Next, Elsa masterminded the first big speedboat races off the Lido, attracting daredevils of all nations. And still more costume parties, masked balls, and evenings of delirious revels attended by the likes of Doris Duke, Cecil Beaton, Fanny Brice, Marie Dressler, and of course Noël and Cole.

Word spread that Elsa, in an outlandish Gay Nineties bathing suit, had sung Cole Porter's latest ditties, including one that contained the line, "Those Lido boys are mere decoys." The old guard had begun to crack, and soon the rival rulers of Venetian society came face-to-face. Princess Jane, having a blast, snapped her long, tapered fingers and shrieked, "Rats to you, Annina Morosini! And rats and rats and rats!" Elsa was delighted, for gaiety had triumphed again.

To celebrate this epic integration, she staged another treasure hunt. This time, participants included Lido boys and ancient noble crones; flappers and gigolos; dazzlers from Hollywood to Berlin and points between; play-boys and tarts; blue bloods and the merely blue. Among the items that the winner must procure was a key from the pocket of a young man. In Italian slang, however, the word *chiave*, key, has sexual overtones, so when various eager treasure hunters began fishing for keys in male Venetian pockets— well, someone called the police, who, under Mussolini's regime were more fascistic than before. A couple of arrests were made. A small riot formed, with much yelling and gesticulating, and the cops pronounced the treasure hunt *finito*. According to Elsa, the spoilsport police unwittingly fused the Morosini and the Faustino camps into a single party of indignant citizens, and from that day on Venetian society flowed like the tides of the Grand Canal.

The British writer Harold Acton, who was there, called Elsa "an astute psychologist of the idle rich. She prescribed strenuous action. Keep them hopping! Persuade them that they are living at top speed; turn them into bloodhounds; let them satisfy their cravings for exhibitionism!" The opera star Frances Alda, who spent much time in Venice in the twenties, recalled in her autobiography that Elsa loved it. "The crowds, the international ce-lebrities, the ex-royalties and aspiring archdukes, the Hollywood queens and the English duchesses. The gossip, the scandal, the atmosphere of a gay, daring, naughty world. With her remarkable flair for knowing exactly the right people, Elsa was in her element."

Fortune concluded its Venetian report with the fact that "whatever you think of Miss Maxwell as a *raconteuse*, it is history that between 1923 and 1929 Venice became a world capital of diversion."*

The importance of Elsa's success, the writer continued, was that "the tourist trade is one of Italy's biggest businesses." In view of the two and a half million tourists expected in Italy in 1934, and the forty million dollars they would spend, it's clear why Elsa should be honored by the government. A few years later, she was invited to meet the dictator—tea with Mussolini, more or less—but, appalled by the Fascists' suppression of civil liberties, she

---

*It is also history that Clare Boothe, inamorata and later wife of Henry Luce, the publisher of *Fortune*, had been a friend of Elsa's for years before the magazine cred-ited Elsa with popularizing Venice. And Luce was no stranger to nepotism.

refused to go. And, in true fairy-tale fashion, Elsa, happily ever after, threw many a Venetian gala long after Mussolini died at the end of a rope.

When resident in Venice, Elsa and Dickie often sojourned at whatever palazzo the Porters had leased for the season: in 1923, the Barbaro; the next year, the Papadopoli; the Rezzonico for several years beginning in 1925. All were splendidly located on the Grand Canal; Robert Browning died in the Rezzonico. Cole's parties rivaled Elsa's (some, of course, were joint efforts), although the guest lists of his more specialized events were limited to gay and bisexual men.

Linda Porter did not share her husband's enthusiasm for Elsa, whom she considered dishonest and an opportunist. Their relationship, cool but polite, suffered a rupture in 1927, when the Porters left Venice for America to attend the funeral of Cole's father. According to Dickie, "Elsa was staying with them at the time. As they were leaving, Linda said, 'No parties while we're away.' And Elsa replied, 'Well, really, Linda, I wouldn't be likely to give a party if you weren't there.' But then Linda sent a telegram to her secretary, from America, reminding her to tell Elsa once more that there were to be no parties. Elsa was furious and moved out." Eventually the women called an uneasy truce.

(One of Cole's biographers, George Eells, recounts a different version from Dickie's. According to him, when Cole's father died, Linda was in Switzerland for her health. Cole, upon leaving Venice, gave Elsa permission to live at the Rezzonico provided that she not draw attention to herself. "Elsa promised, but on the day of the funeral her high spirits got the better of her and she tossed an eye-popping party." When Cole eventually heard about it, he simply shrugged, saying, "That's Elsa." Linda, however, was furious and told Elsa: "Get out of my house!")

Rumors of Cole's wild parties swirled in Venice almost from his first sojourn there. There were drag balls for men only, with gowns that ran the fashion gamut from haute couture to high camp. According to Alfred Allan Lewis, in a book about Elsie de Wolfe's lesbian circle, one of these drag parties "became so raucous that the police were called in. Were it not that one of the gorgeously gowned beauties turned out to be the police chief's son, they would all have been hauled off to jail."

Dickie elaborates: "There was a well known Venetian family, the Brandolin. The head of that family—he was very attractive and he fell for me. He never wanted to meet the Cole Porters, but because of me he finally did meet Cole, and they were very polite and warm to each other. One day, however, he came to me and said, 'You know, I keep fending off the *fascisti* who bring me certain reports. Your Signor Porter cannot go on the way he is going— young gondoliers, that sort of thing. He will be turned out of Venice, whether he has the Rezzonico or not. You'd better warn him.' So I said to Cole, 'Look out. You're heading for real trouble.' After that, things calmed down a bit."

But not quite enough, according to Cole's intimate friend, the actor Monty Woolley. He said, "Cole left Venice reluctantly, just before he would have been officially asked to depart."

During these salad days of the twenties, Cole and Elsa, both of whom loved practical jokes and elaborate hoaxes, collaborated on a prank of novelistic complexity. Cole invented a couple, Mr. and Missus Fitch from Oklahoma, who, like the Beverly Hillbillies forty years later, struck oil while plowing a field. Letters were sent to various newspapers, including the Paris edition of the *Herald-Tribune*, detailing the itinerary of this pair who had come to Europe with their immense fortune. The story spread, especially when Elsa let it be known that they were guests of honor at one of her exclusive dinners. Meanwhile, Cole and various friends supplied frequent items to the columnists: the Fitches attended the races at Longchamps; dined at the Ritz; arrived late at the Opéra; departed early from a ball at the Spanish embassy.

Many Parisians claimed intimacy with the Fitches. Several socialites boasted to envious friends that Monsieur and Madame *Feetch* had dined with them just last night. Cole's delight was boundless. Who needed Scott and Zelda when one had companions of the Fitches' ilk? His joy, however, was short-lived; the *Herald-Tribune* editor smelled a rat. To avoid embarrassment to his society columnist, the editor inserted a news item announcing that Mr. and Mrs. Fitch had been killed in an automobile accident in Italy.

Cole, however, laughed last. A few years later he wrote the song, "Mr. and Missus Fitch," for his show, *Gay Divorce*, which opened on Broadway in 1932. In this updated report, the crash has left them penniless, and now "men who once knew Missus Fitch / Refer to her as a bitch."

20 Sunrise at Monte Carlo

*B*eachfront nations marveled at the flowering of Venice under Elsa's thumb. Next in the queue: Monaco. In the years following World War I, Elsa's repute as a mastermind of fantastically successful events, and huge publicity, radiated from her friends and patrons in Paris and New York to governments, industries, and charities, all curious to learn her trade secrets. Later Greece, the movie colony of Hollywood, and corporate fiefdoms such as the Waldorf became her clients—a word she loathed. Given her druthers, Elsa preferred a crown to a CEO.

Enter Louis Honoré Charles Antoine Grimaldi, who had ruled since 1922 as Louis II, Prince of Monaco. He and his court sought a tonic for its limited pull as a tourist magnet. In this context, it is important to recall that, before the marriage of Grace Kelly and Prince Rainier III in 1956, the minuscule principality of Monaco was better known to stamp collectors than to travelers. Gamblers, of course, bookmarked Monte Carlo, but the country's other amusements were sparse.

There is less ambiguity about Elsa's role in the promotion of Monaco than in her earlier involvement with Venice. Just as Elsa claimed, Prince Louis II did indeed send word to his son-in-law, Prince Pierre de Polignac, in Paris, to invite Mademoiselle Maxwell to lunch. (Prince Pierre was the father of Rainier III.) The son-in-law's assignment: find out how she might seduce more rich visitors to their vest-pocket country, and hire her on the spot if her plans seemed practicable. In spite of bitter tensions between the two princes, both were loyal to the interests of Monaco, and when Elsa's contract was signed, both men were optimistic. (For her creative efforts, Elsa was paid either $6,000, $20,000, or £10,000—she reported all three amounts at various times.)

Why did the Prince of Monaco choose Elsa? Her reputation, of course, had preceded her. Besides that, however, she was a friend of the Princesse de Polignac, née Singer, whom we first encountered in 1919 at Elsa's dinner for Arthur Balfour. And Miss Singer of America had become the *princesse* through her marriage to Prince Edmond de Polignac, uncle of the present Prince de Polignac who has just sat down to lunch with Elsa Maxwell.

Before zooming in on Elsa and the prince at lunch, however, a panoramic sketch of the Riviera in the 1920s provides a useful context for her actual accomplishments versus those she inflated or merely dreamed about. The coastline of the French Riviera, which the French themselves call la Côte d'Azur, stretches more than a hundred miles from Menton, near the Italian border, west to Hyères and Cassis. Inhabited for thousands of years, it attracted vast international attention in the twenties, thanks to the American ex-pats Gerald and Sara Murphy and their circle: Scott and Zelda Fitzgerald, Hemingway, Picasso, Cocteau, Stravinsky, Dorothy Parker, Cole Porter, and many others, all of whom came to the Murphy residence at Cap d'Antibes. Their milieu resembled a miniature Paris because of the famous artists and writers associated with it, most of whom are forever bracketed with modernism in the arts.

Most writers on the subject of the Riviera in that period credit the Murphys with making it *the* fashionable resort. Robert Kanigel, for example, in *High Season*, writes that in 1922 "the Murphys prevailed on the owner of the Hôtel du Cap, the famous Belle Epoque hotel, to remain open for the summer" and to rent them the entire first floor. There at Antibes, throughout those hot summer months, they entertained friends from Paris, swam, rubbed banana oil on their darkening skin, much to the astonishment of the natives, and soaked up what anyone today would consider unhealthy doses of ultraviolet rays. Such cavorting was considered revolutionary, since Riviera regulars avoided Mediterranean sunshine from May to September. *Their* high season was winter.

Peter Mayle, in *Provence A-Z*, traces the sunbathing craze to the unconventional Murphys: "They would take their houseguests to the nearby beach at La Garoupe to swim and soak up the sun. Their friend Picasso would often be there in his capacity as sunbather-in-chief, his skin the color of a well-cured cigar. Little by little, season by season, the habit of the *bronzette* took root and flourished." Up to then, lying on the beach merely to enjoy the sun was eccentric. One swam, then retreated to a cabana or a beach umbrella. Tanned skin was the emblem of peasants and fishermen. But, says Kanigel, "new relationships among sun, sea, and the human body—a new world of summertime leisure—were evolving." One could make the case that these new relationships paralleled modernism in the early twentieth century.

Modernism and suntans—the Murphys centered their lives of pleasure around both, and after summering in 1922 at the Hôtel du Cap, the next year they bought and remodeled a chalet at Cap d'Antibes and named it the Villa America. From the Murphys' villa, Kanigel traces the worship of summer and sun on to Cannes where, in 1923, Coco Chanel arrived, following a Mediterranean cruise, "brown as a cabin boy." She caused a sensation. The hordes couldn't wait to copy her. On to Juan-les-Pins, where the American millionaire Frank Jay Gould started his Riviera empire by buying the local casino and, in 1927, opening a two-hundred-room hotel. Overnight, Cannes was *so* last year, and Juan-les-Pins the happening hot spot.

But as chic France raked in millions from the pink-skinned and nut-brown, Monaco stood by like a wallflower. Something was needed, a brilliant coup that would lure the ultraselect away from Cap d'Antibes, Cannes, Juan-les-Pins, and into the petite principality.

Prince Pierre de Polignac and Elsa ordered lunch, gossiped a bit about goings-on in Monte Carlo and the South of France, and then he came to the point. "What you did in Venice, Elsa—we need a similar effort. Tourists are swarming to other resorts along the coast. Why are we, how shall I say, missing the boat?"

"Simple. You are not rendering proper homage to the new king."

He looked across the table in bafflement. "Which king?"

"*Le soleil*," chirped Elsa. "The sun, my dear, the sun!" She explained to him that life among the leisured had moved outdoors, that those who visited the Riviera came there to escape formality. "They want to play on the beach and in the water. You've got the water. Now get a beach if you want to lure the tourists."

He pointed out that Monaco (smaller than New York's Central Park) had no viable beach. Nature's oversights, however, had not deterred Elsa so far, and she wasn't about to succumb. She explained in prodigious detail, like an engineer from the École Polytechnique, that next door to Monaco, in France, en route to St. Martin, was a strip of unused land, which, she felt sure, could be leased, rented, or purchased, annexed to Monaco, and transformed into glittering beachfront. (The French said *non*.)

"And then," Elsa expanded, "you'll need other attractions. Build a new summer casino with facilities for entertainment. Build a hotel, a swimming pool. Tennis courts. Stage an international tournament every year after Wimbledon. All the great players of the world will already be in Europe for that."

To every one of the prince's demurrals, Elsa had a solution. His chief hesitation was the amount of money that would fly out of Monaco's coffers to inaugurate these plans. Wiping her mouth after a tasty dessert, Elsa said, as though it had never been said before, "You've got to spend money to make money." Before the day was over, he had signed her up as *entrepreneuse*, the closest word he knew to press agent. Her fee was to be paid in quarterly installments.

Elsa, however, immediately lost it all at the roulette wheel, or so she says in *R.S.V.P.*, page 188, forgetting that four pages earlier she had crowed, "I'm still drawing a nice little bonus from the Monte Carlo job."

Elsa's one-paragraph montage of Monaco's emergence as a Riviera butterfly: "The blueprints for a hotel were given to me as a present by Addison Mizner, the architect who practically created Palm Beach in the Florida wilderness. Work was rushed on Le Sporting, the handsome casino and outdoor pavilion, and it was completed in time for a gala opening in July, 1927. Grace Moore was the featured entertainer and King Gustaf V of Sweden headed the list of notables who brought back Monte Carlo's glitter." According to Elsa, her madcap progress encountered a single roadblock.

"The French contractor thought I was crazy for building a huge swimming pool, fifty meters long, next to the sea, and held up work until a clause was inserted in his contract guaranteeing him full payment in the event I later was proved to be mentally incompetent."

Steven Englund, in *Grace of Monaco*, clarifies Elsa's version of Monaco's makeover. The Société des Bains de Mer, administrator of the country's most lucrative enterprises, "teamed up with Elsa Maxwell to build a blue-tiled swimming pool, flanked by a pink stucco hotel of Hollywood-Spanish design [the Monte Carlo Beach Hotel]; it dropped a million and a half dollars completing a country club and another million on terraced tennis courts. The Monte Carlo Grand Prix—a serpentine round-the-principality race of harrowing difficulty—was inaugurated. And later, the International Sporting Club opened, an immense white structure with more gaming rooms, a ballroom, restaurant, nightclub, and bar." He points out that the "Society of Beach Bathing"—i.e., the Société, or SBM—"now had everything except a beach."

Elsa's suggested remedy for that absence perhaps made the French engineer especially glad to have demanded the mental-health clause, for she cooked up a scheme to cover Monte Carlo's uninviting seafront—littered with pebbles and various impedimenta—with large sheets of rubber, held in place with tar, then dump tons of Mediterranean sand on top of that.

Dickie was scandalized. "The tide will wash away the sand faster than you can dump it on the surface, idiot," she jeered. Nevertheless, the SBM found the notion worthy enough to commission a study, which revealed that seawater would destroy the rubber as well as dissipate the golden sand.

Elsa's point, however, is beside the point. Her proposal was a brilliant stroke of press agentry that reaped publicity in Europe and America, and is still written about today. In an interview with the *Daily Express* in 1927, Elsa spoke so convincingly of that rubberized paradise that the reporter didn't lift an eyebrow: "Miss Maxwell caught my imagination when she described the private beach she and her associates are going to build. The rubber will be renewed every year. All day long people will be able to lounge on clean sand, swim, and then take a sun bath, then plunge into the sea again—in and out, in and out, all day long."

The following year, the paper's Riviera correspondent filed a report that "the new Country Club was officially opened a few days ago, and Miss Elsa Maxwell gave a dinner to 150 people in honour of the occasion." The rubber-beach boondoggle, meanwhile, took on a life of its own. In 1928, the *Daily Express*, in a piece on unrest among the citizens of Monaco, reported the beach as a fait accompli. Even now, that imaginary beach lingers as an echo, like a dilapidated Hollywood set or the wan installation of a conceptual artist.

Today, the official Web site of the Monte Carlo Beach Hotel, on its "History" page, mentions Elsa's "extravagant project: a palatial hotel with a beach of artificial sand as lovely as those of the Lido in Venice or Palm Beach. The S.B.M preferred to build an Olympic-sized swimming pool just a few meters from the sea." Eventually, after World War II, Monaco did get a public beach: the Larvotto, man-made but minus rubber. And Elsa visited Monaco every year until shortly before her death. In *The Celebrity Circus*, published in 1963 during Elsa's final year, she wrote: "At the fancy-dress dinner party I gave August before last, to celebrate the opening of the new indoor pool at the Hôtel de Paris, the Prince arrived sporting a fierce black moustache and a bald wig that completely covered his heavy hair. Grace, who came in a rubber mask with fat cheeks and braids beneath a floppy straw hat, was shod in big flippers. Most of my guests departed about five o'clock that morning, after a mad game of water polo that involved some sixty players, but Grace, the Prince, and David Niven stayed for breakfast. We had our scrambled eggs, brioches, and coffee served on the hotel terrace, and the Royal couple, subdued after a swimming race an hour before, sat quietly together and watched, as we all did, the matchless sight of dawn breaking over the Mediterranean."

21 The Rotunda of Generous Matrons

$\mathcal{A}$s the twenties wore on, the years developed crow's feet. Even Elsa's favorite haunts—Paris, Venice, Monte Carlo—began to show fatigue. Newer dances edged the Charleston to one side, and it seemed that nothing could top such marvels as Lindbergh's flight and talking pictures. Money was everywhere, stock markets soared, but pleasures grew repetitive and hedonism wasn't what it used to be. In Elsa's crowd, some were seen leaving parties early for the novelty of sleep. Even the tireless Elsa was caught in the act—by Noël: "One night in the late twenties," he said, "at the height of the Paris season, I encountered Elsa, quite alone, stealing furtively home to bed with a good book." Even such brilliant inventions as murder parties and treasure hunts seemed destined for a short shelf life, and Elsa wished above all to avoid having her entertainments thought of as *vieux chapeau*.

After ten years abroad, she decided it was time to go home. Elsa and Dickie sailed from Le Havre on October 29, 1929—appropriately, perhaps, on Black Tuesday, the day of the stock market crash—and arrived in New York on November 7. (A radio comedian joked that the crash was such a jolt that it even shook Elsa Maxwell out of Europe.)

The crash, she said, had no effect on her finances, immediate or eventual, since she was always broke. Her name, however, had become a trademark, and therein lay her fortune. "Elsa Maxwell," though not registered at the U.S. Patent Office, had such drawing power and publicity value that the

Ritz-Carlton gave her special rates in consideration of the carriage-trade guests her magic name would pull in.

And Elsa was at it again. She threw a "Come As Your Opposite" party for two hundred in the hotel's Crystal Room. George Gershwin came as Groucho Marx. Fanny Brice dressed up as Tosca, Cole Porter as a football player, Frances Alda of the Metropolitan Opera as 1928 presidential candidate Al Smith, and Elsa herself as Republican President Herbert Hoover. Countess Dorothy di Frasso, along with her brother and sister-in-law, danced into the ballroom as an organ grinder, his assistant, and a monkey. The first Mrs. Vincent Astor (née Helen Dinsmore Huntington) sashayed in as a lady of the evening in red wig and scarlet gown. Lady Ribblesdale, hostess of Elsa's famous murder party, as Charlie Chaplin; several socialites dressed in rags and holding out tin cups; stalwart men as chorus boys; and noted anti-Prohibitionists as ladies and gentlemen of the Temperance Union.

The pseudonymous society columnist Cholly Knickerbocker (in reality, Maury Paul, scion of the Philadelphia Biddles) devoted many inches of print to Elsa's "hoopla, whoopee, rah-rah- and whizzbang" success. "I expect to hear no other subject discussed," he predicted, "for some time to come, over the fashionable cocktail trays, tea cups, and dinner platters."

No one present that evening, however, knew the girlhood connection of Elsa and one of her guests, Virginia Fair Vanderbilt, who appeared as—Elsa Maxwell! No one, that is, except Elsa and Mrs. Vanderbilt herself. For this woman, the divorced wife of William K. Vanderbilt Jr., was none other than Virginia Fair, of Nob Hill, whose father, Senator James Fair, supposedly snubbed Elsa's parents by not inviting them to Virginia's engagement party. This story, a motif in many of her subsequent writings, remained an open wound. That snub to her parents became Elsa's Rosebud, and as elusive as Charles Foster Kane's. (Orson Welles himself explained the sled named Rosebud in *Citizen Kane* as "a gimmick, a dollar-book Freudian gag.")

Elsa's, also, may have been some sort of a gimmick, and here's why. As we have seen, her parents belonged to society in San Francisco, and their station was higher than that of Senator Fair's family. The Maxwells were cultured, they attended the opera and the theatre, and celebrities called at their home.

Yet they were no match financially for this very rich ex-senator from Nevada, who left an estate of forty million dollars when he died in 1894. Those millions he earned first in the Gold Rush, and later in the silver mines of Nevada.

"Slippery Jim," as many called the senator, wasn't well liked in San Francisco and, according to one historian, "he made no impression in the Senate save to advertise it as a haunt of millionaires. The gaudiness and irregularity of his life and the social ambitions of his family attracted attention for two decades." Moreover, he was a crook. His wife divorced him and retained custody of three of their four children. He was eventually estranged from his two daughters, despite the millions he bestowed on each one.

Why, then, if there was bad blood between the Fairs and the Maxwells, did the former Virginia Fair turn up at Elsa's exclusive party, which many in New York society had sought in vain to attend? In one version of Elsa's story, the snub came about at the time of Virginia's engagement. In *R.S.V.P.*, however, Fair "was giving a party for his oldest daughter, Theresa." Oddly, though, a friendship existed at the time, for Elsa goes on: "The Fair girls were older than I was, but I knew them well enough to have free run of their spacious grounds and drop into the kitchen for a handout of cookies and cocoa."

If Elsa used that long-ago snub as a gimmick, it surely was a heartfelt one, grounded in reality of a sort, and rife with possibilities. Perhaps friendly feelings between Elsa and the girls did not extend to their elders. Or, no snub was intended because whatever the occasion, it was thought that the Maxwells wouldn't find the gathering of interest. More pointedly, financial dealings between Senator Fair and Elsa's parents may have soured. The Maxwells tried various investment schemes; Fair, according to a historian of San Francisco, "habitually recommended mining stocks he knew to be worthless just for the pleasure of seeing people scramble to buy stock on the strength of his word. When the mines proved worthless and people lost their investments, Fair felt it justified his wisdom. Even his wife was no exception." Knowing she was talkative, he lured her with a worthless stock, she spread the word to her friends, and they all lost a small fortune. "Fair paid his wife what she lost and told her that should be a lesson." (It's unclear whether that triggered their divorce. Such chicanery, however, was not rare: it was a ploy to hold women in check.)

The questions go on and on, unanswered. Elsa's friend Orson Welles might have solved the conundrum like this: Elsa, old and tired, is writing her memoirs. Seated at a desk in her apartment at the Waldorf, she grows agitated. In voice-over, we hear her obsessive repetition of details of the party that no Maxwell was invited to. "I vowed that I would give parties *they* would beg me to attend, and I did it! Now the wheel has turned full circle."

The camera pulls back. We see Elsa open a drawer of the desk and take out a worn and faded envelope. Cut to a close-up of the fancy old-fashioned writing. We read: "My dear Mrs. Fair, We regret that our daughter Elsa cannot attend your party owing to . . ."

The camera pans from Elsa's hand down to the carpet. An instant later, her pen drops and the screen fades to black.

Always broke? Elsa's shibboleth was true as far as it went, for she found it impossible not to squander. Where, then, did she get the funds for a lifestyle that resembled, at first glance, a Rockefeller's? Media accounts, and tittle-tattle, implied that she was handsomely paid for giving parties; that she charged the *nouveaux* for introducing them to the older *riches*; that she blackmailed people for keeping their scandals out of the papers, especially her own columns; and that she collected kickbacks from caterers, orchestra leaders, and others who supplied her parties. These insinuations Elsa vehemently denied.

In *R.S.V.P.*, she also denied receiving "regular handouts" from friends like Mrs. Millicent Hearst and Cole Porter. Then, on the page following, she wrote: "In the last forty years, I have asked a small group of old friends to bail me out of jams from time to time by advancing me modest loans, and they have practically all been paid back." No elaboration is offered on the word "practically," although stories abound that cast Elsa as a Robin Hood in the shape of Friar Tuck—that is, she would beg, borrow, or, failing all else, take from the rich and give to the poor, meaning Elsa herself.

Explaining her finances a bit further, she wrote: "Four old friends—Mrs. Hearst, Mrs. Jessie Donahue, Mrs. Eleanor Loder, and Mrs. Margaret Emerson—who know I'm always strapped for ready money, give me substantial checks at Christmas or on my birthday. The late Mrs. Evalyn Walsh McLean asked me to go to Hollywood with her in 1943 and gave me a check to cover $4,000 worth of radio commitments I could not afford to pass up. The fabulously wealthy Mrs. McLean had such a wonderful time meeting the movie celebrities whom I introduced to her that she threw a mink coat into the bargain."

One of these old friends, and her husband, attended Elsa's "Come As Your Opposite" party: Mr. and Mrs. James P. Donahue. Jessie Donahue was a daughter of F. W. Woolworth, a farmer's son who made millions from his dime-store empire and who, between 1910 and 1913, erected the Woolworth Building in lower Manhattan. One of Jessie Donahue's nieces was Barbara Hutton, perhaps the unhappiest heiress of all time. Jessie's son, Jimmy Donahue, will soon enter Elsa's story owing to his liaison with Elsa's sometime friend, the Duchess of Windsor. Their controversial alliance was a major fuse in the explosion between Elsa and the Duchess.

When F. W. Woolworth died in 1919, he left an estate of some sixty-five million dollars, just short of a billion in present-day value. Jessie's inheritance was vast. It matched the unhappiness of her life, and if the Woolworth fortune had been cursed it could hardly have poisoned the legatees more thoroughly. Jessie's sister, Edna Woolworth Hutton, committed suicide at age thirty-five in 1917, leaving five-year-old Barbara to be shunted from relative to relative.

In 1931, the year after they attended Elsa's party, Jessie's bisexual husband killed himself in a most gruesome way. During a poker game at their home on East Eightieth Street in New York, he left the table, went to his bedroom, and swallowed a bottle of bichloride of mercury. He was said to be desperate owing to financial losses, gambling debts, alcohol, and a sexual entanglement with a sailor. The couple had two young sons, Jimmy and Woolworth Donahue. Whatever her husband's infidelities, Jessie seems to have loved him deeply. Her grief and torment were so great that she never returned to the house after her husband's death. She moved into the Hotel Pierre, and later to a triplex on Fifth Avenue, where Jimmy had his own suite.

Jessie never remarried. She traveled in her private railroad car, which she had commissioned in 1926 and named "Japauldon" for her husband, James Paul Donahue. She and members of her family used the car for trips to Palm Beach and her forty-five-thousand-square-foot estate, Cielito Lindo, built for Jessie in 1927. A year later, she bought Wooldon Manor, a fifty-eight-room English Tudor–style mansion in Southampton, Long Island.

The friendship of Jessie and Elsa began in the teens, when all of New York marveled at this roly-poly, nonstop woman who captured Vanderbilts new and old, governors, mayors, tenors and sopranos, along with shopgirls, taxi drivers, and butlers. Jessie perhaps realized that Elsa was a laissez-passer to the heart of blue-blood society. She herself, with all her millions, was looked upon as "that dime store woman," and even Elsa was unable to boost her very high. Eventually, Elsa became in effect a paid companion and confidante to Mrs. Donahue as she did to other wealthy women. They doted on her not only for her social leverage but also because she kept the ball rolling. And she chased away the blues. Even more important, Elsa knew many secrets and for those who treated her well on Christmas and birthdays her lips were eternally sealed, like a priest of Jessie Donahue's church. Elsa never bit the hand that wrote the checks, although her friendship with Jessie did not survive the infamy of Jimmy Donahue in the 1950s, especially his involvement with the Windsors.

One of Elsa's most thoughtful pieces of journalism was a four-part series published in *Cosmopolitan* in 1938–'39 called "The Truth About Barbara Hutton." Unlike most writers then and now, Elsa looked past the clichés, the isolation, the abuse endured by this woman drowning in money. She portrayed her friend as one who gave not wisely but too well—her "staggering generosity," as Elsa called it, to family, friends, lovers, charities, and a diamond clip to Elsa.*

In 1929, at their first meeting, Elsa said that she and Barbara discussed

---

*Brenda Wineapple, in *Genêt: A Biography of Janet Flanner*, states that Flanner had "undertaken a secret project of ghostwriting a serial biography of heiress Barbara Hutton for Elsa Maxwell at *Cosmopolitan*." The source of this assertion is a letter from Flanner to Katherine White at *The New Yorker* in 1938. The claim is debatable. A comparison of Elsa's style versus Flanner's reveals that Flanner, a labored, unfluent stylist, would have had to be a phenomenal parodist to capture and sustain the rhythms of Elsa's breezy writing style. Then, too, Elsa was a close friend of Barbara Hutton, who later referred, in a letter, to the intimate interview with Elsa. Perhaps Elsa and Flanner collaborated, but the published text belies Flanner's claim of authorship.

music: "It turned out that she was a great admirer of Cole Porter and George Gershwin. She had never met either of them but she knew every tune they had written."

"What else are you interested in?" Elsa pursued.

"Poetry and Chinese art," replied seventeen-year-old Barbara. A few years later, Elsa set to music three of Barbara's poems, all inspired by China: "Lantern Street (Teng Chieh)," "The Temple of Heaven," and "Chu-lu-mai." Lawrence Tibbett, of the Metropolitan Opera, performed them on a radio program in 1935. Elsa said that Lauritz Melchior and Eleanor Steber also sang these songs on different occasions.

Next in the gallery of benefactresses: Millicent Hearst, whose life of sunshine contrasts with the storms and shadows of so many of the female superrich. Best known as the put-upon wife of William Randolph Hearst, who took up with Marion Davies some fifteen years after marrying Millicent, Mrs. Hearst remained Mrs. Hearst. Some said she wouldn't grant him a divorce; others claimed he never asked.

Millicent Veronica Willson, born in Brooklyn, was a sixteen-year-old vaudeville performer in New York when Hearst, already in his thirties, saw her and took a fancy. They married in 1903, and over the next dozen years Millicent bore five sons. During World War I, around the time that Hearst fell for Marion Davies, Millicent met Elsa while they were both engaged in the war effort. Millicent worked tirelessly with many charities, especially the Free Milk Fund for Babies, which she founded in 1921 to provide milk for the poor of New York. She enlisted Elsa in many of her fund-raising schemes. Recalling their first meeting, Elsa described Millicent as "the prettiest creature I had ever seen." And so she was. Easier to understand leaving Marion Davies for Millicent than the other way around.

According to Elsa, "The outstanding facet of Millicent's character is her complete loyalty to those she loves." Diana Vreeland, longtime fashion editor at *Harper's Bazaar*, a Hearst publication, adored the boss's wife. Vreeland emphasized her madcap side. "She was a hearty, lusty, wonderful *blonde* from Brooklyn. If she was going to make a joke, she'd start laughing, so she got you laughing before the joke was made, and by the time the joke *was* made, everybody was hysterical." And you'd know where she came from the moment she opened her mouth. Vreeland again: "Instead of 'the oil of Texas' and 'the Earl of Sefton,' she'd say 'the Oil of Sefton' and 'the earl of Texas.' I think she was just plain too big for old William Randolph Hearst. And that was the reason for Marion Davies."

If Millicent had to refer to Marion, she didn't use a name. It was "that harlot" or "that woman." Yet in 1959 she told W. A. Swanberg, author of *Citizen Hearst*, "W.R. was a great man. Those who thought otherwise just didn't know him."

In the thirties, according to Elsa, Millicent was invited for an audience with Mussolini. The dictator took her for a spin in the Roman countryside, and "drove his Fiat eighty miles an hour. Millicent, who was terrified by reckless driving, suggested to Mussolini that he slow down.

"'Why?' he demanded belligerently.

"'You—you're breaking the speed law,' she said lamely.

"Mussolini laughed uproariously. 'I *am* the law,' he blustered."

For a time in the early forties, Elsa wrote a syndicated column for the Hearst papers. According to her, she injected politics a few times too many into journalism that was contracted as society and celebrity fluff. Dissatisfied with Hearst's constraints, she left in 1942 for the *New York Post*, which ran her column for the next eight years. Then, after Hearst's death in 1951, his son, William Randolph Hearst Jr., made Elsa an attractive offer. She accepted, and stayed with the Hearst papers for the rest of her life. (Around thirty-five newspapers carried Elsa's column.) Elsa doesn't mention the Millicent factor in these deals, though she must have exerted influence: Millicent never relinquished her role in the Hearst empire. Nor did the tolerant Mrs. Hearst take umbrage at Elsa's occasional visits to San Simeon as the guest of Mr. Hearst and Miss Davies.

Margaret Emerson's friends used her maiden name because her many marital changes made it cumbersome, and risky, to attach "Mrs." to the current surname. No one wished to address her as Mrs. Baker when that title had been superceded by Mrs. Amory. First in the marital queue was Dr. McKim of Baltimore; the marriage lasted from 1902 till 1910. Then Alfred Gwynne

Vanderbilt the first (1911 until his death, in 1915, on the RMS *Lusitania*). In 1918, Margaret married Raymond T. Baker, director of the United States Mint, a match that occasioned many predictable jokes, for the bride was said to have more money than the government. Given her sharp tongue, one can only guess her comments upon receipt of President Woodrow Wilson's wedding gift: a complete set of the president's writings. It seems unlikely that Margaret Emerson ever curled up between divorces with *Constitutional Government in the United States*. When they divorced in October 1928, Mr. Baker kept the books.

In November of that year, Margaret married Charles Minot Amory. When reporting on her marital kaleidoscope, the unyieldingly staid *New York Times* veered toward the tabloid arousal of its competitors. DENIES RUMORS OF DIVORCE was a headline in 1922, when Margaret was said to have gone to Paris to establish residence with the idea of obtaining a divorce from Raymond Baker. This she hotly denied, telling the *Times* reporter, "It's getting so that no one can visit Paris without a divorce rumor starting. It's almost as bad as Reno."

Heiress to the Bromo-Seltzer fortune, Margaret had more estates than husbands: seven vast properties in this country and abroad. When her oldest son, Alfred Gwynne Vanderbilt II, turned twenty-one, she gave him a six-hundred-acre horse farm in Maryland.

Eleanor Loder—the name suggests a tall, tailored lady in a smart hat, gloves, and a string of pearls, stepping out of a black 1952 Chrysler at the Congregational Church in Greenwich, Connecticut.

Reality is somewhat different.

Eleanor Curran was born in New Orleans and became a manicurist. An irreverent biographer might concoct a scenario of Eleanor burnishing the fingernails of Sir Mortimer Davis, Canadian manufacturer, financier, philanthropist, and creator of the Imperial Tobacco Company of Canada. She compliments his manly hands and strong cuticles. Their eyes meet, she lays down the nail clippers and— It is true, however, that Eleanor and Sir Mortimer met in the early twenties, while he was still married to Henriette, Lady Davis. In 1924, the couple divorced, and later that year he married the

Countess Moroni—our Eleanor, who previously, it was felt, lacked the proper credentials to become Sir Mortimer's second wife. It was necessary to tweak her pedigree, but how?

A solution was found: Eleanor married the impecunious Italian Count Moroni, whose coffers suddenly filled with Canadian gold. The count and countess soon divorced, and Sir Mortimer married the ex–Contessa Moroni. According to the *Dictionary of Canadian Biography Online*, "Thereafter he seems to have devoted himself to worldly pleasures on the French Riviera, but not for long, since he died suddenly, of a heart attack, at the age of 62."

Elsa presumably made the acquaintance of Sir Mortimer and his new wife in Monaco or the South of France during the twenties. It is reasonable to assume, also, that, after Sir Mortimer's death, she played matchmaker. "My dear," one can almost hear her cooing to Eleanor, "I know the most divine Englishman. Let's give a party and invite him."

What Elsa did say was this: "Eric Loder and I have been friends since 1912, when he was the handsomest Rolls-Royce salesman in London and I was the plumpest songwriter. He was the *beau jeune homme* of London. Some wives resent their husband's former friends, but I saw more of Eric after he married Eleanor. In fact, Eleanor Loder has been my one real friend, with the exceptions of Millicent Hearst and Dickie Gordon, for a quarter century."

From Elsa's sketch, we learn that Eleanor was "a financial genius" who read *The Wall Street Journal* "as if it were authored by Mickey Spillane. But if Eleanor is energetic in regard to business matters, in home matters she has inherited the Southern belle's traditional laziness." Contributing to Eric and Eleanor's marital harmony was the comfortable arrangement they came to: "She looks after their business interests, Eric runs the house, and they are one of the happiest couples I know." Eric Loder was previously married for a year to the beautiful London stage actress Gabrielle Ray, and subsequently to Iris Fitzgerald, of the peerage. The scant information about him suggests that he was the scion of a prominent British family.

Eleanor's wealth, perhaps a legacy of her first marriage, enabled her to buy notable diamonds from Harry Winston, including the Deepdene (104.52 carats) in 1954, and the Louis XIV in 1963, the year of her death. She attempted to advise Elsa on finances, but found a recalcitrant pupil.

"Invest some of your money in a house before you squander it all," Eleanor said. "You're as irresponsible as a child."

"I don't want to be burdened with property," argued Elsa. "I like being free as a bird."

Whereupon Eleanor either gave Elsa a house, lent it to her, or deeded it for life, depending on which one of Elsa's books you read. Elsa hired a staff of eight to clean the house, called Lou Paradou ("paradise" in the Occitan of Provence), which had been vacant for some years. Although Eleanor had understated Lou Paradou as a "nice little place," it was in fact a small estate with five master bedrooms sitting on three acres of land. Elsa's first thought was to give a party. She invited two hundred friends from far and near for August 31, 1939.

By the time Elsa's guests arrived, Hitler had signed the order to attack Poland. German forces moved to the frontier, and in a few hours, on September 1, World War II had begun. Three days later, Britain and France declared war on Germany.

Elsa's guests, looking west from the terrace in the direction of Cannes and in the opposite direction toward Nice, observed a strange phenomenon that Elsa described as "a black carpet" rolling over the entire landscape. In minutes, "the Riviera was shrouded in darkness and silence." Facing the inevitable, the French government had ordered a blackout. Air raids might begin at any time.

When Evalyn Walsh McLean took Elsa to Hollywood in 1943, that lady of uncountable riches was famous for her eccentricities, her generosity, her love of show to the point of exhibitionism, but most of all for the Hope Diamond, which she acquired in 1918. Born among the silver mines of Leadville, Colorado (or Sowbelly Gulch, as she preferred to say, adding, "I ain't a lady"), she had money to burn because *Father Struck It Rich*, the title of her autobiography.

Honeymooning in Paris with her husband Ned, whose father owned the *Cincinnati Enquirer* and the *Washington Post*, Evalyn saw something she liked at Cartier's: a necklace of square links of platinum set with diamonds from which hung three loops of diamonds. Attached to the bottom loop was a pearl of 32¼ grains, the size of a little finger tip; suspended below it was a six-sided emerald weighing 34½ carats, and hanging below that was the Star of the East, a pear-shaped diamond weighing almost 95 carats. She had to have it, so her husband added his $100,000 pocket money to what was left of Evalyn's wedding gift in the same amount, and the necklace was hers. She was twenty-two.

By the time she acquired the Hope Diamond, she had several children, one of whom used his mother's newest gem for teething. Once when a guest asked to see the Hope, Evalyn looked blank for a moment, then said, "What did I do with that necklace?" A bit later she remembered. Going to the window, she called, "Mike! Here, Mike." A few minutes later, a Great Dane galloped into the room, with the Hope and its sister diamonds twisted around his neck.

At Friendship, her estate in Washington, Evalyn hosted American presidents, foreign heads of state, diplomats, generals, and anyone else who struck her fancy. In the twenties, Presidents Harding and Coolidge played golf on the course that Evalyn's husband had built, and Mrs. Coolidge liked to knit on the front porch of the mansion. According to Elsa, during World War II many Allied diplomats and staff officers congregated at Friendship because they "needed a clubhouse where, unhampered by protocol, they could meet to compare notes and exchange off-the-record opinions." In her estimation, "more high-level policies were discussed and formulated there than at any other place except 1600 Pennsylvania Avenue and 10 Downing Street."

Evalyn had a big heart for anyone in need. She helped feed the Bonus Army of veterans who marched on Washington in the early days of the Great Depression. She entertained enlisted men during the war, and set up a club for civilian war workers. Learning of a veteran whose family had been evicted, she took in the man, his wife, and their three children until she could find them a place to live. In an unusual spin on good works, she would sometimes take the Hope Diamond to Walter Reed Army Hospital and let wounded soldiers play catch with it.

Eager to make home movies of her family and friends, Evalyn flew to Hollywood and persuaded Cecil B. DeMille to teach her the rudiments. After Evalyn's death in 1947, Harry Winston bought the bulk of her jewelry collection. In 1958, he donated the Hope Diamond to the Smithsonian Institution, where it has been a major attraction ever since.

22 How to Become a Movie Star at Fifty-five

Given that every day in Elsa's life was tops, a climax, the summit of living, it is difficult to assign one period more importance than another. And yet her beachhead in Hollywood stands out because that rich province, previously unexplored by Elsa, capitulated overnight. Alexander the Great and Napoleon would have gaped at her conquest.

Elsa arrived in Hollywood not starry-eyed but silver-tongued. Anything Hollywood said, Elsa said better, and besides, they couldn't bullshit a bullshitter. She knew already any number of Hollywood names, and while the studios, the stars, the party circuit, the glamour, and the gossip appealed to her celebrity quest, she could take it or leave it. Like Mae West, Elsa was no little girl in a big town; she was a big girl from a big town comin' to make good in a little town.

She spoke her mind from the minute she stepped off the train. From the *Hollywood Citizen-News* in 1932: "Elsa Maxwell, world's most famous party thrower, says our Hollywood variety of party is plain dull." The columnist quoted Elsa at length on the wrongs of entertaining à la Hollywood. Nor did Elsa hide her boredom at a failed Hollywood soiree. The same paper, a week later: "Fifty or so guests at the Lionel Atwill home the other evening waited in vain for an introduction to the guest of honor, Elsa Maxwell. While the guests were left to their own devices, Miss Maxwell sat off in a secluded corner in rapt conversation with Lilyan Tashman. She did not play or sing, neither did she deliver any of the pungent epigrams for which she is noted. The celebrities at that party still are wondering how Miss Maxwell became famous as a hostess. And the Atwills are still making apologies." (Tashman was a big star in her day. When she died in 1934 at age thirty-eight, ten thousand people filled the streets around the Brooklyn cemetery where she was interred.)

Elsa hated the shop talk that dominated Hollywood parties, so she made sure that box office receipts in Omaha would never be discussed where she was hostess. Since actors crave attention always, Elsa asked the stars to perform at her gatherings. According to her, it struck everyone as a revolutionary innovation. "I made the piano, not the bar, the center of activity," she said. One night, to launch the Elsa Maxwell party brand in this new territory, she invited about twenty people to a small house she had rented in Beverly Hills. Among them: Noël Coward, who needed no coaxing. He strolled to the piano and sang one of his latest songs. Next, Marlene Dietrich did "Die Fesche Lola" from *The Blue Angel*. By now, everyone had caught the excitement, and Douglas Fairbanks Jr. did a satirical imitation of Hitler, who, in the early thirties, seemed as much farce as menace. Fanny Brice revived a comic skit from the *Ziegfeld Follies*, and a very young girl from Texas who had a date with someone on the guest list stood up and sang a tune. When asked her name, she said, "Mary Martin."

For Elsa, the road to Hollywood began in Italy. The unlikely instigators of her journey were Gary Cooper and his paramour in 1931, Countess Dorothy di Frasso (née Taylor, from Watertown, New York). In the spring of that year, Cooper was visiting Europe by himself. Although he was handsome, and already a leading man in pictures, he felt lonely and out of place on this continent so different from his own. One day, he received a letter from Walter Wanger in Hollywood. Inside was the telephone number of the Villa Madama, near Rome, the home of Count and Countess di Frasso.

Elsa and Dorothy were old friends, in spite of the occasional hair pulling. Although Elsa had not met Gary Cooper, she had seen him a year or so earlier in *The Virginian*. Elsa filled in the blanks for Dorothy: born on a ranch in Montana; his father was a judge . . . but Dorothy wanted to know what he looked like.

"Oh," replied Elsa with studied conviction, "he's a most unprepossessing fellow. Very short. Very plain."

When Gary Cooper entered the Villa, Dorothy laughed. Then she turned and hissed, "Elsa Maxwell, you rat! I should never believe you."

The honeymoon was on, for Dorothy and the count had a conveniently open marriage. Both were happy in it, for she, as a "dollar princess," had the coveted title, and he a happy share in her twelve million American bucks. Soon a party was under way. Barbara Hutton came, and so did the crown prince of Italy, Prince Umberto; the Duke of York (soon to become King George VI); and dozens of others from royalty and society. Already Princess Dorothy had begun polishing this big rough-cut Cooper jewel. She taught him to dress in the latest, most masculine style, and paid for his wardrobe. Soon, under her tutelage, he could read a menu in French, Italian, or German, and order the proper wine. She took him to museums all over Italy. (Cooper was not as rustic as he often appeared onscreen. He had spent several years in England as a child, and his parents had taught him savoir faire.)

Eventually, Cooper was summoned back to Hollywood for picture work. On a subsequent trip to Europe, he and Dorothy resumed their romance, and in 1932 she returned to America with him. In New York, they dined with Elsa at the Waldorf-Astoria, where she had taken up residence. Along with Dorothy and Gary, Elsa invited David O. Selznick, George Cukor, and Constance Bennett. The latter three would soon leave for Hollywood to film *Our Betters* at RKO, based on a play by W. Somerset Maugham.

As recounted in *The Gary Cooper Story* by George Carpozi Jr., the five were seated in the Sert Room when Dorothy said, "Elsa, why don't you come to Hollywood?"

"Coop reacted enthusiastically. 'Yes, Elsa, why don't you?' he said.

"'Oh, come on, Elsa,' said the countess, 'and you can stay at Gary's place.'

"'I'd love to come,' Miss Maxwell put in, 'but I have to work for a living.'

"'Well, get a job out there—you know a lot of people in Hollywood,' Dorothy persisted.

"Constance Bennett, who was to star in *Our Betters*, turned to Selznick and said, 'David, why don't you engage Elsa in some advisory capacity on the picture?'

"'A wonderful idea,' Selznick replied. 'Would you do it for $500 a week?' "

That amount, of course, came to more than many workers made in a bleak year during the Depression. Since Elsa had never been to Hollywood, Selznick's offer meant a dream vacation among *names*. And vacation it would be, for Elsa knew at once that what Selznick wanted could be done in her sleep.

In the credits, Elsa's name appears as "technical advisor." Her job: informing writers, producer, director, and actors how a duchess would be announced; selecting the proper china and cutlery for upper-class British tables; advising on costumes, jewelry, accents, and manners; and perhaps delineating the difference in body language between American heiresses (played by Constance Bennett and Anita Louise) and the titled British aristocrats they are out to snare.

Dorothy volunteered Gary Cooper's house (rented from Garbo) as Elsa's Hollywood pied-à-terre. Some believed that Elsa was put there to keep tabs on Gary; others joked that the pair were "living in sin." (Two characters in Clare Boothe Luce's *The Women*—the Countess de Lave and her rustic cowboy, Buck—are said to be based on Dorothy di Frasso and Gary Cooper.)

"During my stay," Elsa said, "I met a galaxy of stars—Clark Gable, Carole Lombard, Bob Hope, Cary Grant, Helen Hayes, Fredric March, and many others. Gary, who was a silent, rather inarticulate man, under Dorothy's tutelage became a great host. Dorothy would come every morning to have breakfast with us. That she adored the handsome Cooper was evident." A year later, however, Elsa was a guest at the wedding in New York of Gary Cooper and Veronica Balfe ("Rocky"), his only wife.

Meanwhile, Elsa appeared in the columns as often as many top stars: "Elsa Maxwell, guest of honor at a bridge luncheon given by Mrs. Lionel Barrymore today . . . Elsa Maxwell has taken Hollywood in hand in a very brief time. Between appearances on the RKO lot, she has managed to engineer quite a few parties. A local cafe seems to be her luncheon headquarters, and she generally has a telephone served with her meal." These accounts suggest that Elsa had taken up permanent residence in Hollywood, but such was not the case. Although the 1930s might be thought of as Elsa's movie decade, she was just as active in her other venues during that period.

A montage of her travels: New York in November 1932; a ball at the Waldorf-Astoria in '33; on board the Italian liner *Rex* from France to New York, 1934; sails for the Riviera, spring of 1935; December '36, party at the Waldorf; several crossings in 1937 and 1938; in Hollywood, 1938; in Europe, 1939; leaves France just before the German invasion, September 1939. Dickie sometimes accompanies her, but as often not. Elsa was in and out of Hollywood at least once a year, and always in the local news. It wasn't true, even in that town, that she was only as good as her latest party.

On August 10, 1935, Laura Maxwell died in her home in Los Angeles, where she had lived since the 1920s. The address on her death certificate is 6222 Banner Avenue, a street not far from Paramount Pictures. A few days later, the *San Francisco Chronicle* ran a brief item, MISS ELSA MAXWELL'S MOTHER DIES IN L.A. The three sentences in the item are devoted to Elsa, not to her mother. Laura's name is not even given. The paper reported that "Miss Maxwell is at present traveling in Europe with Mrs. William Randolph Hearst." Elsa's long estrangement from her mother seems never to have ended, for nowhere in Elsa's Hollywood publicity, from her arrival in 1932 up to Laura's death, is there a mention of her mother. If Laura Maxwell had attended one of her daughter's parties, or even a luncheon, it would have made the news. (True, Elsa had a rule against family members at parties: "Believe me, nobody wants to meet your relatives." But minus great disharmony, Elsa and Laura would surely have been spotted at lunch, or attending a concert at the Hollywood Bowl.)

One recalls, unfairly or not, the socialite daughters of Balzac's *Père Goriot*: the old man has bankrupted himself to launch these girls into the Parisian beau monde. When he dies, they are too busy to attend the funeral. Instead they send paid mourners.

Here I include an anecdote from Hedda Hopper that portrays Elsa very badly. If Hedda were the only source, I would omit it, but a slightly different version involves Cole Porter. In *The Whole Truth and Nothing But*, published in 1963, Hedda includes several catty stories about Elsa, but this one is the most disturbing: "Four of Elsa's friends once sat together at luncheon in the Beverly Hills Hotel. Each came from a different city, and each was well up in society. One woman steered the conversation to the subject of their common friend: 'I felt desperately sorry for her when Elsa's mother died in Los Angeles. She sent me a cable from Paris, saying she hadn't a bean and would I cable $3000 so she could bury her mother. Of course, I was happy to.'

"The woman across the table broke in. 'But I had the same kind of cable, and I sent the money. It was I who buried Elsa's mother.'

"The third woman could scarcely believe her ears. 'But I mailed Elsa a check for the same purpose.'

"The fourth of them, who lived in San Francisco, said quietly: 'You are all mistaken. My husband knew Elsa and her mother well. He had several cables from Elsa like that over the years. Finally, she convinced him she was telling the truth one day, but he went down to Los Angeles to make certain. Sure enough, her mother had died. My husband took care of the funeral.' "

George Eells, in *The Life That Late He Led*, wrote of the time that Elsa cabled Cole Porter from France "asking for $5000, saying that her mother was ill. Cole sent it promptly. Shortly after, Lady Mendl arrived in New York and announced that Elsa had asked *her* for $5000 for her sick mother. When Cole said he'd sent Elsa a like amount, Lady Mendl was outraged. Cole simply laughed."

Not only was Elsa a tireless gadfly; the studios frequently tried to put her to work. From the *Los Angeles Times*, 1935: "Elsa Maxwell, the world's most famous party arranger, has been tested by MGM as a possible substitute for the late Marie Dressler." A letter from Elsa's friend, Voldemar Vetluguin, editor of *Redbook*, to the literary agent H. N. Swanson in 1938: "You are not the first man to conceive the idea of hiring Maxwell for a picture. Several producers were after her before, and are now. George Cukor wanted her to play a character bit in a Garbo picture, and Selznick, when last in New York, was having serious conversations with her about different parts he had in mind. The same thing goes for Walter Wanger and Sam Goldwyn." In 1939, Ed Sullivan's column: "Elsa Maxwell, who turned down Paramount's $10,000 offer to come to the Coast, is here doing the tricks for nothing."

In Hollywood, for the first time in her career, Elsa was guest of honor as often as hostess. In 1939, a headline in the *Hollywood Citizen-News*: CELEB-

RITIES TO HONOR ELSA MAXWELL AT PARTIES. The first one, given by Mrs. Edith Wilkerson, whose husband founded *The Hollywood Reporter*, was "a midnight supper for Miss Maxwell in the Louis XVI room at the Trocadero." Next, "the Countess Dorothy di Frasso will be hostess at her Beverly Hills home Friday evening at a red and white ball in honor of the New York visitor, while Mr. and Mrs. Basil Rathbone entertained Miss Maxwell at a dinner party Saturday night at their Los Feliz home." (The guest lists for these events read like a Who's Who of Hollywood for the 1930s—and forever. They include Charles Boyer, Leslie Howard, Marlene Dietrich, Fred Astaire, Irving Thalberg, Darryl Zanuck, Myrna Loy, and dozens more.)

Again in 1939, ELSA MAXWELL, PARTY-GIVER, HONOREE AT TWO GATHERINGS (these given by Constance Bennett, and by Mr. and Mrs. Douglas Fairbanks Sr.). Later the same year, Louella Parsons in the *Los Angeles Examiner*: "What a party the Darryl Zanucks gave Elsa Maxwell, who is my fellow Hearst writer since her interesting articles on Barbara Hutton appeared in *Cosmopolitan Magazine*. Fifty people sat down to dinner—among them all of Elsa's good friends, James Roosevelt, house guest of the Samuel Goldwyns; Tyrone Power, with Annabella; the Henry Fondas; Marlene Dietrich, looking like a picture; Claudette Colbert, Dolores del Rio. . . . Elsa is here for a lecture Wednesday night and all the movie crowd will be on hand, for she is one of the most interesting women in America." (Hedda Hopper, of course, would beg to differ. If Louella liked Elsa, then Hedda must not.)

H. N. Swanson was interested in Elsa as writer, not actor. Though he never became her agent, she was soon writing for *Photoplay* and other fan magazines. She continued to do so up through the 1950s. As if all that were not enough, in 1934 she tried her hand at screenwriting. At the Motion Picture Academy's Margaret Herrick Library, the draft of a script by Elsa for a film to be called *Murieta* (rewritten, and released in 1936 as *The Robin Hood of El Dorado*) fades in on the hacienda of President Antonio López de Santa Anna in Mexico early in 1849. Next, a medium shot of Joaquin Murieta, a handsome young vaquero. The camera pans to Murieta with Clarina Valero, a young girl who cherishes a secret passion for him.

Joaquin: "Why, Clarina, what are you doing here?"

Clarina takes a ring from her finger, holds it out tremulously, and says: "Wear this, so no harm will come to you."

Slightly embarrassed, he puts it on. Cut to a huge snake about to strike. Joaquin, of course, kills the snake . . . and the highly predictable situations and dialogue crawl along to Joaquin's fragrant final line: "I will write my name in blood over *all* California."

"I became a movie actress at the age of fifty-five," Elsa said. It was Darryl Zanuck who "discovered" her. Zanuck's biographers do not record their first encounter, but according to Elsa she and the head of 20th Century-Fox met at a party. He told her, "You have a warm personality that will project well on the screen. How about making a picture for me?" His line, well-worn from use on starlets, in this instance absolves Zanuck of all the -isms: age-, sex-, and looks-. He meant it, and Elsa made her beachhead on the shores of cinema history in 1939 with *Elsa Maxwell's Hotel for Women*, which was also Linda Darnell's debut picture. Ann Sothern received top billing, and Gregory Ratoff, Zanuck's shaggy-dog sidekick, directed. The story idea came from Elsa, who also composed a song used in the picture.

Marcia Bromley, played by Darnell, arrives at the Sherrington, a New York hotel for women only. She has come from Syracuse to marry her boyfriend, who promptly jilts her. With no man of her own, she becomes a model, like several of the other young women in the hotel, and—well, the story is a hybrid of *Grand Hotel* and *Stage Door*, so you can figure it out. In Elsa's first scene, she is bending over to retrieve something she has dropped. Given her girth, this is no easy task. Linda Darnell comes along, picks the object up, and they are best friends forever.

Elsa camera shy? Making her first film, nerves belied her sangfroid. Reports of uncertainty drifted out of the studio, although, as always, when courage failed, she used bravado as its stand-in. After a particularly difficult scene, Elsa took a deep breath, strode to her mark, the camera rolled, and the director shouted, "Great!" Another take; "Colossal!" Quaking before his compliments, preparing for the third take and disgrace, Elsa shivered. She played it well, and— "A miracle!" said Ratoff. Relieved, Elsa retorted, "You know, I ought to be insulted by that compliment, but I'm not. I consider it a miracle myself."

Playing herself in the picture, Elsa is something of a Park Avenue Ma

Kettle: with all the savoir faire in the world, she's still a California gal almost as old as the Gold Rush. She has more screen presence than many a seasoned pro, a quality that helps obscure the lame plot and flabby direction. In fact, you miss Elsa when she's offscreen. *Variety* called it "a picture of exceptional charm and vivid entertainment qualities . . . which will fascinate women audiences down to the remotest hamlet." *The Hollywood Reporter* raved over picture and performers.

Elsa herself was a harsher critic of her talent than those in the trade: "The first feature wasn't too bad. My next vehicle proved the soundness of the old gambling dictum, 'Quit when you're ahead.'" She was referring to *Public Deb No. 1*, which she blithely called "a real flop. . . . The only sop to my aesthetic sensibility is that I did not work on the script. It was a moot question whether anyone did. The story began as a travesty on social climbers and, in some inexplicable manner, ended with a scene showing a dog raising its leg on a copy of Karl Marx's *Das Kapital*."

Released in 1940, it's of interest today because we know that a decade later even a satire on communism would have risked McCarthyite repercussions. Directed by Gregory Ratoff, an ex-Russian, the picture opens with Penny Cooper (played by Brenda Joyce), heiress to the Cooper Soup fortune, arrested for leading a parade of the proletariat through Union Square in New York and thereby disturbing the peace. The resulting publicity causes soup sales to plummet, and Elsa Maxwell is approached to write testimonials for the soup, a PR job that she turns down. Nevertheless, Elsa is soon in the thick of it. She throws an Americana party on Penny's Long Island estate, a set piece that turns out to be the best thing in the picture. Guests come dressed as famous persons in American history, with Elsa as Ben Franklin and Penny herself as Pocahontas. There's an Uncle Sam, a roomful of Abraham Lincolns, Annie Oakley, Betsy Ross, Wild Bill Hickock, and so on. Others in the cast are George Murphy (later elected as a U.S. senator from California), Ralph Bellamy, Charles Ruggles, Franklin Pangborn, and the boxer Maxie Rosenbloom.

When the picture was screened in 1980 at the New School in New York, film historian William K. Everson wrote in the program notes that *Public Deb No. 1* is "a perfect example of how minor movies can record, reflect, and capture the essence of their time. . . . This film achieves some historical importance as a preserved time capsule of Hollywood's self-imposed anti-Communist crusade. The whole ebb-and-flow of Hollywood's attitude towards Russia and Communism (which it never understood, other than knowing it disapproved of it) is a fascinating one. . . . *Public Deb No. 1* is from that uneasy period at the beginning of the War when America was still neutral, and since Hollywood still wasn't supposed to be anti-Nazi, the Communists were fair game and fashionable besides. (And offending Russians didn't pose much of a threat to Hollywood income, which collected but little from the U.S.S.R. anyway.) The ploy at this particular time was to expose Communism as a sham and a racket, and to show that if people of integrity were lured into it, then it was only a matter of time before they realized that they had been tricked and duped. There was never any allowing for the possibility that Communist ranks might include philosophers and statesmen of genuine integrity and idealism." Proving Everson's point, by the end of *Public Deb* Penny renounces communism, realizing she has been tricked and duped.

Real actors in Elsa's position—hired for personal reasons by the studio head, cast in a moderate success and a flop in rapid succession—might find themselves on the street. Elsa, however, merely moved to Warner Bros. There she made three short films that played in theatres before and after main features. Released in 1940 and 1941, these shorts were *Riding Into Society* (based on her long-ago fox hunt in England; here Elsa kills her fox by falling on it); *The Lady and the Lug* (she trains to be a prizefighter with former co-star Maxie Rosenbloom); and *Throwing a Party* (an obvious title). George Reeves, the future Superman, appeared with Elsa in the latter two. She claimed to have earned a total of eighty thousand dollars for these five films.

Elsa had met and befriended Jack Warner and his wife, Ann, in the mid-thirties on the Riviera. Ann Warner, a Hollywood hostess bedazzled by Elsa's triumphs, may well have engineered Elsa's career at Warner Bros. Jack Warner seemed not to mind his wife's manipulation. In his 1965 autobiography, *My First Hundred Years in Hollywood*, he portrays Elsa as a rogue on a par with himself.

"There is a photograph of Miss Elsa Maxwell," he writes, "on my Trophy Room wall which must have been taken with a wide-angle lens because it shows all of her. It is inscribed 'To the dearest boss I ever had.' By 'dearest' she meant about four grand." Elsa and Jack Warner gambled together in Monte Carlo and elsewhere. He claimed she always gave bad advice while looking over his shoulder. She was also a frequent money borrower who prefaced her long-faced requests with "Jack, my dear, I need a favor in the worst way."

Writing two years after Elsa's death, Warner mentioned an unpaid loan of twenty-five hundred dollars that she "took with her." But, he went on, "I really don't mind. Because wherever she went there's going to be action, and she'll spread that cash around with happiness. She was a warm, gay soul, and for many people she made life worth living."

MOVIE STARS AND PAPER PLATES

Joan Fontaine recalls a party that Elsa gave in Hollywood, this one at the home of Evalyn Walsh McLean in the early 1940s: "War had started, no one could get servants, and there were shortages. Elsa gave a dinner party, and she passed out paper plates and boxes of crayons. We made our own dinnerware, and then ate from it. Elsa gave a prize for the best design, but I can't remember who won. I made a floral design on my plate."

At another dinner—this one a cooking party at Romanoff's—Elsa assembled a group of ten stars, each one reputed to be a good cook. On a long table at the restaurant, a variety of foods were spread along with the necessary equipment. "When the guests arrived," Elsa recalled, "they were ushered to one of the chafing dishes, equipped with aprons and chefs' caps, and told to cook whatever they liked." There was a risk factor: the products of those chafing dishes would be dinner for the entire party. According to Elsa, all but one of the dishes turned out superb. She tactfully omitted the name of the failed cook. Clark Gable won the prize, with Ronald Coleman a close second. Joan Fontaine, whom Elsa called "absolute tops" as a hostess, and Claudette Colbert were standouts in the women's division.

These fun times notwithstanding, Joan Fontaine describes Elsa as "dangerous" and "someone to be wary of, because she could easily smash you. But above all, she was a character." Whatever Fontaine's wariness, she often socialized with Elsa.

After Warner Bros., Elsa's screen career was over, though she did appear in *Stage Door Canteen* (1943), a wartime revue with sixty-five guest stars. Each one is onscreen for a couple of minutes, and everyone seems to enjoy his or her cameo immensely. Just a few of the big names: Tallulah Bankhead, Katharine Hepburn, Gypsy Rose Lee, Harpo Marx, and Johnny Weissmuller.

A. C. Lyles, a veteran producer at Paramount, met Elsa during her employment at Fox. "Sometimes," he said, "she was like a slow-motion rose opening up, that sweetness she had. Then, other times, she was a cannon going off. She would rush up and say, 'My darling, do you know who I just had lunch with?'" Lyles, a member of Paramount's publicity department at the time, recalls introducing Elsa to Bing Crosby, Claudette Colbert, Joel McCrea, and Don Ameche. According to him, when the introductions were over, Elsa sized up the Paramount lot and said, "Now when this picture's finished, why don't we all have a big party here?"

Kitty Carlisle Hart, who, with her husband, Moss Hart, was a house guest of the Zanucks in Palm Springs in the late forties when Elsa was also visiting, added a jarring note to the Maxwell symphony. "She was very untidy. That was something that sort of upset me. She had spots all over her dress." In spite of the untidiness, she added, "Elsa was absolutely charming. She had enormous vitality, and that's very attractive. The first time I ever went out with George Gershwin was a big fancy party that Elsa gave at the Sherry Netherland. At the party, George played the piano and I sang—one of his songs, of course."

23 Upstaged by Her Own Underwear

$\mathcal{H}$arold Arlen and Johnny Mercer weren't thinking of Elsa when they wrote "Any Place I Hang My Hat Is Home," but they might have been. The Waldorf-Astoria, where Elsa came to roost in 1931, served as her most nearly permanent domicile over the next thirty years. Her other home—more accurately, her stopping-off place—was a farm that Dickie bought in 1933 at Auribeau, near Cannes. Anyone attempting to catalogue the hundreds of hotels, chateaux, villas, estates, horse farms, suites, and staterooms that Elsa occupied would compile a thick directory indeed.

MY FARM IN THE SOUTH OF FRANCE

$\mathbf{I}$n *R.S.V.P.*, a photo of Elsa, in farm clothes, plowing behind a donkey and a goat yoked together, with the caption "On my farm at Auribeau in southern France." Writing about the Duke and Duchess of Windsor, she mentions that in 1947, "a few days after I moved in with Dickie at her farmhouse in Auribeau, the duchess invited me to dinner at the Château de la Croë." In *Elsa Maxwell's Etiquette Book*, she describes a gift from the duchess—a large brown earthenware setting hen—"in the kitchen of my farm in southern France." And on and on, typically

Elsa: deploring ownership on one page, on the next the proud chatelaine.

If Provence had held its present cachet when Elsa was writing, she would surely have specified that region for its added chic. Dickie's farm was in fact a *mas*, similar to the one that Peter Mayle bought and wrote about in several bestselling books. When Dickie bought Le Sault (meaning "waterfall") from Lord Beaverbrook's daughter, it required much renovation. She described the main house, after remodeling, as having "a dining room, a drawing room, and upstairs two bedrooms, then my bedroom on the next floor, and three bathrooms. The kitchen was off the dining room. Like so many Provençal farmhouses, it had two staircases, and we took away one of them."

Elsa added that the property had a huge millstone converted into an outdoor table, although set so low on a pedestal that comfortable seating was not the norm. (A photograph shows Jack Warner, Tyrone Power, Darryl Zanuck, Elsa, the Duke of Windsor, Clark Gable, and several others with knees not quite fitted under the table.) Peter Mayle defines a *mas* as more substantial than a small farm; Dickie recalled hers as "a charming place, with a waterfall that made a lovely sound. Altogether, about thirty-two acres. I used to grow my own vegetables."

Lord Dudley (William Humble David Ward, fourth Earl of Dudley) recalls visits to Dickie's *mas* and also to Lou Paradou after Elsa took ambiguous possession of it from the Loders. As a youth in the thirties, he attended parties at both places and saw Elsa in Venice, as well. "She had a quick wit," he recalled. "Never drew breath, talked ninety to the dozen. I liked her and thought her fun. A bit grotesque, of course." When I asked him about Elsa's roller-coaster friendship with the Duke and Duchess of Windsor (the duke was Lord Dudley's godfather), he said, "They were regular visitors to Elsa's place. But I didn't keep up with the details of that friendship. Like all young people, I was too busy to think about my elders." I inquired whether he thought that his godfather, as Prince of Wales in the twenties, would have told Elsa on first meeting that he didn't want to be king. Lord Dudley's answer: "I don't think it's impossible."

Ward Morehouse III opens his book *The Waldorf-Astoria* with an evocative paragraph that suggests why Elsa loved the place. "At any time of day," he writes, "the bustle of comings and goings in the main reception lobby is graciously muted; the clatter of the New York streets outside softens as you pass through its gilded doors. Inside the thick walls, traffic horns, shouts, and squeals are lost behind you or somewhere in the air above, and your step slows in the thick carpet that leads to the vaulted central hall. Awaiting in the full city block bounded by Park Avenue to the west and Lexington to the east, Forty-ninth Street to the south and Fiftieth Street to the north, soaring forty-seven stories into the sky, is the world of the Waldorf-Astoria." And Elsa's rent was free, at least for a long time. She moved in the year the hotel opened because, she said, "Lucius Boomer, the president, made the offer thinking my presence might bring other more-desirable guests. Boomer was right; the Towers filled up with friends."

Credible enough, so far. But then: "In 1946, when I resumed my globe-trotting after the war, I became self-conscious tying up badly needed space and made a deal to pay the Waldorf $350 a month for a two-room suite, about one-third the regular rental." Alms for the landlord? Hardly. It's more likely that the management, enjoying the postwar boom, told her she must pay or vacate. No doubt Elsa got a deal, although three hundred and fifty dollars at that time was more than she could hold on to. Fortunately, Mrs. Donahue was nearby.

Among those Elsa lured to the Waldorf were Cole Porter, the Shah of Iran (she once claimed, no doubt to the shah's dismay, that he had let her sit on his Peacock Throne), the Duke and Duchess of Windsor, Marilyn Monroe, and the gangster Benjamin "Bugsy" Siegel. (Elsa did not advertise this underworld connection, but he was the lover of her close friend Dorothy di Frasso until his rubout in 1947. Dickie recalled playing poker with Bugsy until, as she calmly recalled, "They shot him dead one night, right in his own room.") Herbert Hoover, another neighbor, wasn't exactly a friend, though Elsa dressed convincingly as the former president for several masquerades.

A complicated network of gossip brought me this tidbit: according to a maid at the Waldorf during the thirties and forties who cleaned both Hoover's suite and Elsa's, the latter resembled a pigsty. But then, why have maid service if you leave nothing to be cleaned? (Elsa served as technical advisor on the 1945 MGM picture, *Weekend at the Waldorf.*)

Researching his book, Morehouse interviewed several Waldorf managers from Elsa's tenure. With one exception, their recollections are predictably mundane, the sort of statements one could make after reading a few of her columns. Then comes a lurid "revelation" from a source identified only as "a former hotel executive who knew her well."

This man told Morehouse that Elsa was "the Madame of the Waldorf. She would get anything you wanted, women for men, men for men, women for women." That's the only direct quote; the rest is a Morehouse paraphrase: "Her clients didn't indulge their pleasures in her suite, but she would run the operation there, as well as a weekly Sunday buffet for all her pimps. Each of the pimps would throw an unmarked envelope into an empty punch bowl. The envelopes contained sums ranging from $10 upwards to $60 or $70 depending how successful the week had been. But it was a bad night for the Waldorf employee who sometimes assisted her with the buffet—often tuna salad and other low price fare—when as his reward for his job he was permitted to pluck an envelope out of the bowl and it only contained a $10 bill."

Didn't *Confidential* print this first? Whatever the original source, it's preposterous. First of all, such amounts were petty cash to Elsa; those generous matrons, and the legions of friends she borrowed from, kept her in a higher style than meager amounts in envelopes could equal. Nor did Elsa have time for anything so picayune. Then, too, whatever her moral boundaries, Elsa had too much to lose—in court, and in the cruel tribunals of society—to risk any such scandalous, and illegal, enterprise. Finally, anyone looking for an escort service could call up Polly Adler or one of a hundred others in New York, where every taste was catered for. (It's possible that Elsa and friends might have played some naughty version of spin the bottle using a punch bowl and petty cash.) Dickie said that since both she and Elsa adored playing poker, they started a Sunday gambling day that went on for a couple of years. "She would charge ten dollars per person," Dickie recalled, "and for that they got as much food and drink as they wanted." But not a pound of flesh.

The Madame of the Waldorf rumor likely originated in Elsa's meddling, for, like Dolly Levi, she was "a woman who arranges things." Elsa's most famous match was Rita Hayworth and Aly Khan, whom she introduced to each other and who were married for four years. (Tales that Elsa played matchmaker to Grace Kelly and Prince Rainier for a fabulous sum have no basis in fact.) She did relish power and control, however, and Joan Fontaine cited Elsa's relentless matchmaking as one of the ways she was "dangerous," with this example: "After a luncheon with Aly Khan, I was in the car with Elsa back to Paris. 'You're not right for Aly,' she said, 'Aly isn't right for you.' What a friend! She already had us encarnalized. Now, I adored Aly, he was a wonderful friend, but if I had been concerned about our future, I would have had to kowtow to Elsa, send her flowers and champagne to bring her over to my side. Otherwise, she might have sabotaged the romance. Everyone knew to be wary of her."

For many, the decades slacken as age advances. Engagement books stay white, like an untouched snowfall. For Elsa, however, the pages were covered with tracks. As the twentieth century unscrolled, each ten-year allotment ballooned. A schedule that might flatten extreme extroverts caused Elsa no more palpitation than a cup of Sanka.

We know her party life. We know from many a culinary account her hours at table, for three square meals but also elevenses, tiffin, tea, coffee breaks—did she have so much as a bedtime snack without a duchess present? Plus the opera; the theatre; movies; gambling; even ball games—there's a picture of her at bat, with Lefty O'Doul as catcher. Focused on so much bonhomie, one might forget that Elsa was a working woman whose labors required extensive hours. She seems to have relished her jobs as newspaper columnist, radio and TV personality, lecturer, author, composer, actress, and self-appointed ambassador without portfolio for any government that struck her fancy. These duties, obviously, demanded energy, concentration, spunk, and Elsa's own brand of chutzpah. And Nietzschean strength verging on the superhuman. (Perhaps such energy wasn't all that rare before the couch-potato age. Clarence Darrow, Elsa's near contemporary, took part in some two thousand trials.)

Working in movies convinced Elsa that Hollywood was too small for her talents. In 1935, therefore, she made a Broadway "comeback": she had, after all, appeared there briefly with Marie Doro in 1909 in *The Richest Girl*. That play lasted for twenty-four performances; her next one, *De Luxe*, ran for fifteen. It opened in March 1935, and starred Melvyn Douglas. Set in Paris after World War I, the play was top-heavy with disillusion; one reviewer said the characters were "Hemingwayed across the stage." Another wrote of Elsa's performance that "she plays the part of a large, bossy lady who seems to bear a far from faint resemblance to Miss Maxwell herself, and to play it just as Miss Maxwell no doubt would. And, I must add, as all her friends in the audience evidently wanted to see her act it."

But Elsa onstage or in the movies could never surpass reality. She gave her only truly great performance as Elsa Maxwell.

That grandiose presentation of herself continued, even in correspondence. George Cukor, in Hollywood, received a letter from Elsa dated March 12, just before the play closed. "It seems I have made a great success as a comedian," she wrote. "I never expected to get real dramatic notices because, naturally, the critics are always resentful of that mythical thing called social position. However, I walked away with the dramatic notices of the play, which amused me no end. When you have a high comedy Marie Dressler part let me know and I will give you a surprise." She informed him that *De Luxe* was being rewritten and, when revised, "should pull us into a good run." That didn't happen. But Elsa, ever optimistic, closed her letter with "Don't forget that part. I could be a wow in the right part under your direction."

Next came *Who's Who*, produced by Elsa Maxwell (in cahoots with an anonymous moneybags). This revue, which ran for twenty-three performances in 1938, had a cast of some forty singers and musicians; the stand-out name today is Imogene Coca. Elsa herself did not appear onstage.

In 1940, the New York *Daily News* reported that Elsa was under consideration as replacement for the ailing Alexander Woollcott in the Los Angeles production of *The Man Who Came to Dinner*, a huge hit at the time. (Monty Woolley played the role on Broadway, Clifton Webb in Chicago.) Had this whimsical switch come to pass, the producers were prepared to modify the title to *The Gal Who Came to Dinner* or *The Lady Who. . . .* Part of the promo was to be "That's no lady, that's Elsa Maxwell!" It didn't happen, but Elsa's consolation prize was a part in a one-act Noël Coward play at an obscure theatre in Hollywood. Anita Loos, with whom Elsa and Dickie were staying, dutifully attended. "I doubt that Noël would have survived it," she jotted in her diary.

THE ELSA WHO CAME TO DINNER

Although Sheridan Whiteside, the irrespressible man who came to dinner, is based on Alexander Woollcott, of the Algonquin Round Table, one could make the case that George S. Kaufman and Moss Hart also had Elsa in mind when they wrote the play. Whiteside's exuberant opportunism, his compulsive name dropping, unyielding manipulation, self-interested matchmaking, his roomfuls of presents from the world's celebrities—well, we know who fits that description perhaps better than Woollcott. She's even mentioned in the film version, though not in the play. When Lorraine Sheldon (played by Ann Sheridan) arrives from Palm Beach to visit Sheridan Whiteside, she tells him: "Elsa Maxwell gave me a message for you. She wants you to take off twenty-five pounds right away and send them to her. She needs them."

In 1941, Elsa played the Duchess de Surennes in Maugham's *Our Betters* at the Theatre-by-the-Sea in Matunuck, Rhode Island, and in several other venues on the summer theatre circuit. In *The Celebrity Circus*, she recounts an onstage mishap: "In the first act I had to wear a ball dress, with a long white petticoat underneath." Between the first and second acts, Elsa was required to make a quick costume change onstage. There was a blackout, during which she made the successful change in the dark. She left the stage, the lights came up and it was the following day, and Elsa made her act two entrance wearing a tweed hunting suit with a short skirt.

Only one thing went wrong: hanging to the floor under the smart tweed was a redundant petticoat that Elsa had forgotten to remove. "The audience yelled!" she said. "I thought to myself, I'm the greatest actress. I walked around, waiting for them to quiet down. I picked up the gun, pretended to examine it, did this and that. By that time they were screaming, rolling in the aisles, and still I didn't know why." When she told this story to hilarious response on *The Jack Paar Show* in the late fifties, Paar added to the merriment with "You were upstaged by your own underwear."

"She played the whole damn scene just like that," Marguerite Lewis told me, laughing, six decades later, for at the time of the play she was a twenty-year-old assistant stage manager in love with the theatre and breaking in via summer stock. "Maggie" Lewis grew very fond of both Elsa and Dickie, and relished her time with them.

"Surprisingly," she said, "Elsa was highly nervous about forgetting her lines. She knew that she had been booked because she was a celebrity, not because she was an artist, and I think that made her uncomfortable." In her nervousness, Elsa insisted that Maggie stay on one side of the stage as prompter in case she forgot a line, and Dickie on the other side, also with full script.

When Maggie got a tiny part in the play as a street vendor, Dickie taught her to do a genuine Cockney street cry. "And she was a darling," Maggie recalled. "Dickie was distinguished, elegant, and witty. Tall, probably about five feet eight, a handsome, imposing figure with white curly hair. Her head looked like it came off a coin. Dickie giggled about Elsa's nerves. I don't mean as a figure of fun, but in a loving way. Dickie's attitude was 'Well, indulge the dear.'"

Although Maggie and Dickie had to creep under stage-set windows, or climb over backstage contraptions with their scripts in case Elsa lapsed— "We never had to throw her a line. That tells a lot about Elsa and why she was such a successful hostess. She planned everything, she covered every contingency."

Several of the youngsters, including Maggie, resented Elsa before she arrived because she was not of the theatre; it seemed merely a summer pastime. "But as we got to know her, we fell in love with her," Maggie said. "Why? For one thing, she was totally democratic. She gave us kids as much attention as she gave a crowned head. I call that generosity of spirit. Then, too, I can say from my heart that she was a musical genius. The theatre was connected to an inn, and in the lounge of the inn was an old upright piano.

Elsa would sit down at that piano, disregarding the condition of the instrument, and she would play Cole Porter, one tune after another, or whatever anyone asked for. Once, my roommate, who was a devotee of classical music, said, 'Can you play the theme from Borodin's Fourth?' And *boom*! Elsa went right into it."

Determined to explore the far reaches of show business, Elsa—star already of stage, screen, radio—made her nightclub debut in 1935 at the Versailles on East Fiftieth Street in New York. Every night, she came on in a different chinchilla coat—each one borrowed from an intimate friend. Her costar was comedian George Jessel. A columnist in the *New York Evening Journal* claimed that "there hasn't been an opening like this in years and it stamps the Maxwell woman as the biggest night club draw in recent years—and Jessel as the greatest floor entertainer." Society turned out: Vanderbilts, the Grand Duchess Marie, Mrs. Jessie Donahue (proprietress of the opening-night chinchilla), and so did Broadway and Hollywood, represented by Ethel Merman, George Burns and Gracie Allen, Fanny Brice, Cole Porter, and Harpo Marx. The *New York Evening Post* predicted a lucrative run, "for last night they were still arriving from other clubs at 3 o'clock."

In 1943, she returned to the Versailles. This time, she sang a song or two, told a few jokes, and played games with the audience. She told an interviewer that her nightclub stint was like giving a party because her songs and jokes broke the ice, then she enhanced the party mood with a simple game in which she asked her audience of "guests" which animal they would like to be and why. The one with the quickest, cleverest answer won a war bond, a pound of rationed coffee, or perfume.

A couple of winning answers: "A snake, because it would then be easier to make both ends meet."

"A giraffe, so I could do more necking."

Although Elsa's performances stood out as events, even a nightclub visit turned into something of an occasion. In their book *"21": Every Day Was New Year's Eve*, Peter Kriendler and Paul Jeffers wrote that "when Elsa came to '21' she occupied table 3, which not only gave her a commanding view of who came in and left, but put her in a position to be seen by them."

During World War II, according to the authors, Elsa helped bolster the morale of patrons in the armed forces by sending them "copies of current menus and notes filled with gossip so the men wouldn't feel they were missing something."

These nightclubs, and others, glittered as the "in" places of New York in the thirties and forties, like Studio 54 in the seventies and eighties. Near the top of any nightclub A-list was the Stork Club, ground zero of cafe society. Walter Winchell called it "the New Yorkiest place in town." Beneath the surface glamour, however, it was governed by a code of behavior as rigid as the court of Turandot. (No Commies allowed! Table-hopping verboten!) Sherman Billingsley, its owner, was a big-time bootlegger in his native state, Oklahoma. He brought to New York the prejudices of home; these blended well with local bigotries, especially racism. Black celebrities like Josephine Baker, who actually made it into the Stork Club—others didn't get past the door—were treated with icy disdain, especially if accompanied by a white escort.

George Jessel, however, was as tough as Billingsley. When Jessel took Lena Horne to the Stork Club, they were seated at a preferred table owing to Jessel's cachet. Billingsley approached the table and asked, with the faux charm of a televangelist, "Who made your reservation?"

Jessel replied: "Abraham Lincoln!"

I haven't found Elsa's name among frequenters of the Stork Club, though it's hard to believe she would boycott such a definitive spot. When *The Stork Club*, a fifteen-minute TV show, debuted in 1950, Elsa was an early guest. (The show ran for five years, with Yul Brynner as director in its first two seasons. It was broadcast live from a specially designed permanent set at the club itself.) But though this format would seem tailor-made for Elsa, she lacked the rapport with Billingsley that she later had with Jack Paar and other television hosts.

Those who missed Elsa's parties, movies, plays, and nightclub shows could just turn on the radio. She was ubiquitous on the air. Reviewing *Elsa Maxwell's Party Line* in 1936, *Variety* offered a précis of the form that most of her shows took. "Speaks well and her script was clear, crisp, and saucy. She rattled on about how to keep bored people from being bored, and laid down some common sense rules. Then she veered into the Baron Rothschild of Austria and desribed the estate where the Duke of Windsor is now in exile."

Her broadcasts typically originated at her bedside in the Waldorf. According to a 1946 *New Yorker* "Talk of the Town" piece, this was because she felt lethargic before noon and also because her listeners expected "a stylish gadabout to remain supine till all hours of the day." The year before, *Life* ran a photo of her in bed, swaddled in a bathrobe, a tea tray on her lap and a script in her hand, as technicians adjusted microphones as though tweaking the crown of a dowager empress.

Although the exact history of her radio show is difficult to pin down, it ran from 1932 to 1946, with many gaps; for instance, she seems to have been off the air from 1939 to 1942. During all these years, she appeared as guest on any number of programs, including Rudy Vallee's variety show and *Duffy's Tavern*. For all of these she was well paid; a contract for a half hour on *Club Raleigh* in 1944 stipulates a fee of four hundred and fifty dollars. Elsa was often hired for radio commercials and print ads. Here she is, pictured in a 1952 women's magazine with the assurance that "Entertaining Is Easy with a Cook-a-Matic, says Elsa Maxwell, Internationally Famous Hostess." For snob appeal, two recipes were added: *crevettes au champignon* and *friandise grillée*.

Lectures were the equivalent of talk shows in the nineteenth century and, indeed, up to the advent of actual talk shows. Charles Dickens and Oscar Wilde were the Johnny Carson and David Letterman of their day; and, since they had plenty to say, they had no need of guests. By the middle of the twentieth century, according to Tallulah Bankhead in her autobiography, "Everyone of note took to the platform. Authors, polar explorers, Elsa Maxwell, war correspondents, Salvador Dalí, basket weavers, big game hunters, paroled prisoners, and reformed murderers all had a fling at it"— including Tallulah herself.

Many of these events were not dramatically different from the wearisome school assembly programs we were herded to before TV monitors invaded the classroom. Elsa's lectures, though lively and audience-pleasing, sound as memorable as, say, the stump speech of a local politician. But her listeners loved her. In 1939, the *Oakland Tribune* announced Elsa's lecture at the Oakland Auditorium on the topic "Today Society Is Different." More titillating, perhaps, than Elsa's subject was the one proposed by the newspaper: "A more popular subject in Oakland would be 'Do You Remember,' for there are ever so many men and women here who used to know Miss Maxwell when she was 'Elsie' of Belvedere Island. The adventures into which she led most of the youngsters made lasting impressions and they are still discussing the episode of the stolen milk wagon, the time the freight cars were released at Tiburon, and similar escapades which gave the young Maxwell experience in carrying out her philosophy of Let's Have Fun."

Among her venues in the 1940s: New York, Detroit, Houston, Wichita, St. Louis, Des Moines, Knoxville, and a dozen other cities. Her topics: "Social Changes and the War," "Where's Your Sense of Humor?" "Intimate Personality Sketches of Men Behind the War," and "The Ultimate Place of Sports in the War." Elsa's fees were around five hundred dollars per lecture. "Miss Maxwell's program was the biggest success that the Saint Louis Woman's Club has ever had," said Mrs. Henry S. Butler, president. When asked, in Cincinnati, how members might pep up the Woman's Club there, Elsa quipped, "Give a stag party."

The lecture circuit, though lucrative, stimulated Elsa less than her more colorful endeavors. Faced with bleak boredom, however, she could trick her audience—and herself—into hilarity. In Cleveland in the early forties, she said, "I was confronted with the prospect of giving what was advertised as a bright, sophisticated lecture to several hundred clubwomen in the auditorium of a department store at eleven o'clock in the morning." Faced with nothing new or amusing to say, and apprised of resentment owing to overpriced tickets, Elsa turned the Cleveland morning into Mardi Gras. She rushed out and bought all the paper mustaches she could find, which ushers handed out as the ladies entered. ("The mustaches were accepted as though they were dead mice," Elsa recalled.) Finally, however, one lady hooked the contraption to her nose, provoking titters all around. Other ladies followed suit, and soon the huge room was in an uproarious mood. When Elsa walked onstage, wearing the bushiest handlebars of all, she faced two hundred new friends who didn't care at all what she said, for already she had made their day. (A dozen of these ladies are pictured in *R.S.V.P.*, ready, except for mink coats and fine hats, for a gunfight at the O.K. Corral.)

24 When in Doubt, Give a Party

Elsa spent the war years in the United States, but first she had to get there. Since she remained in France until the eleventh hour, her homeward journey took on the shape of melodrama. When we left Elsa at Lou Paradou, she had just moved to the estate, supposedly at the insistence of her patroness, Eleanor Loder, and had thrown a housewarming party for two hundred on August 31, 1939. The following day Germany invaded Poland.

Elsa sent a telegram to Paris to her friend Paul Reynaud, the Minister of Finance. (In *R.S.V.P.*, she identifies him as prime minister; in fact, he did not assume that office until 1940.) In answer to her request for advice on the seriousness of the international situation, Reynaud replied: "*Allez-vous-en.*" (Leave.)

Elsa read the telegram to the crowd of friends who swarmed to her for what they knew might be their last happy time for . . . no one finished the thought. "Everyone was seething with conflicting rumors," she recalled. "My telegram from Reynaud was the most authoritative word anyone had, but it had been sent at noon and there might have been more recent developments in the crisis. I decided to call Joe Kennedy, the American Ambassador in England, for advice."

Elsa first met Joseph P. Kennedy in the mid-thirties. She pursued the Kennedy family, and while they accepted Elsa's overtures, they maintained a remote relationship, carefully nuanced. Elsa's bohemian ways and presumed lesbianism, her occasionally unflattering publicity, and her well-known liberalism did not complement Ambassador Kennedy's relentless—and conservative—political agenda for himself and his sons. On the other hand, Kennedy, like Joan Fontaine, knew Elsa to be "dangerous." He therefore played on her naïve neediness by attending the occasional Maxwell event, especially if it took place far from Boston—and Washington. For instance, her summer ball in 1938, on the Riviera. As a fringe benefit, his current lover, Marlene Dietrich, also showed up. With a quorum of young Kennedys headed to the ball, Marlene allowed her thirteen-year-old daughter, Maria Riva, to come along. From her, we have an arresting glimpse of Elsa's dual character. In her book, *Marlene Dietrich*, Riva recalls Elsa as "shrewd, coarse, an opportunist—and ruthless. But, once your friend, she never stabbed you in the back, never tried to hurt and had a sense of pity for the 'Followers' of this world of which she was one. She recognized my position [as an ill-at-ease adolescent eclipsed by dazzling Marlene]. I was taken to a lot of her parties. She always made sure I sat next to 'nice' people, who rarely asked me to tell them about my mother, even made sure my assigned table was far removed from my famous parent. Being ugly herself, she recognized the insecurities of those who knew they were unattractive in the midst of the beautiful and never forced me into the limelight. As I remember every single person who was ever kind to me, I remember that often maligned woman very well."

Elsa claimed no great intimacy with the Kennedys. She encountered Rose from time to time at important luncheons, and at one such Rose noticed that the zipper on Elsa's snug-fitting dress had jumped its track. Quietly, unobtrusively, she arranged Elsa's coat so that the Maxwell flesh was concealed from fashionable eyes. "Now, Elsa," Rose Kennedy admonished, "don't write something foolish about this in your column." And Elsa didn't. She saved it for *The Celebrity Circus*.

Late in life, when JFK was already in the White House, Elsa wrote that Jacqueline Kennedy "used to spend an occasional afternoon with me at my apartment in the Waldorf Towers when she was awaiting the birth of Caroline." That would have been in 1957, and Senator Kennedy, as he then was, may well have sent his wife to Elsa to insure favorable publicity. Knowing the Kennedy power (they, too, were "dangerous"), Elsa avoided grouping them with her closest friends. She even took pains to justify her phone call to the ambassador by explaining how, earlier in 1939, she had pulled strings at Kennedy's behest to help Arturo Toscanini leave Italy after he had antagonized Mussolini by refusing to play the Fascist anthem at a concert. "Kennedy owed me a favor," Elsa said.

"Where are you now?" the ambassador asked. When Elsa told him, he said, "I would leave if I were you. All Americans should go home immediately. The news is getting grimmer by the hour." Oddly, and uncharacteristically, Elsa omits her harrowing departure from France in her various writings, except for a few uncollected, hard-to-locate newspaper columns in 1939 and 1940.

The invasion of Poland naturally created widespread panic throughout Europe. In France, most foreign visitors, along with many resident aliens, sought to leave the country by any means possible. Although the German invasion did not take place until May 1940, it seemed likely that Hitler's eastern assault on Poland was a dress rehearsal for the conquest of western Europe. In that scenario, he had France in his crosshairs.

Elsa's close friend Grace Moore, the opera singer, remained calm in her villa near Cannes as those around her fell victim to galloping anxiety. After making phone calls to influential friends in Paris who advised her to close the villa and return to the United States, Grace phoned Elsa and other friends and urged them to spread the word. Meanwhile, Grace's husband, the Spanish actor Valentín Parera, packed their car for the drive north. He sent Grace on by train. When she arrived, she set about securing reservations for herself, her husband, Elsa, and several others on the SS *Manhattan*, which was to sail from Le Havre.

After a long delay that caused Grace unspeakable worry, her husband arrived. His difficulties on the road were typical: monstrous traffic jams, convoys of mobilized soldiers, long columns of mules and horses conscripted for the coming battles, even fierce late-summer thunderstorms. Other evacuees: the Duke and Duchess of Windsor, whose drive to northern France took four days; Norma Shearer and her current beau, George Raft, who hired a taxi across France from Antibes to Cherbourg, where they arrived late for the *Normandie* and were ferried out to the departing ship; Maria Riva, her father, and the novelist Erich Maria Remarque (another of Marlene's lovers) in two cars that kept breaking down. When they reached Paris, the Eiffel Tower was dark; Maria saw only its looming outline against the muffled sky.

Grace Moore, in her autobiography, *You're Only Human Once*, recalled that onboard the SS *Manhattan*, "Elsa slept expensively in the captain's bed, and the captain slept outside on a couch; Val and I made shift in rooms shared with others. Some had no rooms at all but bunked in the lounge or on deck. Two days later, out at sea, we all sat around the radio and listened to Chamberlain's declaration of war." (Moore's biographer, Rowena Rutherford Farrar, states that Elsa slept on the bridge, which was laughingly dubbed the "hotel for women.")

THE STARS AND STRIPES FOREVER

Since many of Elsa's benefits for the war effort lacked the swish and splash of her more glittering affairs, they often were reported only locally. Two such entertainments convey the flavor of Elsa's fund-raising in the war years.

In June 1940, at the Clay Theatre in San Francisco, Elsa, in a blue sequin dress, according to the *Examiner*, "took a bow for having put over another successful party—and hearty applause from a socialite audience greeted her report that close to $4,000 had been raised by the affair for the French Mobile Foyer. Thoroughly entertained by the evening's performance were the spectators who filled every one of the theatre's 386 seats. Off to a patriotic start, the program opened with a film depicting the life of Teddy Roosevelt."

Then Elsa thanked those who had helped her produce the program, followed by the San Francisco premiere of the French film *The Baker's Wife*. That was followed by the world premiere of Elsa's Warner Bros. short *The Lady and the Lug*, in which Elsa boxes—convincingly!—in the ring with prizefighter Maxie Rosenbloom. Then, in a dream sequence, these two play the balcony scene from *Romeo and Juliet*. Elsa's line readings are not bad for a star-cross'd sixty-year-old.

In March 1943, in Maryland, the *Fort Meade Post* headlined ELSA WOWS CROWD OF 2000 AT PARTY. When she walked into the assembly hall of the army post, "a shout went up fom the 2,000 soldiers and their guests. The audience obviously had heard of Miss Maxwell's ability as an entertainer, but she probably did not expect to be an audience of one for the soldiers' humor.

"Throughout her stay hearty chuckles shook her (as she calls it) 'wide frame' and at times she was almost convulsed with laughter. Miss Maxwell, who put on display her own brand of wit in speaking to the soldier-and-girl audience, was surprised at their speed on the uptake and roared at some of the comments." The evening apparently took a bawdy turn, which Elsa would have loved. The interactive nature of the event sprang from "an unusual quiz game" in which Elsa awarded prizes for what she considered the snappiest and wittiest answers to questions she posed. "Old, hardened campaigner that Elsa is, even she blushed at some of the answers, roaring at others," the paper reported. Whatever the jokes, they must have been more fun than the patriotic fodder that Hollywood turned out in the forties, which made soldiers look like sexless ninnies.

The ship docked in New York on September 7. "Upon returning to the United States in 1939," Elsa said, "I put frivolity, but not gaiety, behind me for the duration. In the next six years I gave, and helped to arrange, innumerable parties and balls, but only one—to celebrate the liberation of Paris—was purely a social affair. All the others were for American, British, and French war relief organizations."

Elsa's despair was double-edged. Like any person of feeling, she grieved for the world. She keened especially for France, a country she adored. But added to this sorrow was personal heartbreak, for Elsa had broken up with Dickie. The quarrel seems to have been the most serious one of their half-century partnership, and it involved another woman, who had moved into Dickie's heart, and then her house.

In 1939, this curious item appeared in Maury Paul's syndicated column:

"Elsa Maxwell in Cannes, on the French Riviera, occupying the charming cottage of Mrs. Eric Loder's estate which the kindly Eleanor Loder placed at La Maxwell's disposal following last summer's unfortunate mix-up in which Elsa is said to have ordered Isabel Townsend Pell out of Dickie Fellowes-Gordon's house and Dickie is reported, as a result, to have slammed the door of that same house in Elsa's face—after a friendship of almost a quarter of a century."

To a casual reader, the item might seem less than momentous: a noisy row among strong women. Based on what we know, however, it's impossible *not* to read between the lines. But first, meet Isabel Townsend Pell.

Pell was born in 1901 into a socially prominent family in New York, sent to exclusive schools, and given a coming-out party in 1920—after which she shocked other debutantes, and their mothers, by taking a job in a dress shop. "Life had grown stupid," she said. "I was bored with it all." A little later, she shocked those ladies once more by taking up acting, although briefly. Life upon the stage gave her entrée to a circle of artistic, financially secure women who pursued one another more diligently than they pursued careers. Mercedes de Acosta, a premier lesbian of her day, befriended Isabel, whom she called "a lovable person." Eventually Isabel settled in France with her lover, Claire, Marquise de Forbin. They lived at Auribeau, near Dickie's *mas*.

The door slamming in Maury Paul's report obviously amounts to a lovers' quarrel, a very serious one, fueled by jealousy and reaching the incandescence of a cat fight. Although it's impossible to fix the date when Dickie and Isabel began their affair, it was certainly in progress by 1938, for Dickie, arriving late that year in New York by ship, listed Isabel Townsend Pell as her arrival contact. In previous arrivals, she had always listed Elsa.

Estranged from Dickie, and kicked out into a country lane, Elsa needed another roof and thus Eleanor Loder's gift, or loan, of Lou Paradou. Maury Paul's word "kindly" as applied to Eleanor means not only that she took in the homeless Elsa, but that she also nursed Elsa's fractured heart. As rumors of war thundered louder and closer, it must have been wrenching for Elsa to leave France without Dickie, who stayed on until 1940. Did she wait so long because of Isabel? Dickie finally arrived in New York on January 12, 1940, on the Italian liner *Rex*, which sailed from Genoa. (A curious choice of ship

for Dickie, who, as a British subject resident in France, risked serious consequences in Italy and even onboard an Italian ship. Five months later, Mussolini declared war on France and Great Britain.)

Isabel stayed on, and when Germany and Italy invaded France in 1940,
she and the marquise joined the Résistance. When Axis agents discovered
weapons, anti-Nazi propaganda, and a radio in their house, Isabel was arrested. Here the story becomes muddled, because, while some accounts have
her using a gun on dangerous missions against the enemy, and rescuing
American paratroopers stranded behind enemy lines, another version claims
that she collaborated with the Nazis. This assertion was reported by Eve Pell,
a distant cousin, who wrote about Isabel in the spring 2005 issue of *Ms.*
magazine.

If Isabel truly held Axis sympathies—and this accusation seems tenuous,
outweighed by reports of her bravery—might she have influenced Dickie to
take the Italian liner? Dickie's allegiance to the Allied nations is never in
question. If besotted by love of Isabel, however, her judgment might have
lapsed. In fairness to Isabel, it's entirely possible that she acted as a double
agent on behalf of the Résistance. Isabel died in New York in 1952.

Elsa and Dickie made up in the early forties, and from then on "we"
meant the two of them again. Dickie told Hugo Vickers, when he questioned
her about her work for the war effort, "Oh yes, fund-raising, and hospital
work, quite a bit. And I worked with the Stage Door Canteen. I spent the war
years in New York and Hollywood. Douglas Fairbanks Jr. was a great friend
of ours. We knew the Zanucks very well. Jack Warner and his wife were
great friends of ours, too."

"Our friends," part of "our" life together. But then, in 1944, after the
liberation of France, Isabel once more invaded the household, although via
letter. But first, a reminder that Elsa's writings were sometimes ghosted: for
instance, *R.S.V.P.*, her most important book. Speaking with disapproval,
Dickie told Hugo Vickers: "It's not a good enough book. She should have
done it herself. She shouldn't have had a ghostwriter; he was no good. Ghostwriters always hate you, you know. Although she was full of vitality, she was
lazy. And also a little bit frightened. She didn't think she had enough talent,
when she really did."

Dickie also revealed that she sometimes wrote Elsa's columns, especially if Elsa was ailing: "It was nothing, I could do it like that." She might also have added that Elsa could not possibly have written all that appeared under her byline and also have kept up her pace. Elsa's secretaries pitched in, basing their work on Elsa's dictaphone notes. This practice was not unusual, then or now. Columns under the names of Hedda, Louella, Walter Winchell, and most others might more accurately have been credited to "the staff of." (Rare also is the presidential memoir crafted by an ex-president; or the celebrity cookbook whose recipes were star-cooked, and so on down the bestseller list.)

I suspect, therefore, that Dickie wrote Elsa's column of November 8, 1944, which starts out with De Gaulle as head of the war-torn French government, Elsa's great love of France, and—"I want to pass on to you a trenchant letter. This letter illustrates, in part, how France can become a part of a person. . . . One of my greatest friends, Dorothy Fellowes-Gordon, owns a beautiful farm in the south of France, where I have spent too many summers to count.

"After the fall of Paris, Miss Fellowes-Gordon came over here to try to raise some money for the children and wives of the French soldiers who had gone off to war. She worked hard, as did her friend, Isabel Pell, of Boston [sic], who had been staying with her when war broke out. Isabel, a wild, dashing creature, made a wonderful record in this war. She chose to stay, while Miss Fellowes-Gordon got stuck over here—for, being British, she could not get back. Isabel Pell stayed and, as you have probably learned recently, she fought with the Maquis against the Germans, barely escaping with her life. She is certainly a real heroine—as correspondents who went into the south of France with our task forces describe her.

"Here are excerpts from a letter within a letter. The first letter was sent by Isabel to a friend in Pennsylvania. The references are to Dickie Fellowes-Gordon:

"Tell Dickie the house has suffered comparatively little damage; but the beautiful woods, except just in front of the house, was burnt to the ground by the Boches, who are not human beings but beasts of the lowest type. I succeeded in saving Dickie's silver and all her furniture and most of the broken windows are fixed.

"Tell her her house was a very famous house for the resistance and today stands proudly as a monument to the great work of the Maquis. Tell her the love I have for France is very great and I thank her for leaving her place in my care during the last five years."

The style isn't Elsa's. This column is less breezy, slightly elevated in the way of those who don't write professionally, but more than anything, a farewell wave to Isabel across the Atlantic. And not from Elsa, who more likely would stick out her tongue. One imagines Elsa's silent displeasure at Dickie's tribute, even though Elsa had triumphed: for she had Dickie, and Isabel had Dickie's good-bye.

In May 1943, Dickie gave a sixtieth birthday party for Elsa (or so Elsa called it in her column; it was, in truth, her sixty-second). Many old friends turned up, including Eric and Eleanor Loder, Grace Moore and her husband, Valentín Parera. Elsa suspected something special when Fritz Kreisler and Nathan Milstein arrived together—"the first and second greatest violinists in the world," to Elsa's mind. When the time came for entertainment, these two walked over to the piano where their accompanist had been playing already.

"I looked at [Fritz's wife] Harriet Kreisler," Elsa wrote, "a wonderful woman who arranges these things in some magical way. 'Not,' my lips formed the words incredulously, 'the Bach double violin concerto.'

" 'Yes,' countered Harriet. 'Now shut up.' "

Elsa's heartfelt thank-you:

"At the end of this incomparable work, not a word was spoken. It was too moving, too stupendous for mere words. What a tragedy that this work cannot be shared with millions, for this is the greatest comfort and builder of morale that exists. But I do not need to say, God bless Fritz Kreisler, for God has already taken care of that."

"On July 27, 1944," Elsa wrote, "while the Allied armies still were fighting in the hedgerows of Normandy, I sent out invitations for a party in Hollywood on September 9, to celebrate the liberation of Paris. The Allies then were 150 miles from Paris and rival columnists had a field day ridiculing me as a military expert. I was wrong—but on the side of the angels. A Free

French armored division entered Paris on August 25, fifteen days before the date I selected. I borrowed Dorothy di Frasso's home for the party, and the talent that performed was worthy of the occasion commemorated."

Elsa's victory party opened with Alicia Markova and Anton Dolin dancing *Les Sylphides*, to the piano accompaniment of Artur Rubinstein playing Chopin. Next, in order of appearance: Lauritz Melchior, Judy Garland, Frank Sinatra, Danny Kaye, each one singing a song about Paris. Edgar Bergen did a French routine with his dummy, Charlie McCarthy, and for the finale, Elsa played "The Star Spangled Banner," then her 130 guests (including Greer Garson, Anita Loos, Lady Mendl, and Evalyn Walsh McLean, wearing the Hope Diamond) joined Charles Boyer in "La Marseillaise."

If Elsa's long train of schemes and enterprises had a caboose, it was her role as political camp follower. After the Paris Peace Conference in 1919, she turned her attention away from politics except for the 1940s war effort, occasional columns of admiration for Eleanor Roosevelt and heroic generals, and recurring visits to the White House. In these, she ran neck-and-neck with Billy Graham, for Elsa was a guest of Presidents Roosevelt, Truman, Eisenhower, and Kennedy, and of their respective first ladies. (Elsa was too frail for a White House visit during Camelot. Various Kennedys, however, had entertained her since the thirties.)

When Elsa wrote on political topics, she took the moderate-liberal stance of a traditional Democrat. In 1948, however, she supported Thomas E. Dewey, the liberal Republican. (The term was not an oxymoron then.) Arriving by train in Mason City, Iowa, in the early hours of the morning after election day, she inquired confidently whether Dewey had won. Told of Harry Truman's surprise victory, she exclaimed, "No! It can't be! When I left New York last evening it was in the bag." The Mason City *Globe Gazette* reported that in her lecture she devoted more time than planned to the subject of politics: "She pleased the audience with her glib thoughts and fine delivery." The paper reported further that, owing to Truman's victory, Elsa found it difficult to eat all day.

The reasons for Elsa's early dislike of Truman are obscure; later, however, she incurred his wrath by daring to criticize his daughter's singing.

Certainly, he was a strong advocate of the United Nations, whose founding conference in San Francisco in April 1945 he addressed, and which Elsa attended, although with something less than her usual hoopla. In this case, Elsa's news value was overshadowed. Impossible, or so it seemed, for her to capture page one when the city teemed with delegations from some fifty countries, many of them headed by famous statesmen. Their eight hundred and fifty delegates, unlike Elsa's regular coterie of bored socialites and unemployed royalty, had serious work to do, and two thousand five hundred journalists, photographers, and broadcasters covered every syllable of the conference, which took place at the Opera House. Despite the zany fringe of Hedda Hopper and her ilk ("I'm here now," she proclaimed upon arrival. "All other columnists can go home."), the carnage of the recent war added gravity even to after-hours relaxation. To be sure, the city was awash in parties: Helen Russell (of the San Francisco Crocker family), who had been a hostess at the New York World's Fair in 1939, was chosen as hospitality chairwoman of the conference. In this capacity, she organized over five hundred official dinners and some two hundred and fifty cocktail parties for a cost of a million dollars.

Did Elsa feel eclipsed? Probably not, for such responsibility as Mrs. Russell's would have left her scant time to enjoy the multitude of events. More important, she attended the conference as a working journalist, and as such rushed from one plenary session to the next in search of frothy material for her columns and broadcasts. These she made from bed, a station that had become her trademark—in this case, her bivouac at the St. Francis Hotel. Like her lecture in Mason City, Elsa's reporting from the United Nations conference was notable for glib thoughts and fine delivery.

Every reporter covets an exclusive interview, especially with the exotic and controversial, and Elsa was no exception. Enter Molotov.

Stalin's protégé, Vyacheslav Mikhailovich Molotov, had been named People's Commissar for Foreign Affairs in 1939 and headed the Soviet delegation to San Francisco. On April 25, 1945, the first day of the conference, Molotov entered the Opera House surrounded by stern bodyguards. Realizing that the theme of the conference was peace, he soon dismissed his protectors and, at the first recess, strode into the lobby surrounded by noisy reporters hurling questions. Elsa, though far from lithe and one of the older members of the press that day, broke through the barrier, overtook the fearsome Molotov, and addressed him straight on. (Her question, alas, has been lost to history.) "Molotov," said Elsa, "did not speak a word to me as we hurried down the aisle together." Just then, a photographer snapped a picture of the impromptu couple for an extra edition of a local paper. A few hours later, there was Elsa, on page one after all, identified as Mrs. Molotov! (The caption writer may be forgiven, since Elsa's outline matched the stereotype of Soviet tractor-driving womanhood.)

Those among the delegates who knew Elsa, or had heard of her, had a merry time with the misprint, and so did many a San Franciscan. Undeterred, Elsa marched that night to the Molotov suite at the St. Francis, brandished the newspaper to unsmiling secret police in hopes of an interview, and saw no more than the butt of a rifle. The following year, in London, several British reporters approached Elsa to ask a favor. "We're appealing to you as a colleague to intercede with Molotov and ask him to let our families join us in England," they said, to Elsa's bafflement. Further explanation revealed that while on assignment in Moscow during the war, these journalists had married Russian women who had not been allowed to join their husbands in England.

The rumor had spread that Elsa was en route to Moscow as the guest of Commissar Molotov and his *real* wife. Somehow the San Francisco mistake had morphed into a supposed intimacy between Elsa and the Molotovs. Onboard the *Queen Mary*, the commissar's interpreter had issued an "official" invitation to come to Russia and "tell the truth about the Soviet Union to the American public." Elsa doubted the veracity of the invitation, especially the stipulation that she must not stay at the American embassy but in the bosom of the Molotov family. Eventually, Tass, the Soviet news agency, got hold of the propaganda and implied that Miss Maxwell was on her way. Perhaps a "Come Dressed As Your Favorite Captive Nation" party crossed her mind, but Elsa never saw the Kremlin. She suggested that the Russians wooed her as a vehicle to present Molotov more favorably in the Western press.

In spite of her fourth-estate shenanigans in San Francisco, Elsa hosted one major blowout while there: a dinner for eighty guests, selected from among the delegations. "Each country's table was decorated by a product historically associated with it," she said, "a chore that took a good deal of ingenuity. Saudi Arabia left me stumped until I borrowed two exquisite miniature Arabian horses which I found in an antique shop." Prince Faisal ibn Abd al Aziz Al Saud, a future king of the country, swept in with his entourage, all in white robes and jeweled scimitars. One of the prince's chamberlains found the miniature horses so enchanting he tried to wheedle them from Elsa. Since they were on loan, however, she could not present them in a gallant beau geste.

After dinner, Elsa lamented, one of the horses disappeared—"and it cost me $250 to make good with the antique shop. I wouldn't vouch for it, but I think that was the first time I ever entertained a horse thief."

25 Put the Blame on Elsa

Elsa's sojourn in the United States from 1939 until her first postwar trip to Europe, in December 1946, was her longest since 1909. Arriving in London, she found England "the bleakest and, paradoxically, the brightest spot in Western Europe. It was broke, but not morally bankrupt." She brought in a thousand dollars' worth of tinned foods for British friends deprived by war and still heavily rationed. Elsa didn't name the recipients of her bounty, although the status of her hotel—Claridge's—suggests trickle-up charity.

Before sailing from New York on the *Queen Mary*, Elsa had made the acquaintance of Sir Hartley Shawcross, attorney-general of the United Kingdom and soon to be Britain's chief prosecutor at the Nuremberg war trials. Invited by Sir Hartley to a luncheon in the House of Commons hosted by Ernest Bevin, foreign secretary in the newly formed Labour government, Elsa regaled a flush of cabinet ministers. She reported the dining room frigid but the soup, though thin and watery, palatably warm. "Food was the least of the attractions the occasion held for me," she said, "but I could not help bridling with surprise, then revulsion, when we were served thick, juicy steaks." The average Briton got by on four ounces of rationed meat per week, while here, in the House of Commons—outraged, Elsa folded her napkin in a theatrical gesture, crossed her arms, and leaned back from the table.

"What's the matter, Elsa?" asked Bevin. "Eat your steak. You're not a vegetarian, are you?"

"You'll have to excuse me," she replied. "I have lost my appetite. Much as I appreciate your hospitality, I think this lunch is a disgrace." And she lectured the foreign secretary on how his constituents would give the world for such a meal, and also her shock that a Labour government, especially, should fail to set an example for the country. Ernest Bevin said only, "Go on, eat your steak."

Having spoken her mind, Elsa took a bite—and spat the fishy mouthful into her napkin. Bevin, a former truck driver with few pretensions, roared at Elsa's discomfiture. "That's whale steak, Elsa. We're planning to introduce it to augment the meat ration. You're our first guinea pig." Then he took his own first bite, and shuddered. "This could cost us the general election," he winced, leaving Labour's culinary experiment unfinished on his plate. (Whale steaks—even served as "Moby Dick and chips"—did not charm the British palate.)

On to France, where Elsa disliked what she found: a state of demoralization and haunted disgrace, the residue of Vichy collaboration. Nor did the existentialist poobahs of Paris offer any dab of useful philosophy for an optimistic bon vivant like Elsa. Dickie, meanwhile, arrived at Auribeau in 1946, bringing with her a large amount of stores and medical supplies. Soon her farm was restored, and in a year or so she and Elsa resumed, in summers, their colorful country life.

Days and nights among the waterfall and vegetable patch at Le Sault did not much resemble the slow, seasonal rhythms of neighboring farmsteads. Nor did the guest list, despite Elsa's professed love for "the ordinary people of my class." There was Prince Aly Khan, for example, and Rita Hayworth, along with the Duke and Duchess of Windsor, and a rainbow of wealthy celebrities eager to forget the privations of war.

Aly Khan stands apart from the barnful of international studs so obsessively reported on during the 1950s by such publications as *Confidential* and *Whisper*. Unlike Porfirio Rubirosa, for instance, Aly Khan had no interest in wealthy heiresses, since he owned half the Moslem world himself, or so it seemed. By most accounts, this "boudoir Bonaparte" treated his female conquests very well. Nor did he seek out trophy wives à la Aristotle Onassis. Aly Khan was married twice: first to Joan Guinness, of the brewery family, and next to Rita Hayworth. In the latter instance, he seems to have dealt sympathetically with his wife's emotional hardships.

He belonged to the royal family of the Ismaili sect of Islam, which—detouring past a theological mountain—we can identify as tracing its lineage back to Fatimah, daughter of the Prophet. Aly's father, the Aga Khan III (1877–1957), was both spiritual leader of the Ismailis and a royal personage internationally recognized. Expecting to succeed his father, Aly was shocked and disappointed when the Aga Khan's will revealed that the title of Aga Khan IV would go to Aly's son, Karim (born 1936, and still on the throne.)

The Ismaili Moslems might be called the Unitarians of Islam. That is, they don't much care for jihads and fatwas, they generally promote peace and avoid conflicts, and they're on the liberal side, socially and politically, as religionists go. Lacking a definitive census, estimates of the Ismaili population range from fifteen to twenty million worldwide.

Elsa adored Aly Khan, and wrote about him with the ardor of one of his conquests. "Every facet of women delights him," she rhapsodized. "When he is with a woman, he makes her feel no other person exists for him. He talks to her with breathless excitement. His eyes burn her intently. He dances with her slowly and rapturously, as though it is the last time he ever will hold her in his arms. He even acts that way with me, for heaven's sake." In Leonard Slater's biography, *Aly*, there's a photograph of Elsa and Aly Khan dancing. And, confirming Elsa's Harlequin Romance prose, he holds her as though she were Kim Novak.

Elsa took credit for introducing Rita Hayworth to Aly, and it came about like this. Meeting Aly for the first time in 1947, Elsa found him charming but assumed he was just another playboy. She saw him next in 1948, in Cannes, where she invited him to a dinner party at the Summer Casino "to dress up the party." Knowing his predilection for beautiful women, Elsa rounded up as many as she could find. "I like pretty girls, too, at parties," she confessed. "They're cheaper and more decorative than flowers." At the time, the most attractive prospect for Elsa's soiree was Rita Hayworth, who was awaiting her divorce decree from Orson Welles at Cap d'Antibes.

Elsa found Rita in the doldrums, and unwilling to decorate anyone's dinner party. "I don't have anything to wear," Rita said. Her disingenuous-ness didn't work. Elsa packed her off to a fine dress shop in Cannes and an-nounced the festivities for nine thirty. "But I want you to be late," Elsa added. "Make a grand entrance. It'll be good for your morale."

Shortly after ten o'clock, Elsa and Aly were deeply involved in a card game when, suddenly, Aly's gaze jumped across the room. Such a disconnect happened rarely, even when a beautiful woman came in sight. But this one— "My God!" he said. "Who is that?"

"That's your dinner partner," Elsa crowed. "I asked her especially for you." Rita Hayworth stood in the doorway in "an exquisite white bouffant dress and looking more beautiful than the law should allow," according to Elsa. The couple married May 27, 1949, and divorced in 1953. Barbara Leaming, in her biography *Orson Welles*, offers a different version of their initial meeting. According to her, Aly Khan asked Elsa "to arrange a gather-ing for which he secretly paid," his sole purpose being to meet the movie star whose films had excited him for years.

"A fascinating footnote to history can be attributed to Aly's romantic al-lure," Elsa wrote in *R.S.V.P.* "Edward VIII might still be on the throne of England if not for Aly. In 1934, Lady Thelma Furness, for years the then Prince of Wales's favorite companion, fell in love with Aly, who was only twenty-three, and followed him to America when he came to this country on business connected to his racing stable. During Thelma's absence, Wallis Simpson moved into the orbit of Edward's serious attention and affections."

J. Bryan III and Charles J.V. Murphy, in *The Windsor Story*, contradict Elsa with precisely the opposite version: Thelma Furness met Aly at a dinner party in New York, and he was smitten. He begged her to delay her depar-ture for England. When she refused, he booked passage on the same ship and surprised her with a phone call from his suite to hers a few miles out of New York harbor: "Will you lunch with me today?"

The shipboard romance heated up in proportion as the Prince of Wales's shoulder grew cold. Did he have spies on the ship, as some suspected? In any event, when Thelma arrived in England, her royal paramour had found comfort in Wallis Simpson. These authors (who, like Elsa, knew the Windsors well) concur with Elsa that "but for Aly, Thelma Furness might never have lost the Prince's favor; King Edward VIII might never have abdicated; and almost certainly he would have died at home in England, full of years and honors, beloved by his Empire."

For Elsa and Dickie in the South of France in the late forties, however, those royal romances had retreated like spring snow. The king did abdicate; he did marry the woman he loved; Thelma lived—where, exactly? She had not been in the news for years; and Elsa and Dickie are en route, on this summer night in 1947, to the Château de la Croë at Antibes, to dine with the Windsors.

26 Enigma Variations

The first time Dickie met the Windsors, she recalled that "all the ladies curtsied to the Duchess, but she, knowing that I was Scottish, put her hand out." Dickie's feelings for them were unambiguous: "I liked her very much. I found him uninteresting."

Nevertheless: "I always gave him a bob, because he had been my king, of course. I never did curtsey to her." Recalling visits to another Windsor residence, Dickie said, "It was wonderful to stay with them at the Mill. They had wonderful food. They loved entertaining, but they were not the giving type. I always used to take something when I went there, either special chocolates or, at Christmas, an American fruit cake, which he loved. But they never gave you anything, never." ("The Mill" was Le Moulin de la Tuilerie, a property of twenty-six acres not far from Paris, which served as the Windsors' country home.)

Dickie's opinions of the duke and duchess remained unchanged throughout their acquaintance. She never considered them close friends. Elsa, on the other hand, spun around like a weathercock at the mention of this pair. Her vexed friendship, especially with the duchess, dropped, year by year, from a barometric high of admiration and flattery to the lows of an impending tropical cyclone. If the duchess had ended up at a murder party on a stormy night, Elsa's temptation might have been prodigious.

After meeting the Prince of Wales occasionally in the twenties and early thirties, Elsa rarely encountered him after his coronation as Edward VIII, and his subsequent abdication, in 1936. She did, however, write about him in the June 1937 issue of *Hearst's International Combined with Cosmopolitan* (which later dropped all but the final word of its title). That article, titled "Edward's 'Set' As I Knew Them," is a strong defense of the former king. In it, Elsa took as her starting point the accusation, made during the abdication crisis by the Archbishop of Canterbury, that the king had sought his happiness "within a social circle whose standards and ways of life are alien to all the best instincts of his people."

"I know most of those who surrounded the King and Mrs. Simpson during their all-too-brief reign over London society," Elsa wrote. "Many, indeed, have been dear friends of years' standing, and if they are 'alien' to the 'best instincts' of Britain, then so are roast beef and small beer." Those in the king's "set," in Elsa's round-up, are all well-known to abdication theorists: Thelma Furness, Major E. D. Metcalfe and Lady Metcalfe, and so on. Elsa's article was no doubt read with interest just six months after the abdication. Today, however, it adds little to the story. She ends it with the rousing apostrophe, "Yes, my British friends, with all his infirmities on him, I think you have lost a great sovereign."

Three months earlier, however, in March 1937, Lord Brownlow, who had been lord-in-waiting to the king during his short reign, cabled Lord Beaverbrook, publisher of many British newspapers and the Rupert Murdoch of his day, asking him not to publish "Elsa Maxwell's second article," which he had been told "is of a very derogatory character to the Duke of Windsor," particularly regarding his past life and friendships. Lord Brownlow was referring to another article that Elsa wrote for *Cosmopolitan*, which was subsequently reprinted in Lord Beaverbrook's *Sunday Express*. This piece need not have concerned the former king nor his retinue unduly, though it might have seemed bold at the time. The "derogatory" aspect was no more than Elsa's saying, in circumlocution, that the king was a man with a man's needs, and that those needs had been met before Mrs. Simpson, and with her. All of this was tasteful enough not to have shocked Queen Victoria beyond recovery.

———

Elsa gleaned the content of her abdication articles from common knowledge and not from any exclusive source, though readers might have inferred, erroneously, that she herself belonged to "Edward's set." Only in 1946 did she come to have more than a passing acquaintance with the Duke of Windsor. That was the year, also, when she met his notorious wife, for Elsa became the Windsors' neighbor when they took a suite in the Waldorf-Astoria Tower Apartments a few floors above Elsa's own. One day, Elsa received a telephone call from Mrs. Charles Suydam Cutting, a New York socialite. "The Duke of Windsor would like you to have tea with him tomorrow afternoon at five in his apartment," she said. "He is anxious to see an old friend again after all these years."

Elsa was received by the duke, and a bit later the duchess made a theatrical entrance, saying, "I simply had to meet the famous Elsa Maxwell." Elsa claimed not to know what to make of "this tiny, rather ordinary woman who had climbed from a middle-class home in Baltimore to the threshold of Buckingham Palace. She had assurance and poise. Her clothes were perfect. But I could detect none of the strong physical attraction she obviously held for the Duke."

Elsa encountered the duchess twice in the following weeks in New York. Then the Windsors left for the Riviera, and Elsa did not see them again until the night she and Dickie dined at the Château de la Croë in the summer of 1947. After that, the duke and duchess sometimes came to Auribeau. They frequently entertained Elsa, who was sometimes accompanied by Dickie, at their chateau on the Riviera, at the Moulin de la Tuilerie near Paris, and at their Parisian mansion in the Bois de Boulogne. In the coming years, they attended Elsa's parties and charity balls in Paris, Monte Carlo, New York, and other fashionable venues. For a long time, the friendship was a happy one.

In 1952, Mrs. Lytle Hull, a patron of the arts in New York, asked Elsa to stage a benefit for the Musicians Emergency Fund. The money raised would aid hospitalized veterans. Elsa, believing it would be "a splendid publicity gimmick to have the Duchess of Windsor lend her name to the affair and participate in a fashion show," either secured permission of the duchess to do just that, or else she neglected to do so. (No one ever gave a complete and believable account of events that fueled the Maxwell-Windsor explosion, least of all the principals.)

Elsa expected to call out the name of the Duchess of Windsor with great fanfare, not only to raise huge sums for the benefit but also to prove, yet again, that she, Elsa Maxwell, could command the most grandiose names to her worthy, and glamorous, causes. "On the night of the ball," Elsa said, "just as I was going to the microphone to express my gratitude to everyone who had contributed to the success of the event, the Duchess said to me, 'Please don't mention my name.' I obeyed." One reason put forth for this demurral is that the duchess constantly claimed a shortage of funds in an effort to escape high taxes in the countries where she resided, namely the United States and France. In this scenario, keeping a lower profile was part of her tax dodge. The obvious question is this: How many tax officials could she hope to convince, given her lavish lifestyle?

Even noble events like the musicians benefit are replete with ignoble tongues. Immediately the scorpion gossip stung Elsa, for she was accused of deliberatly snubbing the duchess. "A number of silly stories were written commenting on it," lamented Elsa, to whose tremendous annoyance the duchess made no attempt to set the record straight, neither publicly nor among their mutual friends. Humiliated, Elsa nevertheless let it pass . . . this time. After all, the duke and duchess were big fish in anybody's pond. Having landed them, Elsa recognized the folly of cutting them loose.

But then it happened again.

The following year, 1953, Elsa once more engineered Mrs. Hull's charity event. Minus the Duchess of Windsor. "My original plan," Elsa explained, "was to have a costume ball sponsored by four duchesses representing distinguished houses of their respective countries. The friends I selected were the Duchess of Argyle (England), the Duchess de Brissac (France), the Duchess of Alba (Spain), and the Duchess di Sera (Italy)." This plan was soon changed, though not before reporters reached the Duchess of Windsor to ask what she thought. "It would take four ordinary duchesses to make one Duchess of Windsor," quoth the maven.

It may come as a surprise, given Elsa's printed pieties, that she knew how to cuss. Words remembered from the bawdy streets of San Francisco, and from decades among the internationally uninhibited, spewed from her tongue in four and five letters. Publicly, she wrote her side in *The American Weekly*, a Sunday magazine supplement distributed nationwide with Hearst newspapers. Elsa had her say in the issue of December 5, 1954, in "My Troubles with the Windsors."

"When I read that quote in the papers about four duchesses making one Duchess of Windsor," Elsa wrote, "a sharp feeling of revulsion swept over me, for I thought the duchess was too hard, too possessive, with a destructive quality within, to be a friend. I suddenly resolved to cut all my ties with the duchess. My only regret was the loss of the duke's friendship."

Elsa's article had immense appeal at the time, comparable to revelations in later decades about Diana, Princess of Wales. Even today the Windsors remain a hot topic. In 2001, *The New Yorker* ran a cartoon of two matrons walking down Fifth Avenue, with this caption: "I just don't want to turn into one of those women who never shut up about the Duchess of Windsor." Elsa, in fact, did turn into one of those women.

Although the duke represented the weakest side of this Bermuda Triangle, Elsa scorched him with her rhetoric nonetheless. In *R.S.V.P.*, published in the white heat of the feud, Elsa no longer believed, as she did in 1937, that the British lost a great sovereign when he abdicated. In her autobiography she wrote: "Forgetting sentiment and looking at the king's abdication realistically, it was an extraordinary stroke of luck for the British Empire and its wartime allies. Edward simply did not have the strength of character or the *noblesse oblige* of King George VI and Queen Elizabeth, his successors." This volte-face, though perhaps a part of Elsa's anti-Windsor campaign, has less to do with fickle friendship than with history, for World War II had happened in the meantime. Historians, world leaders, and many in Britain, even those loyal to Edward VIII, had come to believe that he would have made an unfortunate wartime monarch.

Elsa's quarrel with the Windsors dragged on and on in American newspapers. The duchess, for her part, maintained a granite silence. Her loudest comment is the absence of Elsa's name from *The Heart Has Its Reasons: The Memoirs of the Duchess of Windsor*, published in 1956 when she and Elsa were still at daggers drawn.

The Windsors, meanwhile, learned that *R.S.V.P.* was to be published, and that in it Elsa had elaborated on the feud. The duchess sent word to

Elsa asking whether they might have a little talk. In the same note, showing her famous talons, the duchess warned that she and the duke had already consulted their lawyers, having heard though the grapevine that in the book Elsa was "saying things that should be prohibited." Their anxiety seems extreme, since libel laws at the time were stricter than now, and also because of media punctilio. One wonders exactly what Elsa knew about the couple, and about the duchess in particular, to cause such anxiety, and also how many pages were eventually deleted from *R.S.V.P.* by the publisher. Elsa duly called on her former friend in the spring of 1954, when the book was still in manuscript. She took along the relevant pages, and after a politely formal meeting, left an unedited chapter in the Windsor suite.

Next day the duchess wrote Elsa a short note, saying that some of the things Elsa had written "certainly did hurt," and she questioned the accuracy of others. She ended the note with this sentence: "I also dared to correct the spelling of two words as I know you would want me *too*." [emphasis added] This line Elsa included, with great relish, later that year in "My Troubles with the Windsors." Those looking for evidence of the Duchess of Windsor as a vulgar arriviste pounced upon that misused homophone, as Elsa knew they would.

The following summer, Elsa and Dickie spent a week in Venice, where Elsa gave a party at the Hotel Danieli. She invited the Windsors, who were also in town. Ignoring the invitation, they let it be widely known that they were turning in early in their suite at the Gritti Palace. A few days later, as Elsa strolled on the Lido, she spied the duke and duchess advancing toward her. She turned to speak, but they shot her unfriendly glances and moved away.

In their overlapping social circles, however, complete avoidance was not possible. At a housewarming for Mr. and Mrs. Byron C. Foy (he was a vice president of the Chrysler Corporation; Thelma Foy, a socialite and art collector and daughter of the boss, Walter Chrysler, who financed the Chrysler Building) in their new apartment on Park Avenue, Elsa was chatting with Cole Porter and Prince Filippo Caracciolo when the Windsors swept in. With great aplomb, the duchess made straight for Elsa as every guest turned to gape. Putting out her hand, she said, "Elsa, I am so very glad to see you."

Elsa, with equal friendliness, shook hands with the duchess, saying, "Wallis, I am glad to see you, too."

And their enmity continued.

Behind the smokescreen of insults, jibes, and knaveries, a presence loomed that, in Elsa, produced the social equivalent of anaphylactic shock and, in Wallis Warfield Windsor, the antidote to years of secrets and frustration. His name: James Paul Donahue Jr., called Jimmy, who lived from 1915 to 1966. His mother, Jessie Donahue, was one of Elsa's intimates. His first cousin, Barbara Hutton, wove in and out of Elsa's inner circle, so that, by rights, Jimmy should have been at least a casual friend of Elsa's. But she never mentioned him in print.

The main reason for her loathing had to do with Jimmy's flamboyant homosexuality. Like many deeply closeted women and men, Elsa felt intense discomfort when near those who might, by words or actions, "give her away"—that is, call attention to her own presumed sexual preference. Gay men like Cole Porter were acceptable because of their talent, their savoir faire, and often, their wives. Noël Coward caused no anxiety because he was famous for partnering glamorous women onstage, and also because Elsa was crazy about him. And such men usually conducted their affairs with discretion.

Not so Jimmy Donahue. Ladies and gentlemen of Elsa's vintage, especially those of Anglo-American breeding, considered him a cad, or worse. So great was his notoriety that he still pops up in ducal biographies. Indeed, in 2000, Christopher Wilson, a demon writer of Fleet Street, published *Dancing with the Devil: The Windsors and Jimmy Donahue*. Filling his book with hearsay—along with much that is factual—Wilson asserts that Donahue and the duchess carried on a four-year love affair, beginning around 1950.

"It was money that first attracted the Windsors to the Donahues, mother and son," writes Wilson, and he follows with details of the many presents—jewels, cash, lavish entertainments—that Jessie Donahue and Jimmy bestowed on the duke and duchess. Since Elsa, too, was a beneficiary of Mrs. Donahue's largesse, she might understandably have begrudged the dollars spent on those she considered less needy than herself.

Some of Jimmy Donahue's exploits are sophomorically amusing. According to Wilson, he "once turned up at '21' in a dress stuffed with pillows, wearing odd shoes and a five o'clock shadow, claiming to be Miss Maxwell, and noisily demanding her table." Others make you wince, like the time he rigged up a tape recorder in the loo of a restaurant where the Windsors were dining and later played the tape so that friends could hear the "royal wee." Some of Jimmy's "pranks" were criminal, if true: more than one account of male prostitutes and Waldorf waiters raped and/or castrated. Although some of these tales came from dubious sources like Truman Capote, enough of Jimmy's misbehavior is documented to explain Elsa's revulsion.

Such crimes and misdemeanors on Jimmy's part blazed as lurid, open secrets in cafe society. Elsa, outraged by what she considered Jimmy's nonstop debauchery, and even more by his sordid liaison with the duchess, spoke her mind. (Dickie remembered that Elsa "disapproved of the goings-on with Jimmy Donahue, and she said so.") Elsa lectured Wallis on the imminent ruin of the duke's reputation, which his wife must guard even if she cared little for her own. She even referred in print to the "perverseness" in Wallis's character, warning that it would be "tragic if the duchess utterly destroyed the greatest love story of all time."

Although ostensibly offered as constructive criticism, Elsa's admonitions to the duchess—before the two stopped speaking—were not welcomed by a woman long shielded from lèse-majesté, even without benefit of crown and throne. Such advice not only fueled but prolonged the feud. When another friend, the heir to a chain of food purveyors, whispered similar remonstrances, Wallis glared at him. "The Duchess of Windsor does not take advice from grocery boys," she snapped.

But what if Jimmy Donahue was a red herring? Nicholas Haslam, the designer and man-about-the-world, a shrewd observer who knew the Windsors and Jimmy, said, "I really can't think he could ever have touched any woman, let alone one as rigidly undressable as Wallis. My reading of the situation was that, more probably, Jimmy Donahue had originally caught the eye of the duke, and a sisterly rivalry developed with Wallis." On the other hand, goes another line of gossip, when the duke warned Wallis of the vicious talk about her and Jimmy, she laughed at the notion. "*Really*, David? Come along—his friends call me the Queen of the Fairies."

Suddenly it stops. Jimmy is banished. Elsa, like an exiled jester, returns to her stool of honor, even though it must always bear the taint of her disloyalty. There is general agreement among the commentariat that Jimmy's downfall came about because, risking his mother's wrath, and having worn out his welcome, he made a final, ghastly mistake.

I return to Bryan and Murphy in *The Windsor Story*. They write that Jessie Donahue had threatened to cut Jimmy out of her will if the duchess left her husband for him. "The breaking point came one evening when the three of them were having supper in the Windsors' rooms in a hotel at Baden-Baden. Something the Duchess said piqued Jimmy into a burst of temper; he kicked at her under the table. She yelped with pain and jumped up. Her stocking was torn, and her shin bled. The Duke called for the maid to fetch towels and Mercurochrome and helped the Duchess to a sofa, where he wiped away the blood and dressed the scrape. Only then did he turn to Donahue. 'We've had enough of you, Jimmy. Get out!' They never saw each other again."

Christopher Wilson, in *Dancing with the Devil*, adds the detail that a drunken Jimmy kicked the duchess when she upbraided him for having garlic on his breath. This is a credible particular when you recall that upper-class Anglo-Saxons in the fifties feared garlic as much as Count Dracula once had.

"The Duchess of Windsor and I wasted three and a half years by our social estrangement," proclaimed Elsa in 1957, "but we get along now like a house afire." This rapprochement came slowly. The Windsors kicked Jimmy out in 1955, but not for a couple of years did Elsa return to their fold, or they to hers. To readers languishing for still more news of Elsa and the Windsors, the pages of *The American Weekly* opened once again, on December 1, 1957, for Elsa to recount "My Apology to the Duchess."

Elsa explained that for three and a half years she and the Duchess of

Windsor had neither spoken nor shaken hands. Then, at the April in Paris ball of 1957, "both the Duchess and I had tables," Elsa wrote. At both tables sat many guests of distinction, including, at Elsa's, the mayor of New York, Robert Wagner, and his wife, along with Millicent Hearst. That very afternoon, however, Elsa had entertained a far more illustrious name than any of these: Marilyn Monroe.

AH, DID YOU ONCE SEE WALLIS PLAIN?

In 2004, at Christie's in Rome, nineteen letters from Elsa to the Duchess of Windsor went up for auction. Most were dated 1957, in the months after their reconciliation. The letters, some typewritten and others written by hand, often bore the salutation "Dear little Duchess," followed by fulsome endearments. In August of that year, for instance, Elsa wrote: "You really are an amazing creature. I think you are amusing, sweet, wicked, sometimes cataclysmic and always fun." The estimate was $4,800 to $6,000, but the letters did not sell.

Elsa invited Marilyn and her husband, Arthur Miller, to the ball, and to her surprise they came—late, of course. Marilyn triggered a stampede, and next day the New York tabloids ran headlines to the effect that ELSA STEALS THE SHOW and ELSA OUTDOES THE DUCHESS. Aghast at the implication that she had schemed to outshine a Windsor, Elsa wrote the duchess a note explaining that she had invited Marilyn to meet Millicent Hearst and also to give the ball a lift for charity purposes. Since Elsa and Millicent were soon to sail for Europe on the same ship as the Windsors, Elsa added that she would tell reporters onboard exactly what she was now saying to the duchess by letter.

Elsa kept her promise. On the SS *United States*, she told reporters how much she deplored those headlines and that her hand was outstretched any time the duchess wished to take it. The next day, Elsa and Millicent received an invitation for cocktails in the Windsor suite. "We accepted," Elsa said, "and when we arrived the Duchess greeted me as if the past three and a half years had flown out of the porthole. I cannot help but regret the time we lost. For the Duchess and I always have fun together, her delightful sense of humor meeting mine head on." Elsa ended her article with a slice of humble pie: "In this Sunday magazine I once said things, in anger, about the Duchess. Now, in friendship, I regret those words and write for all to read: My apology to the Duchess."

Fast-forward to 1962. Elsa, suffering serious health problems, has gone on a diet, which she honors in the breach more than the observance. At a United Nations luncheon, she and the duchess are seated at the same table, although not side by side. For dessert, a waiter brings a large dish of strawberries in cream. "Just as I picked up my fork," Elsa said ruefully, "the Duchess leaned forward and called to me down the table, 'Don't do that! Remember your health!' " Elsa's comment—"She treats me like a child, and frankly I love it"—suggests that Elsa was like many who miss out on maternal love: they seek it in surrogates. The Duchess of Windsor, whatever her true feelings for Elsa, possessed the knack of pleasing and manipulating the powerful. (By many accounts, she ruled the duke as he had never ruled his kingdom.) We can almost hear Elsa saying to Dickie, as they approach the Windsor domain that night in 1947, "Had Wallis been allowed on the throne, she might have made a remarkable king."

27 And Say Hello to My Niece, Princess Margaret

This greeting the Duke of Windsor emphatically did *not* convey via Elsa. They were still on the outs when, in 1954, Elsa took part in an odd little amateur theatrical codirected by the princess. For Elsa, the experience was more embittering than otherwise, although, when she first wrote about it in *How to Do It, or The Lively Art of Entertaining*, published in 1957, her account glittered. "There is no doubt that wherever Princess Margaret goes she scatters a special magic," Elsa gushed. "I came to know her quite well when we took part together in a production of *The Frog*," a drama by Ian Hay based on a thriller by Edgar Wallace.

Judy Montagu, a socialite and close friend of Princess Margaret, staged the play at the Scala Theatre in London to raise money for needy children. Elsa wrote that, following the first rehearsal, the cast was asked to assemble and discuss rough spots in the performance. This discussion took place on the floor. "I tried dutifully to lower my bulk," Elsa said, "but the princess instantly sensed my distress." She said to a stagehand, "Miss Maxwell will sit here with me. Please bring her a chair." Elsa praised the princess for her gaiety, her sense of humor, her talent for piano playing and cooking. According to Elsa, often after rehearsals they would go to Judy Montagu's house in Trevor Place where "Princess Margaret would roll up her sleeves and scramble eggs, and very good eggs they were."

By the time of *The Celebrity Circus*, however, Elsa recalled that "things were not all rosy" between her and the princess. At the time of their theatrical venture, Britain was embroiled in one of its periodic quarrels with the Mediterranean island of Cyprus, then a part of the British Empire. Cyprus sometimes sought to unite with Greece, and at others demanded independence. Owing to the tussle, tensions between Britain and Greece often ran high. Therefore, when a Greek friend of Elsa's presented a check for five hundred pounds for a box seat at one of the five performances, it struck a sour note with Princess Margaret. Elsa handed her the check, but when she saw the Greek name on it she raged that "We won't accept that! Tear it right up! He can't have a box, nor a seat!" Elsa reminded her that the money was for the Invalid Children's Homes, adding that in any case the Greek friend didn't plan to attend. "Finally," Elsa said, "she coldly and reluctantly accepted the gift."

In the play, Elsa pantomimed singing the words to "Some of These Days," while an offstage gramophone played a recording by Sophie Tucker. *The Frog* was the place to be for title chasers, for the cast included Maureen, Marchioness of Dufferin and Ava, as a ladies' lavatory attendant; Colin Tenant, the future Lord Glenconner, as a serial killer; Lord Porchester, the seventh Earl of Carnarvon; Raine Legge, Lady Dartmouth; Baroness Hornsby-Smith; Douglas Fairbanks Jr.; Billy Wallace, a paramour of the princess; and others of the London smart set.

According to some accounts, critics reviewed the play tongue-in-cheek. Elsa's perception, however, was that "the London critics tore us unmercifully to pieces, quite unfairly, as none of us claimed to be professionals." She labeled her costars as "the ungifted amateurs of the British aristocracy" and rated herself equally low.

Noël Coward, who attended with Vivien Leigh, reviewed the play in his diary with uncharacteristic bile: "The whole evening was one of the most fascinating exhibitions of incompetence, conceit, and bloody impertinence that I have ever seen in my life. Elsa Maxwell appeared in a cabaret scene and made a cracking ass of herself. Those high-born characters we watched mumbling and stumbling about on stage are the ones who come to our productions and criticise us! In the dressing room afterwards, we found Princess Margaret eating foie gras sandwiches, sipping champagne, and complaining that the audience laughed in the wrong places. We commiserated politely and left." (An offer from the American impresario Lee Sobel to bring the play and original cast to the Hollywood Bowl for a week, at fourteen thousand pounds, was declined owing to scheduling conflicts.)

On opening night, banks of flowers crowded Elsa's dressing room. They were sent by well-wishers of the London smart set from a couple of generations back, as well as by her current friends in Britain and elsewhere. The following night, Elsa was closer to Queen Elizabeth and the Duke of Edinburgh than ever before or after. They, with other members of the royal family, sat in the front row of the balcony. Elsa must surely have felt the smallness of all previous triumphs.

That night, when she entered her dressing room to change into her costume, she found the flowers all gone. They had been removed to the balcony to honor the royal visitors without so much as a by-your-leave. Elsa soon learned that "Princess Margaret was the pilferer," as she put it, using language that once would have landed her in the Tower. She faced the awful truth: "Princess Margaret was not nearly as charming or as nice as I had imagined her to be. I realized that she was thoughtless and heedless. To top it off, she did not even bother to thank me for coming to England, at my own expense, or for giving up two weeks in June to devote myself to her charity, in the most idiotic and senseless performance of my life."

And why did Elsa not reveal these royal shortcomings in her 1957 book? Because she was part of a Windsor intrigue. I have no proof, and yet the plot lines are neatly in place for any amateur detective. The Duchess of Windsor was loathed by everyone in the royal family, for her perceived vulgarity, her vandalism of the throne, and its consequences—namely, forcing King George VI, father of Princess Elizabeth and Princess Margaret, to assume the heavy duties of kingship for which he was ill prepared. It was widely felt that the rigors of that office hastened his death.

Elsa's feud with the Windsors was well publicized in Britain, as in the United States. The Queen Mother, who knew her from Paris and London in the twenties, was shrewdly aware that Elsa lacked immunity to anything royal, no matter how trivial. And in spite of the Queen Mother's public image as a dear old lady with a twinkle in her blue eyes, she packed a bare bodkin among her lace hankies—if not a literal one, then a figurative one every bit as deadly.

Which brings us to the script that won't be produced by the BBC: The Queen Mother summons her daughters, and in Macbethish conference not around a cauldron but seated at tea, they cast Elsa Maxwell in the play, at no detriment to the palace because their motives will never be guessed. And yet how the American duchess will gnash her teeth to see her enemy cavorting where she herself will never penetrate.

Elsa was the perfect pawn not only because of enmity between her and the duchess, but also because the prestige she had once held in Britain had now evaporated. In this connection, I consulted the historian and journalist Jan Morris, who, as James Morris, reported for the *Times* of London and the *Manchester Guardian* in the fifties and who, in her own spheres, got around even more than Elsa. In an e-mail from her home in Wales, Morris wrote: "I don't believe that even in the forties and fifties she meant much over here, and the two neighbours I have just this minute consulted—both in middle-age—have never heard of her."

Elsa, shrewd and incapable of being deceived except when she wished it, probably guessed that Princess Margaret had only one use for her. After that, she was as disposable as a royal handkerchief. Elsa's gain, of course, matched that of the royal family: spite for the Duchess of Windsor. After Elsa and the duchess ended their quarrel, however, and spent considerable time together, Elsa realized that the duchess really was her friend—or, at least, a fine facsimile. And so, in 1963, Elsa decided to reveal the rascality of Princess Margaret. Besides, at that late hour, she knew that her one great wish, which might have been so easily granted by the princess, would never come true. Princess Margaret did not present her to the queen.

28 The Isles of Greece

$\mathcal{E}$lsa's rhapsodies about her friendship with the Greek royal family always sound off-key. In *The Celebrity Circus* she wrote of having met Queen Frederika in the early fifties, and: "Then, as now, I admired her more than any other living sovereign.* It was she who saved Greece from communism after the occupation. She went alone into the mountains and spoke to her subjects in person. 'Be Greeks first,' she pleaded, 'and Communists afterward, if you must!' "

Like her husband, Paul, King of the Hellenes, who ruled Greece from 1947 to 1964, Frederika of Hanover (1917–1981) was related to Queen Victoria and to the vast root system of Victoria's forebears and descendants who held countless European titles. Without taking on the byzantine history of the Greek monarchy and violent opposition to it, we may point out that she was widely considered "inherently undemocratic" (by G. S. Kaloudis, in *Modern Greek Democracy*, published in 2000 by University Press of America). Robert V. Keeley, a former American ambassador to Greece, described the queen as "notorious for her numerous arbitrary and unconstitutional interventions in Greek politics."

To balance Elsa's Hollywood-studio thumbnail, one should know that

---

*Elsa erred in calling Queen Frederika the sovereign. The sovereign was her husband, King Paul. Frederika was his consort.

during the Communist insurgency, the king and queen toured northern Greece under elaborate security to appeal for help in propping up their shaky regime. In no sense did Frederika "save" Greece from communism. Elsa's mountaintop image of the brave, lone queen winning over grizzled legions of guerrillas with Hanoverian charm is outrageous even for a sometime scriptwriter from Warner Bros. It's Elsa's royalty worship caramelized into Graustark hokum. Even *Time* magazine, which burned incense to the queen in its cover story in 1953, pointed out her "Teutonic inclination toward rigid government," and mentioned in passing that "three of her brothers were officers in Hitler's Wehrmacht."

Behind Elsa's billet-doux to Frederika, however, lies an intriguing rumor. In 1936, an article by the reporter Jane Eads appeared in a number of newspapers through the King Features Syndicate, a service owned by the Hearst Corporation. Eads led with: "Mayfair is waiting expectantly for newly restored King George of Greece to bestow some special mark of favor upon Elsa Maxwell and Elsie de Wolf Mendl, confident that stories that Elsa and Elsie 'carpetbagged' the Hohenzollern Greek back to his throne are substantially true and that he will not prove ungrateful." (This was George II of Greece, who ruled from 1922 to 1924, was deposed, and went into exile for eleven years until his restoration to the throne in 1935. He then ruled until his death in 1947, and was succeeded by his younger brother, Paul, whose queen consort was Elsa's beloved Frederika.)

Elsa and Elsie denied the rumor. "But the story persists nevertheless," continued Eads, "that Elsa together with her socially and financially potent friends in Paris and London did a great deal of maneuvering behind the scenes with the right people and thus brought about the restoration." If one burrowed in the secret archives of Greece, one might find evidence to support the rumor. For our purposes, what stands out is that more than a few took Elsa seriously as a minor kingmaker. It's likely that she fostered this image of herself as possessed of political powers. Indeed, given her vast network of friends and associates, it is plausible that she could exert influence. Governments might have found her useful as war threatened, and also during World War II. As for Elsie de Wolf, Lady Mendl, her husband was a British diplomat whose country had many reasons to wish for a monarch on the Greek throne—especially a blood relative of the Saxe-Coburg-Gothas who occupied Buckingham Palace.

If Elsa did play some part in the restoration of George II, that would help to explain why Queen Frederika, two decades later, invited her to lunch. In September 1954 Elsa was on a Greek island cruise aboard the *Gaviota*, owned by the Chilean industrialist and patron of the arts Arturo Lopez-Willshaw, whose father, said Elsa, founded a tin empire—other sources say guano, but Elsa was incapable of writing that word—and whose house in Paris Elsa described as "Louis XVI throughout." Also on the cruise were Baroness Lo Monaco (sketched by Elsa as "American-born, gay, loving, an ardent Christian Scientist, incapable of saying an unkind word of anyone"); Count and Countess Rossi, Baron de Rédé, Count Alex Castaja, and Henry ("Chips") Channon, born in Chicago and later a British subject who was elected to Parliament. Before the *Gaviota* docked at Piraeus, Elsa wired the queen the time of her arrival as one might an old school chum. Meanwhile, she also promised her illustrious fellow passengers an audience with the queen.

BARON DE REDE

B ob Kingdom, a British actor coming up in a later chapter, called on Baron Alexis de Rédé (1922–2004) a few years before the baron's death. Recalling that visit, which took place at the appropriately baronial seventeenth-century Hôtel Lambert, on the Ile Saint-Louis in Paris, Bob said: "The place was so camp. A flunky answered the door, or rather the gate, in a powdered wig and breeches. The whole place was dripping with gilt and velvet. The baron had been the best-kept boy in Europe, by millionaire Arturo Lopez-Willshaw. He told me that he liked Elsa, and thought her fun."

Born Alexis Dieter Rudolf Oscar von Rosenberg in Switzerland, he derived from a distinguished line of Jewish bankers. He met Lopez-Willshaw in New York, and they were soon acknowledged as a couple; Nancy Mitford called Alexis "La Pompadour *de nos jours*." Madame Lopez-Willshaw was hardly overjoyed at her husband's new amour, though she seems eventually to have adjusted. Officially he lived with her; in reality he spent most nights at the Hôtel Lambert. When Lopez-Willshaw died in 1962, Baron de Rédé inherited many millions, said to be half the fortune. To insure proper management of the money, the baron, with a partner, acquired a controlling interest in a British bank.

As a friend of Elsie de Wolfe, Alexis often visited her at the Villa Trianon. One day, according to her biographer Jane Smith, Elsie "took him aside and showed him a table. 'I want you to have it,' she said. 'I'm going to leave it to you in my will.' The baron demurred. 'No, really,' she insisted. 'You should have it. I want you to take it now.' Reluctantly, he accepted the gift, only to get a telephone call two weeks later from Elsie's secretary. The table cost six thousand dollars, she announced, and he could pay for it in three installments if he wished.'"

The queen's equerry met Elsa at the boat with an invitation to lunch with Their Majesties the next day at Tatoi, the summer palace located in the suburbs of Athens. None of the titled Europeans, nor the acerbic Chips Channon, were included, even though, since they outranked Elsa, strict protocol would have dictated that they be on the guest list. Elsa's red-carpet treatment hints that the royal family was somehow in her debt.

Not only the king and queen, but also two of their three children— Princess Sophia and Prince Constantine—celebrated Elsa's arrival in their kingdom. Later, she wrote about the occasion: "The talk was good—better, I am compelled to admit, than the food. I suppose I had expected something typically Greek, but there was nothing Greek about lunch at the Queen's table that day. It was plain, pleasant food in the English style: eggs Benedict first, then a chicken dish with vegetables; salad, cheese, and a simple blanc-mange for the sweet. All very good, but hardly inspired. I don't think the Queen gives much thought to food."

To welcome Elsa further, her hosts invited her to sit at the king's table at an important dinner at the Royal Jockey Club (in one of Elsa's books; the Royal Yacht Club in another) a few days later. Elsa's neglected co-voyagers were invited to this dinner, but according to her, "they were relegated to a separate table." It's no wonder that Frederika was Elsa's favorite queen.

At this dinner, the royal couple, having heard of Elsa's miracles in Venice and Monaco thirty years earlier, brought up the matter of tourism. Greece needed the money visitors would bring in. Elsa proposed "a Dutch-treat cruise through the islands, with a hundred of the world's biggest celebrities. Think of the publicity!" Already it sounds like a backyard musical with Mickey Rooney, Judy Garland, and "Let's put on a show!"

"But where would you get a ship large enough?" asked the queen.

Stavros Niarchos, the shipping tycoon, happened to be at a nearby table. "He will know how to get a ship," said Elsa.

And he did. He chartered the *Achilleus*, and when Elsa asked how much it would cost, Niarchos replied, "Consider it a *cadeau de Noël*." In the end he paid for everything from caviar to buses and cars to take Elsa's celebrities sightseeing among the ancient ruins. One of Elsa's favorite counts donated several hundred bottles of Moët et Chandon. When Niarchos asked Elsa whether she could get a hundred people, she exclaimed, "I can get a thousand!" She sent out one hundred fifty invitations, and got back a hundred and ten acceptances.

These would not qualify as "the world's biggest celebrities," however. Such a list might have included, for instance, Picasso, Elizabeth Taylor, Chanel, Frank Lloyd Wright. Instead, the biggest name on Elsa's ship when it sailed from Venice in September 1955 was Olivia de Havilland. She was accompanied by her husband, the journalist Pierre Galante. Others on the cruise were former French premier Paul Reynaud who, in 1939, had advised Elsa to leave France before the Germans arrived, and Madame Reynaud; Broadway producer Gilbert Miller and his wife, Kitty; Cesare Siepi, of the Metropolitan Opera; novelist and poet Frederic Prokosch; Millicent Hearst; the Duke and Duchess of Argyll; the Duc and Duchesse de Brissac; Count and Countess Crespi of Italy; Mr. and Mrs. Byron Foy of New York; the designer Valerian Rybar. In Athens, Aly Khan and Perle Mesta joined the group. (As the *Achilleus* was preparing to sail, the Duchess of Windsor arrived in Venice, having timed her entrance to match the arrival of Elsa's illustrious guests. "His Royal Highness and I come here," she said with poisonous innocence, "expressly not to take part in the social life.")

PERLE MESTA

Then—and now—some found it easy to confuse Elsa and Perle Mesta (1889–1975), an understandable perplexity, since both women were famous for their parties. But there the similiarity ends. Mrs. Mesta (as she was deferentially called) grew up wealthy and married money. When her husband died in 1925, he left her seventy-eight million dollars. Eminently respectable, she worked quietly for women's political rights, and in 1940 changed her affiliation to the Democratic Party. In 1949, President Truman named her as ambassador to Luxembourg, a post she held until 1953.

Poor Perle must have tired of the tag line that followed her forever once Irving Berlin bestowed it: "the hostess with the mostes' on the ball," from one of the hit songs in his Broadway show *Call Me Madam.* Ethel Merman played Mrs. Mesta—or Sally Adams, who of course resembled no person living or dead—onstage and in the 1953 film version. Sally was the full-throated American emissary to "Lichtenburg." (As part of the in-joke, Elsa's name is dropped in the song.)

Perle Mesta's parties usually took place in Washington, where they were populated by senators, members of Congress, ambassadors, and others who cranked the engines of government. Her influence as a hostess to the political establishment lasted only two decades, from about 1940 until 1960. To youthful Camelot, she seemed as passé as Mamie Eisenhower's fudge recipe. Like her parties, Perle seemed bland on the surface. Beneath her matronly smile, however, she packed a lively tongue. Her quiet comebacks lacked initial sting, though like the bite of a tiny sandfly, they raised a delayed welt.

Columnists craved a feud between Perle and Elsa. They thought they had it when Elsa described Perle as "a great hostess," but with the qualifier, "If anything, she's too good. She welcomes anyone and everyone, and a good many shameless climbers get in on others' coattails, but Perle is just too kindhearted to turn them away." To feud mongers who telephoned for Perle's response she said, like a true diplomat, "I think she's got something there. But how can I say 'no' to anybody who's dying to come?" Later she added, "I like Elsa and go to her parties and she comes to mine. We disagree on many things. She thinks political people are dull, and I don't." Elsa probably found Perle's parties staid, in need of a dash of controversy, and woefully deprived of the *Almanach de Gotha*.

No Greeks were invited—"That would be bringing coals to Newcastle," said Elsa. Then she decided against having any royalty on board, since, according to her, "they never have any money to spend." And surely she would know. "It's better to bring rich people to Greece who will spend money than poor kings and queens who won't." Among other things, Elsa planned the cruise as an exercise in democratic luxury. There was no seating protocol; passengers pulled their seat assignments out of a hat. Those who became seasick were fined, and Elsa added another innovation: "If a person wears his hat on the side of his head, that means he doesn't want anyone to talk to him." Spyros Skouras, president of 20th Century-Fox, sent twenty new movies to show.

As the *Achilleus* sails on, I turn the narrative over to Elsa, whose column of September 17 was wired to the *Journal-American* from the ship. "The most interesting places to me were Mycene and Epidaurus and Delos—of course, after Athens. We were fortunate to reach Athens at the beginning of their fabulous Music Festival, which took place under a full moon at the steps of the Acropolis in the beautiful frame of the ancient Herod Atticus theatre. The performance of Gluck's *Orfeo ed Euridice*, with our own Risë Stevens giving the most eloquent performance of her career in one of the oldest theatres in the world and with acoustics so perfect that no sound amplifiers or microphones were needed, was even more beautiful than Mozart's *Idomeneo*, which I also heard in the presence of the King and Queen of Greece, the Duchess of Kent, Princess Olga of Yugoslavia, and Princess Alexandra of Kent. Eleanor Steber in the Mozart opera made us all proud of our American singers.

"Speaking of singers, my own guest, Cesare Siepi, star bass-baritone, honored us with a little concert on the ship after dinner. I had caught a bad cold so I was unable to accompany him, but he rehearsed the songs with the ship's pianist and he could not give the audience enough. To my surprise and delight he had learned a song of mine which he had to repeat as an encore.

"Mycene, the birthplace of Agamemnon, has always fascinated me beyond words. His tomb was stark and realistic, and adjoining it, the superb gate of the lions, where Clytemnestra awaited his return, looked sinister and sombre. I am ashamed to say that after half an hour of one of our brilliant guides' lectures, one of my guests was heard to say, 'So this is Troy.' Considering that Troy is near the Dardenelles, I fear my guest had little knowledge of geography.

"Delos, the birthplace of my favorite god, Apollo, was absolutely bewitching. One friend was heard to ask, 'Is this where Apollo conquered the Turks?' and our patient guide set her straight."

This breathless travelogue sounds like *Edith Hamilton for Dummies,* and yet it suggests reasons for Elsa's unique position among the rich and high-born. Brainier than most of them, better educated even though self-taught, and also possessed of greater energy and imagination, she charmed, persuaded, and browbeat her followers, even as she flattered them in person and in print. Most important, she filled many a monotonous hour with games and merriment, so that even the dullest among them preferred to pay for Elsa's entertainments rather than to save their money and be bored.

Two guests—Broadway producer Gilbert Miller and his wife, Kitty—became obnoxious during the cruise, she by attempting to commandeer two staterooms, one as an oversize closet for her clothes, and he by bathing, "with plenty of soap," Elsa said, each morning in the ship's tiny swimming pool. Everyone on board was scandalized. To make matters worse, "both were gossips and troublemakers," and finally Elsa had enough. With the backing of the other guests, she told the Millers to leave the ship and get home the best way they could.

Elsa's immediate goal was publicity, which, she hoped, would lead to an influx of tourists to Greece. She said, "I don't believe there was an important popular magazine or newspaper in North America, South America, Britain or Free Europe that did not carry the story of our cruise, and a number of them supplemented text with pictures." Based on a random sample, I believe she had a point. On my desk now is a half-page article from *Time*, with a picture of Olivia de Havilland and Elsa; and similar features from the *New York Herald-Tribune*, the *San Francisco Chronicle*, the *San Francisco Examiner*, and of course Elsa's own column. To Elsa's surprise, the photograph that most publications ran was not a group shot of lords and ladies clustered around broken Corinthian columns, with the Acropolis in the background. Instead, they pictured Elsa attired in a blue-and-gold admiral's jacket and matching cap, and looking like Tugboat Annie crossed with Captain Queeg. Elsa's friend Jean Dessès designed the outfit for her as a joke. Elsa was nonplussed that her getup lured more attention than the glory that was Greece. Of her outfit, *Time* said it resembled "the official uniform of a six-star admiral of the Nepalese navy."

As the ship sailed from Santorini under a full moon, its owner, Markos Nomikos, lit up the coastline with torches, a spectacular effect that Elsa called both Wagnerian and eerie. Elsa was satisfied, for the cruise, she said, "had measured up on all counts to my canon of what a good party should be: it was novel, it was fun, and it did good." A few years later, she reported that Greek tourism had increased by some forty-five percent.

A few days after Christmas that year, 1955, Elsa gave a ball in honor of Stavros Niarchos and his September "*cadeau de Noël*" that had taken her and her guests through the Greek islands. Cholly Knickerbocker titled his column "Soiree for Tycoons and Tiaras," calling Elsa's latest "a triumph of elegance and gaiety . . . her affairs never fail to amuse because, like a good bartender, she knows the secret of the right mixture—enough imposing names to make it impressive but not too many to make it boring, masses of beautiful women, and enough youth to make it gay."

In Elsa's mix were two ambassadors dancing together: Clare Boothe Luce, the United States ambassador to Italy, and Greek ambassador to the United States George Melas. Among the other guests, Elsa's friends Mrs. Lytle Hull and Millicent Hearst . . . Marcos Nomikos, owner of the *Achilleus*, and another shipping tycoon, Basil Goulandris . . . bunches of princesses and duchesses . . . and a list of those women whom the columnist considered "beauties," all of them wearing tiaras, including C. Z. Guest, Jinx Falkenburg, and Mrs. Jack Kennedy, wife of the Massachusetts senator. Elsa had asked the ladies to wear tiaras for added elegance. Her own, lent by Harry Winston, dazzled with entwined diamond roses, making Elsa literally worth half a million, for a few hours at least.

No one knew it that night, but Jacqueline Kennedy foreshadowed the end of Elsa's era and the beginning of what would later be called "the sixties." Just as the fifties ended sometime between 1960 and 1963, so Elsa and her world were already hurtling toward oblivion. We know the story. One quick glimpse of the future convinces us that Elsa would have withered in a post-Eisenhower, post-Kennedy world.

What on earth would she have made of Truman Capote's black and white ball in 1966? Would she even have been on the guest list? Surely the host, and his party, were the antithesis of Elsa and the parties that made her famous. Elsa's entertainments—whether vast, intimate, plain, or glittery—sprang from her impulse of conviviality and a good time for all present. "Gaiety" was one of her favorite words. To Elsa, spontaneity within the planned structure of a party added sparkle and pizzazz.

Capote's stiff, vainglorious affair violated almost every one of Elsa's theories of party giving. Over five hundred imposing names, with egos to match—Elsa would surely have disapproved of the motley. Look at photographs taken that evening, and you see faces more strained than smiling. Did anyone really have fun? All were relieved, rather than elated—relieved to be there and not among the uninvited castaways. You might almost mistake the photos for a Diane Arbus exhibition, or those disturbing society candids by Weegee. Unlike many of Elsa's parties, no charity benefited from this one. It was Capote's present to himself, and as such the perfect prelude to the narcissicistic decades to follow. Elsa's summing up at the end of the Greek cruise is worth repeating: ". . . it was novel, it was fun, it did good." Truman Capote's ball wasn't even novel; Edgar Allan Poe had the idea first.

Of all the guests at Capote's ball, Lee Radziwill and Frank Sinatra might serve as figures in an allegory of the evening—*Boredom in the Ruins of Camelot*. Her icy face barely stretches into a wan smile. Sinatra looks as though he'd rather be anywhere else in the world. Indeed, he left early with his entourage even though Capote begged him to stay.

The New York Times, describing the arrival of guests, perhaps got it right: "They rolled off the assembly line like dolls, newly painted and freshly coiffed, packaged in silk, satin, and jewels, and addressed to Truman Capote, the Plaza Hotel." Packaged indeed: all those silks and satins were like ribbons that Capote would eventually rip from his evening of five hundred presents done up in black and white, to pile them up in a joyless heap like a sour brat.

29 One God, One Callas

*W*hat is it like to be in love with the greatest opera singer of the age? Elsa's infatuation with Maria Callas, that magnificent melomaniac, flamed high and hot, and had Elsa's devotion not been so absurdly impossible it might be counted as the second great love of Maria's life, after Aristotle Onassis. The embarrassing attachment, however, remained unreciprocated. Callas regarded the squat Elsa by turns as convenient factotum and chattering monkey. But also, in certain recesses of her heart, as more besides.

Soon after the pair first met, in 1956, Elsa, age seventy-six, was imparadised by this *monstre sacré*. For a time, Elsa lived in the tropic of Callas, buffeted by the torrid voice, the winds of tragedy, the heavy black clouds of anger . . . but lulled, also, by the gardenia sweetness of a Callas smile, or a rare caress. Maria, the volcanic island, beckoned, and Elsa answered the siren song.

Just as Elsa invented herself, so did Callas. Eventually there lived, inside the same body, Maria the woman and Callas the star. Maria, in private, referred to her other self as "Callas" and "her." Regarding the strange Callas beauty, few remembered, at the height of her greatness, that she had started out with an inauspicious face and body. A gawky girl with a slightly simian hairline, Callas rebranded herself as few had done before. No one knew exactly how she got the new body and the Helen of Troy face. (Later her husband claimed that she employed a tapeworm.) The voice, of course, was always there—except when it rebelled and zoomed out of control—that voice of incendiary emotions: murderous passion, rage, naked heartbreak previously unheard on the opera stage. Elsa marveled at this musical Mona Lisa with a streak of coarseness swiped across her art.

When Callas made her debut at the Met on October 29, 1956, in *Norma*, Elsa's avid anticipation—this was, after all, the great event of the season—slumped. In her column of November 3 she wrote: "Her 'Casta Diva' was a great disappointment. Perhaps she was nervous, or maybe, through dieting, she's lost some of the magnificent voice we have heard so much about. The voice I heard was hollow, denuded of the luscious tones I was listening for; but as the opera went on, her softer passages, when she did not force the tone, were supremely beautiful—so she's got it there somewhere, but only occasionally. It seemed like the voices of two different women singing."

(In *The Celebrity Circus*, which Elsa dedicated "To M.C., with great admiration and affection and love," she devoted seventeen pages to Callas. In those pages are some of her best writing, along with astute criticism of the vagaries, and the greatness, of the Callas voice. There, her account of their friendship is mostly level-headed, and balances the extravagant hearsay of many a subsequent Callas biography.)

For a long time, Elsa had been a friend and partisan of Maria's supposed archrival, Renata Tebaldi, whose acting, even Elsa admitted, failed to excite although her singing was impeccable. (Asked by Elsa, in 1957, whether she would consider teaming up with Callas in a grand-diva *Turandot* benefit, Tebaldi shook her head. "Ah, Elsa" she sighed, "God would never bless such a charity.")

Like many opera devotées, Elsa had long searched for "the perfect blend of actress and singer, a great voice combined with stage genius." It took a while for her to recognize it in this irregular, witchy Greek swan worshiped by half the world and spat on by the other half.

After Callas's debut performance, Elsa was at supper in the Ambassador Hotel's Trianon Room with Dario Soria, of Angel Records, who planned to introduce her to the diva. Recalling the evening, Elsa said, "I gathered Mrs. Lytle Hull; Lauder Greenway, president of the Met's board of directors;

Wally Toscanini, daughter of the conductor; Count Lanfranco Rasponi, a writer on society and the arts; and we saved three places for Mario del Monaco, Fedora Barbieri, and Cesare Siepi (the latter three had also performed that night in *Norma*.)"

Just as their meal arrived, Dario Soria dashed up to their table and said to the singers, "You must come and sit with Madame Callas."

"We want to stay here!" caroled Barbieri and Del Monaco, who had perhaps been delighted enough by their imperious colleague.

"You must go," said Elsa, and shooed them away. Then Soria invited Elsa, who declined, saying, "She has given me the greatest disappointment I have ever suffered from an artist." All of this Elsa included in her column. Seven years later, as she reread it for inclusion in *The Celebrity Circus*, she reflected on "whether the total experience of hearing her for the first time was not more disturbing than it was disappointing. Something about her had struck me, though I was hardly aware of it then."

Elsa returned to the Met on November 15 for the first Callas *Tosca*. Having seen "most of the great Toscas," Elsa catalogued them for her readers: "Milka Ternina, years ago; Emmy Destinn, who looked like a cook and sang like an angel; Geraldine Farrar, whose voice was not great, but who was lovely to watch (I heard her sing *Tosca* with Caruso and Scotti, and Toscanini conducting). I even remember Mary Garden as Tosca. Her voice was small, but she was a magnificent actress. I heard Germaine Lubin at the Paris Opéra; but perhaps the most memorable of all my Toscas was Claudia Muzio."

At the end of that blazing roll call, Elsa added her impressions of Callas in one of her greatest roles. "Again I felt disappointment. Callas' first act, I thought, was particularly poor." Elsa's description of Callas as Tosca that night is unique in its details. "Her voice thrilled me, but I found myself silently quarreling with the stage business she had assigned herself. At the end of the jealous scene with Cavaradossi over the portrait he is painting, she abruptly took from her bag a *minaudière* and powdered her nose. When Scarpia told her that Cavaradossi had betrayed her, in spite of her anguish she again powdered her nose. In the second act she sang 'Vissi d'arte' dead center, almost on top of the prompter's box. Though she sings to God in this aria, she sings to Scarpia as well, to try to soften his heart. It seemed to me that Callas' appeal for applause was far more important to her than an appeal to either Scarpia or God."

When Elsa returned to the Met in early December for a third Callas performance—*Lucia di Lammermoor*—she said that "my reserve began to break." In her next column, she wrote that *Lucia* was by far the best thing Callas had done in New York. A few nights later, at the Knickerbocker ball, Elsa glimpsed, from a distance, Maria and her entourage seated with Spyros Skouras, the Greek-born president of 20th Century-Fox. Next day, Elsa predicted that he would star Callas in a movie. (The terrible irony here is that Callas was never filmed in a complete opera performance. Act Two of her *Tosca* at Covent Garden in 1964 was filmed, and to see it is to behold her greatness. She starred in Pasolini's *Medea*, in 1969, and though she's far from her best, the picture at least suggests what she might have done on film.)

Late in 1956, Elsa was involved with the so-called Greek ball (officially, the American Hellenic Welfare Fund) at the Waldorf. Again, Spyros Skouras was in attendance, and this time, as Elsa passed his table, he jumped up, grabbed her hand, and said, "Come with me."

"I can't," Elsa replied. "I have to get the show going."

"Someone at my table wants to meet you," he said, pulling the reluctant Elsa along with some effort.

"I don't think Madame Callas would enjoy meeting me," Elsa said, loudly and distinctly, knowing that her unflattering columns would have reached the diva, who was now within earshot.

"On the contrary!" called out Maria, reaching long, elegantly tapered hands toward Elsa. Like a bejeweled octopus, she entwined the Maxwell hands in her own, and squeezed. "Miss Maxwell," she breathed, "you are the one woman in New York I do want to meet, because—you are honest."

Even brazen Elsa was taken aback. "That is nice of you indeed, Madame Callas," she managed. "One day we must have tea or a cocktail together and talk it over."

Whose come-on line was better? Maria's, surely, for she had prepared a script. The scene ends with Callas, in her international accent and slightly brassy speaking voice, devouring Elsa with great feline eyes and the smile of a sorceress. "I will ring you, if I may?"

Scripted, indeed, like the plot of a verismo opera. Elsa, in her columns, had detracted more than the quotes above might indicate. Certainly, to Maria and her husband, Giovanni Battista Meneghini, these writings amounted to "attacks." But then, their joint paranoia created enemies behind every pilaster. "We have to shut her up!" preached Meneghini, again and again.

Finally Maria said, "Leave it to me." At the Greek ball, the soprano's adversary stood exposed and vulnerable. That's when, as Meneghini put it, "Maria decided to go into action."

Who would fail to succumb to those Callas blandishments? Certainly not Elsa. The tone of her columns brightened. If she could have written little Xs at the bottom, for kisses, she might have done so. "When I looked into her amazing eyes," Elsa swooned, "I realized she is an extraordinary person." From that day on, Elsa championed Callas as no one else in journalism did. Elsa was cheerleader, lapdog, fan club prez, and serving wench to the goddess. And Callas encouraged her simpering slave, cooing endearments to her and, with friends an hour later, raging that she had wasted time with "that fat old son of a bitch."

Elsa's approval burnished the Callas image, or so Meneghini believed. In New York, at least, she morphed in the mind of society from the fishwife diva to a beloved New Yorker come home at last. "Maria was invited to appear on television programs and to attend balls and important receptions," he said. She had escaped her shy cocoon, perched on Elsa's back.

Christmas 1956. A special messenger arrived at Elsa's apartment in the Waldorf bringing a large berry tree and a note from Maria. "Dear Elsa," it read, "I want to see you. We must have a talk. I wish everything for you for Christmas and the New Year. With my great friendship and affection, Maria Callas." Elsa, head over heels, sighed as she imagined a future reaching toward the stars.

Callas finished her short season at the Met on December 19 and had several weeks before her next commitments. Soon after the New Year, Elsa and Maria met up at the Imperial ball at the Waldorf *en costume*. The theme that year was famous persons in history. Elsa went as Catherine the Great, Maria as Hatshepsut. Meneghini said her jewels were valued at a million dollars. Photographs of her arrival, with two strong men holding her train, were published in newspapers around the world. She and Elsa chatted briefly, and were photographed together.

Then Callas flew to engagements in Chicago, London, and Milan. Elsa, as usual, seemed everywhere at once, and owing to full schedules they didn't spend time together until well into 1957. Meneghini said that, pending closer acquaintance, Elsa "followed us everywhere with telephone calls, letters, and telegrams. She even telephoned during the night. It was obvious that she had a crush on my wife, and Maria was aware of it. There were serious and unfair insinuations about my wife and Elsa Maxwell at the time. Some people, aware of Maxwell's proclivities, assumed that Callas also shared these tendencies."

The "affair" became as drawn-out and labyrinthine as the doomed love in an opera. Meneghini described Elsa's letters as "oppressive . . . overflowing with affection and full of the most grotesque inanities." And, he added, "Maria was nauseated by them." Eventually she stopped reading Elsa's billets-doux, and passed them to her husband unopened. Having made her conquest, Maria determined to hold the devotion of this one true media acolyte. Every other journalist was fickle and, Callas believed, grossly unfair. "I was persecuted," she railed.

Elsa apparently believed that Callas, in some form or fashion, would return her tender affection. Meneghini, in *My Wife, Maria Callas*, exercised no restraint in quoting intimate passages from Elsa's love letters: "I do not dare to write all that I feel, or you would consider me mad. But I am not that at all; I am only a person different from the others." And, "Maria, the only thing that sends me into ecstasy is your face and your smile."

By September 1957, Elsa seemed to think of nothing but promoting the happiness and the social success of Maria Callas. Although we cannot know for sure, it's reasonable to assume that, during their conversations, Maria expressed the wish to join Elsa's flashbulb parade of crowned heads, lords and ladies, and big-screen celebrities, and to savor their nonstop nightlife. Callas had reached the pinnacle of artistic fame, but Maria had worked since girlhood with hardly a day off. She felt every year more deprived of—

what? Sexual satisfaction may well have been her unexpressed longing. She told Franco Zeffirelli that marital relations with her husband occurred no more than once a year. Other friends speculated that the marriage was never consummated. And Maria, conservative and pious, did not condone affairs.

Another key to Maria's strange relationship with Elsa is this: long estranged from her own mother, she seems to have usurped Elsa as a mother figure. Onto this surrogate she then projected her need for maternal love, along with the full hatred she felt toward Evangelia Callas, the implacable parent who inflicted some incurable secret wound on the young Maria. Added to this dangerous formula was Elsa's own long-ago maternal rupture from Laura Maxwell.

Elsa, of course, saw herself as anything but a mother figure for Callas. In her beclouded imagination, she was a suitor on the threshold of bliss. And so she did the natural thing, for her: to celebrate such happiness, she planned a great sparkling party in Venice to honor Maria. The subtext of this event, for those who could decode the semiotics: After tonight, Maria belongs to me.

Yet another strand of this muddled DNA is Elsa's wish to experience vicariously, through the Callas beauty, what it must feel like to attract the eyes of desire. Although Elsa made endless sport of herself—her looks, her weight, her clumsiness—somewhere in her soul she must have craved the opposite image. Along comes Callas, who had transcended homeliness and fat to become a ravishing Venus. How could Elsa not succumb?

Had a clairvoyant warned Elsa, Maria, and Meneghini of the consequences to spring from that Venetian gala on September 3, 1957, all three might have trembled like Verdi heroines, and rushed off to church to light candles for deliverance.

Elsa never forgot Cole Porter's birthday. *(Courtesy of Mabel Mercer Foundation Archive)*

I get a kick out of you! Elsa and Cole, ca. 1938. *(Courtesy of Mabel Mercer Foundation Archive)*

May Boley in *Jubilee,* the 1935 Cole Porter musical. Her character is Eva Standing—*standing* in for Elsa Maxwell. Moss Hart, who wrote the book, described Eva as "a delicate mouselike creature" who was "as helpless as the Bethlehem Steel Company and as delicate as Jack the Ripper." *(Photofest)*

Though often *in* Hollywood, Elsa was not *of* Hollywood. With Constance Bennett and Darryl F. Zanuck, 1939. *(Photofest)*

Elsa and Cary Grant, 1943.
(Photofest)

Elsa's greatest love, she said, was music, and she could play anything by ear after one hearing, from show tunes to symphonies. *(Photofest)*

"All dressed up and nowhere to go except to *you* this Xmas day with my love, Elsa." *(Collection of the author)*

Elsa adored Aly Khan, and resented the intrusive photographer who trespassed on their dinner. *(Collection of the author)*

Elsa and Marilyn Monroe, ca. 1955 *(Photofest)*

Elsa and Joan Crawford at the party hosted by 20th Century-Fox for Joan's 1947 film *Daisy Kenyon*. *(Photofest)*

Elsa and Gina Lollobrigida at the Berlin Film Festival, 1958. *(Photofest)*

Elsa and debutantes. *(Collection of the author)*

Elsa and Princess Vasili at barnyard
party, 1939. *(Photofest)*

Elsa, by Hollywood caricaturist
Jacques Kapralik. *(Jacques Kapralik
Collection, American Heritage Center,
University of Wyoming)*

Elsa arrives in New York on board the *Queen Elizabeth*, 1947. *(Photofest)*

Elsa in Venice, 1954. Few of her readers guessed that she often used ghostwriters. *(Photofest)*

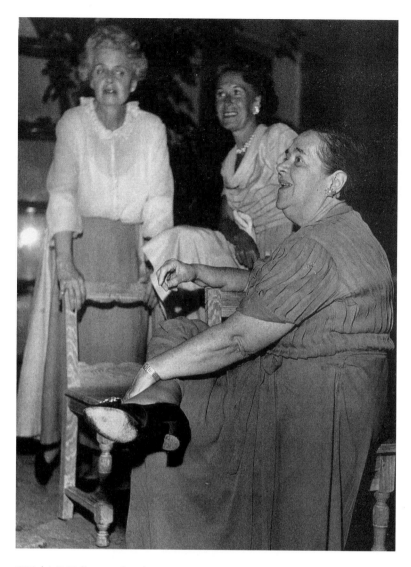

"Dickie" Fellowes-Gordon, Virginia (Mrs. Darryl) Zanuck, and Elsa in the South of France. Owing to precautions of the closet, Elsa and "Dickie" were rarely photographed together. *(Jean Howard Collection, American Heritage Center, University of Wyoming)*

Elsa used this happy image for a holiday card. Inside, the greeting read, "Happiness for the New Year from Elsa." *(Courtesy of Fredrick Tucker)*

Iran's representative to the United Nations presents a rare Persian rug to Elsa in 1959, a gift from the Shah in gratitude for Elsa's efforts on behalf of his country. Did she mistake it for a pashmina? *(Photofest)*

Elsa fell desperately in love with Maria Callas in 1957. *(Collection of the late Peter Urbanek)*

Aristotle Onassis, Maria Callas, unidentified man, and Elsa at El Morocco in New York, ca. 1960. *(Collection of the author)*

C. Z. Guest, Mrs. Edgar Leonard, and Elsa, cochairs of a charity ball in the early 1950s. *(Photofest)*

Elsa became a regular guest on *The Jack Paar Show* in the late fifties. *(Photofest)*

Elsa and Jack, angry at Walter Winchell. Their blazing feud with the columnist made the network nervous when Winchell threatened to sue. *(Photofest)*

Geneviève, the Parisian chanteuse, was also a frequent guest on *The Jack Paar Show*. She and Elsa gossiped in French while Paar scratched his head. *(Collection of the author)*

Elsa in 1963, shortly before her death. *(Photofest)*

British actor Bob Kingdom played both Elsa and her sometime friend, J. Edgar Hoover, in a one-man show in London and New York in the late 1990s and in 2000. *(Courtesy of Bob Kingdom)*

Bob Kingdom in costume as Elsa Maxwell. *(Courtesy of Bob Kingdom)*

30 Snakes on a Plane

In *The Celebrity Circus*, there is a single fleeting reference to the party in Venice. In Callas lore, however, the event figures as a watershed, for it marks the first unraveling of her career. That decline began in the months before Elsa's party, and it resulted from ill health, extremely bad publicity, lack of a press agent, quarrels with the management of half a dozen world-famous opera companies—one might as well throw in hubris and nemesis for good measure.

More than anything, however, fate struck that night in the person of Aristotle Onassis, whom Callas met for the first time when introduced by Elsa. For the past fifty years, dark rumors have spread that Elsa, in some occult way, foresaw Callas in thrall to Onassis and labored to bring about their deadly liaison, along with the wreck of both lives. Elsa's motive, in that scenario, is revenge on Callas for spurning her advances. This, of course, is tabloid malarky.

Elsa simply introduced the two Greeks, who at first took a distanced interest in each other. Owing to exhaustion, low blood pressure, anemia, depression, and irritability, Callas at the time lacked curiosity. Her strength had run out. In recent months, she had quarreled with Herbert von Karajan at the Vienna Staatsoper over money. The upshot was that she never sang again in Vienna. In August, shortly before Elsa's party, Callas had caused a kerfuffle in Scotland, and had borne the fury of the British press, when she supposedly walked out of an obligation at the Edinburgh Festival.

She was innocent. Having signed a contract for four performances, which she gave in spite of ill health and a damp climate that adversely affected her voice, she learned to her dismay and outrage that the manager of La Scala, under whose auspices she had traveled to Edinburgh, had volunteered her for a fifth performance. She refused and left for Venice instead, where she had agreed to attend Elsa's party. If she felt ambivalent toward this soiree, she at least knew that the climate of Venice, a city she loved, would heal her voice and raise her spirits. Her departure from Scotland was portrayed in the headlines as the caprice of a fickle diva who preferred partying to work. No one mentioned that her doctors had cautioned her not to go in the first place.

On the night of Elsa's ball, which took place at the Hotel Danieli, Maria still looked pale and gaunt. In *Greek Fire: The Story of Maria Callas and Aristotle Onassis*, Nicholas Gage describes her outfit as "a gown with a tight black bodice, a white satin cummerbund, and a voluminous skirt of white polka-dotted satin. Her arms were encased in long black gloves." The theme of the party was a fancy-headdress competition. One countess, according to Gage, "created a balloon, enveloping herself in a striped paper sphere, and the Marquise de Cadava managed to construct on top of her head a miniature Venetian campanile. Princess Forta Ruspoli was unrecognizable as a white Persian cat and won second prize for her costume. The white feathered headdress of Tina Onassis [wife of Aristotle] stretched like an egret's crest two feet high, but was not spectacular enough to win her the first prize of a brooch, which went to Baroness Lo Monaco, who, according to Elsa, came as 'an elderly bride with a great nose: she was quite the funniest thing I have ever seen.'" Elsa herself wore a lace dress that resembled a tablecloth, with a mink stole and a rakish doge's hat that could have passed for a mushroom, and that she misplaced before the end of the evening.

Among the other one hundred seventy guests were Henry Fonda and his fourth wife, Afdera Franchetti; Mr. and Mrs. Artur Rubinstein; Contessa Natalia Volpi di Misurata, Merle Oberon, and Arturo Lopez-Willshaw. When, sometime after midnight, Elsa finally introduced "the two most famous living Greeks in the world" to each other, they exchanged the usual pleasantries, then Tina Onassis joined them and the three chatted for a while. No erotic fireworks were visible, though Callas and Onassis seemed to find more and more topics of common interest. They spoke the same language, literally and figuratively; Greek, of course, and both came from lower-middle-class families. From inauspicious origins, they had conquered their respective worlds of opera and shipping.

After the party, Maria and Meneghini stayed on for five days in Venice. Onassis, whose yacht, the *Christina*, was anchored nearby, offered to put his fancy motorboat, with two crewmen, at Maria's disposal for the remainder of her stay. Elsa called those five days "Callas Week." The two couples—Onassis and Tina, Meneghini and Maria—went everywhere together: another all-night party in the palazzo of Count Volpi; drinks in Harry's Bar; dinner at Florian's; strolling the Lido at sunset with the Fondas; then back to the *Christina* for cocktails.

During those warm September days, as Elsa's party receded in memory, she wrote a column describing it in frilly detail. By distorting the facts of Maria's attendance, she fueled the continuing storm back in Britain over "another Callas walkout," as the headlines wrongly persisted in labeling her departure from Edinburgh. Elsa wrote: "I have never given a better dinner and ball in my life. It had a flare of such joy and happiness. I played the piano and Callas sat on the platform by me humming 'Stormy Weather.' I have had many presents in my life but *I have never had a star give up a performance in an opera because she felt she was breaking her word to a friend*." [emphasis added] Those who accuse Elsa of setting out to sabotage Callas—as in this piece of sloppy, egotistic journalism—forget that September of 1957 was a continuing aria for Elsa. At last, it seemed, she had triumphed with a party that enveloped her heart. All the same, Elsa's disregard for facts helped to stain the Callas reputation throughout the opera world. A less self-serving press agent might have controlled the damage, but Elsa was the only one on duty. (Strictly speaking, Elsa did not prevaricate. Callas, who had fulfilled all her Edinburgh obligations and was free to go where she chose, may well have told Elsa something like, "I wouldn't break a promise to a friend." Elsa apparently heard something quite different, more like a declaration of love.)

Returning to Milan on September 8, Maria faced battalions of enemies. La Scala, her home opera house, had decided to cut her down. Antonio

Ghiringhelli, the general manager, refused to issue a statement establishing her innocence in the Edinburgh debacle. Meanwhile, in mid-September, on orders from her doctors, Callas canceled a performance scheduled to open the season at the San Francisco Opera. Although she promised to honor her October appearances, the director, Kurt Adler, flew into a rage, canceled all of her performances, and sued her for breach of contract.

My flippant suggestion, some pages back, that Elsa's love might almost be counted as the second great passion of Maria's life, looks a bit less absurd as evidence stacks up. They spent countless hours together, from 1957 until a year or two before Elsa's death, and one wonders why, if Maria detested Elsa so much, she didn't shoo her away. In March 1957 Elsa flew to Milan, at Maria's invitation, to hear Callas in *Anna Bolena* at La Scala. They were photographed in a close embrace at the airport. Maria had taken time off from rehearsals to meet Elsa, who was to be her house guest. The payoff: a torrent of worshipful columns on Callas.

In June, Elsa took Maria on a whirlwind tour of Paris. The Windsors invited them to tea. They touched down at a Rothschild cocktail party, followed by dinner at Maxim's, and the next day they took in the races with Aly Khan. In November 1957 Elsa rose at four in the morning to meet Callas and Meneghini at Idlewild (now JFK) Airport. "It was a grueling hour," Elsa proclaimed in her next column, "the time I sometimes go to bed." A few days later, Millicent Hearst and Elsa gave a dinner party for Maria, including entertainment by Bobby Short, who sang Cole Porter songs as the composer sat among the dinner guests. Dickie was there, too, but her views on Maria Callas went unrecorded.

November 1957 was surely "Callas Month" in Elsa's engagement calendar: a week later she flew to Dallas to support Maria in her debut there. Elsa had a secondary mission, one that for most writers would have been paramount: she had come to sign copies of her latest book, *How to Do It, or The Lively Art of Entertaining*. For Elsa, however, the book launch at Neiman-Marcus played second fiddle to the Callas concert at State Fair Music Hall. Local papers made no mention of Elsa's dedication page, but to Elsa that page mattered greatly. For the book was dedicated "To Maria."

Callas had come to town at the invitation of a trusted friend, Lawrence Kelly, formerly with the Lyric Opera of Chicago, where, in 1954, he had organized Callas's American debut. Now, in 1957, having just chartered the Dallas Civic Opera, he easily persuaded Callas to give the inaugural concert. Callas was never impressed by the big shots of opera: Rudolf Bing at the Met, Ghiringhelli at La Scala, von Karajan in Vienna. Those who, in her opinion, "served music," to use a favorite Callas expression, were the ones who really mattered. For them, she would sing in a pup tent. Dallas, a comparative backwater in 1957, seemed startingly unaware of the megastar whose plane would soon land at tiny Love Field.

Indeed, a few days before the concert barely half the tickets had sold. For patrons of the opera, this embarrassing neglect foretold disaster for their new company. And how would Callas react? Would she even go on? When Elsa got wind of the sagging box office, she flew into action. "My friend Maria Callas is too great an artist to sing to an empty house," she announced to an influential Dallas lady. Elsa promoted the concert on local radio and television shows (for she was better known to the population at large than Maria was), and in all her newspaper interviews. And then she spent two thousand dollars to buy up the remaining tickets. Pulling strings all over town, she arranged for employees of Neiman-Marcus and other department stores to attend the concert gratis, along with teachers and students from high schools and colleges. Even so, the large house was not full when Callas came onstage.

Mary Carter, a young Dallas woman at the time who became a close friend of Maria Callas and also a friend of Elsa's, recently filled me in on events. "If Elsa was your friend," she said, "she was a really good friend. There wasn't a phony bone in her body. And it was always exciting to be with her. So smart—brilliant, really. And she enjoyed every second she was alive."

Knowing that Mary Carter's family was among those who sponsored the annual Met tour to Dallas in those days, I asked about her involvement with the fledgling Civic Opera. "I stood on a street corner with a tambourine raising money," she said, and after I stopped laughing, she added, "That's not much of an exaggeration!"

Mary knew Callas through Lawrence Kelly, a close friend of hers as well as of Callas. "A few days before that inaugural concert, I went with

Lawrence to meet her and Meneghini at the airport." One would expect a sumptuous luncheon to await Maria Callas and entourage at the finest table in Dallas. Instead: "We had lunch in whatever greasy spoon there was at Love Field in 1957: Maria, Meneghini, Lawrence, and me. And her maid!"

I had to know more about Callas and airport food. "Oh, I think she enjoyed it. She wasn't that particular. Once we went to Disneyland, and she loved the corn dogs and cotton candy."

Mary Carter concurs that Elsa had a crush on Callas. "It was not mutual. I remember once in New York Maria asked me to join her for lunch with Elsa to avoid an awkward tête-à-tête. That's the way it was." Asked about Meneghini, Mary said: "He was crude. The marriage was expedient, but Maria took it very seriously."

Mary recalled that while in Dallas, Callas and Meneghini stayed at the Adolphus, *the* celebrity hotel in those days. Elsa, however, stayed with a prominent family she had befriended on previous visits. "She accepted their invitation, and in a letter she announced what she would like for breakfast and also the china pattern that she preferred!" When I said this seemed greatly out of character, Mary said, "I think they found it very amusing. Being good sports, they went out and bought the china." (All the same, I suspect it was a private joke among friends. I can imagine Elsa's tease: "Now you know I can't face Blue Willow in autumn," or something similar. Elsa had many friends in town, for she had been coming to Dallas since 1939, when she staged an elaborate coming-out party for a local debutante and her five hundred guests.)

LA STUPENDA

Whenever one diva or duchess slipped from Elsa's grasp, a replacement was quickly found. Enter Joan Sutherland, who made her American debut in 1960 in Handel's *Alcina* at the Dallas Opera. Journalists, fans, and critics from everywhere flocked to Dallas, including Elsa, who stayed for several weeks. In her autobiography, *A Prima*

Donna's Progress, Dame Joan recalled that "in my dressing-room for the opening matinée performance I found a huge vase of four dozen red roses from Elsa Maxwell. At the party after the opera I thanked her for her lovely thought, at which she roared laughing. 'Oh,' she said, 'enjoy them. I arrived today and found them in a hotel room. It's Sunday and I don't know where to get flowers, so I had them delivered to you at the theatre.' Her honesty gained my respect." A Sutherland biographer added a remark that Elsa either made, or should have: "Besides, I saved eighty dollars."

The following year, in New York, Dame Joan and her husband, Richard Bonynge, had lunch at the Colony with Elsa and the Duchess of Windsor: "Elsa kept the conversation spinning in her inimitable style. She confessed that she felt responsible for Callas's vocal decline, having introduced her into the whirl of the social jet-setters. This increased our admiration for her apparent candour and directness."

Returning to New York after the concert, Callas, her maid, Meneghini, and Elsa took the same plane. Something drastic happened on board, but details were hushed up. Since Meneghini didn't speak English, he reported only that "during the return flight to New York, there were heated words between the two which generated considerable surprise." The reason: "By that time my wife had finally had it with Elsa, and she was certain that she now had the upper hand." According to him, "reporters learned of it and the news that the friendship between Callas and Elsa Maxwell had gone up in smoke was circulated as if it were some big event. The press had a field day with it."

Such an event today might make the evening news. In those days of placid air travel, however, flight attendants were not unduly concerned. Perhaps fresh cocktails were offered as balm. At any rate, Maria refused to speak to Elsa for the remainder of the flight. Back in New York, however, a ripple of gossip reached the tabloids. And *Time*.

In *Greek Fire*, Nicholas Gage, a reliable chronicler, suggests that, although no exact explanation exists for the quarrel, "there is strong evidence that it stemmed from Maria's rebuffing Elsa's sexual overtures." Maria and Meneghini left immediately for Milan, but Elsa felt the heat. Rumors had her worried. Since Meneghini handled not only his wife's career but her correspondence, as well, Elsa cabled him: "Tell Maria that if *Time* magazine asks if our friendship ended in Dallas, as they asked me, she should deny everything categorically, as I did. I wanted to discover the origin of this gossip which has been picked up by all the American television networks, and I learned that it began with an indiscreet remark on the part of a member of the crew on the plane. This news item must be stopped."

Then, on December 15, Elsa wrote Maria an eight-page letter, parts of which appear in Meneghini's book, and similar versions in other Callas biographies. Nicholas Gage, however, obtained a copy of the original, which he describes as a "farewell letter" from Elsa that is "a fascinating fabric of self-pity, boasting, veiled threats, and the anguished recriminations of a broken-hearted lover."

Excerpts from this astonishing document: "I had to write to thank you for having been the innocent victim of the greatest love one human being could feel for another . . . it exists no longer . . . it brought no happiness to you and after a few wonderful weeks it brought only misery to me. You killed my love that day on the plane from Dallas . . . That I could have fallen with such a supreme state of madness and insanity now fills me with self-disgust."

Scrutinizing the letter, one wonders whether Elsa was in love, or love-sick. That's because she is healing as she writes. The very ink from her pen is like a therapy drip in reverse: it drains the bile from her heart. Writing near Christmas, she mentions that peace and goodwill should guide one's thoughts. She tells Maria that all is forgotten, "a thing of the past," and that when they meet again they must be kind to each other—to avoid the world's gossip. Elsa promises that she will continue to be Callas's "greatest champion," and that nothing can take away from her the unspeakable joy of beholding Callas on the stage. Then she reveals to Callas that she, Elsa, bought half the tickets for the Dallas concert. Rambling a bit, Elsa claims to tell this secret only for fear that Maria might hear it from someone else.

Elsa mentions that she will be in Rome for the Callas *Norma* the following month, and that Callas had better be good. Elsa's implication: or else.

That's because now that she is no longer in love, the scales have fallen from her eyes as a critic. Winding up with conventional holiday wishes, Elsa writes once more as a friend, and not a woman scorned: "I think of you always with kindness and tenderness Maria—may you keep well may you sing beautifully and may God always bless you."

This sudden turnabout suggests that Elsa was too wise to lose her heart—or all of it—to Callas. Instead, she may have had an opera queen's crush on the phenomenon: awed by the art; agog at the Pygmalion transformation engineered by Callas herself; dazzled by the beautiful calamity always on the verge of happening, and the Callas sorcery that kept it at bay. Surely Elsa knew that Maria Callas would never love her in return. Elsa took the gamble—but she didn't play all of her chips.

31 Rome Trembled

On January 2, 1958, all Rome gazed in the same direction: toward the Teatro dell'Opera, where Callas would sing *Norma* that evening. Two nights earlier, on New Year's Eve, she had gone out on the town with friends, she had stayed up late, and on New Year's Day she awoke with a scratchy throat. By the day of performance, she had a vocal emergency.

Meneghini calls the resulting "situation" the ugliest in her career, "one which is still remembered as the most publicized scandal in the history of opera in this century." And he's right. The president of Italy was in the audience that night, along with enough celebrities to populate a Fellini spectacle. Newsreel footage shows the arrival of Gina Lollobrigida, Anna Magnani, the painter Giorgio de Chirico, European high society, politicians, and clergy just short of the pope.

Despite the parlous state of her health, the pressure on Callas was enormous. *She must not cancel.* The management refused to find a substitute, reasoning, correctly, that no one could replace Callas. Meneghini urged her to try, given the importance of the occasion and also the fact that the performance was scheduled to be broadcast throughout the country. Doctors rushed to Maria's side. She sprayed her throat hourly, drank her medicine, applied poultices, prayed to her favorite icon, crossed herself repeatedly, and hoped for a miracle. Elsa, as promised, had come to Rome. Letting bygones be bygones, she rushed to the side of the speechless diva. As dedicated a drama queen as Callas, Elsa relished this foreign crisis. Gladly did she spray the golden throat. She offered motherly advice to the hapless woman who, two weeks earlier, she was ready to forget. Elsa, too, cautioned Maria not to cancel, even as she hovered by the bedside like a Madonna at the foot of the cross.

Finally, Maria went on. At the end of Act One, near collapse in her dressing room, she told the manager that she could not continue. He begged her to try. The director, Margherita Wallmann, reiterated that the most difficult musical moments were over. If nothing else, she suggested, Callas might speak the lines and not sing them. Desperation mounted. The conductor, Gabriele Santini, appealed to her as Elsa, once more the Callas handmaiden, dabbed Maria's face with cologne. The intermission dragged on for close to an hour, until finally it was announced that the performance had been canceled. The management cravenly omitted the detail that the prima donna had a very sore throat.

Fortunately, Maria and Meneghini left the opera house by an underground passage leading to their hotel. Angry crowds blocked the theatre exits. The furor went on all night, with apoplectic mobs surrounding the opera house and eventually moving on to the Meneghinis' hotel, where they shouted abuse in the street all night. Even by the emotional standards of Italy, the outrage was unprecedented. Every newspaper in the counry attacked Callas, and at least one included Elsa in its assault. *Il Giorno* called Callas a second-rate artist and referred to her "dangerous friendship with Elsa Maxwell." Headlines resounded with words like "*scandalo,*" "*insulta,*" "*disgrazia.*"

Elsa retaliated, not for herself but for Callas. Unlike Maria, she did not refuse to be interviewed. Lecturing an Italian journalist on the horrific treatment of a great artist, she called their stories about the "Rome Walkout" nothing less than "false, idiotic, and ridiculous." And Rome, she went on, "has always been a city where human beings were thrown before beasts." At an impromptu press conference in the street outside her hotel, she upbraided the Roman press, calling the papers "utterly ungenerous to treat in such a way a really sick woman." Then she struck even closer to Roman pride. "You threw Callas to the lions," she roared, "as you did in the days when you ate with your fingers. You forget that Maria Callas came from a land [Greece] that taught Rome such refinements as eating with a knife and fork."

The public raged. Newspapers, fuming about "insults to the national honor," reported the Italian government ready to deliver an official protest to the American embassy. Many wanted "*la signorina* Maxwell" declared persona non grata and kicked out of Italy. (Elsa must have sighed for the relative quiet of Mussolini.) As loud as the racket grew, it did not in reality reach the point of a diplomatic crisis. No protest reached the American embassy. The Italian foreign minister denied knowledge of such intention, but added, "I must recognize that the statements of Elsa Maxwell cannot be considered in very good taste." On January 5, as blood pressures sank toward normal, Elsa boarded a flight for New York.

Facing brigades of enemies, Maria perhaps decided that Elsa wasn't so bad after all. Back at the Met in February, where her performances were acclaimed, Maria depended on Elsa for distraction: the usual round of dinners, masquerades, charity balls, and photo ops. After New York, Maria went to Spain, Portugal, Milan, to London, Atlanta, Montreal, and finally, on October 31, 1958, back to Dallas.

Despite the triumphs of the year, and the relative calm after Rome, a deadly shark swam in the Callas ocean. That mighty monster, as Callas perceived it, was none other than Rudolf Bing, general manager of the Met, who, understandably, wanted to complete next season's schedule. His communiqués notwithstanding, Callas refused to commit. The many points of her discontent need not detain us here. It is likely, however, that Elsa encouraged an uncompromising stance.

In her biography *Maria Callas: The Woman Behind the Legend*, Arianna Stassinopoulos (now Huffington) sums up neatly why Callas sought a haven of refuge in Dallas. "On October 31," she writes, "the opening night of the Dallas *Traviata*, she received a telegram of congratulations from Bing. 'But why in Dallas?' was the question at the end of the good wishes." Stassinopoulos understands precisely *why Dallas*—"Perhaps," she continues, "Dallas had given her everything she could have wished for, and more," and here Stassinopoulos lists the pleasing new productions and the congenial conductors, directors, and costars, along with "unconditional enthusiasm and gratitude" from the city. Furthermore, "Maria was tired of fighting, tired of being attacked and misrepresented in the New York press, tired of once again having to seduce the blasé Met audience into surrender."

Elsa, always resilient, now seemed as hand-in-glove with Callas as ever. She had brought her own colorful contingent to town, including Clare Boothe Luce, Spyros Skouras, and Dame Eva Turner (a British prima donna of yesteryear). This time, Elsa didn't have to paper the house. All four thousand seats at the Music Hall were occupied, and not once but nightly. (No doubt the Callas notoriety packed them in as much as the voice.)

Callas, having triumphed in two *Traviata*s, absorbed herself in rehearsals for two *Medea*s, set for November 6 and 8. Professionally happy in Dallas, and given total artistic freedom, she was in danger all the same. From the Met, Rudolf Bing sent a telegram demanding that she sign the contract for which a binding agreement was already in place. Time was running out to settle his spring season once and for all, with twelve Callas performances, plus the Met summer tour. She and Meneghini had many reservations about the productions that Bing proposed, and so no reply was sent. Phone calls followed from Bing, whose exasperation was ready to boil over. On one occasion, he hung up on Meneghini. Next day, Bing sent an ultimatum: they must wire back within two hours accepting his terms, or else. The deadline passed. That afternoon Bing called a press conference in New York to inform the media that he had fired Maria Callas.

Yet another operatic storm broke over Callas on the very day of her first *Medea*. IMPETUOUS DIVA DEFIES BOSS OF MET read one headline. Dallas papers came to her defense, and several Texas millionaires offered to *buy* a New York *Medea* for the little lady. Elsa, of course, stood on the right hand of Callas like St. Peter beside the Lord. In photographs, her expression at this latest crucifixion is one of suffering beatitude. Elsa's face suggests that Callas is now hers, other disciples having fled like a thief in the night.

But Elsa misjudged. In the spring of 1959, Aristotle Onassis invited Callas and Meneghini to join him, his wife, and his sister on a cruise on the *Christina*. Finally, over her husband's objections, Maria prevailed. In mid-July they boarded the yacht in Monte Carlo. Other guests included Sir Winston and Clementine, Lady Churchill.

After meeting at Elsa's party in Venice in 1957, Callas and Onassis had encountered each other only a few times before this cruise. Some biographers believe that he had lain in wait, planning his conquest, from that first night. At any rate, their affair began during the cruise. Callas divorced Meneghini, Onassis divorced Tina, and over the next decade Callas expected Onassis to marry her. Since the story of their romance has been chronicled in every particular, I will skip a rerun and instead focus on Elsa and Callas at one of their final meetings.

Elsa happened to be in Monte Carlo that July of 1959—"like a bird of ill omen," in Meneghini's sour phrase. From her hotel she sent a letter to Callas, wishing her a splendid voyage but also pointing out, somewhat maliciously, that "you are taking the place of Garbo, now too old, on board the *Christina*. Good luck. I never cared for Garbo, but I loved you." Like a sticktight, Elsa would not exit. She added a P.S. that sprang out like a jack-in-the-box: "Yesterday Ari and Tina invited me to dinner with you. I couldn't say no."

TWO-FACED WOMAN

Elsa had no patience with Garbo, whom she and Dickie encountered from time to time in Hollywood, New York, and the South of France. Garbo's self-pity over aging, along with what Elsa considered her narcissism, made Elsa want to shake her. Not to mention her appearance in the years after she left the screen—"drab to the point of eccentricity," Elsa said. "I ran into her at Maxim's in Paris in the spring of 1951. She was wearing a loose polo coat and a shapeless slouch hat and her divine face was disfigured by an expression of stark despair."

A few years later, Dickie took action. "One morning," she said, "I was walking in New York, and I saw this figure in a rather shabby macintosh and a battered looking hat, and glasses. I saw that it was Garbo, and I said, 'You look awful!' She had the remains of some purple lipstick on, and no other makeup. I told her, 'You oughtn't to go around looking like that.' She laughed and said, 'I don't care.' I said, 'Well, you should care. I'm going to have some makeup sent to you.' I phoned someone I knew at Helena Rubinstein's and told him, 'Please send Garbo everything she needs,' and he did."

Elsa must have pined to go on the cruise. If she had been invited, the story might have ended differently, for like the kick-up-your-heels fairy godmother she liked to project, and the benevolent witch she often was in reality, Elsa would have warned Callas away from Onassis, the demon lover—even blocked her path. Perhaps in league with Meneghini and Tina Onassis, Elsa would have badgered and harangued Maria, talked her ears off, scandalized her (while making her weak with laughter) by prancing on deck in a designer bathing suit; would have worn them all out with costume balls, bridge games, all-night gambling, pop songs and conga lines, treasure hunts, outrageous contests, even jumping overboard if necessary.

But Elsa didn't take the cruise, and in view of the ensuing scandal, she lost her illusions. Arianna Stassinopoulos again: "Maria had expected support from her most loyal and least tactful champion so far, Elsa Maxwell. She did not get it. Throughout, Elsa maintained the dignified silence of a betrayed lover, and when she finally broke it, in her role as a self-appointed watchdog of public ethics, it was to side unequivocally with Tina. While Elsa was seen with Tina often, she deliberately kept out of Maria's way, and when she was asked at her suite in the Hotel Danieli in Venice whether her friend Ari was going to marry her friend Maria, she emitted only an openly disapproving 'I guess not.' "

Stelios Galatopoulos, author of *Maria Callas: Sacred Monster*, was acquainted with Callas, Meneghini, and Elsa. Near the end of that book, he recounts the last meeting, in Greece, of Elsa and Maria. "In 1961 I was asked to escort Maxwell for the last hundred metres (motor cars cannot go beyond this point) to the theatre at Epidaurus where Callas was singing in *Medea*. She asked me a thousand questions about Maria and the dress rehearsal of *Medea* which had taken place two days previously. At one moment she reminisced about the ball in New York when Maria went as the female pharaoh Hatshepsut. Maxwell could not hold back the tears and we stopped walking for a few minutes. She then smiled and exclaimed, 'On with the show!' "

Later that year, Elsa bumped into Onassis at a nightclub in New York. He shouted, "Come on, Elsa, let's twist!" He led her onto the dance floor and as they began the vigorous new dance, Elsa felt the world spin around her.

"Take me home, Ari. Please," she said, not realizing that her dizziness and confusion might be the result of a stroke.

"Don't go home yet!" was his heedless reply. "From here we'll go to El Morocco."

"I hardly heard him," Elsa wrote in *The Celebrity Circus*. "I remember someone slipping a coat around me and getting me to the street and into a taxi. That was all I knew for the next ten days. I spent the rest of the winter and part of the spring recovering from what turned out to be a desperately serious illness."

Onassis's insouciance when told by an elderly woman that she isn't well suggests his unfeeling treatment of Maria, as well. It's almost as if he doomed both. Once captured for his collection, Callas ceased to hold his attention. Her career suffered and finally ended, in 1965. After he dropped her for Jacqueline Kennedy, whom he married in 1968, Callas began the long descent into hopelessness that ended in 1977, with her death.

Near the end of *The Celebrity Circus*, Elsa recounts her final conversation with Callas: "Last spring [i.e., May 1962] I was in bed with a cold when the telephone rang. 'Elsa!' said the unmistakable voice at the other end of the line. 'This is Maria.' "

Elsa claimed that she had resolved to have no further contact with Callas. Yet "all my resolutions dissolved in an instant, and we had a long, lively talk." Maria had come to town to sing at President Kennedy's forty-fifth birthday celebration, at Madison Square Garden. The Callas voice was already in serious trouble, and she apparently sought Elsa's advice on what to sing.

"You'd make a marvelous Carmen," Elsa blurted. "Why don't you sing the 'Habañera' for Jack Kennedy tonight?"

According to Elsa, "The program was changed at the last minute. Madame Callas sang *Carmen* for Kennedy." But of course, the chanteuse who gave the legendary performance that night was Marilyn Monroe, who sang "Happy Birthday, Mr. President" in that notorious breathy version that later come to resemble a funeral dirge. And Callas did not feel upstaged. When she posed with Marilyn after the show, the two of them looked almost like girls who had grown up together, who understood each other and who couldn't have been happier to meet again.

As for Elsa, she didn't pine. After all, she had Dickie. She couldn't ask for Callas, as well.

32 "Jack's Guests Tonight Are . . ."

*A*lthough it might seem that Elsa devoted the last full decade of her life—the fifties—to Callas and the Windsors, such was not the case. If anything, she opened her social umbrella even wider to include regular appearances on the *Tonight* show from 1957, when Jack Paar followed Steve Allen as host. (Two years later, NBC renamed it *The Jack Paar Show*.) Like many of Jack's guests, Elsa popped up often when she happened to be in New York. Given her travels and the never-ending kaleidoscope of parties, she appeared with surprising frequency.

Elsa was in France when Jack Paar invited her to be a guest. (They first met in 1954, when Elsa plugged *R.S.V.P.* on *The Morning Show*, which Jack hosted on CBS.) Marie Torre, a columnist for the *New York Herald-Tribune*, announced in her column of July 18, 1957, that Paar was "trying to contact Elsa Maxwell by transatlantic phone to find out just when she aims to bid farewell to the socialites of Europe and report to his new *Tonight* show, which has a July 29 starting date. Paar's last cabled plea was: 'Pay off Farouk and come home!'

"Elsa Maxwell's wire in reply: 'How could I possibly refuse to be with my favorite glamour boy of television? Farouk already paid off. Love, Elsa.'" (They were referring to ex-King Farouk of Egypt and his libel action against Elsa, covered in Chapter 1.)

It is often said that Jack Paar invented the talk show, but that's a facile characterization. If one added that his show was about intelligent, literate conversations that veered from witty repartee to the serious, and from barbs to bonhomie, the description would be more accurate. But the Paar show also had singers, stand-up comedians, skits, and variety acts. By television standards then and later, the show was sophisticated. Even the opening theme, "Everything's Coming Up Roses," had a big-city sound. The stay-up-late time slot, also—11:15 P.M. to 1:00 A.M. EST—appealed to the hip and excluded early-to-bed squares. Unlike any other TV show I can think of, it resembled a party at the home of your smartest friends—a place to relax, tell stories, laugh, talk politics or books or current events, gossip, meet all kinds of new people, gripe, gather around the piano, and sometimes encounter a big name such as John F. Kennedy, Fidel Castro, or Judy Garland. Perhaps it was the party atmosphere that lured Elsa.

Tom Shales, television critic of the *Washington Post*, wrote that "Jack Paar, like Ernie Kovacs and Rod Serling and a few others, was one of TV's true auteurs, producing his own show as well as starring in it, overseeing every aspect." I would add that when Paar left late night in 1962 for a weekly show in prime time, he lost much of the intimacy and the extemporaneous feel of the years 1957 to '62.

Ron Simon, writing in Horace Newcomb's *Encyclopedia of Television*, adds that the late-night Paar surrounded himself with "a salon of eccentrics," among them pianist and professional hypochondriac Oscar Levant; Alexander King, a bohemian raconteur whom *Time* magazine described as "an ex-illustrator, ex-cartoonist, ex-adman, ex-editor, ex-playwright, ex-dope addict, ex-painter, ex-Viennese, and ex-husband of three wives"; Cliff Arquette, who appeared on TV as his alter ego "Charley Weaver," a folksy, gamey ancestor to the denizens of Garrison Keillor's Lake Wobegon; a bevy of British wits—Robert Morley, Bea Lillie, Peter Ustinov, Hermione Gingold; Geneviève, the French chanteuse who sounded like Piaf without the tragedies; scratchy-voiced comediennes Peggy Cass (Boston Irish) and Selma Diamond (New York Jewish); ditzy Dody Goodman; and Elsa. Nice-guy Hugh

Downs, Jack's announcer and fellow Ohioan, stood out for his lack of quirks. For added star power, on any night you might see Richard Burton, Zsa Zsa or Eva Gabor, Jayne Mansfield, Billy Graham, Eleanor Roosevelt, and a conga line of celebrities almost as long as Elsa's own. Each guest was paid three hundred and twenty dollars. Five weeks before the Beatles appeared live on *The Ed Sullivan Show* in 1964, Jack showed a film of the four singing "Yeah, yeah, yeah" in front of a frenzied teen audience in England. It was their first exposure on American television.

When Jack Paar first tried to locate Elsa in the summer of 1957, she had just celebrated what was reported as her seventy-fourth birthday (we know it was her seventy-sixth). In late May, Elsa was guest of honor at a party for three hundred in Paris at the home of Norman K. Winston, a New York construction magnate. The hostess was Mrs. Winston. (Once when Elsa gave a dinner for Cole Porter in the Empire Room at the Waldorf, then presented him with the bill, the Winstons paid for the flowers.)

"Everyone I know and love in France is here tonight," Elsa said. "And never did I dream that at seventy-four [sic] I would feel so young and full of life." She barely sat down from the start of her birthday party until long past dawn, when dancing was still in progress. Aristotle Onassis, in attendance, posed repeatedly for photographers as he hugged and kissed the ebullient Elsa. Jazz singer Hazel Scott and a Peruvian guitarist entertained Elsa's well-wishers, among them Prince and Princess Alexander of Yugoslavia; the Duc and Duchesse de Noailles (he had recently translated *R.S.V.P.* into French as *J'ai reçu le monde entier*); Millicent Hearst; Aly Khan and the fashion model Bettina, his fiancée; Stavros Niarchos; and the usual assortment of titles, politicians, and capitalist moguls. Asked what she would like if any birthday wish could be granted, Elsa replied: "I would have the most beautiful voice in the world with the art of interpretation, or I would be able to conduct a great symphony orchestra."

Given her musical passions, it's odd that Elsa never performed on the Paar show. She played for everyone else. Why didn't she volunteer, or why didn't Jack form an impromptu jam session? Even Richard Nixon, not long after his defeat in 1960, played his own piano composition, accompanied, said Jack, by "fifteen Democratic violinists." Perhaps Elsa never stopped talking long enough to be asked.

BACKWARD GLANCES

In Jack Paar's first book, *I Kid You Not*, published in 1960, he recounted funny incidents from Elsa's appearances on his show. By the time his last book came out, in 1983, Elsa had been dead twenty years, Paar was long retired from television, and the book—*P.S. Jack Paar*—was his last published retrospective on his life and times. It turned out he was not entirely enchanted by Elsa.

Excerpts: "Elsa Maxwell was hardly a new face. She looked like Ernest Borgnine in drag but became a big hit on the first years of the program. Elsa wrote a silly society column for the Hearst papers and was so serious on television when discussing the wealthy that it became funny; rather *we* became funny. She was not actually witty, just so brazen and outspoken that my look of astonishment sitting next to her became hilarious.

"She was democratic only in the sense that she seemed to prefer old, half-assed, deposed royalty, rather than ruling sovereigns. 'They need me more,' she said stoutly. Elsa really had no visible means of support, but I felt that she was given donations by society figures for mentions in her column and on the program. Oscar Levant once called her 'the oldest living woman on a scholarship.'

"She was really a harmless old fraud, but 'our act' became the talk of television. She attacked people and governments, and there were many threatened law suits, but nothing came of them."

In *The Celebrity Circus*, Elsa devoted twenty-six complimentary pages to the Paar experience. For instance: "Jack is a master comedian, and a man with firm opinions he is not afraid to express. He knows how to make friends *and* enemies; perhaps that's why he is one of the most dynamic, attractive celebrities I know."

According to several sources, most tapes of the Paar show were destroyed. Why, and by whom, is a matter of debate. Footage available on DVD and on YouTube is valuable but limited, and most of it is post-1960, meaning that Elsa turns up only in snippets. Existing transcripts of exchanges between Elsa and Jack lack the sparkle that the two actually ignited. For that reason, I include a montage of Jack's introductions—each time Elsa entered, he tried for a bigger laugh than the time before, and she, of course, guffawed the loudest.

"And here she is, the Orphan Annie of the Waldorf . . . Here is Elsa Maxwell, the Peter Pan of society . . . Here's the den mother of El Morocco, Elsa Maxwell . . . It's twelve midnight in New York, and here's our Cinderella, Elsa Maxwell . . . Tonight we have the winner of an award—the room service award at the Waldorf-Astoria . . . And now, directly back from Europe, only arrived on the pier this morning, is our old friend, the winner of the Nobel Prize for Catering—Elsa Maxwell! Please welcome the grandmother of the world, Miss Elsa Maxwell . . . A big welcome for Elsa Maxwell, who lists her vital measurements as 60-60-60."

Elsa's explanation for her departure, in 1960, from the Paar show differs from other versions. Jack Paar himself did not address the issue in print. She decided to leave, she wrote in *The Celebrity Circus*, because Jack "aimed a particularly violent blast at my paper, the *Journal-American*. Of course he was entitled to his own opinions, but I had to think the matter over, and I decided because I wished to remain loyal to my old friend Millicent Hearst and to her son Willie, the paper's publisher, that I must decline to appear further on what I truly believed to be the show of shows."

Elsa's account is plausible, but so are those which suggest that she wore out her welcome. From the start, Elsa had been highly outspoken on the air. She had, for instance, attacked Elvis Presley, Jayne Mansfield, Zsa Zsa Gabor, and Liberace, all of whom offended her sense of aesthetics or her standards of decorum. In the case of Elvis, Elsa heard that he had autographed the chests of eight teenage girls after one of his concerts. "Horribly dreadful," she cried out. "A menace to our country!" (One wonders whether her vehemence would have been as great had the autographer been a duke.) On

Jayne Mansfield: "Vulgar and overbusted. I think it's disgraceful that she was allowed to meet the queen." Elsa used this broadcast forum to start vendettas, settle scores, and speak her mind on politics, society, movies, and any other topic that came to mind. She enjoyed not only the resulting publicity but also the hundreds of letters she received each week. Much of that publicity was unfavorable, and with reason, for, becoming disinhibited, she revealed a side of her character that she had always sought to conceal from the public. Increasingly, her repartee became ribald but not funny, peppered with sophomoric sexual innuendos that detracted from the show's sophistication rather than enhancing it. Her own vulgarity matched that of Jayne Mansfield and Elvis.

Then one night her target was one of the most powerful columnists in the country, Walter Winchell. He had recently printed unfounded rumors about Jack Paar (that his marriage was in trouble), and cast aspersions on Elsa's musical talents. When Winchell's name came up one night in April 1958, Jack said that the columnist was "after him." Whether intended or not, Elsa took that as her cue. "He's never voted and never registered! Is that a good patriotic American or not?" (She later claimed that her information was based on a series in the *New York Post* in 1952.) Jack added that Winchell's "high, hysterical voice" resulted from wearing "too-tight underwear." He implied that Winchell was envious of the success of the Paar show, Winchell himself having tried television and failed.

Winchell retaliated in his column. What couldn't be printed he said aloud: he called Elsa "a fat, sloppy, smelly cunt." Claiming that her accusations had endangered contributions to the Damon Runyon Cancer Fund, a charity that Winchell had founded, he threatened to sue all of Paar's sponsors. He also threatened legal action against Elsa. Then he produced a photograph of himself entering a voting booth in New York.

Elsa, with no money to lose in a lawsuit, barked still louder. NBC, and the sponsors, grew nervous. Network brass pressured Jack to show the Winchell voting-booth picture on the air as a way of setting the record straight without an outright apology. They also warned him that Elsa was out of control. Some wanted her banned from the Paar show. Nevertheless, she continued to appear until 1960, which lends credence to her stated reason for leaving. (Hal Gurnee, a director of the Paar show, told me he's reasonably sure that Elsa appeared once or twice on Jack's weekly show, which began in 1962.)

Elsa's amplification on her ill-advised attack: "Winchell had gotten the notion that I'd not really written the songs I sang in a record album I'd recently made [the 1958 LP titled *Elsa Maxwell*]. When he printed as much in his column, my hackles rose, and in a fit of pique I told Jack's audience that he had never cast a ballot, had, indeed, never even registered." The closest Elsa came to a retraction was in *The Celebrity Circus* three years later: "I admit that we turned out to be somewhat off base with that particular accusation." Winchell didn't follow through with his threatened lawsuits, which raises the question: Was Elsa right all along? After all, the photo of him in a voting booth might have been posed for a PR stunt.

33 Cocktails and Laughter, but What Comes After?

Elsa's appearances on the Paar show swept her to the climax of fame, where one might have supposed her already ensconced. She had long been a household name in penthouse and palace. Now her recognition spread to modest homes in towns and rural tracts far removed from Fifth Avenue and the Ritz. Suddenly, bookstores needed fresh copies of *R.S.V.P.*, which was no longer in print. Magazines such as *McCall's* and *Photoplay* ran mail-order ads for *Elsa Maxwell's Etiquette Book* (with glowing blurbs from Joan Crawford, Doris Day, and Gordon MacRae) for one dollar, postage paid. Although for decades Elsa had received two or three hundred letters a month, secretaries now handled up to a thousand a week. Questions about the Windsors, Marilyn Monroe, and any other name in the news arrived daily. Many correspondents asked how they, on meager budgets, might entertain with flair, or sought recipes for canapés, steak au poivre, and the like. Others solicited Elsa's opinions on everything from the arms race to hula hoops. Still others complimented or chided her for outspokenness on the air, and of course some were vile and full of abuse. Unlike most celebrity mail, Elsa's contained relatively few requests for autographed glossies. And all the while, she kept up the roller-coaster pace that had become as natural for her, and as necessary, as a pulse.

Although parties occupied roughly half of Elsa's vast social panorama, they are still thought of as her raison d'être. This seems the proper time, therefore, to look back at a few of the ones that helped make her such a curious twentieth-century phenomenon. We start by revisiting those that Elsa described in a magazine article in 1952: "These Are the 10 Parties I'll Never Forget."

Surprisingly, Elsa's number one party on that list was not especially fabulous. It was the one in Paris after World War I at the home of Louise Brooks, with General Pershing and Brigadier General Douglas MacArthur among the guests. Elsa recalled in particular the duel outside her window in the small hours of the morning. Next, the event she attended as Prime Minister Edouard Herriot, again in Paris, followed by the "Come As Your Opposite" party in New York. Then the famous murder party in London; the London scavenger hunt; the Paris scavenger hunt; a Palm Beach party at Millicent Hearst's where Elsa, in Gypsy garb, told fortunes; a circus party at the Plaza in New York where Gloria Swanson, dressed as Jenny Lind, mouthed the words to a famous aria until the actual singer emerged from the wings to join her: it was the diva Lily Pons.

Elsa's number nine was a shooting party in Austria. Never having handled a gun, she bribed an attendant to produce a brace of pheasants that won Elsa the prize as sportswoman of the year—without firing a shot of her own. And finally, the 1952 April in Paris ball at the Waldorf. Elsa disguised herself as a beturbaned maharajah from India, Bea Lillie was a harem favorite, and they planned to ride in on an elephant. Pachyderm behavior being unpredictable, they were persuaded instead to follow the animal with brooms and buckets. Elsa concluded: "I'm pleased to say that the fake maharajah and his favorite, at work, got applause from real royalty. Juliana, Queen of the Netherlands, was one of the guests."

Here's the party I least expected to encounter among the thousands that Elsa gave. It took place in Italy in April 1931, in honor of King Alfonso XIII of Spain. He had just arrived there as an exile from his own country upon proclamation of the Second Spanish Republic. (He did not abdicate, however, until ten years later.) The king enjoyed describing his exploits, including the seven assassination attempts he had foiled; driving his thirty-thousand-dollar Bugatti at eighty miles per hour along the Grand Corniche on the Riviera; trying to purchase Marion Davies for a night; and, given half an hour to pack and leave Spain, destroying over two hundred compromising photographs of female companions and then packing a single suitcase for his journey.

Here Elsa takes up the narrative: "I saw Alfonso the day he began his exile in Rome. The superstitious Italians believed there was a curse on Alfonso and muttered 'malocchio' (evil eye) behind his back, then brushed their clothes with their little and index fingers to ward off the malign spirits that followed him. Alfonso gave no indication that he noticed it. Later, I invited twenty titled Italians to a dinner party for Alfonso in Venice, but all refused to come because of the malocchio superstition." And so, in lonely splendor, Elsa dined with the king as her only guest. She proclaimed that "Alfonso never was more charming." Alfonso's looks may have inspired terror in susceptible Italians, for he had the sunken eyes and spectral mien of an Iberian Nosferatu.

I wish I had many more details of Elsa's "Hate Party" in Paris in the fifties. According to Susan Smith in the *San Francisco Examiner*, "each guest was asked to represent the person he or she most intensely disliked." Elsa came as King Farouk of Egypt, whom she seems to have detested even more than Hitler and Mussolini.* In a similar deconstructive spirit, Elsa's annual masked ball in Venice, at the Hotel Danieli, took a louche turn in 1959. She decreed that everyone was to wear or carry something "very ugly." Some guests wore frightful, grotesque masks. Elsa herself sported a huge false nose. Tina Onassis carried a string bag through which all could see a large, evil-looking eel. (In 1937, Elsa's Venetian masquerade had a more conventional theme. Guests came as their favorite movie stars. Barbara Hutton chose Constance Bennett, whom she resembled, while her husband, Count Reventlow, appeared as Erich von Stroheim, with cape, saber, sash, and monocle.)

---

*Elsa loathed dictators, and yet upon arrival in Madrid in 1961, she was met at the airport by a limousine sent by the ruthless Franco, whom she never actually met. She often partied, however, with Franco's daughter and son-in-law.

———

For unmitigated gall, the prize goes to Elsa's party for Alec Guinness and other cast members of T. S. Eliot's *The Cocktail Party*. Elsa's invitation to a supper party arrived in January 1951, toward the end of the play's Broadway run, and before he was Sir Alec. A few years later, his title might have spared him the bizarre event. "We were flattered," he wrote in *A Positively Final Exposure*, "and taxied off under the guidance of Cathleen Nesbitt, who was a friend of Elsa's, to an unlikely venue which turned out to be a commercial-looking building on Sixth Avenue." They took an elevator to the twentieth floor, where "another bevy of somewhat bewildered Maxwell guests" joined them. They realized the party was already in progress when, somewhat startled, they heard a woman singing. Just then a young man wearing headphones opened an oversize door to admit the latecomers, putting a finger to his lips to warn them that their chatter must cease. "Then," Guinness continued, "a tall, pretty girl beckoned us over coils of heavy cables which squirmed across a linoleum floor and, ducking under TV camera lighting equipment, she shoved us into various sofas and chairs scattered across the vast bleak studio. Maxwell was somewhere in the middle of it all interviewing people. The focus of attention changed and an even taller, prettier girl, wielding a microphone, descended on me as I was sitting primly on my sofa, kissed the top of my balding head—with a knowing wink at the cameras—and belted out 'True to You, Darling, in My Fashion' from *Kiss Me, Kate*."

If Sir Alec were a less credible witness, I would swear he had mixed up this New York evening with the plot of one of those Ealing comedies for which he is so well remembered—*Kind Hearts and Coronets*, perhaps. And is it too late to turn this into a mad British comedy starring, say, John Cleese?

"None of us, I am sure, in accepting the invitation to supper, had anticipated that we were to be stooges in a TV commercial. Actors are always ready for food after a performance and by midnight we were decidedly peckish. But hope reassured our greedy eyes; on the far side of the studio we could see a sumptuous cold meal laid out on a long table covered with a dazzling white cloth. Sides of ham, turkey, chicken, lobsters, salmon, and salads looked like a millionaire's picnic."

Suddenly Elsa clapped her hands and called out, "À *table*," adding a Gallic gourmet touch that set off a salivary rush. Immediately there was a well-mannered stampede to the buffet, with a stop at a side table for gleaming plates, sparkling silver, and heavy cloth dinner napkins.

"The camera zoomed in on Maxwell as she handed me plate, knife, and fork," Guinness added. (Ordinarily a gentleman of Sir Alec's stature would refer to "Miss Maxwell," but writing many years later he still held a grudge.) As director-apparent of the gracious-living commercial, Elsa commanded, "Now give that to the lovely lady at your side," and when he had done so, "take this yourself. And everyone, help yourselves. My, these knives and forks are so pretty!"

The lady to whom Alec Guinness had handed the plate approached. He asked what she would like and she said turkey. As he lifted the fork to carve, someone yelled "Cut!" and suddenly all the bright TV lights went out.

"Not only were we left in dingy semi-darkness but Maxwell had the temerity to shout again, 'Don't touch what's on the table; your food is in another room.'" Soon it dawned upon the crestfallen crowd: all those delicious viands were plastic, like the sushi in the window of a Japanese fast-food restaurant. The commercial had been filmed to promote some distant purveyor of silverware and bone china.

"The real food," concluded the actor so piteously that you almost hear his stomach grumble, "proffered in a small grotty room, was some sort of rice salad to be eaten off cardboard plates. "Let's get out of here before worse befalls," he said to a couple of fellow cast members from *The Cocktail Party*. "There is bound to be a drugstore nearby where we can have eggs, sunny-side up."

Without a word to their hostess, they escaped by bleak freight elevator into the unfestive street.

Elsa pulled no such low tricks in 1933 when she welcomed Vita Sackville-West and Harold Nicolson to San Francisco. Few details are available apart from society notices like this one from the San Mateo *Times and Daily Ledger*: "Entertaining yesterday at luncheon, Mr. and Mrs. Nion Tucker of Hillsborough were hosts for Miss Elsa Maxwell. Included in the guest list were Lady Sackville-West and her husband, Hon. Harold Nicolson." Half a dozen other guests were mentioned, but Elsa, obviously, was held in the Bay Area's highest esteem, where Bloomsbury trailed as an afterthought.

In the year 1958, Susan Smith in the *Examiner* again recalled a New York trip she made in the thirties. "I received a hush-hush telephone call from one of Elsa's closest friends. If I could meet the owner of the voice for lunch the following day I would find out what was up. The next afternoon I learned there was a surprise in store for Elsa. Five of her friends were to attend a costume party Elsa was giving, and they were going as Elsa herself—representing five stages of her life. Peggy (Mrs. Harold Talbott) was to come as Elsa when a baby. I had been earmarked for Elsa today (in those years I was just as stout as the hostess). She had a black beaded Patou gown I could wear. Through some pre-arranged plot the dress was to be smuggled out of Elsa's closet hours before the start of the ball. It was a gown she had worn to so many of the winter's parties it had become a definite part of her personality.

"I agreed to attempt the part when I learned that a skilled artist had succeeded in making a mask of her face from a photograph. Elsa's coiffeur had briefed him on face measurements, flesh tones, etc. I would wear a wig. Nothing had been forgotten.

"I don't think I ever enjoyed a party more. When I entered the ballroom, the shout went up, 'There's Elsa!' Many of the guests, who never saw the real Elsa during the evening (she had first been detained by several members of our group and then, realizing what was up, kept very much in the background to enjoy the fun), thought that I *was* the hostess. I was the recipient of several handsome presents which, when I turned them over to Elsa, she laughingly told me to keep."

Did anyone wince at Elsa's Blitz Party in Palm Beach in 1941? True, her intentions were good, for the event raised money for British war charities. Guests were asked to come in dressing gowns, siren suits (i.e., jumpsuits with zippered front to slip on in a hurry during air raids), or their oldest clothes, and a large tent was scattered with fake debris from which dummy figures were extricated and carried off on stretchers.

Diana Vreeland's looks were not much better than Elsa's, in spite of her *Harper's Bazaar* and *Vogue* connections, and her italicized prose is both frothy and espaliered, unlike Elsa's, which seems to gush from a river of enthusiasm deep inside. Vreeland's establishment credentials, however, saved her from derision. She liked Elsa well enough not to go beyond the usual epithets: "plump old Elsa Maxwell" and the like. "Elsa wasn't a vulgar woman," Vreeland wrote in her autobiography. "This is hard to explain to someone who never knew her, because she *looked* vulgar. The end of her nose was vulgar. Why wasn't she? I don't know. Maybe it was because she adored music so much. She was a sublime pianist."

Vreeland writes about a luncheon that Elsa invited her to, with Christine Jorgensen (1926–1989), one of the first persons to undergo gender reassignment surgery—in this case, male to female—and certainly the most famous one in the fifties. If Vreeland's account is accurate, it must have been a stiff affair. But perhaps Elsa realized, too late, that apart from Jorgensen and herself, the wrong people were seated at her table.

"The lunch was in Elsa's private room upstairs in a hotel salon," Vreeland wrote. "Leland Hayward [the Broadway and Hollywood producer] was there. Fulco di Verdura, the great jewelry designer, and several other very fascinating men I can't remember. And no one could think of a single word to say to this very well-mannered, very charming person called Christine Jorgensen. We stared at her and had no idea how to begin. What *would* one ask: 'What's the first thing you did—blow up your bazooms?' She did the best *she* could to keep the ball in the air, talking about the food and the weather and, mmm . . . my God, the changes in this world! Elsa was *bouleversée*. It was the *only* time I ever saw her like that, and I knew her very well." (Elsa ill at ease? I'm not convinced. Maybe Vreeland perceived the emotions of all present as identical to her own.)

No awkward pauses, no casting about for what to say, at Elsa's party in 1940 for children of Hollywood stars and journalists. Amid the cacaphony and the clack of shiny toys, a few tears fell, all quickly dried, and a few knees were skinned and patched up. Steffi Sidney, the daughter of Hollywood columnist Sidney Skolsky, attended, though she was too young at the time to remember very much. She does recall, however, that "the party was lavish with balloons. Elsa was very gracious with all the children, and reminded us of a nice grandmother."

Steffi sent me several clippings from her baby book, one of which shows Elsa holding the wailing toddler Peter B. Good. The article explains that "The party was in honor of the premiere of Peter's first starring picture, *Brother Rat and a Baby*," which also starred Priscilla Lane, Jane Wyman, and Ronald Reagan. The party took place at the Hollywood Roosevelt Hotel. No adults were admitted unless accompanied by their young, and in lieu of cocktails, milk was served. Among the guests: Ronnie and Sandra Burns, whose parents were George Burns and Gracie Allen; Freddie Astaire; Gary, Denny, and Philip Crosby; Joan Benny (daughter of Jack Benny and Mary Livingstone); and Jeffrey Selznick.

THE "COME DRESSED AS THE SICK SOUL OF EUROPE" PARTY

First, to clarify two points: I purloined this title from Pauline Kael's *I Lost It at the Movies*, and then, no one gave such a party, though if Elsa had been alive when Kael's book was published in 1965, it might have given her ideas. Toward the end of her life, Elsa had become as disenchanted with the international set as Kael with the films in her piece: *La Notte*, *La Dolce Vita*, and *Last Year at Marienbad*.

I want to indulge a moment of fantasy with a drive-by look at a few parties that Elsa *didn't* give. The idea comes from Janet Flanner's *Paris Was Yesterday*, in which she quotes Elsa as saying of a party given in 1939 by Mrs. Louise Macy that "it was one of the most successful parties I never gave." The chic Mrs. Macy, a Paris editor of *Harper's Bazaar*, rented a disused historical mansion, the Hôtel Salé, for one night, installed temporary furnishings and plumbing, a makeshift kitchen, and thousands of candles. Guests were required to wear diadems and costumes appropriate to the period of the mansion's construction in the seventeenth century. Flanner reports another party that Elsa surely would have loved to host, this one a "Racine Party" given by Comte Etienne de Beaumont, to which guests came dressed as characters from the plays or period of Racine, whose tercentenary was being celebrated in 1939.

In 1935, *Time* magazine reported that Elsa was "mad as a hornet" because she hadn't thought up the Surrealist Party in Manhattan to honor Salvador Dalí. Socialites bedecked themselves in lamb chops, mushrooms, alarm clocks, hot water bottles, sausages, and anything else from their dreams that might approximate one of the artist's paintings. So attired, they gathered in a nightclub where a bathtub full of mud and oysters served as a giant ashtray. Dalí himself wore a glass case containing a brassiere on his chest.

Elsa disliked out-of-control rowdiness, but she enjoyed the raucous jollity of the "Come As You Were" party she gave in Paris in 1927. (These are more commonly known as "Come As You Are" parties.) In advance, she required pledges from sixty guests that they would show up at the party in the state of dress—or undress—they were in when the invitation arrived. "To make sure of a wide variety of getups," Elsa said, "I had the invitations delivered by messengers at odd hours of the day and night."

Well aware of the vagaries of her Parisian friends, Elsa insured against mayhem by chartering two buses to pick them up on the day of the party. Elsa: "The Marquis de Polignac was attired in full evening dress save for one conspicuous omission. He wasn't wearing his trousers. Daisy Fellowes carried her lace panties in her hand. A half-dozen women who are respectable grandmothers today [Elsa was writing in 1954] came in slips that definitely were not shadowproof. Bébé Bérard [Christian Bérard, the artist and designer] wore a dressing gown, had a telephone attached to his ear, and had white makeup on his face to simulate shaving cream. Several men who rated honor above vanity came in hairnets. Jay O'Brien [the sportsman and dancer] was a fashion plate in tails, except for one minor detail. He wasn't wearing a white tie and somehow he looked more disreputable than anyone else."

Elsa admitted that she made two mistakes in planning this party. She installed a bar in each bus. And she forgot to allow for the traffic jams in Paris, even in 1927. The buses began collecting partygoers at seven in the evening, but only arrived at nine o'clock at the apartment in Montparnasse that Elsa had borrowed for the occasion. It belonged to Meraud Guevara, the painter, who was the daughter of Elsa's longtime friend Mrs. Bridget Guinness. The guests were smashed, and a number of the outfits they had left home in were now ripped or otherwise drastically altered.

"Countess Gabriella Robilant, an Italian, lost her skirt," Elsa recalled. "Gabriella was unconcerned, but Countess Elisabeth de Breteuil, a French-woman, was outraged. 'I refuse to be seen in my country with anyone in that scandalous condition,' she said.

"'To the Bastille!' Gabriella cried, yanking off Elisabeth's skirt. 'Now a French countess and an Italian countess are equals.'"

Elsa doesn't elaborate further, though she hints at the evening's main preoccupation: "It looked like the rehearsal of a French bedroom farce."

I wish I could have attended one of Elsa's "Barnyard Parties," where she gathered various farm animals as objects of laughter and merriment. I would have told her, "Don't do this again!" True, in Elsa's day few people considered animal welfare, and it's unlikely that the animals underwent more than fright and mild discomfort at Elsa's parties. Nevertheless, if she resisted my warning I would add, "You'll find enough jackasses among your guests." Since these parties did take place, however, we'll look in on them to see just how repellent such animal exploitation really is, even under fairly humane circumstances.

Elsa first attempted this questionable practice in 1924. The *Daily Express* in London reported that "performing seals have been barred from the dining room of the Ritz Hotel. The animals were to figure at a dinner party given by Miss Elsa Maxwell, a member of the American colony in Paris. Their trainer protested that the seals were well behaved, but the Ritz management were adamant." A few years later she succeeded. A newspaper in 1932 reported that she did indeed give a party at the Ritz with a troupe of trained seals as the evening's novelty. They were turned loose during the fish course and guests were astonished to find the animals' cold noses pressing against them for a share of the banquet.

A year earlier, Elsa staged a *fête champetre* for four hundred "peasants" at the home of Baron Nicky de Gunzburg, of Paris *Vogue*, in the Bois de Boulogne. "The house," Elsa said, "was transformed into a glorified farm-house by the brilliant artist and scene designer Christian (Bébé) Bérard, who painted a fantastic farmyard on wood frames and covered the entire house with blue satin. Cole Porter had composed a special score for the orchestra, and Lauritz Melchior and Frida Leider sang the love duet from *Tristan und Isolde*. Serge Lifar, the ballet dancer, made a grand entrance on a white horse, his body painted in gold. The Cole Porters arrived in a Sicilian don-key cart loaded with orchids and gardenias. Daisy Fellowes came as Circe, with the Baroness Lo Monaco as her bewitched swine."

Back in New York, Elsa's Park Avenue hoedown at the Waldorf in 1937 made the papers from San Francisco to London. Guests—financial moguls, actors, European royalty—were required to have hay in their hair, and they had to climb a stile to get into the party. The *Chronicle* reported that "guests arrived in ginghams, calicos, and overalls as farmerettes, country lasses, and milkmaids, country squires and farmhands, shepherdesses and farmers' daughters. Bewildered passersby stopped in the streets as cows mooed, sheep baa-ed, chickens cackled and laid eggs in the elevators, and a donkey brayed. Tom Bevington of Chardon, Ohio, was announced as 'champeen hog caller of the world.' He gave demonstrations, using six hogs loaned by millionaire Leonard Hanna of Cleveland, then acted as judge as society tried its hand at hog calling."

Elsa rounded up the women for a milking contest. Then, a greased pig contest, which the London *Daily Mirror* headlined as SCREAMING WOMEN CHASED BY PIGS AT FREAK BALL. John Gielgud, invited but unable to attend, wrote to his mother after hearing reports of the hogs: "Very biblical and odd! So do the idle rich recreate themselves." Asked the reason for her party, Elsa said, "Society is too sophisticated. It must be taken back to nature now and then." Marie Antoinette thought so, too, cavorting in the pastures of Versailles with golden milk pail and bejeweled shepherd's crook.

———

Elsa re-created her barn dance at the St. Francis Hotel in San Francisco in 1938. Again, guests came as froufrou farmers. This time there was a country store, and hillbilly fiddlers alternated with an orchestra playing reels and waltzes from a stage at one end of the ballroom. At the other end stood a "beer well"—that is, a replica of an old well with rope and pulley, and a bucket from which to take a swig of cold beer. Once more livestock roamed among the guests: pigs, a donkey, a horse, a cow, and several perfumed goats. The most popular animal, however, stood unmoving in the center of the room. She was a papier-mâché cow, full size and covered in gold foil. When squealing guests squeezed her udder, Marguerite—French for "Bossy," more or less—produced fresh champagne.

Had I reprimanded Elsa for insensitivity toward animals, she might have come back—disingenuously—as she did in *The Celebrity Circus* to those who criticized her taking part in a bullfight. "I sympathize with the point of view, but when I think of prize fights, it seems to me that beating a man, a human being, sometimes until he is critically injured, is worse than engaging in a contest with an animal who is trained to fight. We pen up thousands of wretched animals every day, kill them by pounding them on the head, and serve them up for the dinners of America. Is fighting a trained bull, who has a fair chance of winning, and who dies quickly if he must die, really more cruel?"

34 When Death Occurs*

P hilip Ziegler, in his biography *King Edward VIII*: "There comes a point in nearly everybody's life when he must accept the fact that he is old; from that moment onwards all that is left is a melancholy process of decay, sometimes mitigated by remissions or apparent recoveries, sometimes proceeding headlong to total degeneration."

For Elsa, the moment struck that night in 1961 when she danced the ill-fated twist with Aristotle Onassis. From then, her health declined. Few in society, and none in the media, knew the gravity of her condition. Perhaps Elsa herself didn't know. If she did, she used her enormous will to bulldoze illness aside as she had dislodged so many potential obstructions throughout her life—her looks, her poverty real or imagined, her womanhood in a man's world. If she appeared less frequently in the New York papers, it was because she was whirling through Europe at top speed.

The Celebrity Circus is aptly named: it's a dizzying, three-ring, high-wire act with Elsa as ringmaster, clown, acrobat, and audience. Surrounding her at the spectacle are countless new acquaintances, most of them eligible for friendship—from the next generation of royalty and the younger nobility to stars, ambassadors, socialites, and maîtres d'hôtel. Much of the book is

---

*The title, in *Elsa Maxwell's Etiquette Book*, of her chapter on obituaries, funerals, burials, and mourning.

devoted to her feverish travels in Europe in the early sixties. By the end of 1962, however, Elsa felt the necessity of rest. She spent more time in bed than she had done since infancy, although not at the Waldorf, for at some point she had moved uptown to the Delmonico Hotel at Park Avenue and Fifty-ninth Street. It was said, and noted in some of the gossip columns, that she had worn out her welcome at the Waldorf; had been surly to staff; had created an unpleasant scene in the lobby. In truth, Elsa no longer had the drawing power that had lured so many of her wealthy, glamorous friends to the hotel she came to think of almost as her own. Her circus had devolved to a sideshow. (Nevertheless, she is still pictured, along with other luminaries, in a promotional booklet placed in every guest room.)

Early shadows of senility had fallen across the Maxwell landscape, along with the melancholy process of decay. Nicholas Haslam, whose life has been almost as vivid as Elsa's, recalls in his memoir, *Redeeming Features*, that Elsa was incontinent at a cocktail party in London given by the playwright Terence Rattigan. Dickie "followed her movements, solicitously covering up the evidence with yet another of Rattigan's apricot silk cushions."

On May 24, 1963, *The New York Times* reported that Elsa had celebrated her eightieth birthday at a small party. (It was, of course, her eighty-second.) The host was Jacques Sarlie, a secretive international financier and art collector who had once owned twenty-nine Picassos. A few years earlier Elsa had publicly disparaged him, then patched up the rift.

The *Times* reporter gave few details of Elsa's present condition, focusing instead on her colorful past: Monaco, Noël Coward, playing cards with Winston Churchill, and the like. He did reveal that "Miss Maxwell admits she is a little lame." Elsa seemed determined to throw him off track. She was sailing for France in a few days, she said. (It would be her final visit to the country she considered her second homeland.) She was planning a party for the Duke and Duchess of Windsor, to take place five days before departure. And she read aloud several of the eight hundred telegrams and birthday greetings, by Elsa's count, that had poured in from around the world.

"Adlai Stevenson asked me the other day how I have so much vitality left," she chatted to the reporter. "The secret, I told him, is that I have no position or capacity. That means I don't have to see anyone I don't want to see." On her dress the wore "the little red ribbon of the French Légion d'Honneur," presented to her, she said, by "that amazing man, General de Gaulle." (The actual presentation, by Ambassador Henri Bonnet, took place at the French embassy in Washington in 1947.) Elsa told the *Times* reporter that she was looking forward, on her return from France, to the next April in Paris ball, which, despite its name, took place each year in October.

In the early fifties, Elsa was one of the originators of the April in Paris ball, an annual charity event still held at the Waldorf. She called it "the benefit that is dearest to my heart." During Elsa's time, it was rated the biggest money raiser of all the New York charity balls, and benefited numerous causes in France and the United States. (While such events do raise money for worthy causes, they also benefit those who attend by shining the spotlight of recognition on them.)

Leaving France at summer's end, 1963, Elsa had grown feeble. Janet Flanner wrote in a letter, "I saw her at the Ritz Bar, walking with a stick, Dickie Gordon with her. Saw Dickie later about to take her to the boat to New York to die. When I said to Dickie, 'Are you going with her?' she said in her quick Scottish snarl, 'What on earth would she do without me?'" Despite her incapacitation, Elsa enjoyed that last summer in France with Dickie. While there, she saw a number of old friends, including Prince Rainier and Princess Grace, who had sent her "some lovely roses" with birthday wishes in May. With them, Elsa reminisced about Monaco as she had known it before their time.

On Friday, October 25, Elsa attended the twelfth annual April in Paris ball in a wheelchair. The event had moved from the Waldorf to the Americana Hotel, and among those in attendance were Maurice Chevalier and Liza Minnelli. Elsa had lost a great deal of weight and her face looked gaunt, drawn. Although stylishly dressed in a floral print evening gown with matching jacket and elbow-length white gloves, she didn't smile for the camera. The photograph that later appeared in the *Times* was a sad study of the ravages of vanishing years.

Six days later, on Thursday, October 31, Elsa entered New York Hospital for treatment of a heart ailment. On Friday evening, November 1, 1963, she died.

The next day, and for several days thereafter, every major newspaper in the United States and Western Europe reported her death, as well as papers throughout the British Commonwealth. The larger papers printed appreciations of Elsa's accomplishments, along with tributes. Perle Mesta said, "There won't be another Elsa Maxwell in this era. I think she was a great hostess. She was amusing and a good friend." Millicent Hearst: "In Miss Maxwell's passing, I lost a very dear friend of many years. Elsa was happiest when entertaining and giving pleasure to others." Mayor Robert F. Wagner of New York: "Mrs. Wagner and I regret the death of Elsa Maxwell, an old and valued friend."

The French ambassador to the United States, Herve Alphand, spoke on behalf of France: "Her passing is a great loss to us. She had always been a great friend of mine and of my country." Another Frenchman, Claude Philippe, cofounder with Elsa of the April in Paris ball, spoke warmly and eloquently through his grief: "I am terribly shocked. She was a very great woman whose generosity and affectionate friendship made many, many people's lives happier. She was one of the most unselfish persons I have ever known. She had a great love for music and knew more operatic scores by heart than any other amateur in the world." On November 5, Noël Coward wrote in his diary, "A great sadness. Poor old Elsa died. Another old friend gone. How glad I am that I went to see her a couple of weeks ago and made her laugh. I had a feeling that she was on her way, poor old duck."

In the weeks and months following Elsa's death, magazines ran features on her life, which they had covered for years. *Time* devoted almost a full page to Elsa, with a photograph of her, taken in 1958, in a moment of great happiness: she is standing between Aly Khan and Maria Callas. The long obituary began, "Elsa Maxwell gave to the world of society, in which boredom is the occupational disease, an illusion that it was composed of marvelously amusing people having a wonderful time. They thanked her for it by giving her a free ride through the caviar-and-champagne life, the gaspygossipy life, which she enjoyed so much that she made lots of other people enjoy it too." A fitting eulogy, tinged with knowing irony: "Elsa was a great matchmaker, but that kind of love was not for her. In the numerous costume parties she attended, she often came as a man."

Henry Luce, the publisher of *Time*, and his wife, Clare Boothe Luce, were in Elsa's debt. She was there the night they met, in 1933, and she kept their affair a secret, for Luce was married at the time. Through the years, Elsa retained her high admiration of Clare Boothe Luce, who, as a teenager, had been a protegée of Elsa's friend Mrs. O.H.P. Belmont.

An unusual circumstance delayed Elsa's funeral and burial for almost two weeks, until Tuesday, November 12. Her lawyer, Sol A. Rosenblatt (who also represented such clients as Alfred Vanderbilt and Stavros Niarchos), deferred final arrangements because of accounts published in several newspapers saying that Elsa had expressed a wish to be cremated and her ashes scattered over the Adriatic Sea, near Venice. No such stipulation was found in her will, however, and so Rosenblatt decided on local burial. (Dickie, of course, had no legal standing in the matter, even though she was Elsa's sole legatee. In the eyes of the law, she was just another friend.)

The funeral was held at the Frank E. Campbell Funeral Chapel, at Madison Avenue and Eighty-first Street. Before the service, an organist played one of Elsa's compositions, "The Singer." (In *R.S.V.P.*, Elsa wrote that this song was used by Dame Nellie Melba and by Frances Alda as an encore in recitals.) The Reverend Leonard Helie, minister of the Universalist Church of New York, conducted the service, which included prayers and a reading of Psalm XXIII. *The New York Times*, listing some of the one hundred or so who attended the funeral, named Mrs. Robert F. Wagner, representing the mayor; Newbold Morris, Commissioner of Parks and chairman of the New York City Center of Music and Drama; and Jean Dalrymple, director of the center's light opera company. Elsa had served on the board of City Center for a number of years.

"DEAR GOD, HOW SMALL A SINGER AM I"

The soprano Frances Alda (1879–1952), in her autobiography, *Men, Women, and Tenors*: "Another song, called 'The Singer,' Elsa dedicated to me. Frank La Forge and I fixed it up a bit, and I sang it on my concert programs all through one season. It was sentimental, but it was one of those songs that people will drop a tear over, and love for the emotion it arouses in them. All about a singer who thought she was pretty good until she heard a little bird warbling in a tree. Then she cried, 'Dear God! How small a singer am I!' And, presumably, never sang again."

The *Times* continued, "Others attending the service included Douglas Fairbanks, Jr. and Zachary Scott, actors; Anton Dolin, choreographer; Mrs. Whitelaw Reid, Mrs. Stephen R. Sanford, Mrs. Winston Guest, and Dorothy Fellowes-Gordon."

Among those who spoke were Newbold Morris, who praised Elsa for her efforts on behalf of City Center, and Sol Rosenblatt, whose cliché in this case was absolutely true: "With the passing of this great lady, there has passed almost an era."

More than three decades later, in 1999, I spoke to Mrs. Winston Guest (1920–2003), better known in society as C.Z. She was one of the few persons then alive who had attended Elsa's funeral. "We became good friends," Mrs. Guest began. "I loved her. Oh, she was wonderful." I asked what made Elsa so wonderful, and she replied, "She was such fun, and she never, never complained. Everything she had, she gave away. When she came to my house she brought a case of champagne. She always brought toys to my children. She was a giver, not a taker." Then Mrs. Guest reminisced about Elsa's piano playing, her love of opera, the April in Paris ball, which she herself had chaired for two years, Elsa's Warner Bros. short *Riding Into Society* ("Funniest thing I ever saw, I almost died laughing"), and then: "She came to my house here on Long Island for lunch a week before her death."

I asked what Elsa was like in those final days. "I didn't realize how desperately sick she was. She always tried to put a good face on things." Then she said something quite surprising. "Mrs. Elsie Woodward wanted to arrange a beautiful funeral, and various members of the Metropolitan Opera were going to sing, but Dickie Gordon wouldn't allow it. They had the most terrible fight."

I probed for details, but C.Z. Guest either did not remember, or she wasn't telling. "How do I know?" she said. "I only know about it because of Sol Rosenblatt, Elsa's lawyer." She added that very few people even knew when Elsa's funeral was to take place; otherwise, more would have attended. "I only found out because Sol called me up and said, 'Elsa's funeral is tomorrow.'"

While her account seemed convincing, certain details did not match the report published in the *Times*. For instance, Mrs. Guest reiterated that "very few people attended, there was only a handful in the chapel." Yet surely a hundred people is a respectable number for any elderly person. Then she said that Mrs. Woodward had secured Maria Callas as one of the singers, and Cesare Siepi. After these intriguing details there were no more. Why did Mrs. Woodward take it upon herself to plan Elsa's funeral when she, like all of Elsa's friends, knew that Dickie was Elsa's companion? Was Dickie still affronted by Elsa's crush on Callas, and is that why she vetoed the Woodward plans? Or did she disdain Elsa's society friends in New York? Dickie, we recall, was not enraptured even by her former king.

One may speculate endlessly, but these questions, I'm afraid, find no answers among Mrs. Guest's broken memories. The past, ever changing, goes by faster than the present. While Mrs. Guest could not, or would not, say more about Elsa's funeral, she repeated, with variations, much of the high praise she had already paid Elsa. Then, suddenly remembering some gossip that Elsa had told her in 1962, when *Lawrence of Arabia* was released, she said: "I don't know how Elsa knew, but she told me about Lawrence of Arabia and the shah. Apparently they had an affair. Or maybe he had been sodomized by the shah. I don't know. But Elsa said it."

This passed across the conversation like a trailing whiff of strong cigar smoke, and then was gone. Inquiries as to which shah this would have been led nowhere, though I knew it wasn't the last Shah of Iran, who was barely born in time for T. E. Lawrence's exploits in the Middle East. I repeat the gossip here not because it's new, but because this posthumous eavesdropping recalls a side of Elsa—her perpetual fascination with carnal gossip—that is absent from her writing. Dickie, too, loved the *on-dit*, and in conversation with Hugo Vickers at age one hundred, she still relished the whispered tales of a century gone by.

After the funeral service, a private burial took place in Ferncliff Cemetery, in Hartsdale, New York, some forty miles from Manhattan. Later a plain, flat marker was placed at the head of the grave. On it was inscribed

ELSA MAXWELL
1883–1963

Elsa's lawyer filed her will for probate on the day of the funeral. This last will and testament was terse and to the point. Everything was left to Dorothy Fellowes-Gordon, including $7,600 in a bank account, $1,200 in French francs, and $15.74 in pocket money. Personal belongings and jewelry were valued at $2,190, including a worn-out mink coat, a dilapidated white fox scarf, thirty-odd pieces of luggage in bad condition, and a gold bridge for teeth appraised at eight dollars. Her total estate was worth some twelve thousand dollars, and her debts (to Saks Fifth Avenue, Elizabeth Arden, and a furrier) came to around four hundred.

Elsa loved to say that she owned nothing, and at her death it was proved to be true. All the gifts she received over the years, from the unlikely medal given her as winner of the beautiful-baby contest in San Francisco, to diamond bracelets, brooches, emerald rings, silver bowls—where were they? I suspect that Elsa hocked each one as soon as she had written a thank-you note to the donor. When friends gave her gifts, they often attached a note saying something like "I selected this scarf with Mary's color in mind, because I know you'll be passing it on to her." Elsa herself, writing in *Harper's*

Bazaar in 1938, admitted that when facing an overdrawn bank account, "I dispose of this or that trinket which I happen to possess at the moment," including a "ruby ring, I loved it dearly but I was about to give a party and I needed cash."

But what about the voluminous correspondence of eight decades? Letters and telegrams from Noël, Cole, and a hundred friends barely touched on in these pages, such as Vladimir Horowitz, Dorothy Parker, Nathan Milstein, David Niven, Rebecca West, Elizabeth Taylor, Coco Chanel, Gene Tierney, George Bernard Shaw (who called her "the eighth wonder of the world"), and that long queue of nobility, dollar princesses, heads crowned and uncrowned, presidents, ambassadors, Hollywood moguls, and, yes, her mother Laura Wyman Maxwell—surely this is an archive that, if preserved, might now reside in the hushed precincts of a Yale library, as neighbor to the Cole Porter papers; or in the British Library, the Academy of Motion Picture Arts and Sciences, or even the Sorbonne.

There is, alas, no Elsa Maxwell Collection. Was she so blasé that, when a letter arrived from Jean Cocteau, with a whimsical drawing of herself included, she dropped it into her wastebasket at the Waldorf? The same for a note from Callas? Or when the Duchess of Windsor threatened legal action at the time of *R.S.V.P.*, did Elsa forward the letter to Sol Rosenblatt, or did she drop it beside her desk for the maid to collect?

It's true, of course, that nomads like Elsa must focus on portable property. I raise the question because the presumed loss of these memorabilia is poignant, but also because maybe, somewhere in the world, someone saved them, and one day they will resurface. In that regard, I'm as distantly hopeful as those who launched the *Voyager* spacecraft in 1977, containing sounds and images of Earth, a message from President Carter and the secretary-general of the UN, and destined for beings in interstellar space who might eventually respond.

Elsie Woodward did not forget Elsa Maxwell. Although Dickie would not permit the spectacular funeral that Mrs. Woodward wanted, a year later she helped bring about a different kind of tribute. In October 1964, at the April in Paris ball, twelve hundred people raised two hundred thousand dollars to fund a scholarship honoring Elsa at the Columbia University School of Journalism. Officially named the American-French Scholarship in Memory of Elsa Maxwell, it was funded to pay out over a period of ten years, and therefore ended in the mid-1970s. I learned from the Development Office at the School of Journalism that Elsie Woodward was "stewarded for the scholarships," meaning that she was the person kept abreast of anything pertaining to them, including each year's recipients. The first awards were made in 1966, to the colorful, witty columnist Molly Ivins, and to Carole Ashkinaze, a distinguished journalist and author. Elsa surely would have been pleased to count these women among her friends.

35 Renewer of Hearts

The many obituaries published after Elsa's passing emphasized her four decades of party giving, and rightly so. My aim in these pages has been to show the spirit of Elsa's parties and why they succeeded so well, and also to spotlight the less familiar facets of her voluminous life. Now, nearing the end, I realize that no obituary—indeed, no book—delivers a full-length portrait of Elsa Maxwell. She remains vast and elusive, a quicksilver personality who constructed "Elsa Maxwell," world citizen and bon vivant extraordinaire, out of raw materials from that Elsie Wyman Maxwell who grew up on the lower slopes of Nob Hill. Around that name in quotation marks, a mythology evolved as fastastic as any concocted by a press agent— Elsa included.

Once, at a party, she had her guests play a game that some perhaps found disconcerting. It was Write Your Own Epitaph, and according to Elsa it was then that Samuel Goldwyn jotted his famous phrase, "Include me out." I wish she had listed others, including her own, but she didn't. Later, however, in interviews, she stated what, in effect, might serve as her epitaph of choice: "I die happy."

In context: "If I knew I were to die tomorrow, I'd want my epitaph to be, 'I die happy.' For I was born gay, and my life has been glorious, transcendently magical, full of glamour." In another interview, she said, "My credo is, Do good and have fun," which, with a bit of tweaking, might also serve on a tombstone.

Elsa spoke often of her greatest treasure, her friends, and I've quoted them to prove that her affection was largely reciprocated. "I have more friends than any living person," she said shortly before her death. "They are my riches." Toward the end of *R.S.V.P.*, Elsa philosophized about her own life and about life in general. "The ultimate perfection is happiness," she wrote, "and my parties helped to achieve it. Giving parties is a trivial avocation, but it pays the dues for my union card in humanity."

What she would have preferred to all the fame and glitter, she told Tom Cochran, a producer of *The Jack Paar Show*, was a very simple thing that never happened. "I have known seven presidents of the United States, and entertained a dozen kings. But I'd trade places with anyone who knows a man I have never seen: Albert Schweitzer," the medical missionary to Africa and winner of the Nobel Peace Prize in 1952.

She never tired of paying tribute to those who had created the happiness in her life. In 1961, on one of her last visits to France, a group of Elsa's Parisian friends gave a luncheon in her honor on the day before her departure for New York. Before the meal, they drank a toast to her and then called out, "Speech! Speech!" Elsa stood up, raised her glass of champagne, and said, "I drink to myself. I drink to Elsa Maxwell, because I am so lucky to have such dear friends. And in drinking to myself, you see, I really drink to you."

And yet no one knew better than Elsa herself that not all the world lifted its collective champagne glass to toast her in return. Like Maria Callas, who often seemed more infatuated with persecutors than with friends, Elsa relished a feud, a good fight, and she boasted of her enemies. Perhaps she found a drop of venom stimulating when mixed with so much ambrosia. And, despite her relentless bonhomie, Elsa understood human nature. She recognized the heartbreaks and treacheries of life, and also the tragic truth that, ultimately, all relationships end. To counteract the chaos of living, she sought to create a parallel life, this one social, even theatrical—a hothouse atmosphere as it were, planned, controlled, directed, its denizens beautifully attired and on best behavior making their entrances and exits. Elsa's idea of the perfect party resembled a work of art whose effect, though transitory, might create as much pleasure as a play, a painting, a poem, an opera, or a piano concerto. "In the final analysis," she said, "it is not the *who* that counts in entertaining. It is not the money you spend, nor the prestige you may reap—it is what is in your heart. More, it is what you leave in the hearts of others."

In *How to Do It, or The Lively Art of Entertaining*, Elsa wrote a charming passage in which she likened herself to Hatshepsut. Listing several of the ancient ruler's many titles—"Bestower of Years," "Goddess and Lady of All Lands"—Elsa zoomed in on the epithet that, she felt, also applied to her: "Renewer of Hearts! That is the one that appeals to me—an appeal in no way diminished by the strong likelihood that Hatshepsut wrote it herself. The phrase sings through the ages, touching the countless generations of people who have wakened one morning and thought, 'I think I'll give a party—the best party ever!' I like to think that I am simply a twentieth-century addition to that gaudy, wonderful crew—a sort of latter-day *Renewer of Hearts*."

Although Elsa put little store in astrology, she once elaborated on her dual nature, for she was born under the sign of Gemini, the twins. "One side of me is reckless, debonair, impulsive, the other is conservative, constructive, and occasionally quite puritan." Many readers of the *New York Post* were surely surprised in 1942, when the paper profiled Elsa, to learn of her interest in philosophy. Capable of discussing the works of Rousseau, Voltaire, Montaigne, Thoreau, Dostoyevsky, and Tolstoy—"*War and Peace* is probably the greatest book ever written," she declared—she revealed one of her greatest influences as Lao Tse, the father of Taoism. (A Taoist saying that seems particularly apt for Elsa: "Whether one dispassionately sees to the core of life, or passionately sees the surface, the core and the surface are essentially the same.") And though Elsa was far too busy to devote great chunks of time to profound thoughts, sometimes her aphorisms sounded as pithy—and as French—as those of La Rochefoucauld. "Charm," she said, "is completely innate and cannot be acquired. Glamour can be bought and manufactured."

Pressed by a reporter for examples of both qualities, she cited the stage actress Lynn Fontanne as "utterly and completely charming," and though she considered Eleanor Roosevelt "a wonderful woman," the first lady lacked charm. In Elsa's eyes, Orson Welles possessed charm, which Tallulah Bankhead lacked in spite of her tremendous vitality. Elsewhere in Hollywood, Elsa considered Charles Boyer and Maurice Chevalier full of charm, along with Luise Rainer and Joan Fontaine.

And Elsa Maxwell herself had all the charm in the world, though not everyone found her charming.

For all her goodness, and her good heart, Elsa had her share of Gemini flaws. Those tall tales about her destitute youth, the endless denials that anyone but she herself ever paid for her parties (and, in the next breath, the avowals of bankruptcy)—from our vantage point, these traits detract but little. They add a roguish touch, like white worn defiantly after Labor Day by Mrs. Astor. "We live through our imperfections," Elsa said.

And yet . . . Elsa on the topic of homosexuality is regrettable, even when you allow for the fact that she was writing in a homophobic era, the fifties. The conservative, puritan side of her personality was nowhere more unattractive than in those pages of *R.S.V.P.* where she pontificates on "the shocking increase in homosexuality as further evidence of decadence in the top levels of American and European society. Thirty years ago, lesbians and sash boys—a euphemism for commoner terms I prefer not to use—were almost unknown in America. There were homosexuals in theatrical and artistic circles, of course, and guarded references were made to effeminate men in certain fields such as interior decoration and fashion designing. But the average American rarely, if ever, encountered a sexually maladjusted person. Perhaps I was naive, but I never saw a woman who was an obvious lesbian until I went to Europe." (Could a San Francisco sophisticate really have been so ingenuous? Most unlikely.)

"I AM NOT A LESBIAN, EVEN THOUGH I'D LIKE TO BE ONE WHEN I GROW UP"—DAWN FRENCH

Writing about her childhood on Belvedere Island, Elsa mentioned "George Cameron and Larry Harris, two well-known bachelors who lived next door to us." Written records from the nineteenth century reveal very little about homosexual relationships, but beginning with the Gold Rush, and its overwhelmingly male population, faint clues suggest many liaisons among men. Adding to San Francisco's Sodom and Gomorrah reputation are hints that lesbianism existed there less secretly than elsewhere in the country. For example, when a hundred-year-old time capsule was opened in Washington Square in 1979, a pamphlet was found inside titled *The Great Geysers of California*. On the flyleaf was this handwritten note by the author, Laura De Force Gordon: "If this little book should see the light after its 100 years of entombment, I would like its readers to know that the author was a lover of her own sex and devoted the best years of her life in striving for the political equality and social and moral elevation of women." (That ambiguous inscription can be read as feminist, or as lesbian-feminist.) According to Mick Sinclair, in *San Francisco: A Cultural and Literary History*, "In 1908 the city's first known gay bar, The Dash, at 574 Pacific Street, was closed by a police raid."

For Elsa to have lived as a bohemian gadabout in San Francisco until the age of twenty-six, and never seen a lesbian, is a comical remark. Who would believe such a claim?

Like Savonarola on the down low, Elsa rants on for two long paragraphs, attributing the prevalence of "sash boys" in England to the custom of sending British boys to all-male boarding schools, and of homosexuality in general to boredom and "indolent leisure." She also blames women of her own generation who, losing their physical attractiveness, seek out "safe" young men as escorts and companions.

I have no real explanation for the inclusion of this tirade, nor did Dickie.

Speaking to Hugo Vickers in 1991, she said in reference to *R.S.V.P.*, "I shouldn't have allowed some bits to be in. I should have cut out the bit where she talks about homosexuals, it's ridiculous. Our friends were. That should never have been allowed in the book."

Curiously, the word "homosexuality" was omitted from the index of the British edition, titled *I Married the World*, even though Elsa rattled on at greater length than in the American edition. She took it upon herself to discuss rich widows who took up with "homosexual gigolos," mothers who loved their sons almost incestuously, the trial of Oscar Wilde and its long stigmatization of "perversion." Then she asked herself rhetorically, "How can you take up this attitude when you know very well a number of these men are among your friends and acquaintances?"

Her response: "It is quite true. I am guilty of contradictions here. But I just cannot apply the same rules to genius. It may be morally indefensible but I feel there must be one law for the especially rich in mind and another for the remainder." Elsa's unrelenting viciousness in those pages has no excuse. One reason for it, however, is not far to seek: the widespread homosexual self-hatred that began to dissipate only with Stonewall in 1969. Elsa claimed to have no interest in sex. I believe her erotic drive was low, and that she sublimated it to a hectic social life. Based on scant evidence, however, and educated guesses, it seems that she and Dickie did have a physical relationship, perhaps short-lived or intermittent, but a lesbian partnership nonetheless—which Elsa, sadly, was unable to acknowledge, even to herself. So conflicted was she, on the other hand, that I wonder whether she herself believed a word of those unfortunate passages.

Another reason for her harangue is this: her homophobic gun was pointed at the head of Jimmy Donahue, though custom and the libel laws required a silencer. Such was her hatred of him that she also mowed down her friends with her spiteful volleys. And the Duchess of Windsor, too, who, losing her "physical attractiveness" had taken up with a "safe" young man, a "homosexual gigolo," as escort and companion. Elsa's victims, and everyone else in the know, would have guessed the omitted names on first reading.

Only once did she face the question head-on in print. From September 1937 through February 1938, *Harper's Bazaar* serialized what purported to

be "Elsa Maxwell's Autobiography." On the first page of the first install-
ment, as she sweeps aside various accusations ("They say that someone is
always paying for my parties, but the bills that I get and the checks that I
write tell a different story"), she discloses, boldly for the time: "They say
that I am a lesbian because I don't pop into bed with every man I see, but
they overlook my fat—and fat is the greatest protection to a woman's vir-
tue." In Elsa's case, of course, "they" knew all the reasons why she didn't
sleep with men, and fat had nothing to do with it.

Contemporary readers who find Elsa's homophobia abhorrent will, on the
other hand, applaud her lack of racial prejudice. To write as she did on
American bigotry and discrimination required a measure of courage in the
forties and fifties.

Not many white writers went so far as Elsa in her column in the *New
York Post* on November 16, 1943. I quoted part of it in chapter 1; a con-
densed version, titled "Glamour vs. Prejudice," appeared in *The Negro Di-
gest* in January 1944. There, Elsa led with: "The glamorous and great artists
of the Negro race are gradually turning the whole race 'problem'—which is
not, and never was, a problem—into a glorious absurdity. When stiff-necked
whites are faced with the beauty and charm of a Katherine Dunham or a
Lena Horne, or nettled by the magnificent talent and intellect of Paul Robeson, the idea of 'prejudice' seems a matter for concern only in lunatic asy-
lums."

Then Elsa recounted a recent incident involving Katherine Dunham—"a
great beauty and a startling dancer"—who was invited to a dinner given by
a New York producer. Elsa wasn't present, but an unnamed woman friend
of Elsa's was invited to the dinner. The host asked this woman to stop by in
her car and pick up Katherine Dunham. The woman had never heard of
Dunham, and when her car stopped at a midtown hotel and Dunham stepped
in, "as gay, delightful, and poised as a wood nymph," according to Elsa, "my
friend was flabbergasted. She made what little conversation she could, then
relapsed into stony silence."

At dinner, the woman continued her frigid demeanor, even though everyone else had a jolly time. As soon as possible, she left. Next day she phoned the producer: "What do you mean, inflicting this on me?"

"You should have been honored," he replied. "Katherine Dunham is one of the greatest dancers of our time—and you, my dear, can't even rhumba."

Elsa went on to list outstanding "Negro intellectuals" such as George Washington Carver, Richard Wright, Walter White, Countee Cullen, and James Weldon Johnson, who had not been included for membership in the American Academy of Arts and Letters but who, she wrote, "would be a credit to any national academy." Then she listed "Negro artists such as Marian Anderson, Dorothy Maynor, Paul Robeson, Duke Ellington, and Dean Dixon, the conductor, who are outstanding in their respective fields."

Elsa devoted other columns in the forties to racism, often in reaction to particular events or court decisions. On May 2, 1944, she wrote that "the organized attempts of a number of southern whites to keep [the black population] from having any say in its own government makes Hitler rise up and cry 'Brother.'" A year earlier, she had written, "Here's a pat on the back all the way from California to New York's Governor Dewey, who had the courage to appoint to the bench two lawyers of the Negro race."

On her birthday in 1950, Elsa gave a party for thirty friends at the Ritz Hotel in Paris. She hired Marian Anderson to sing. This was five years before Anderson became the first person of color to sing at the Metropolitan Opera in New York. In *The Celebrity Circus*, Elsa recalled that "years ago I gave a luncheon at the Waldorf Towers for several great singers, and among them were Marian Anderson, Dorothy Maynor, Paul Robeson, and several other Negroes. Just before they were due to arrive, it suddenly dawned on me that restrictions for colored people then existed at the Waldorf perhaps more than any other place in New York. At that time they were not even allowed to come in the front door."

Elsa telephoned the front desk and said, "I am expecting some very great artists to lunch today, and among them are some members of the Negro race. They must be allowed to come up in the regular elevators to my apartment. Not one of these gifted people is to be put in the service car. This I expect, this I demand." (If Elsa was indeed "dangerous," she sometimes used her power for good.)

"My instructions were followed to the letter," Elsa concluded. "I believe that on that day, so long ago, I broke the color bar at the Waldorf."

But what are we to make of Elsa's association with the FBI? Her file, which I obtained—minus four withheld pages—through the Freedom of Information and Privacy Acts, raises more questions than it answers, one reason being the endless blacking-out of names and other pertinent facts in correspondence, memoranda, and the like. In chapter 1, I quoted from a 1945 memo that apparently ended whatever association she had with the agency. Three years earlier, when the outcome of World War II was by no means certain, the FBI approached her to supply information regarding any friends and acquaintances who might sympathize with the Germans, or conversely, with Russian Communists.

At the same time, Elsa herself was looked on as slightly suspicious. For one thing, J. Edgar Hoover, director of the FBI and a closeted homosexual, didn't trust "deviants," not even those "of genius" whom Elsa so easily pardoned. He would, of course, have recognized Elsa as "family," to use current gay jargon, from the moment he first heard of her.

Then, too, in the eyes of the FBI Elsa seemed to know too much. In a four-page latter from P. E. Foxworth, assistant director, to Hoover, dated October 15, 1942, it was mentioned in passing that Elsa, at a party, had explained to _____, an FBI informant, how hard she was working "getting together sufficient games to be played on ten Army transports that were leaving that night."

The main thrust of the letter, however, was to inform Hoover that Elsa had been asked to furnish details about the author Louis Bromfield and his association with the Joint Anti-Fascist Refugee Committee. "During the conversation with Miss Maxwell today," Foxworth reported, "she stated that Louis Bromfield is an old friend of hers and that she knew of the organization, Joint Anti-Fascist Refugee Committee. She stated that she had recently refused to give her name or to speak at the meeting of this organization to be held late in October." (This committee was thought to be a Communist front because it opposed Franco in Spain and, of course, all other Nazi fellow travelers. In the early fifties, eleven of its members served prison sentences, including the novelist Howard Fast, author of *Spartacus*, which Stanley Kubrick adapted for his 1960 film.)

Foxworth quotes Elsa as saying, of Bromfield's connection with the committee, that he was "an adolescent non-grown-up fool" whom she considered harmless even though she conceded that he might indeed be acting as a "front." Also during her meeting with Foxworth, Elsa named other friends and acquaintances who belonged to the committee, including Dorothy Parker, Paul Robeson, and Lillian Hellman. (These names, of course, would not have been new to the FBI.) The conversation moved on to Frenchmen, and others, whom Elsa considered friendly toward the puppet government in Vichy. Owing to the many deletions in her file, however, it is difficult to follow her discussion with Foxworth.

As to the suspicion that Elsa knew too much, several memoranda in the file express surprise and displeasure that "such a woman" would know "the movements of our Army transports." (Today this strikes us as an instance of FBI paranoia, but during wartime such precautions were not necessarily misplaced. In Britain, the dictum "loose lips sink ships" was taken very seriously.)

From J. Edgar Hoover himself, to "SAC, New York," on January 8, 1943: "Dear Sir, There are enclosed copies of a C-2 report concerning the activities of Elsa Maxwell which is self-explanatory. The copies of the report are furnished you for your information and guidance." Handwritten at the bottom of the letter, presumably by an agent in the New York office, is this note: "In view of attached report this contact should be handled very cautiously & no work assigned except where possibly _____." (Hoover's report is not included in Elsa's file; I suspect that it comprises the four withheld pages mentioned above.)

Hoover's Stalinist methods are so well known that we needn't linger over them. I prefer to think that Elsa's association with him, and with the FBI, stemmed from genuine patriotic impulses. And patriotism, in Elsa's time, had not acquired the pejorative connotation that sullied it from the era of Vietnam. To Elsa's credit, she had no connection with the FBI after the forties, nor would she, in my opinion, have approved of the tactics of McCarthyism. She may well have worried, in the early fifties, that she herself was under suspicion on any number of counts, from that photograph of her with Molotov at the UN conference, and her antiracist writings, to her friendship with the Windsors and others considered a bit too pro-German. It's even possible that Elsa's antihomosexual tirade in *R.S.V.P.* was the lesbian equivalent of draping herself in the flag.

36 Dickie Revisited

In Dickie's twenty-eight years after Elsa, the blanks recur like the ones in Elsa's FBI file. Those unfilled decades resemble negative space in a painting, with Elsa as the vanished subject, and Dickie's old age, up to the time of her interviews with Hugo Vickers, the area lacking shapes.

The immediate question is, How did Dickie handle her grief? Gary Carey, in his biography of Anita Loos, told of a train trip that Anita took with Dickie and several others in 1965. "Since Elsa Maxwell's death," he wrote, "Dickie had been querulous and so very helpless, acting as though never in her life had she opened a door or made a phone call for herself." (Age, too, may have depleted her, for by then Dickie had reached her mid-seventies.)

Carey's information came from Anita's diaries, correspondence, and from his interviews with her. Anita Loos herself, writing *A Girl Like I* in 1966, mentioned only the happy times with Elsa and Dickie. "Dickie loved to laugh and she remained more or less in Elsa's background," Loos recalled, "preferring better company than that of Elsa's overprivileged friends. Together with Dickie, I indulged in a favorite pastime, which was to take long walks with which Elsa's fat little feet were unable to cope. During the many years of our friendship, Dickie and I have walked miles along the Seine, in Chelsea, in Beverly Hills, and through offbeat neighborhoods of New York."

One wonders how long Dickie remained in New York following Elsa's burial. Did she leave immediately for London? For France? Certainly not for Auribeau, for she had sold the farm there in 1958. "It broke my heart to let it go," she said, "but I had to." The reason: "I spent too much money, instead of putting it away, which I should have done. I spent it on an apartment in Venice and things like that and I shouldn't have, but I had a great time, too." Elsa's legacy of twelve thousand plus in 1963 dollars amounted to perhaps six figures today, and this presumably kept Dickie going for some years.

Dickie told Hugo Vickers of living in a hotel in Paris, apparently not long after Elsa's death. Then she bought a house at Antibes, but, she said, "I took a dislike to it, it was so noisy, all the schoolchildren used to congregate there, so I decided to sell it."

In 1965, she returned to London and settled there permanently. "That was when I got my annuity, which gave me three thousand pounds a year, a very nice income in the sixties. It was wonderful living in Pont Street, five minutes from Harrods. But I had to move. I went to Lower Belgrave Street, in the basement of some friends. I was very happy there, and I stayed for about ten years. But it was expensive."

"When did you move to Tachbrook Street?" Hugo Vickers asked her in 1991.

"About eight years ago," she answered. "I never thought I'd end in a Council flat, I must say. I was lucky to get one, of course." ("Council housing" refers to subsidized houses and apartments for lower-income persons, the elderly, and others in distressed circumstances. Throughout Britain, these dwellings range from comfortable and attractive to run-down.) On a recent stroll through Pimlico, Dickie's last neighborhood, the buildings I saw in Tachbrook Street and elsewhere looked, from the outside at least, cheerful and well maintained.

On the tape recordings made by Hugo Vickers, Dickie's voice is strong despite a bronchial cough. In her bed at Westminster Hospital in London, her recall seems nearly total, for she recites incidents, names, dates, love affairs, and gossip going back almost a century. She quotes bon mots in French from her school days around 1900, and her hearing has diminished but little. Her only regret, it seems, is that she didn't save enough money.

"Do you see people from the past?" Hugo asked. "No," replied Dickie in a matter-of-fact tone, "everybody else has died. I had so many friends in London. We used to have canasta almost every night, and things like that. I used to belong to the library at Harrods, until I couldn't afford it any longer. Then I went to the public library, but I was finding the walk a bit hard. Then I learned that they deliver. I read a great deal. Every three weeks they bring ten books. Not always what I want, of course, but you have to take what they've got."

Dickie recalled visiting Noël Coward in London not long before his death. Setting up Noël's punch line, she said, "I was known for my bad temper, I'm sorry to say. I was easily irritated, easily inflamed. I used to scream at people sometimes, including Elsa. That day, I said to Noël, 'You know, darling, I'm eighty years old.'

"He said, 'I don't believe it! You just don't look it.'

"I said, 'It must be my beautiful nature.'

"Noël said, 'If that were so, you'd be on crutches.'"

Just shy of one hundred, Dickie's opinions remained unfiltered. When certain names came up, she didn't hesitate to describe the person Hugo mentioned as "very stupid," "quite plain," "a half-wit." A certain countess struck Dickie as "a common little thing."

In spite of old age and penury, Dickie kept up. Her thoughts could jump from the late Victorian years of her girlhood to Andy Warhol: "I never thought he was that talented, did you?" she asked Hugo Vickers. "He was very good at making a name for himself." That reminded her of the time she met Picasso and sat beside him at a film. Asked which changes she liked and which ones she didn't, Dickie said, "There were no automobiles when I was born. Then, when they came in, my stepfather was very keen on cars. He had two, a French car and an English one. The roads were terribly dusty in those days, so you had to put on a veil." And flying? "I hate that. I wish they'd never invented planes. I used to love traveling on the big ocean liners."

Elsa's many friends, and society in general, soon lost track of Dickie after 1963. By the time of her death, she was one of the last survivors of Edwardian London, New York in the teens, Paris in the twenties, and so much besides. Hugo Vickers spent many hours with Dickie, at her bedside, in May of 1991, and visited her regularly thereafter, along with Philip Hoare, who had befriended Dickie while writing *Noël Coward: A Biography*, published in 1995.

August 3, 1991, was Dickie's hundredth birthday, and the queen sent her a congratulatory telegram, as she does to all centenarians in the United Kingdom. Dickie, who had known many varieties of royalty without being swept away, nevertheless felt a certain warmth toward Queen Elizabeth II. She said to Hugo, "Well, I rather think I ought to reply, don't you?"

He answered, "I think that would be most splendid and most unexpected and unusual." A few days later, when he called to see her, Dickie dictated a letter to the queen. I reprint it here with Hugo's permission:

Your Majesty,
I would like to send my gratitude for your kindness in sending a telegram on my 100th birthday.

Your Majesty might be interested to know that in the early 1920s some friends told me that Lady Elizabeth Bowes-Lyon was in Paris and would very much like to visit the club run by Elsa Maxwell called l'Acacia, so I said that all she had to do was to ask for Elsa's table and she would arrange that. And she arrived with a very rich young American millionaire from Chicago, who obviously adored her and gazed at her throughout the evening. And she was her usual charming smiling self and charmed everybody. I have always treasured the memory of that myself and wondered if she remembered that evening.

I am in hospital at the moment and I celebrated my birthday there with members of my family, who came from Ireland and Scotland.

(signed)
Dorothy Fellowes-Gordon

"I popped it in the post," Hugo said, "and five days later, on August 11, she was dead."

———

I wish I could quote all of Philip Hoare's long obituary, which appeared in the *Independent* on August 16, 1991. A few lines, however, must suffice.

"Dickie's anecdotes were many and varied, and mostly ribald. She recalled accidentally opening a door at the Grand Hotel in Venice, and discovering Violet Trefusis being whipped by the Princesse Edmond de Polignac with a riding crop."

In old age, Dickie "admitted with glee to stealing French cheese from Harrods, not from penury but rather as a gesture of defiance. With her thick white hair cropped short, clad in a long flowing emerald gown, she entertained me with tales of Noël Coward over incredibly strong vodka tonics in heavily-smeared glasses. At 100 years of age, she was resolute, indefinably chic, and fearsomely charismatic to the last."

37 Elsa's Kingdom

Elsa, at her most breathlessly superlative and full of adjectives, might have started a column like this: The other day in London I rang up one of my dearest friends, the brilliant actor Bob Kingdom, who is blessed with that greatest of all gifts, a British sense of humor. "Bob," I said, "I'm giving a luncheon at the V and A and you simply must join me there." Bob, who is no stranger to theatregoers throughout the UK and in New York, grew up in Wales, that most romantic land of crags and castles. Imagine my surprise when he arrived with Steve Ross, the marvelous cabaret singer, and the three of us sat down to a spectacular meal in the museum's cafe, surrounded by the lavish designs of William Morris and those fantastically beautiful stained-glass windows by Edward Burne-Jones. Sitting not far away were my old friends Sir John and Lady Jane . . .

Well, Bob Kingdom is a friend of mine, we did meet for lunch in the cafe of the Victoria and Albert Museum, he did indeed bring along Steve Ross, but I spied no titled friends in the room. I first met Bob in New York in 1999 when he starred in his one-man, two-character play *Elsa/Edgar* at Primary Stages, an off-Broadway theatre on West Forty-fifth Street. Written by Bob Kingdom and Neil Bartlett, the eighty-minute theatre piece is set first at the Waldorf, where Elsa is broadcasting her radio show, and then at FBI headquarters in Washington, D.C., where J. Edgar Hoover, seated at his desk, more or less threatens the entire world.

Pairing these two monumental characters was a clever idea, one that worked well onstage. As one reviewer pointed out, the play is "heavily weighted (in a couple of ways) toward Elsa Maxwell," meaning, of course, that she's the heavier of the two and also by far the more sympathetic character. That reviewer accurately summed up Bob's performance as "a pitiless and at the same time compassionate comparison of two lonelinesses, the pain and peril of the unpretty and the unhandsome, and the burden of being constantly on the inside, while equally and constantly feeling on the outside."

In less than an hour, Bob brought Elsa to life by suggesting her traits, her passions, and her foibles. He re-created her deep voice and her Anglo-American accent along with her staccato vocal rhythms. This Elsa is a chatterbox who lives to gossip, to drop names, and to regale her radio audience with accounts of glittering parties. Elsa's intelligence and her drollery are also there in the characterization, as well as underlying anger that veers toward desperation. As Elsa, Bob Kingdom summoned up the Maxwell ego—tough as an armadillo shell—as well as the web of fragile feelings and wounded tissue underneath. He is not only a fine actor but also an impeccable researcher. He read everything available on Elsa, and watched hours of video footage, before he wrote a word. (As J. Edgar Hoover he was equally convincing. Hoover's most chilling line is this one, hurled at a member of the audience: "You are a Communist if I say so.")

When the play opened, I was planning an eventual biography of Elsa, so of course I attended and I also interviewed Bob one day at lunch. Here's a note I jotted at the time: "Elsa watched silently over Bob Kingdom and me at Joe Allen's this cold winter day, for a photograph of her hung over our table, just like Julie Newmar's picture on the wall behind Patrick Swayze, Wesley Snipes, and John Leguizano in *To Wong Foo, Thanks for Everything, Julie Newmar.*" It seemed a good omen.

Lunch was long that day, for Bob told me not only of his preparations for *Elsa/Edgar* but also the backstory, and I'll divulge his punch line right off: Elaine Stritch was originally picked to star. When a workshop version was in rehearsal in 1998 at the Bay Street Theatre on Long Island, Stritch played both roles. Suddenly, on the night of dress rehearsal, she withdrew.

Local papers quoted the theatre's executive director as attributing her departure to "the unhappy feeling that the role was not right for her." Those words amount to one of the great understatements in theatre history. Such grotesque miscasting is hard to top.

Fortunately, Bob as author was on hand, and even more fortunately, he had recently performed *Elsa/Edgar* at the Edinburgh Festival and also at the Lyric Hammersmith Studio in London. One preview was canceled pending the arrival, from London, of Bob's wigs and costumes. Then the show went on, to excellent reviews in the local press and in *Newsday*. The following year, during its limited run in New York, the play was also well received.

One reason for continuing interest in Elsa—onstage, and especially on the Internet, with a couple of million possibilities—is the amazing phenomenon she invented: "Elsa Maxwell." During her lifetime Elsa was unique, and she remains so. Beside her, other party givers seem like mere event planners placing paper napkins on card tables in a church basement. But then, those vibrant, theatrical occasions that bore the stamp of Elsa Maxwell began to disappear even before her death. How could her great, whirling, manufactured world survive without glamour, whose obituary we might almost include with Elsa's own? A few years later, the concept of glamour was a hollow husk, strangled perhaps by the egalitarian sixties. To be sure, no sane person would wish to resume the oppressions and injustices of Elsa's era for the sake of glamorous frosting on a poison cake. Those days, and the goneness of them, seem safe and refreshing on short visits from the present, when we view only the *nicer* side, knowing the ugliness is there, but hidden. Elsa herself, however, had no time for nostalgia. Her best party was always the one coming up tonight.

Acknowledgments

Grateful acknowledgment to those who died before publication: John Ardoin, Raymond Daum, Rick Dawn, John Galliher, Bob Grimes, C. Z. Guest, Kitty Carlisle Hart, Maggie Lewis, Jerry Sachs, Charles Stumpf, Dame Joan Sutherland, and Peter Urbanek.

When I did my first research on Elsa Maxwell in 1999, I couldn't have known that a decade, and the writing of three other books, would take place before I sat down to write Elsa's story. Now, recalling those who helped in so many ways, I feel as if I have almost as many friends as Elsa.

Although every person named here contributed some vital piece to the vast Maxwell mosaic, I must single out two friends without whose allegiance to the project that mosaic would have remained a preliminary sketch. To them the book is dedicated; they are Joann Kaplet Duff, in Ohio, and Ron Bowers, in New York. From the start, both took as keen an interest in my project as in one of their own. They sent me, over the years, countless books, clippings, photocopies, contact information, leads of every sort, and spent a thousand hours at least e-mailing and talking to me about Elsa on the phone. They read the book either chapter by chapter or upon completion, making incisive editorial comments on every page. I thank them, and everyone else acknowledged here, for the book's strengths, while claiming any faults as my own.

To describe the services rendered by the volunteer army named below, and to list their professional affiliations, would stretch on for many pages. I resort, therefore, to alphabetical order, hoping that all will remember how they put aside their own work and attended mine.

Bruce Abbott, Michael Henry Adams, Tricia Allen, Luana Almares, Tavo Amador, Robyn Asleson, Kirsten Baldock, Donald Bastin, Elizabeth Beier, Rita Belda, Aimee Bell, Matthew Bernstein, Carole Betts, Tonya Boltz, Linda Booth, Tim Boss, Kathy Breen, Beverly Bridger, Curtis F. Brown, Zoe Burman, Cindy Byers, Tom Carey, Mary Carter, Clarence Dargie, Ronald Davis, Jim Donovan, Kathleen Dowling, Hugh Downs, the Earl of Dudley, Jonathan Eaker, John Edwards, Bernard Fitzgerald, Ramona Foley, Joan Fontaine, Nicholas Gage, Tom Gardner, J. R. Giesen, Cordelia Brooke Gilder, Ilan Goddard, Martha A. Crosley Graham, Karen Greco, Marilyn Greenwald, Stephanie Guest, Hal Gurnee, Barbara Hall, G. D. Hamann, Marianne Hansen, Judy Hawkins, Steven Hayes, Kimberley Heatherington, Ron Henggler, Howard Hook, Chi Howell, Steven Hughes, Stacy Hutchins, Vernon Jordan, Robert Kanigel, Brian Kellow, Sharon Kelly, J. Gerald Kennedy, David Kessler, Bob Kingdom, Terry Kingsley-Smith, Miles Kreuger, Daniel Kusner, Steve Lambert, Wayne Lawson, Ken Leavens, Rosie Leonetti, Scott Lindsey, Carl Lundberg, A. C. Lyles, Nancy F. Lyon, Berri McBride, Brad McCulley, Howard Mandelbaum, Ron Mandelbaum, Bill Mann, Judith Martin, Evan Matthews, Ann Maxwell, Jimmy Maxwell, Tyson Meierotto, Dina Merrill, Hank Moonjean, Alison Moore, Jan Morris, Kristin Morris, Karola Noetel, Sharon Norris, Viscount Norwich, William Norwich, Brian O'Connell, James Robert Parish, Joan Allene Graziano Perry, Glenn Plaskin, Nancy Reddick, Mark Ricci, Michelle Richter, Jacque Roethler, Ron Ross, Steve Ross, Glenn Russell, Leigh W. Rutledge, Cynthia Sainsbury, Robert Sanchez, Brian Saumes, Carolyn Schroeder, Marvin Schulman, Sandy Seabold, Pat Sheehan, Steffi Sidney-Splaver, David Sinkler, David L. Smith, Donald Smith, Carly Sommerstein, Leonard Stanley, Kevin Sweeney, Kirsten Tanaka, Nigel Toft, Bruno Tosi, Fredrick Tucker, Tony Turtu, Sally Ingles Van Dyke, Hugo Vickers, Claus von Bülow, John R. Waggener, Robert Wagner, James Watters, Christi Weindorf, Susan Kohner Weitz, Betty Ann Wells, Bart Williams, and Hailey Kaylene Woodall.

Selected Bibliography

Elsa Maxwell turns up in several thousand books, and even more periodicals, published in many countries. I have limited these entries to books that seemed most trustworthy and most informative. I have omitted end notes because to annotate every source and every quoted statement would have made the book as bottomheavy as Elsa with documentation. I decided, therefore, to mention the sources in the text except where doing so would have proved cumbersome and distracting.

Alda, Frances. *Men, Women, and Tenors*. Boston: Houghton Mifflin, 1937.

Altrocchi, Julia Cooley. *The Spectacular San Franciscans*. New York: Dutton, 1949.

Amory, Cleveland. *The Last Resorts*. New York: Harper & Brothers, 1952.

———. *Who Killed Society?* New York: Harper & Brothers, 1960.

Andelman, David A. *A Shattered Peace: Versailles 1919 and the Price We Pay Today*. Hoboken, NJ: John Wiley & Sons, 2008.

Applebaum, Stanley, ed. *Great Actors and Actresses of the American Stage in Historic Photographs*. New York: Dover, 1983.

Auchincloss, Louis. *The Vanderbilt Era: Profiles in a Gilded Age*. New York: Collier Books/Macmillan, 1989.

Bach, Steven. *Dazzler: The Life and Times of Moss Hart*. New York: Knopf, 2001.

Balsan, Consuelo Vanderbilt. *The Glitter and the Gold*. New York: Harper & Brothers, 1952.

Beaton, Cecil. *Self Portrait with Friends: The Selected Diaries of Cecil Beaton, 1926–1974*. Edited by Richard Buckle. New York: Times Books, 1979.

Bernstein, Matthew. *Walter Wanger: Hollywood Independent*. Berkeley: University of California Press, 1994.

Binns, Archie, and Olive Kooken. *Mrs. Fiske and the American Theatre*. New York: Crown, 1955.

Blumenthal, Ralph. *Stork Club: America's Most Famous Nightspot and the World of Cafe Society*. Boston: Little, Brown, 2000.

Bodley, R.V.C. *Indiscretions of a Young Man*. London: Harold Shaylor, 1931.

Borden, Mary. *A Woman with White Eyes*. Garden City, NY: Doubleday, Doran & Co., 1930.

Bricktop, with James Haskins. *Bricktop*. New York: Atheneum, 1983.

Burke's Geneological and Heraldic History of the Landed Gentry. London: Burke's Peerage, Ltd., various editions., 1939–1972.

Cannadine, David. *The Decline and Fall of the British Aristocracy*. New Haven, CT: Yale University Press, 1990.

Carey, Gary. *Anita Loos: A Biography*. New York: Knopf, 1988.

Carpozi, George, Jr. *The Gary Cooper Story*. New Rochelle, NY: Arlington House, 1970.

Castellane, Boni de. *Confessions of the Marquis de Castellane*. London: Thornton Butterworth, Ltd., 1924.

Chaney, Lindsay, and Michael Cieply. *The Hearsts: Family and Empire— The Later Years*. New York: Simon & Schuster, 1981.

Collier, Richard. *The Rainbow People: A Gaudy World of the Very Rich and Those Who Served Them*. New York: Dodd, Mead, 1984.

Cooper, Duff. *The Duff Cooper Diaries*. Edited by John Julius Norwich. London: Weidenfeld & Nicolson, 2005.

Coward, Noël. *The Letters of Noël Coward*. Edited by Barry Day. New York: Knopf, 2008.

———. *The Noël Coward Diaries*. Edited by Graham Payn and Sheridan Morley. Boston: Little, Brown, 1982.

———. *Present Indicative*. Garden City, NY: Doubleday, Doran and Co., 1937.

Davis, Ronald L. *La Scala West: The Dallas Opera Under Kelly and Rescigno*. Dallas: Southern Methodist University Press, 2000.

De Wolfe, Elsie. *After All*. New York: Harper & Brothers, 1935.

Dunning, John. *On the Air: The Encyclopedia of Old-Time Radio*. New York: Oxford University Press, 1998.

Edwards, Anne. *The Grimaldis of Monaco*. New York: William Morrow, 1992.

———. *Throne of Gold: The Lives of the Aga Khans*. New York: William Morrow, 1995.

Eells, George. *The Life That Late He Led: A Biography of Cole Porter*. New York: G. P. Putnam's Sons, 1967.

Etherington-Smith, Meredith. *Patou*. New York: St. Martin's Press, 1983.

Farrar, Rowena Rutherford. *Grace Moore and Her Many Worlds*. New York: Cornwall Books, 1982.

Flanner, Janet. *An American in Paris: Profile of an Interlude Between Two Wars*. New York: Simon & Schuster, 1940.

———. *Darlinghissima: Letters to a Friend*. New York: Random House, 1985.

———. *Paris Was Yesterday, 1925–1939*. New York: Viking, 1972.

Fontaine, Joan. *No Bed of Roses*. New York: William Morrow, 1978.

Forbes-Robertson, Diana. *My Aunt Maxine: The Story of Maxine Elliott*. New York: Viking, 1964.

Gage, Nicholas. *Greek Fire: The Story of Maria Callas and Aristotle Onassis*. New York: Knopf, 2000.

Gagey, Edmond M. *The San Francisco Stage: A History*. Westport, CT: Greenwood Press, 1970 (original 1950, Columbia University Press).

Galatopoulos, Stelios. *Maria Callas: Sacred Monster*. New York: Simon & Schuster, 1998.

Garrison, Raymond E. *Tales of Early Keokuk Homes*. Hamilton, IL: The Hamilton Press, 1959.

General and Business Directory of the City of Keokuk for 1882–83. Keokuk, IA: J. A. Dull, 1882.

Genthe, Arnold. *As I Remember*. New York: Reynal and Hitchcock, 1936.

Gielgud, John. *A Life in Letters*. New York: Arcade, 2004.

Graves, Charles. *The Big Gamble: The Story of Monte Carlo*. London: Hutchinson & Co., 1951.

Guinness, Alec. *A Positively Final Exposure*. New York: Viking, 1999.

Hart, Kitty Carlisle. *Kitty: An Autobiography*. New York: St. Martin's Press, 1988.

Haslam, Nicholas. *Redeeming Features: A Memoir*. New York: Knopf, 2009.

Heymann, C. David. *Poor Little Rich Girl: The Life and Legend of Barbara Hutton*. New York: Random House, 1983.

Hoare, Philip. *Noël Coward: A Biography*. New York: Simon & Schuster, 1995.

Holland's Keokuk City Directory for 1871–72, Containing an Historical Sketch of the City, and Complete List of All the Residents, also a Classified Business Directory. Chicago: Western Publishing Co., 1871.

Hopper, Hedda, and James Brough. *The Truth and Nothing But*. Garden City, NY: Doubleday, 1963.

Howard, Jean. *Jean Howard's Hollywood*. Photographs by Jean Howard, with text by James Watters. New York: Harry N. Abrams, 1989.

———. *Travels with Cole Porter*. New York: Harry N. Abrams, 1991.

Jablonski, Edward. *Gershwin*. New York: Doubleday, 1987.

Jackson, Stanley. *Inside Monte Carlo*. New York: Stein and Day, 1975.

James, Robert Rhodes, ed. *Chips: The Diaries of Sir Henry Channon*. London: Weidenfeld & Nicolson, 1967.

Jellinek, George. *Callas: Portrait of a Prima Donna*. New York: Ziff-Davis, 1960.

Kanigel, Robert. *High Season: How One French Riviera Town Has Seduced Travelers for Two Thousand Years*. New York: Viking, 2002.

Kimball, Robert, ed. *Cole*. New York: Holt, Rinehart and Winston, 1971.

Klurfeld, Herman. *Winchell: His Life and Times*. New York: Praeger, 1976.

Kurzman, Dan. *Disaster!: The Great San Francisco Earthquake and Fire of 1906*. New York: William Morrow, 2001.

Laffey, Bruce. *Beatrice Lillie: The Funniest Woman in the World*. New York: Wynwood Press, 1989.

Leaming, Barbara. *If This Was Happiness: A Biography of Rita Hayworth*. New York: Viking, 1989.

———. *Orson Welles*. New York: Viking, 1985.

Lee, Betty. *Marie Dressler: The Unlikeliest Star*. Lexington, KY: University Press of Kentucky, 1997.

Lerman, Leo. *The Grand Surprise*. New York: Knopf, 2007.

Lewis, Alfred Allan. *Ladies and Not-So-Gentle Women*. New York: Viking, 2000.

Loos, Anita. *Cast of Thousands*. New York: Grosset and Dunlap, 1977.

———. *A Girl Like I*. New York: Viking, 1966.

———. *Kiss Hollywood Goodbye*. New York: Viking, 1974.

McKibbin, Ross: *Classes and Cultures: England 1918–1951*. Oxford: Oxford University Press, 1998.

McLean, Evalyn Walsh. *Father Struck It Rich*. Boston: Little, Brown, 1936.

Mann, William J. *Behind the Screen: How Gays and Lesbians Shaped Hollywood, 1910–1969*. New York: Viking, 2001.

Martin, Ralph G. *The Woman He Loved*. New York: Simon & Schuster, 1974.

Maxwell, Elsa. *The Celebrity Circus*. New York: Appleton-Century, 1963.

———. *Elsa Maxwell's Etiquette Book*. New York: Bartholomew House, 1951.

———. *How to Do It, or The Lively Art of Entertaining*. Boston: Little, Brown, 1957.

———. *I Married the World*. London: Heinemann, 1955 (British edition of *R.S.V.P.*).

———. *J'ai reçu le monde entier*. Paris: Amiot-Dumont, 1955 (French edition of *R.S.V.P.*).

———. *R.S.V.P.: Elsa Maxwell's Own Story*. Boston: Little, Brown, 1954.

Meneghini, Giovanni Battista. *My Wife Maria Callas*. New York: Farrar, Straus and Giroux, 1982.

Mesta, Perle, with Robert Cahn. *Perle: My Story by Perle Mesta*. New York: McGraw-Hill, 1960.

Metz, Robert. *The Tonight Show*. New York: Playboy Press, 1980.

Moats, Alice-Leone. *The Million Dollar Studs*. New York: Delacorte, 1977.

Moffat, Frances. *Dancing on the Brink of the World: The Rise and Fall of San Francisco Society*. New York: G. P. Putnam's Sons, 1977.

Moore, Grace. *You're Only Human Once*. Garden City, NY: Doubleday, 1944.

Mordden, Ethan. *Sing for Your Supper: The Broadway Musical in the 1930s*. New York: Palgrave Macmillan, 2005.

Moorehouse, Ward III. *The Waldorf-Astoria: America's Gilded Dream*. New York: M. Evans Co., 1991.

Morris, Sylvia Jukes. *Rage for Fame: The Ascent of Clare Boothe Luce*. New York: Random House, 1997.

Muscatine, Doris. *Old San Francisco: The Biography of a City from Early Days to the Earthquake*. New York: G. P. Putnam's Sons, 1975.

Paar, Jack. *I Kid You Not*. Boston: Little, Brown, 1960.

———. *My Saber Is Bent*. New York: Trident Press/Simon & Schuster, 1961.

———. *P.S. Jack Paar*. Garden City, NY: Doubleday, 1983.

Peters, Margot. *The House of Barrymore*. New York: Knopf, 1990.

Porter, Cole. *The Unpublished Cole Porter*. New York: Simon & Schuster, 1975.

Powell, Dawn. *The Diaries of Dawn Powell, 1931–1965*. South Royalton, VT: Steerforth Press, 1995.

Preston, Charles, and Edward A. Hamilton, eds. *Mike Wallace Asks: Highlights from 46 Controversial Interviews*. New York: Simon & Schuster, 1958.

Reeder, Colonel Red. *Bold Leaders of World War I*. Boston: Little, Brown, 1974.

Ritz, Marie-Louise. *César Ritz: Host to the World*. Philadelphia: J. B. Lippincott, 1938.

Riva, Maria. *Marlene Dietrich*. New York: Knopf, 1993.

Rose, Kenneth. *Kings, Queens, and Courtiers: Intimate Portraits of the Royal House of Windsor from Its Foundation to the Present Day*. London: Weidenfeld & Nicolson, 1985.

Schwartz, Charles. *Cole Porter: A Biography*. New York: DaCapo, 1979.

Silverman, Stephen M. *Where There's a Will: Who Inherited What and Why*. New York: HarperCollins, 1991.

Sinclair, Mick. *San Francisco: A Cultural and Literary History*. Northampton, MA: Interlink Books, 2004.

Smith, Jane S. *Elsie de Wolfe: A Life in the High Style*. New York: Atheneum, 1982.

Stassinopoulos, Arianna. *Maria Callas: The Woman Behind the Legend.* New York: Simon & Schuster, 1981.

Strange, Michael [pseud. of Blanche Oelrichs]. *Who Tells Me True.* New York: Charles Scribner's Sons, 1940.

Stuart, Amanda Mackenzie. *Consuelo and Alva Vanderbilt: The Story of a Mother in the Gilded Age.* New York: HarperCollins, 2005.

Sutherland, Joan. *A Prima Donna's Progress.* Washington, D.C.: Regnery, 1997.

Swanberg, W. A. *Citizen Hearst.* New York: Charles Scribner's Sons, 1961.

Vickers, Hugo. *Behind Closed Doors: The Untold Story of the Duchess of Windsor.* London: Hutchinson, 2011.

————. *Cecil Beaton: A Biography.* Boston: Little, Brown, 1985.

————. *Elizabeth the Queen Mother.* London: Hutchinson, 2005.

Vreeland, Diana. *D.V.* New York: DaCapo, 1997.

Wagenknecht, Edward. *American Profile, 1900–1909.* Amherst, MA: University of Massachusetts Press, 1982.

Warner, Jack L. *My First Hundred Years in Hollywood.* New York: Random House, 1965.

Wells, Evelyn. *Champagne Days of San Francisco.* New York: D. Appleton-Century, 1939.

Wilson, Christopher. *Dancing with the Devil: The Windsors and Jimmy Donahue.* New York: St. Martin's Press, 2000.

Winchell, Walter. *Winchell Exclusive.* Englewood Cliffs, NJ: Prentice-Hall, 1975.

Winchester, Simon. *A Crack in the Edge of the World: America and the Great California Earthquake of 1906.* New York: HarperCollins, 2005.

Wineapple, Brenda. *Genêt: A Biography of Janet Flanner.* New York: Ticknor & Fields, 1989.

Wisneski, Henry. *Maria Callas: The Art Behind the Legend.* Garden City, NY: Doubleday and Co., 1975.

Zerbe, Jerome. *The Art of Social Climbing.* Garden City, NY: Doubleday and Co., 1965.

Ziegler, Philip. *King Edward VIII: A Biography.* New York: Knopf, 1991.

Index